A Kodansha Trade Paperback Original

Blue Lock 2 copyright © 2019 Muneyuki Kaneshiro/Yusuke Nomura
English translation copyright © 2022 Muneyuki Kaneshiro/Yusuke Nomura

All rights reserved.

Published in the United States by
Kodansha USA Publishing, LLC, New York.

Publication rights for this English edition arranged through
Kodansha Ltd., Tokyo.

First published in Japan in 2019 by Kodansha Ltd., Tokyo
as *Buruu rokku*, volume 2.

ISBN 978-1-64651-655-1

Printed in the United States of America.

1st Printing

Translation: Nate Derr
Lettering: Chris Burgener
Additional lettering and layout: Scott O. Brown
Editing: Thalia Sutton, Maggie Le
YKS Services LLC/SKY JAPAN, Inc.
Kodansha USA Publishing edition cover design by Matthew Akuginow

Publisher: Kiichiro Sugawara

Director of Publishing Services: Ben Applegate
Director of Publishing Operations: Dave Barrett
Associate Director of Publishing Operations: Stephen Pakula
Publishing Services Managing Editors: Alanna Ruse, Madison Salters
Senior Production Manager: Angela Zurlo

KODANSHA.US

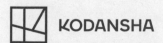

KODANSHA

"Clever, sassy, and original....*xxxHOLiC* has the inherent hallmarks of a runaway hit."
—NewType magazine

Beautifully seductive artwork and uniquely Japanese depictions of the supernatural will hypnotize CLAMP fans!

Kimihiro Watanuki is haunted by visions of ghosts and spirits. He seeks help from a mysterious woman named Yuko, who claims she can help. However, Watanuki must work for Yuko in order to pay for her aid. Soon Watanuki finds himself employed in Yuko's shop, where he sees things and meets customers that are stranger than anything he could have ever imagined.

KC
KODANSHA COMICS

The beloved characters from *Cardcaptor Sakura* return in a brand new, reimagined fantasy adventure!

RESERVoir CHRoNiCLE
TSUBASA
OMNIBUS
1
CLAMP

TSUBASA
WoRLD CHRoNiCLE: NIRAIKANAI
1
CLAMP

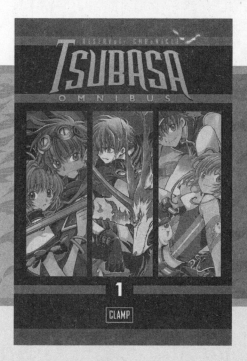

"[*Tsubasa*] takes readers on a fantastic ride that only gets more exhilarating with each successive chapter." —Anime News Network

In the Kingdom of Clow, an archaeological dig unleashes an incredible power, causing Princess Sakura to lose her memories. To save her, her childhood friend Syaoran must follow the orders of the Dimension Witch and travel alongside Kurogane, an unrivaled warrior; Fai, a powerful magician; and Mokona, a curiously strange creature, to retrieve Sakura's dispersed memories!

KC KODANSHA COMICS

The adorable new odd-couple cat comedy manga from the creator of the beloved *Chi's Sweet Home*, in full color!

Sue & Tai-chan

Konami Kanata

Sue is an aging housecat who's looking forward to living out her life in peace... but her plans change when the mischievous black tomcat Tai-chan enters the picture! Hey! Sue never signed up to be a catsitter! *Sue & Tai-chan* is the latest from the reigning meow-narch of cute kitty comics, Konami Kanata.

KC KODANSHA COMICS

THE SWEET SCENT OF LOVE IS IN THE AIR! FOR FANS OF OFFBEAT ROMANCES LIKE *WOTAKOI*

Sweat and Soap © Kintetsu Yamada / Kodansha Ltd.

In an office romance, there's a fine line between sexy and awkward... and that line is where Asako — a woman who sweats copiously — meets Koutarou — a perfume developer who can't get enough of Asako's, er, scent. Don't miss a romcom manga like no other!

SAINT ☆ YOUNG MEN

A LONG AWAITED ARRIVAL IN PREMIUM 2-IN-1 HARDCOVER

After centuries of hard work, Jesus and Buddha take a break from their heavenly duties to relax among the people of Japan, and their adventures in this lighthearted buddy comedy are sure to bring mirth and merriment to all!

"Brilliant…the physical comedy and facial expressions will make you literally LOL."
—Sam Humphries
(host of *DC Daily*;
writer, *Green Lanterns,
Legendary Star-Lord*)

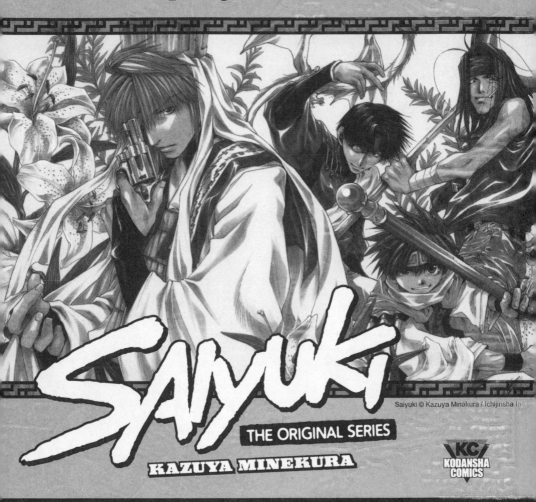

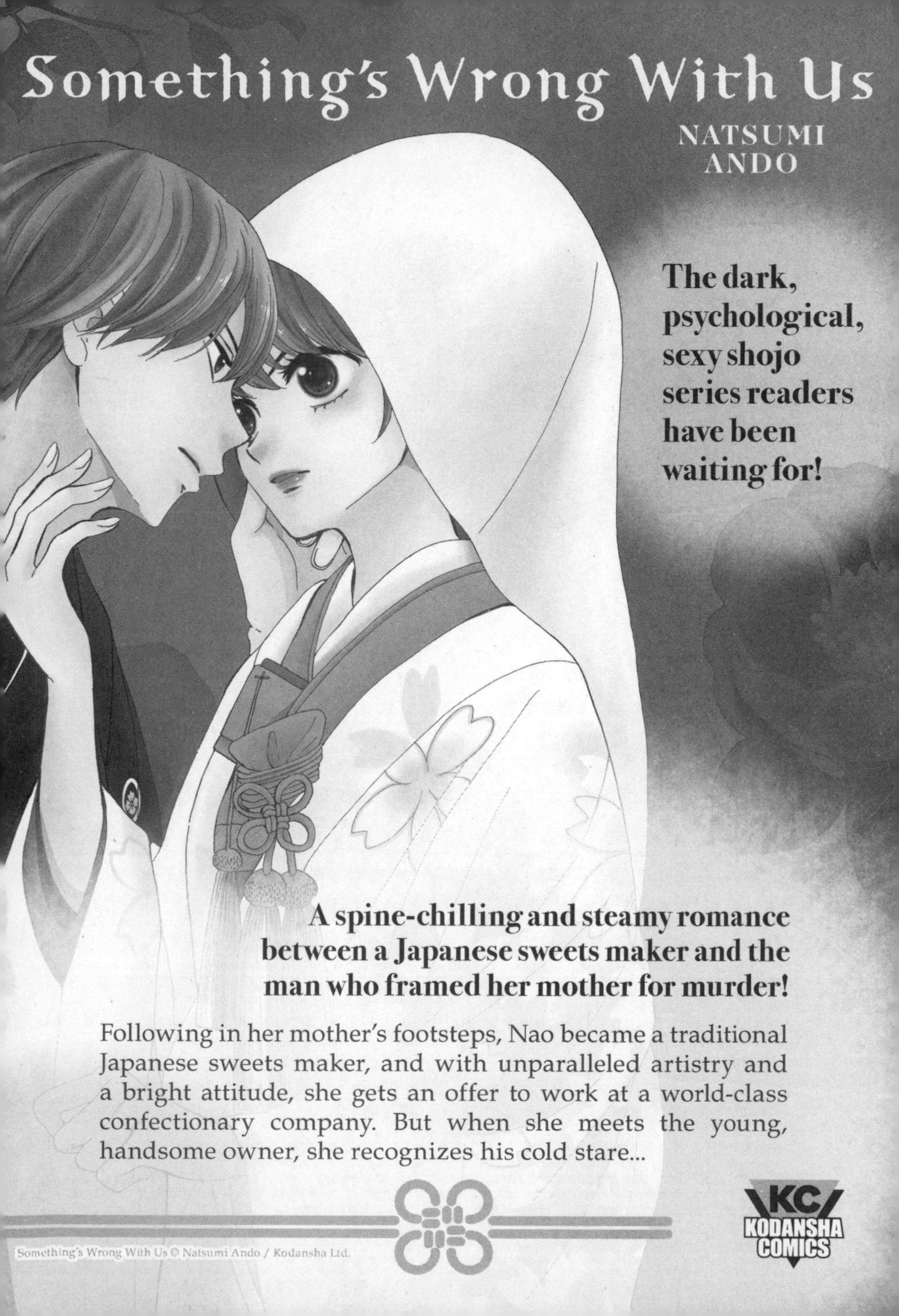
Something's Wrong With Us
NATSUMI ANDO
The dark, psychological, sexy shojo series readers have been waiting for!
A spine-chilling and steamy romance between a Japanese sweets maker and the man who framed her mother for murder!
Following in her mother's footsteps, Nao became a traditional Japanese sweets maker, and with unparalleled artistry and a bright attitude, she gets an offer to work at a world-class confectionary company. But when she meets the young, handsome owner, she recognizes his cold stare...
KC KODANSHA COMICS
Something's Wrong With Us © Natsumi Ando / Kodansha Ltd.

PERFECT WORLD

Rie Aruga

A TOUCHING NEW SERIES ABOUT LOVE AND COPING WITH DISABILITY

An office party reunites Tsugumi with her high school crush Itsuki. He's realized his dream of becoming an architect, but along the way, he experienced a spinal injury that put him in a wheelchair. Now Tsugumi's rekindled feelings will butt up against prejudices she never considered — and Itsuki will have to decide if he's ready to let someone into his heart...

"Depicts with great delicacy and courage the difficulties some with disabilities experience getting involved in romantic relationships... Rie Aruga refuses to romanticize, pushing her heroine to face the reality of disability. She invites her readers to the same tasks of empathy, knowledge and recognition."
—Slate.fr

"An important entry [in manga romance]... The emotional core of both plot and characters indicates thoughtfulness... [Aruga's] research is readily apparent in the text and artwork, making this feel like a real story."
—Anime News Network

KC KODANSHA COMICS

A SMART, NEW ROMANTIC COMEDY FOR FANS OF *SHORTCAKE CAKE* AND *TERRACE HOUSE*!

A romance manga starring high school girl Meeko, who learns to live on her own in a boarding house whose living room is home to the odd (but handsome) Matsunaga-san. She begins to adjust to her new life away from her parents, but Meeko soon learns that no matter how far away from home she is, she's still a young girl at heart — especially when she finds herself falling for Matsunaga-san.

Knight of the ICE

Yayoi Ogawa

Knight of the Ice ©Yayoi Ogawa/Kodansha Ltd.

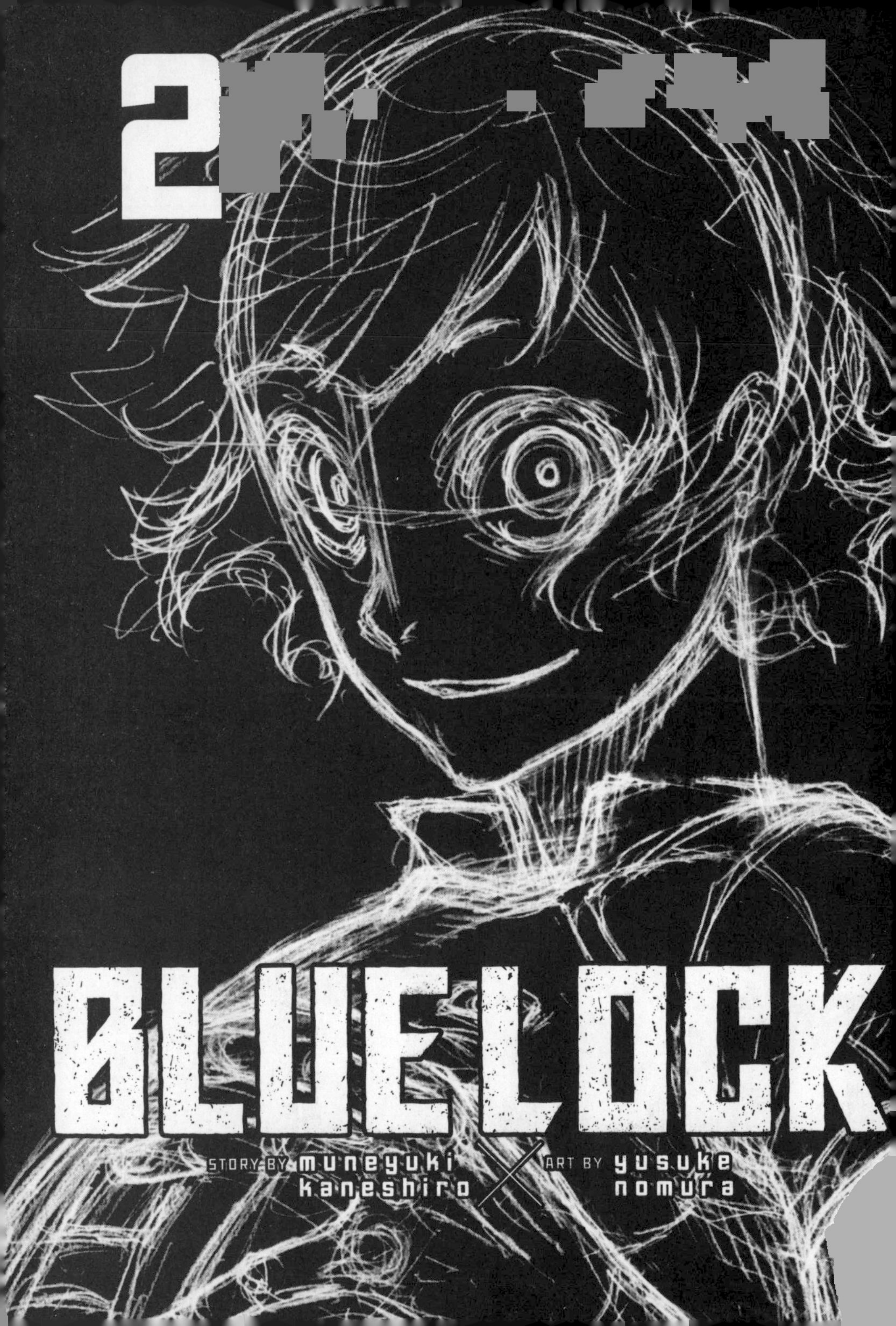
2 [redacted]
BLUE LOCK
STORY BY muneyuki kaneshiro
ART BY yusuke nomura

CONTENTS

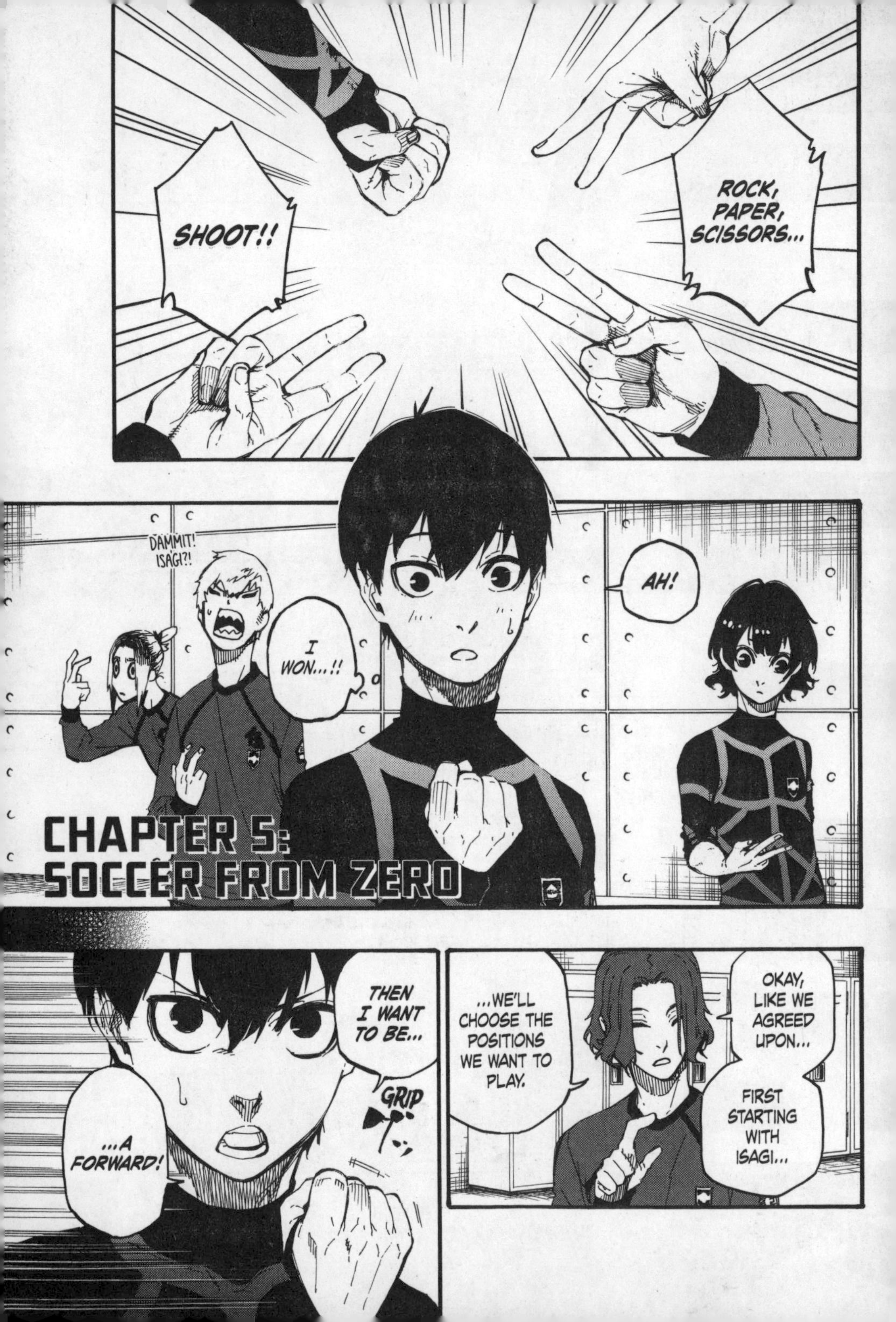
ROCK, PAPER, SCISSORS...
SHOOT!!
AH!
I WON...!!
DAMMIT! ISAGI?!
CHAPTER 5: SOCCER FROM ZERO
OKAY, LIKE WE AGREED UPON...
FIRST STARTING WITH ISAGI...
...WE'LL CHOOSE THE POSITIONS WE WANT TO PLAY.
THEN I WANT TO BE...
GRIP
...A FORWARD!

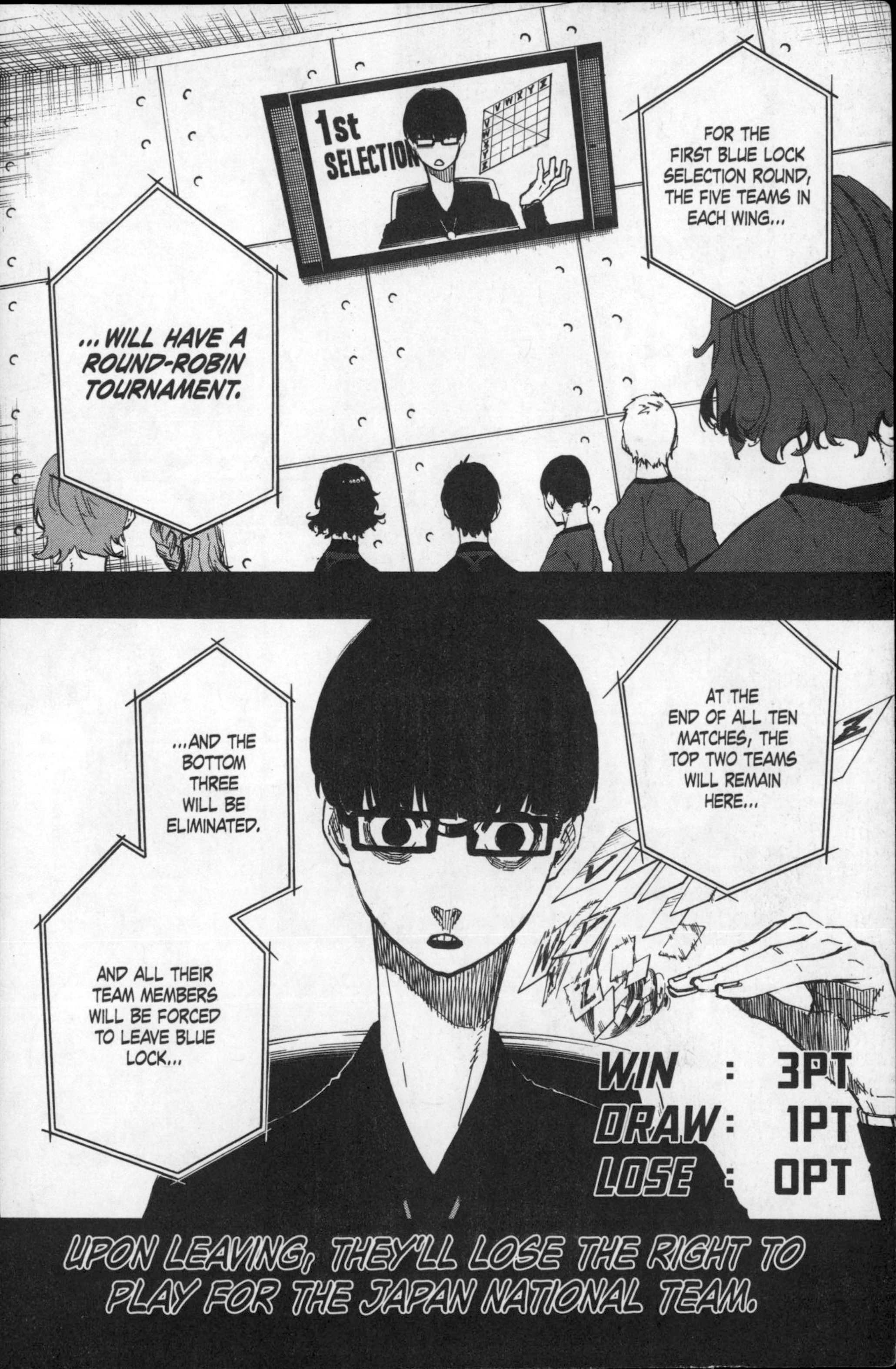
1st SELECTION
FOR THE FIRST BLUE LOCK SELECTION ROUND, THE FIVE TEAMS IN EACH WING...
...WILL HAVE A ROUND-ROBIN TOURNAMENT.
AT THE END OF ALL TEN MATCHES, THE TOP TWO TEAMS WILL REMAIN HERE...
...AND THE BOTTOM THREE WILL BE ELIMINATED.
AND ALL THEIR TEAM MEMBERS WILL BE FORCED TO LEAVE BLUE LOCK...
WIN : 3PT
DRAW : 1PT
LOSE : 0PT
UPON LEAVING, THEY'LL LOSE THE RIGHT TO PLAY FOR THE JAPAN NATIONAL TEAM.

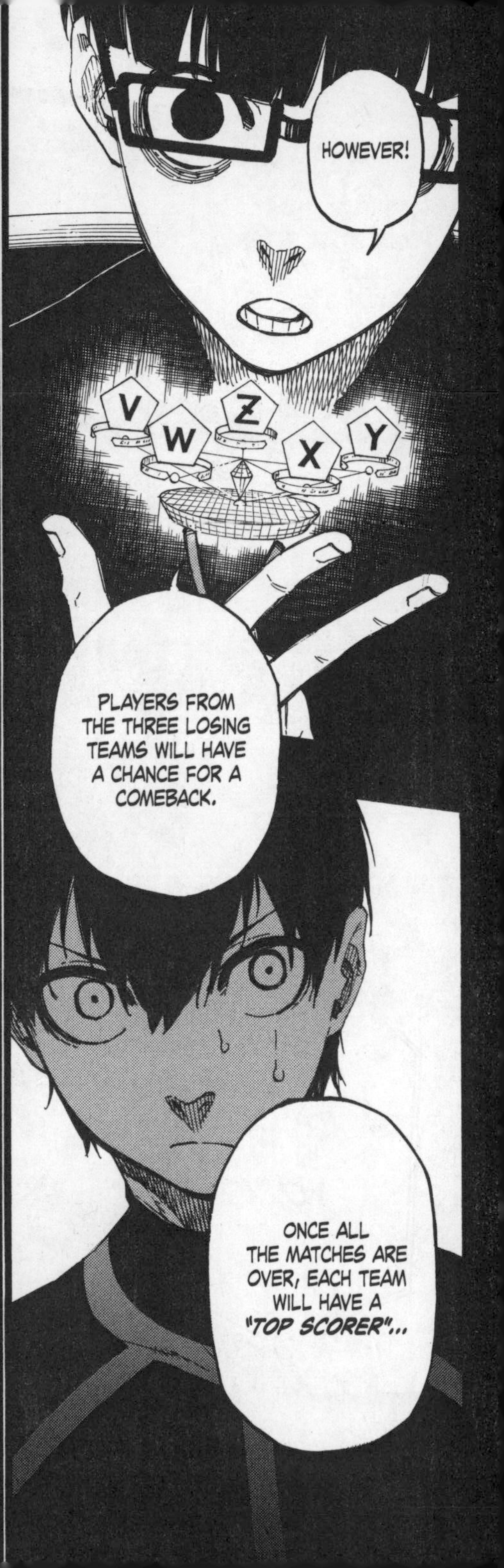
HOWEVER!
V W Z X Y
PLAYERS FROM THE THREE LOSING TEAMS WILL HAVE A CHANCE FOR A COMEBACK.
ONCE ALL THE MATCHES ARE OVER, EACH TEAM WILL HAVE A *"TOP SCORER"*...

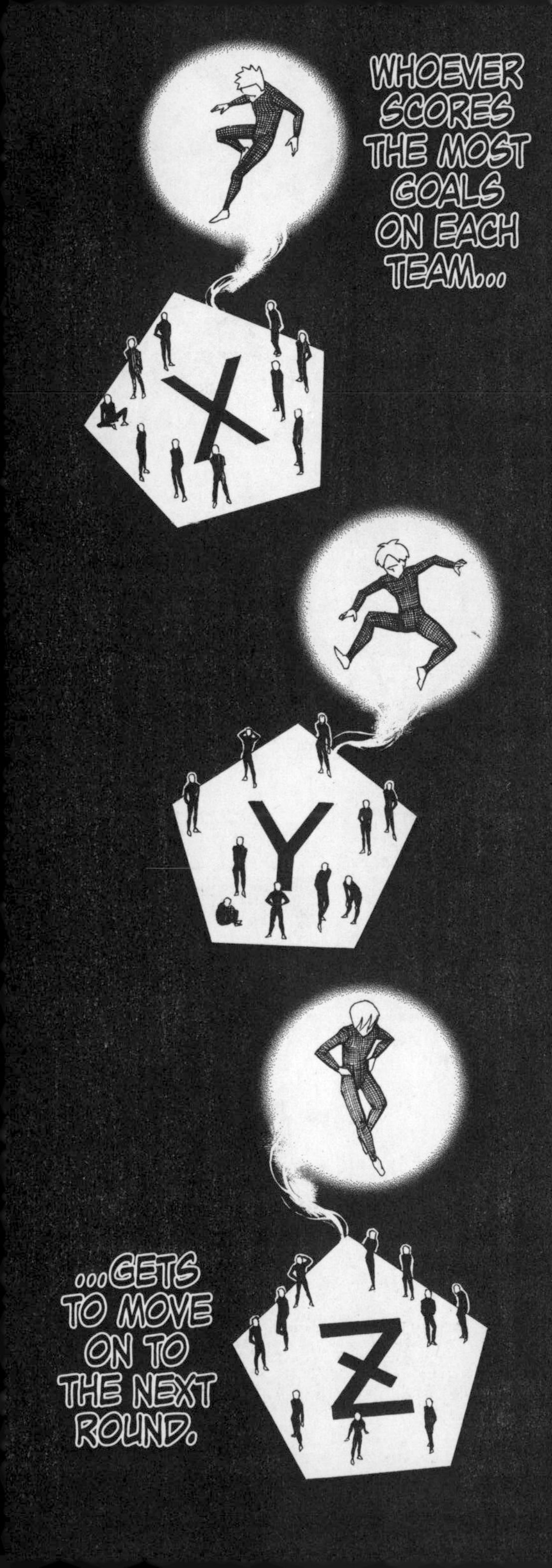
WHOEVER SCORES THE MOST GOALS ON EACH TEAM...
X
Y
Z
...GETS TO MOVE ON TO THE NEXT ROUND.

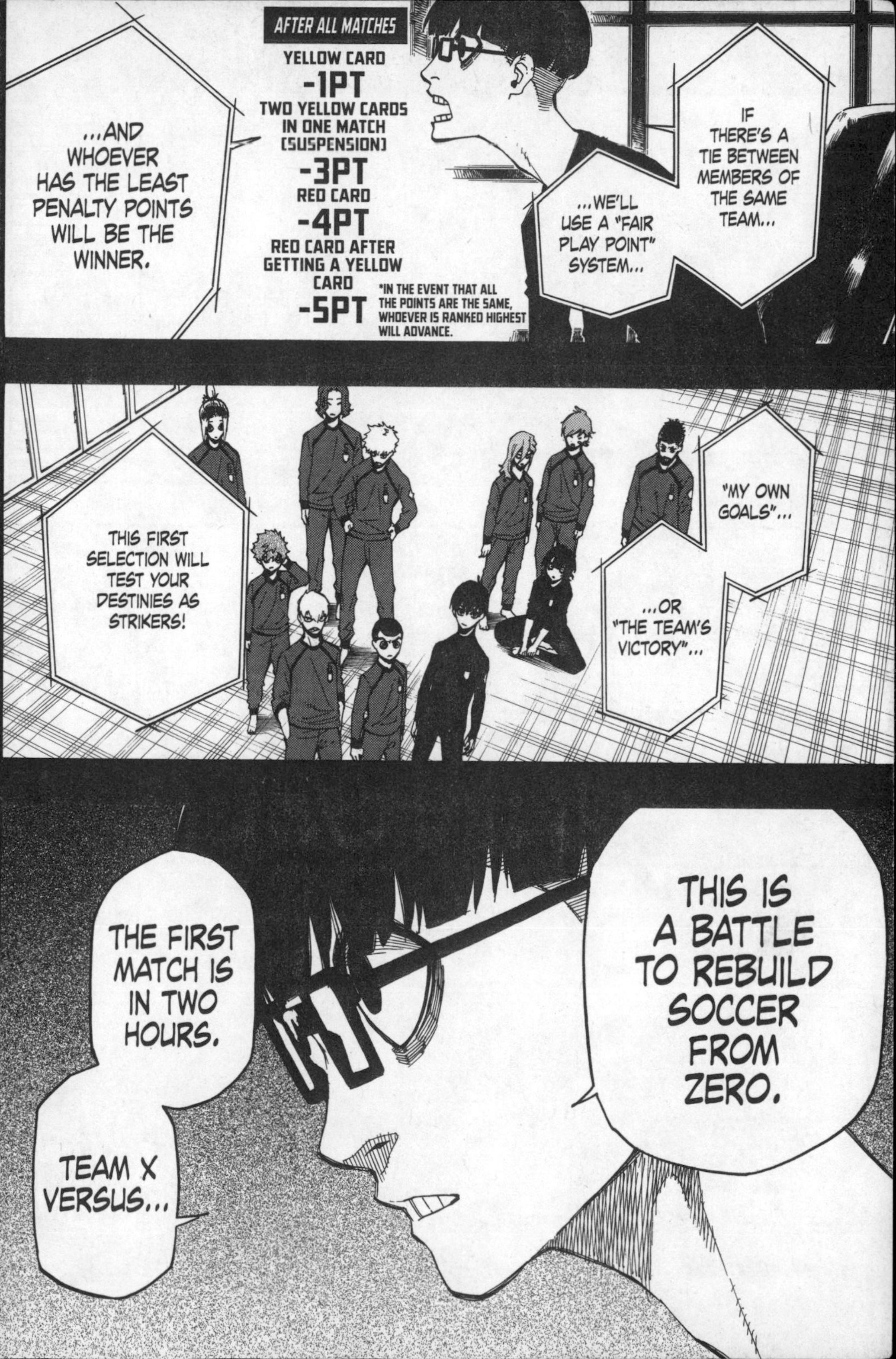
IF THERE'S A TIE BETWEEN MEMBERS OF THE SAME TEAM...
...WE'LL USE A "FAIR PLAY POINT" SYSTEM...
AFTER ALL MATCHES
YELLOW CARD -1PT
TWO YELLOW CARDS IN ONE MATCH [SUSPENSION] -3PT
RED CARD -4PT
RED CARD AFTER GETTING A YELLOW CARD -5PT
*IN THE EVENT THAT ALL THE POINTS ARE THE SAME, WHOEVER IS RANKED HIGHEST WILL ADVANCE.
...AND WHOEVER HAS THE LEAST PENALTY POINTS WILL BE THE WINNER.
"MY OWN GOALS"...
...OR "THE TEAM'S VICTORY"...
THIS FIRST SELECTION WILL TEST YOUR DESTINIES AS STRIKERS!
THIS IS A BATTLE TO REBUILD SOCCER FROM ZERO.
THE FIRST MATCH IS IN TWO HOURS.
TEAM X VERSUS...

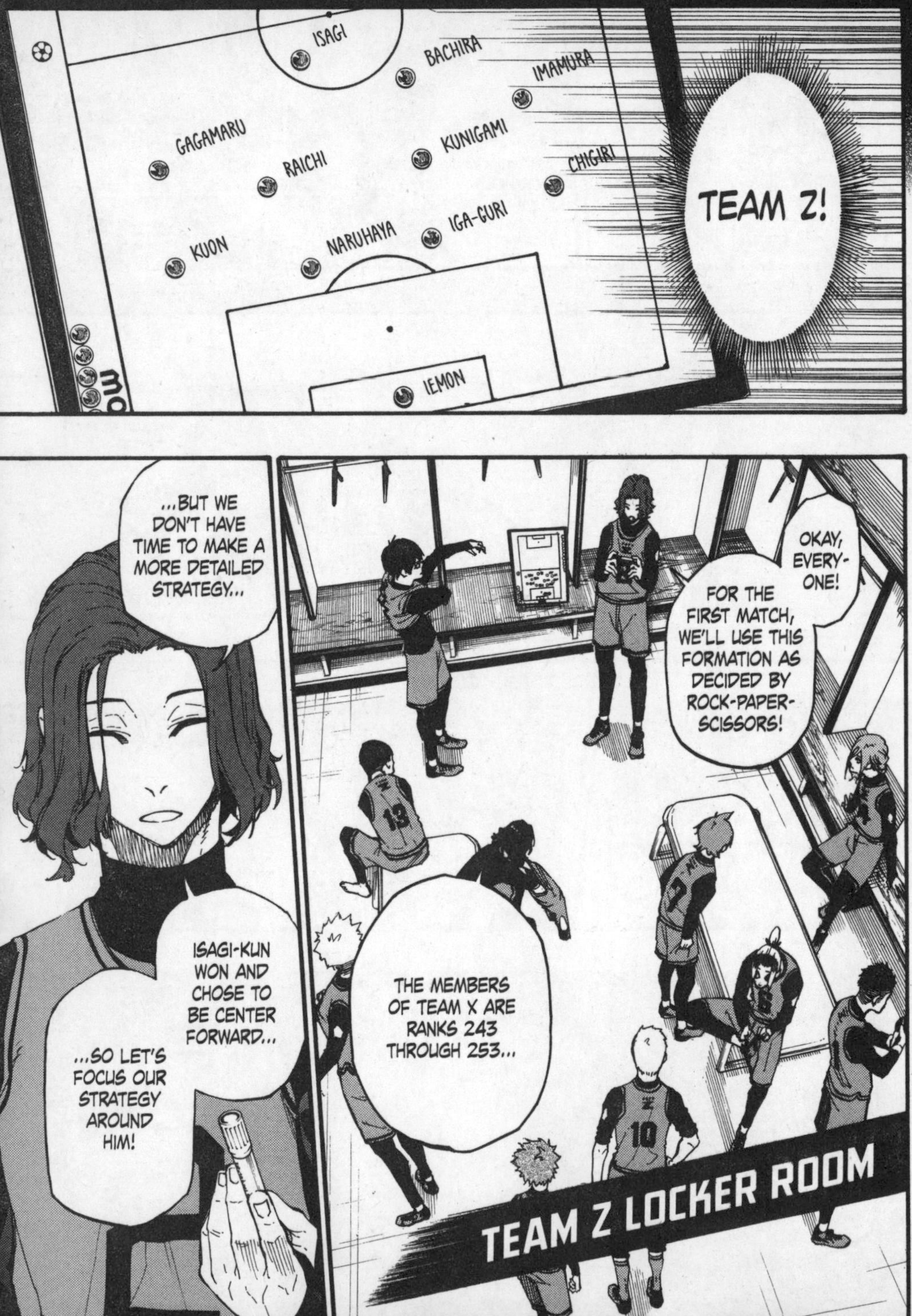
TEAM Z!
ISAGI
BACHIRA
IMAMURA
GAGAMARU
KUNIGAMI
RAICHI
CHIGIRI
KUON
NARUHAYA
IGA-GURI
IEMON
OKAY, EVERYONE!
FOR THE FIRST MATCH, WE'LL USE THIS FORMATION AS DECIDED BY ROCK-PAPER-SCISSORS!
THE MEMBERS OF TEAM X ARE RANKS 243 THROUGH 253...
TEAM Z LOCKER ROOM
...BUT WE DON'T HAVE TIME TO MAKE A MORE DETAILED STRATEGY...
ISAGI-KUN WON AND CHOSE TO BE CENTER FORWARD...
...SO LET'S FOCUS OUR STRATEGY AROUND HIM!

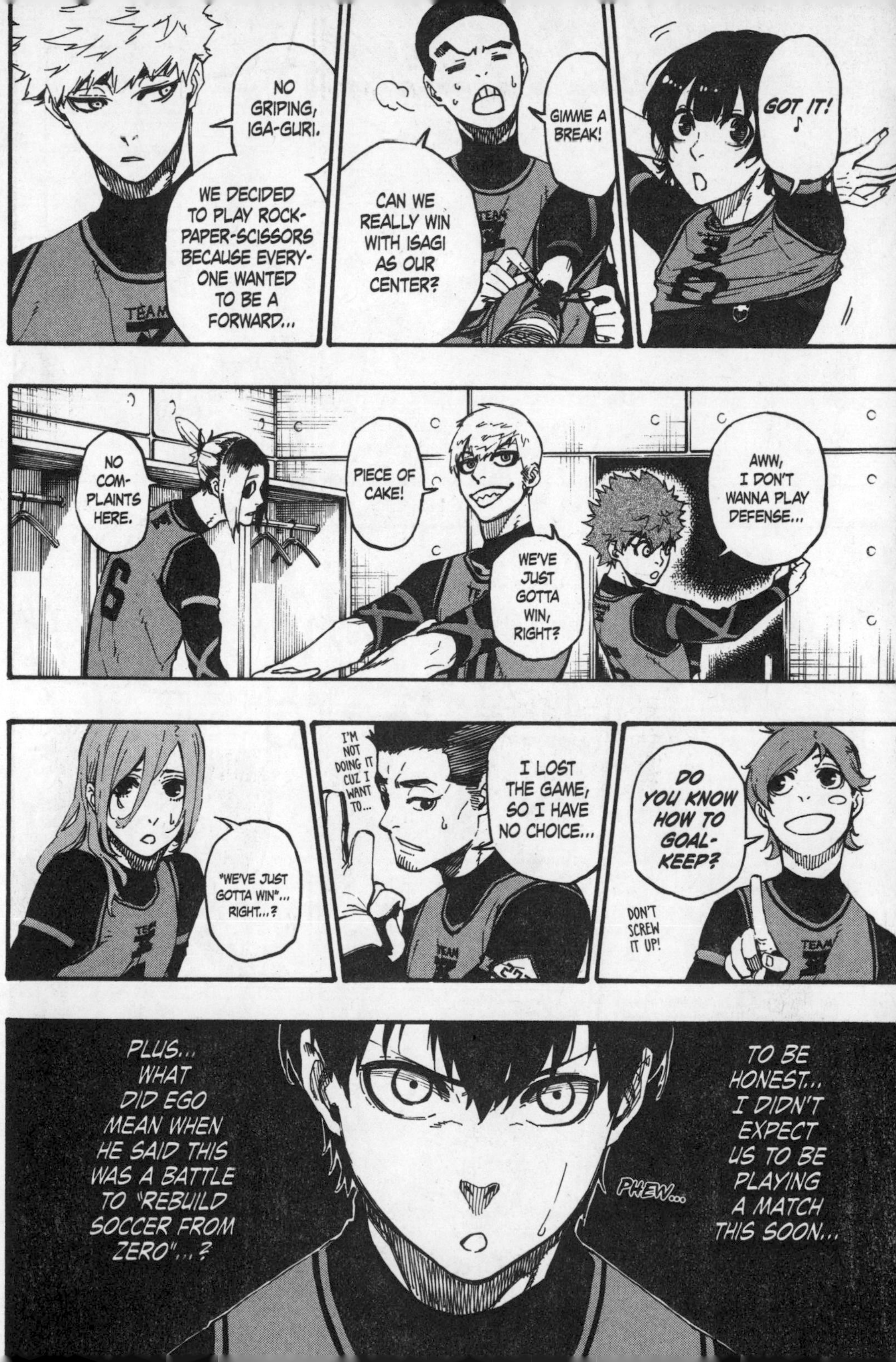
GOT IT! ♪
GIMME A BREAK!
CAN WE REALLY WIN WITH ISAGI AS OUR CENTER?
NO GRIPING, IGA-GURI.
WE DECIDED TO PLAY ROCK-PAPER-SCISSORS BECAUSE EVERYONE WANTED TO BE A FORWARD...
AWW, I DON'T WANNA PLAY DEFENSE...
PIECE OF CAKE!
WE'VE JUST GOTTA WIN, RIGHT?
NO COMPLAINTS HERE.
DO YOU KNOW HOW TO GOALKEEP?
DON'T SCREW IT UP!
I LOST THE GAME, SO I HAVE NO CHOICE...
I'M NOT DOING IT CUZ I WANT TO...
"WE'VE JUST GOTTA WIN"... RIGHT...?
TO BE HONEST... I DIDN'T EXPECT US TO BE PLAYING A MATCH THIS SOON...
PHEW...
PLUS... WHAT DID EGO MEAN WHEN HE SAID THIS WAS A BATTLE TO "REBUILD SOCCER FROM ZERO"...?

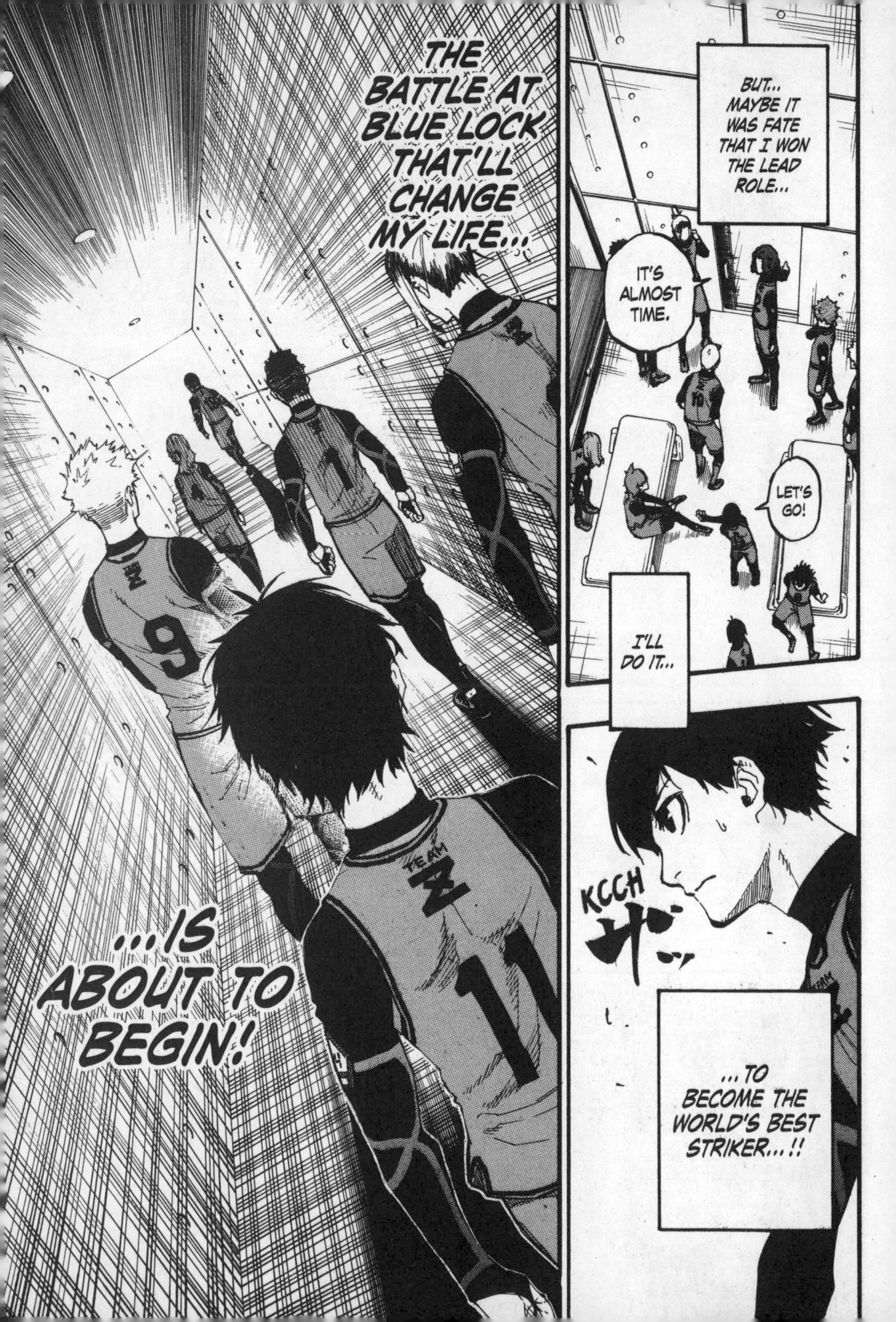
BUT... MAYBE IT WAS FATE THAT I WON THE LEAD ROLE...
IT'S ALMOST TIME.
LET'S GO!
I'LL DO IT...
KCCH
...TO BECOME THE WORLD'S BEST STRIKER...!!
THE BATTLE AT BLUE LOCK THAT'LL CHANGE MY LIFE...
...IS ABOUT TO BEGIN!

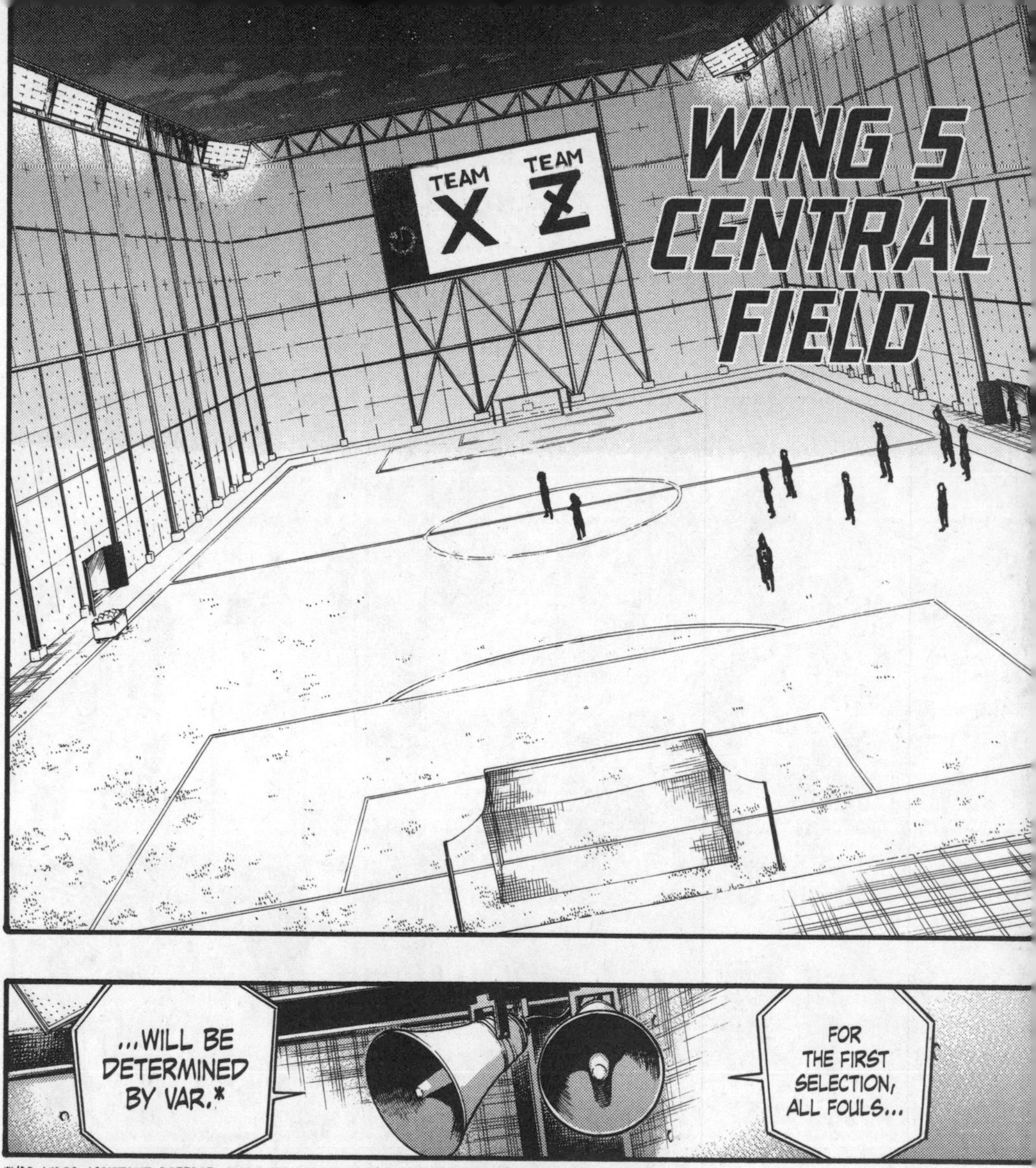
WING 5 CENTRAL FIELD
TEAM X
TEAM Z
FOR THE FIRST SELECTION, ALL FOULS...
...WILL BE DETERMINED BY VAR.*

*VAR=VIDEO ASSISTANT REFEREE. MADE ITS DEBUT IN THE 2018 RUSSIA WORLD CUP.

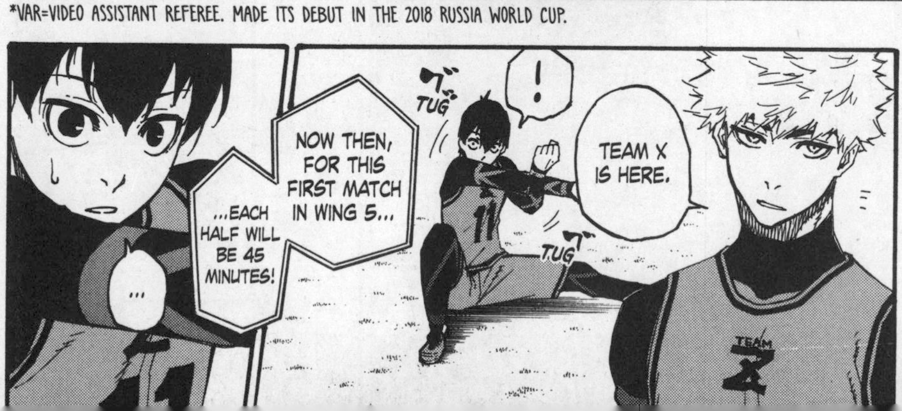
TEAM X IS HERE.
!
TUG
NOW THEN, FOR THIS FIRST MATCH IN WING 5...
...EACH HALF WILL BE 45 MINUTES!
TUG
TEAM Z
...

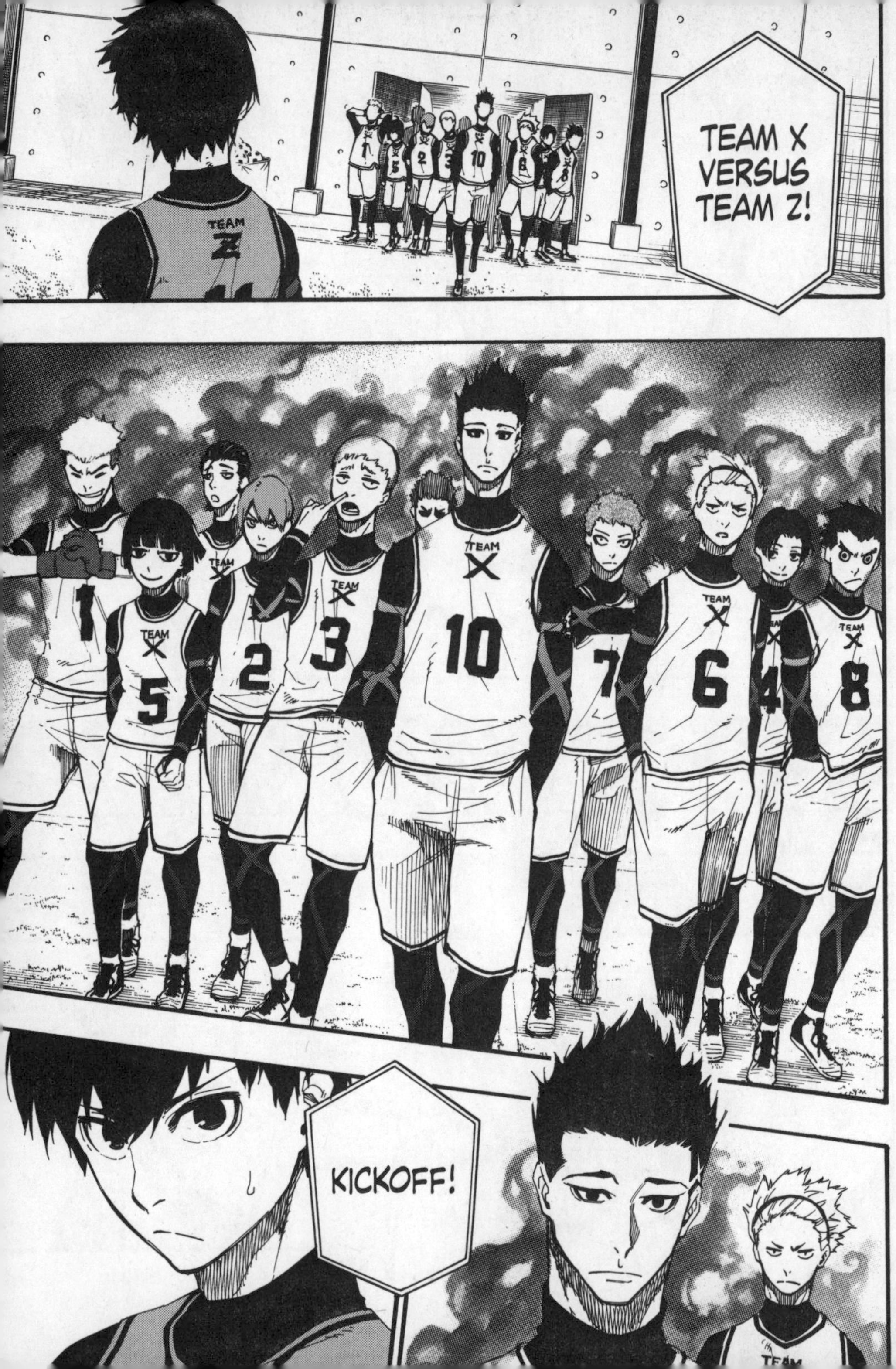
TEAM X VERSUS TEAM Z!
KICKOFF!

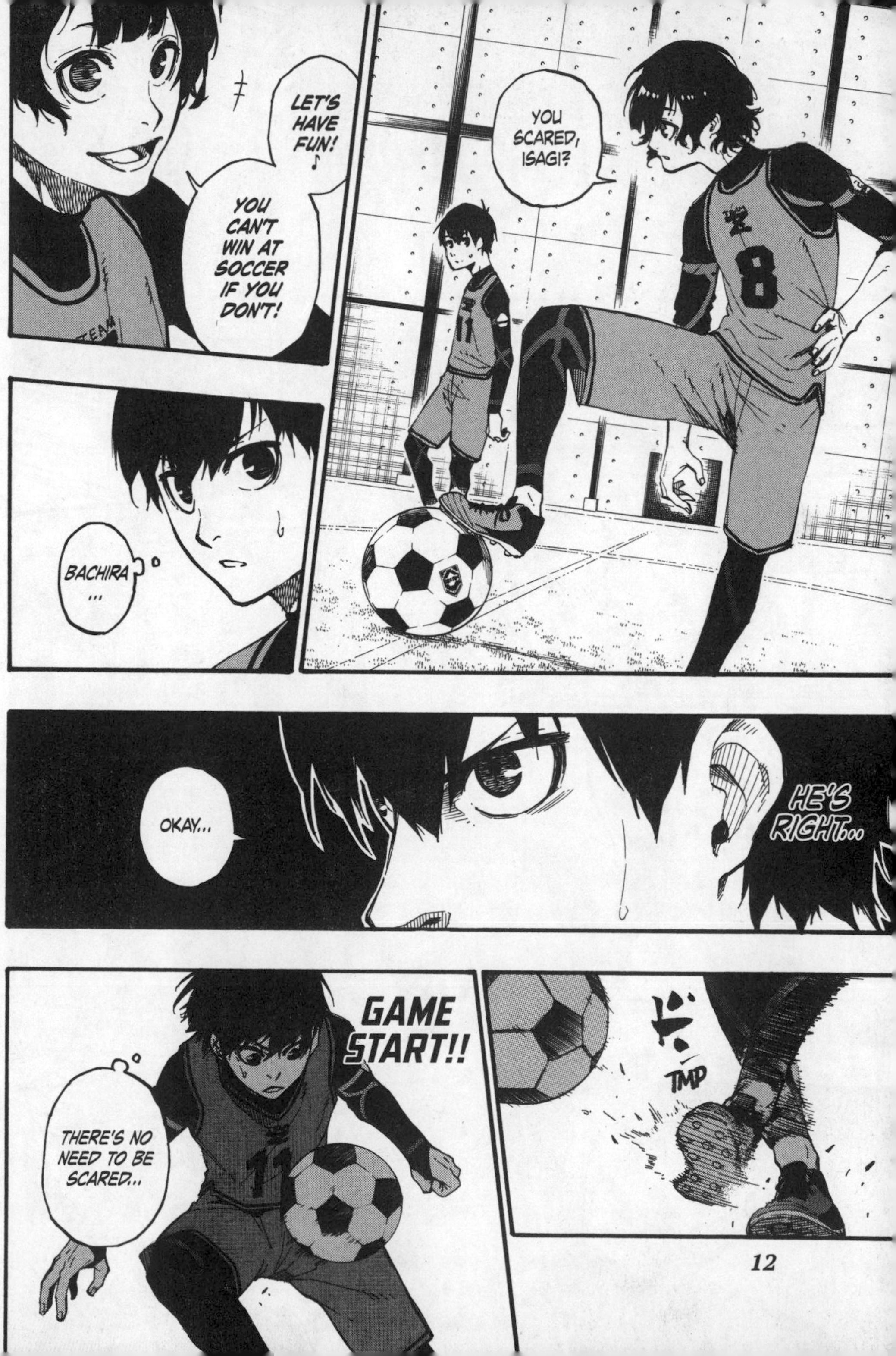
YOU SCARED, ISAGI?
LET'S HAVE FUN! ♪
YOU CAN'T WIN AT SOCCER IF YOU DON'T!
BACHIRA...
HE'S RIGHT...
OKAY...
TMP
GAME START!!
THERE'S NO NEED TO BE SCARED...

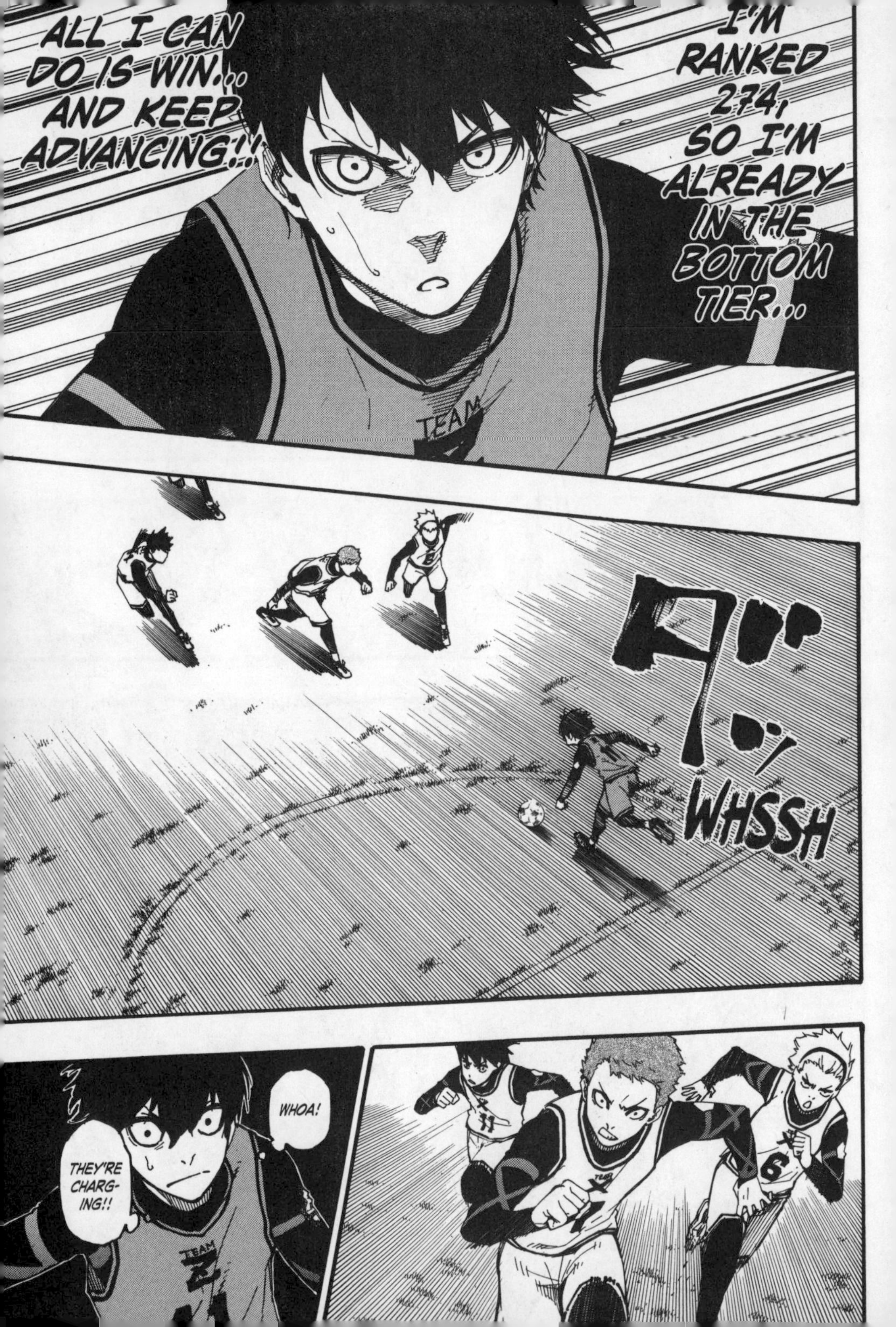
I'M RANKED 274, SO I'M ALREADY IN THE BOTTOM TIER...
ALL I CAN DO IS WIN... AND KEEP ADVANCING!!
WHSSH
WHOA!
THEY'RE CHARG-ING!!

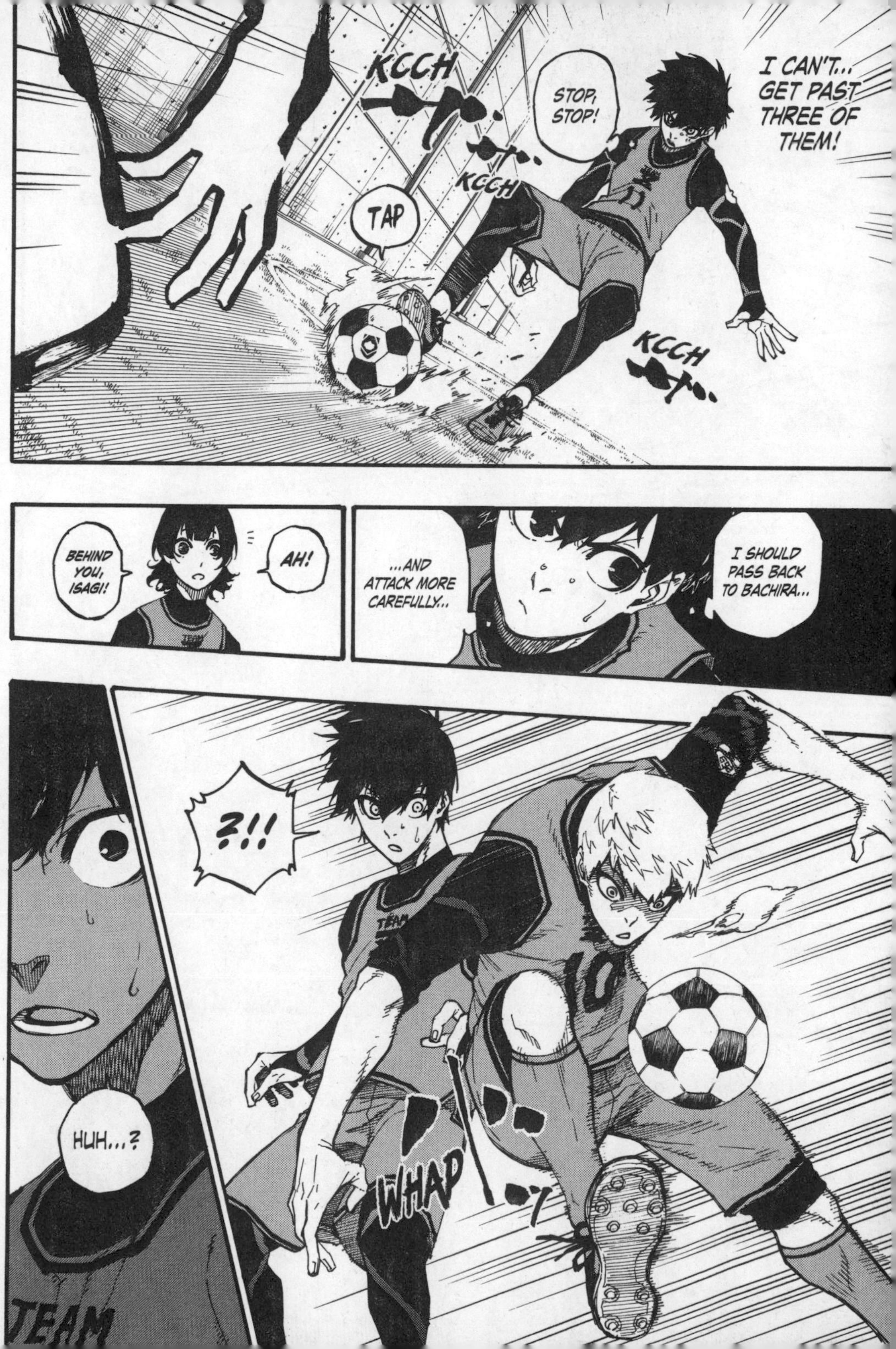

I CAN'T... GET PAST THREE OF THEM!
STOP, STOP!
KCCH
KCCH
TAP
KCCH
I SHOULD PASS BACK TO BACHIRA...
...AND ATTACK MORE CAREFULLY...
AH!
BEHIND YOU, ISAGI!
?!!
WHAP
HUH...?
TEAM

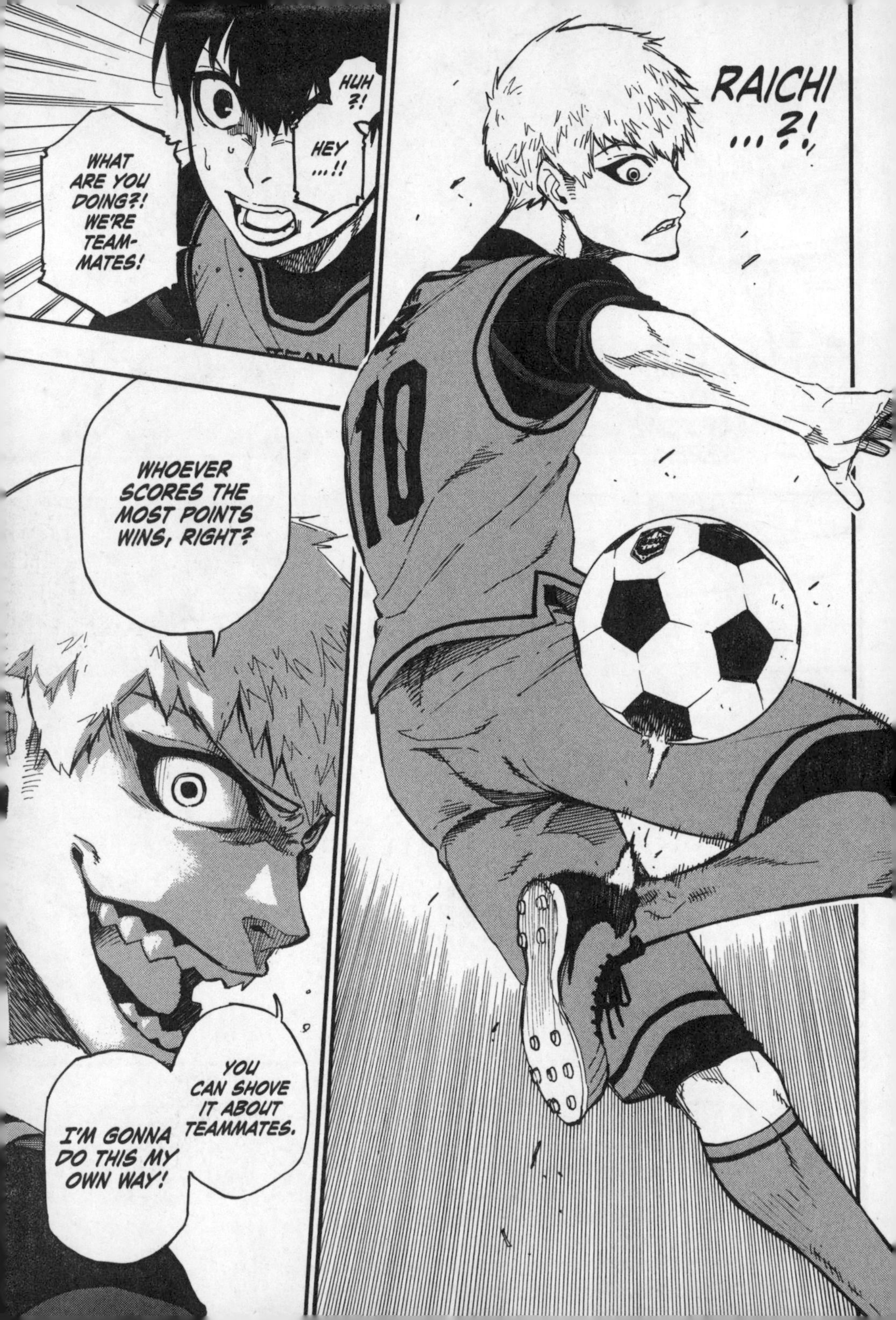
RAICHI ...?!
HUH ?!
HEY ...!!
WHAT ARE YOU DOING?! WE'RE TEAM-MATES!
WHOEVER SCORES THE MOST POINTS WINS, RIGHT?
YOU CAN SHOVE IT ABOUT TEAMMATES.
I'M GONNA DO THIS MY OWN WAY!

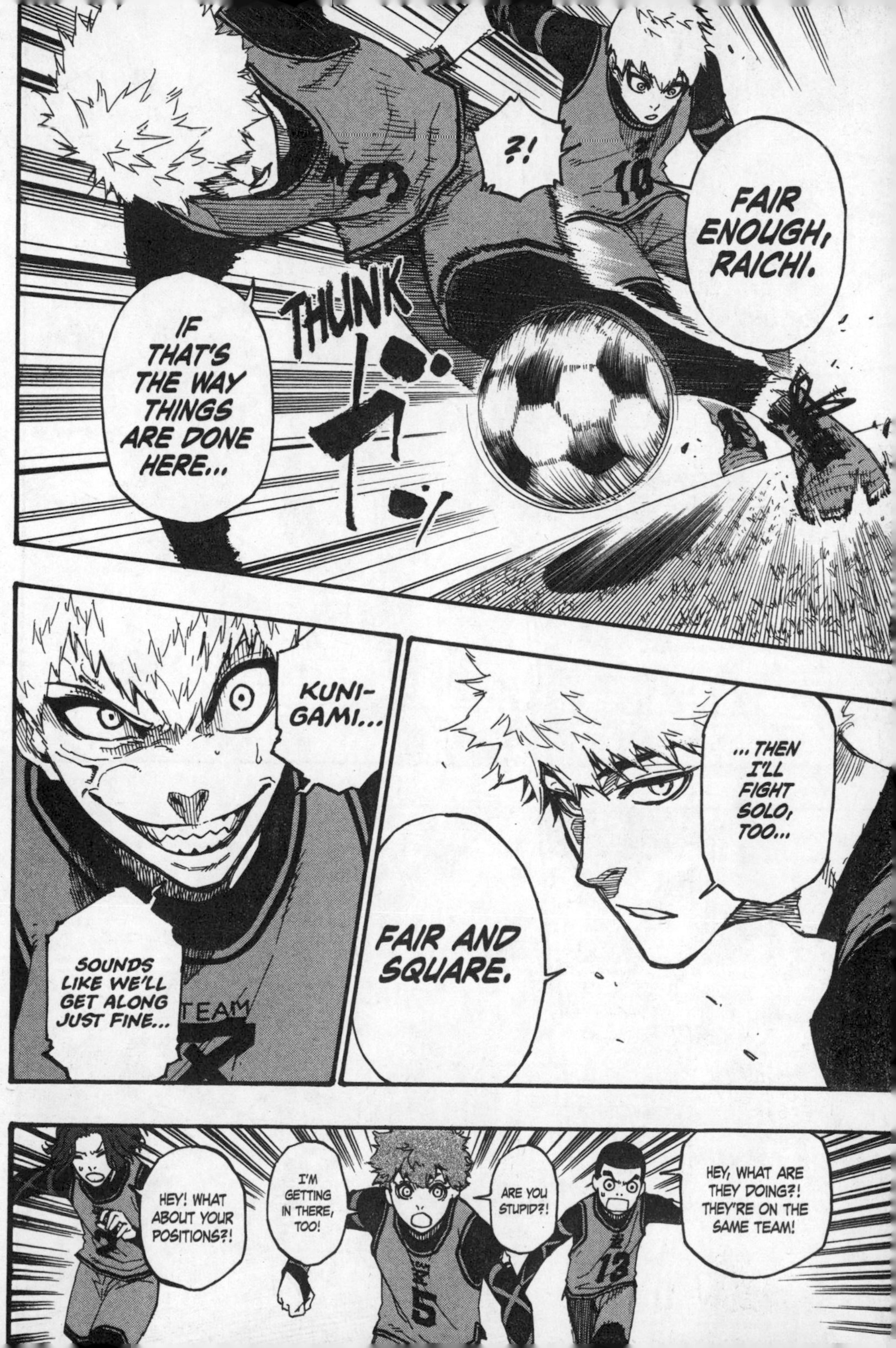
FAIR ENOUGH, RAICHI.
?!
THUNK
IF THAT'S THE WAY THINGS ARE DONE HERE...
...THEN I'LL FIGHT SOLO, TOO...
FAIR AND SQUARE.
KUNI-GAMI...
SOUNDS LIKE WE'LL GET ALONG JUST FINE...
TEAM
HEY, WHAT ARE THEY DOING?! THEY'RE ON THE SAME TEAM!
ARE YOU STUPID?!
I'M GETTING IN THERE, TOO!
HEY! WHAT ABOUT YOUR POSITIONS?!

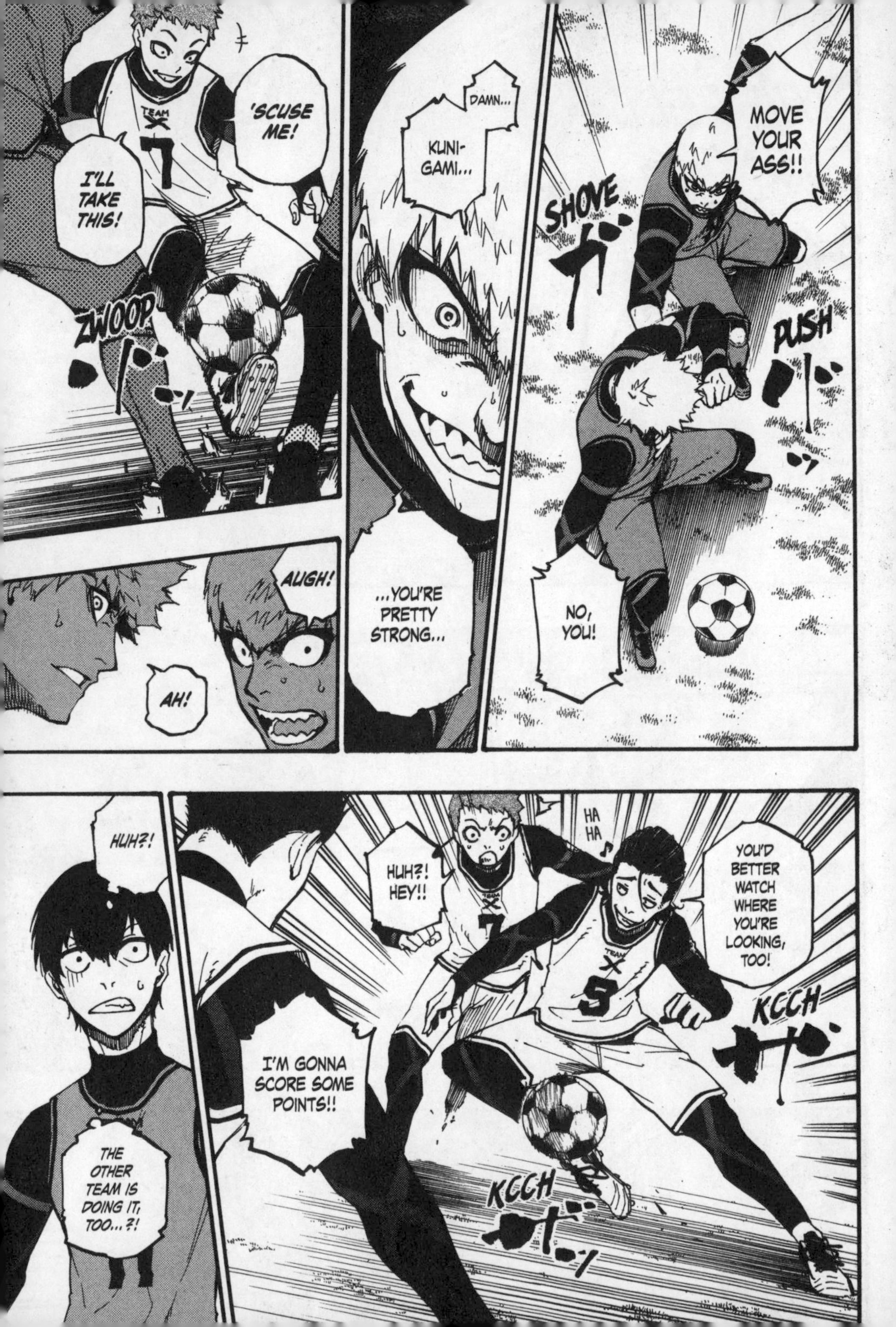
MOVE YOUR ASS!!
SHOVE
PUSH
NO, YOU!
DAMN...
KUNI-GAMI...
...YOU'RE PRETTY STRONG...
'SCUSE ME!
I'LL TAKE THIS!
ZWOOP
AUGH!
AH!
HA HA
YOU'D BETTER WATCH WHERE YOU'RE LOOKING, TOO!
HUH?! HEY!!
KCCH
I'M GONNA SCORE SOME POINTS!!
KCCH
HUH?!
THE OTHER TEAM IS DOING IT, TOO...?!

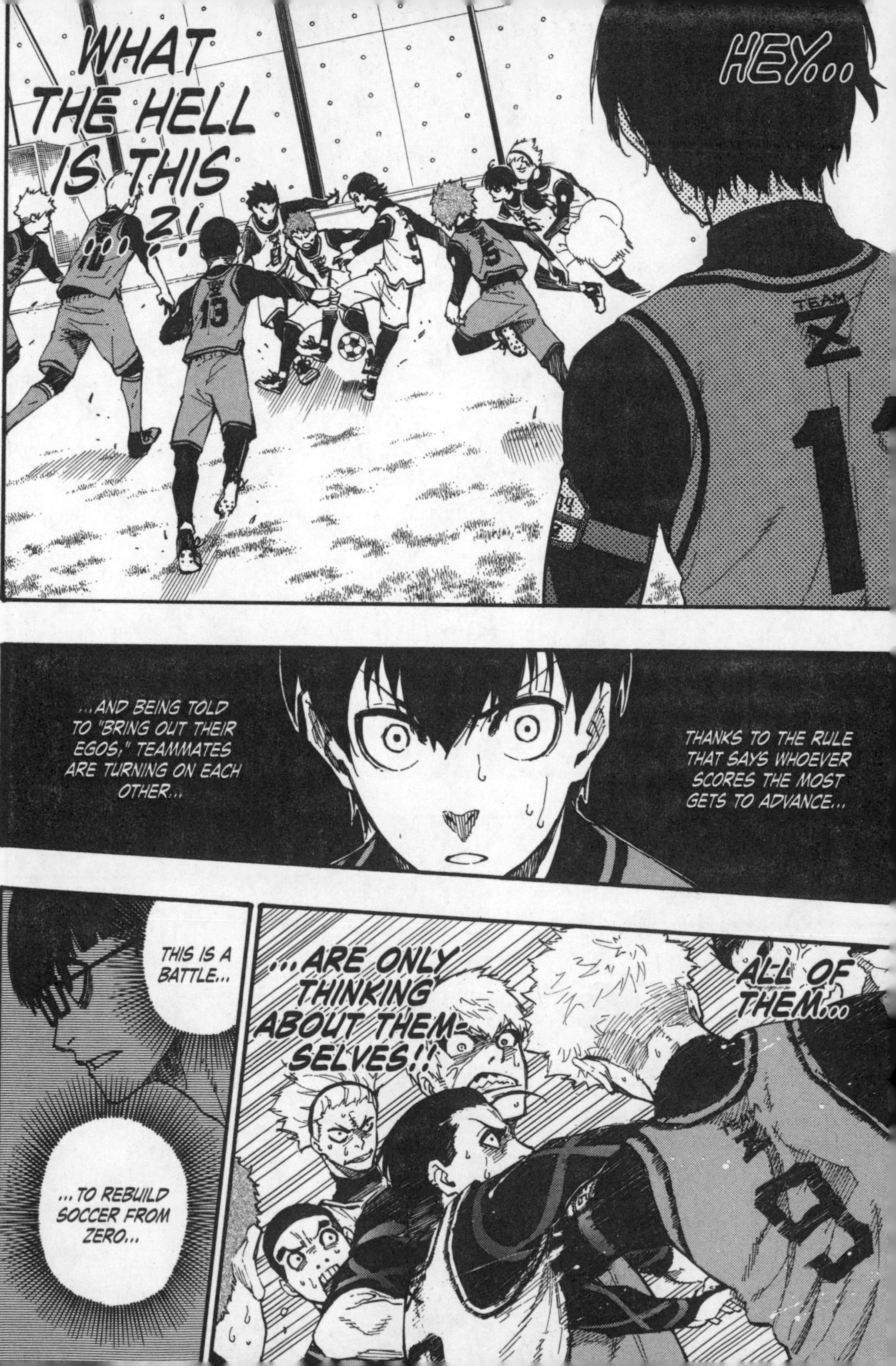
HEY...
WHAT THE HELL IS THIS ?!
THANKS TO THE RULE THAT SAYS WHOEVER SCORES THE MOST GETS TO ADVANCE...
...AND BEING TOLD TO "BRING OUT THEIR EGOS," TEAMMATES ARE TURNING ON EACH OTHER...
ALL OF THEM...
...ARE ONLY THINKING ABOUT THEMSELVES!!
THIS IS A BATTLE...
...TO REBUILD SOCCER FROM ZERO...

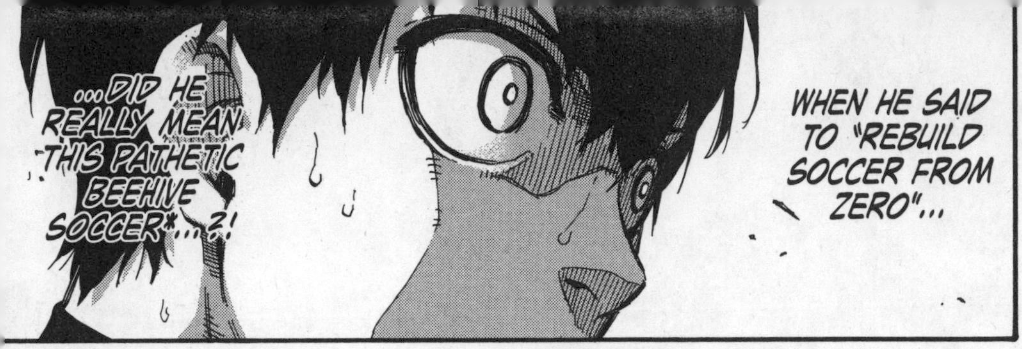
WHEN HE SAID TO "REBUILD SOCCER FROM ZERO"...
...DID HE REALLY MEAN THIS PATHETIC BEEHIVE SOCCER*...?!

*A TYPE OF PLAY IN WHICH THE PLAYERS ALL TRY TO STEAL THE BALL, COMMON IN EARLY ELEMENTARY SCHOOL SOCCER. ALSO KNOWN AS "THE BLOB" OR "THE SWARM."

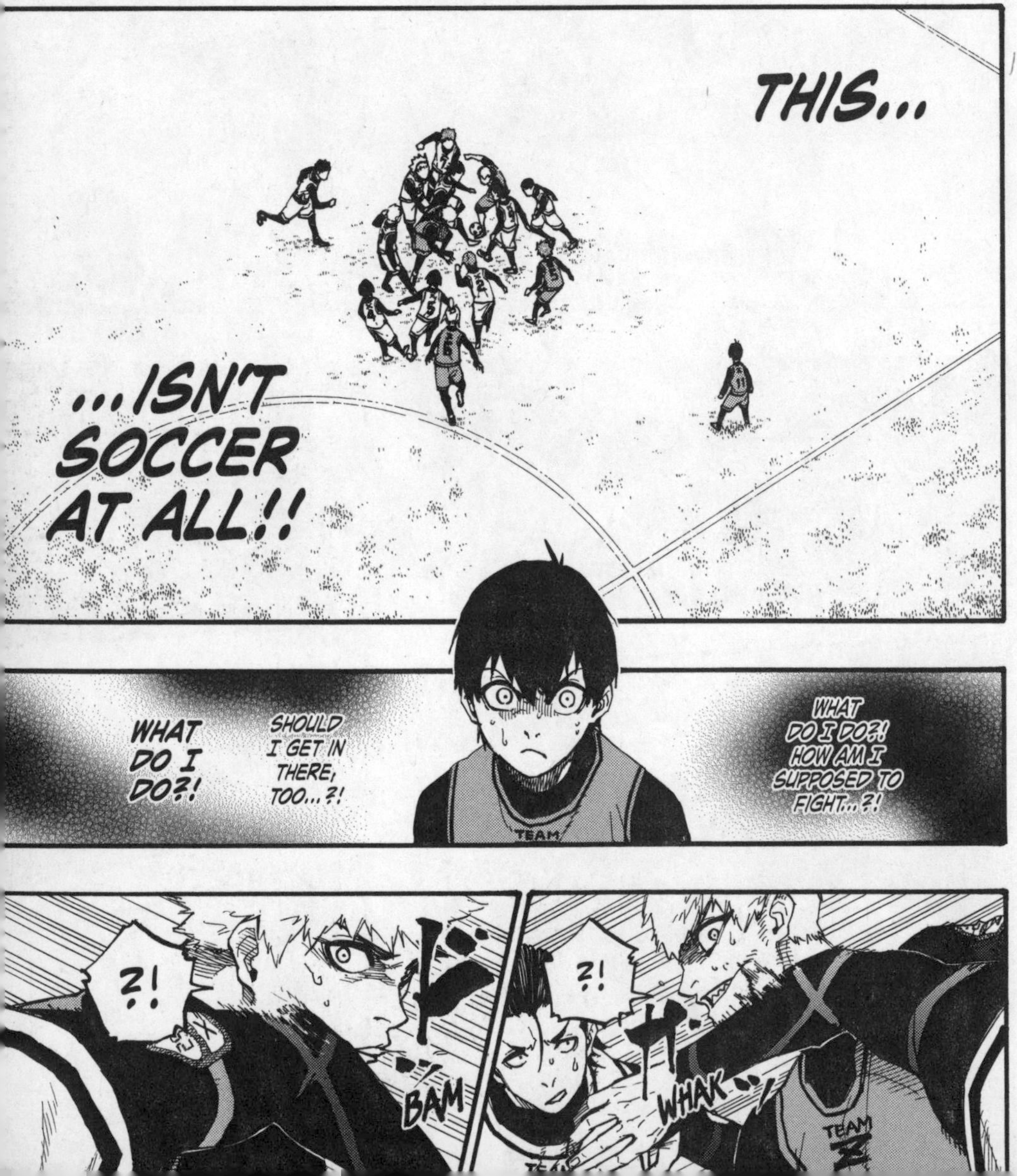
THIS...
...ISN'T SOCCER AT ALL!!
WHAT DO I DO?! HOW AM I SUPPOSED TO FIGHT...?!
SHOULD I GET IN THERE, TOO...?!
WHAT DO I DO?!
?!
WHAK
?!
BAM

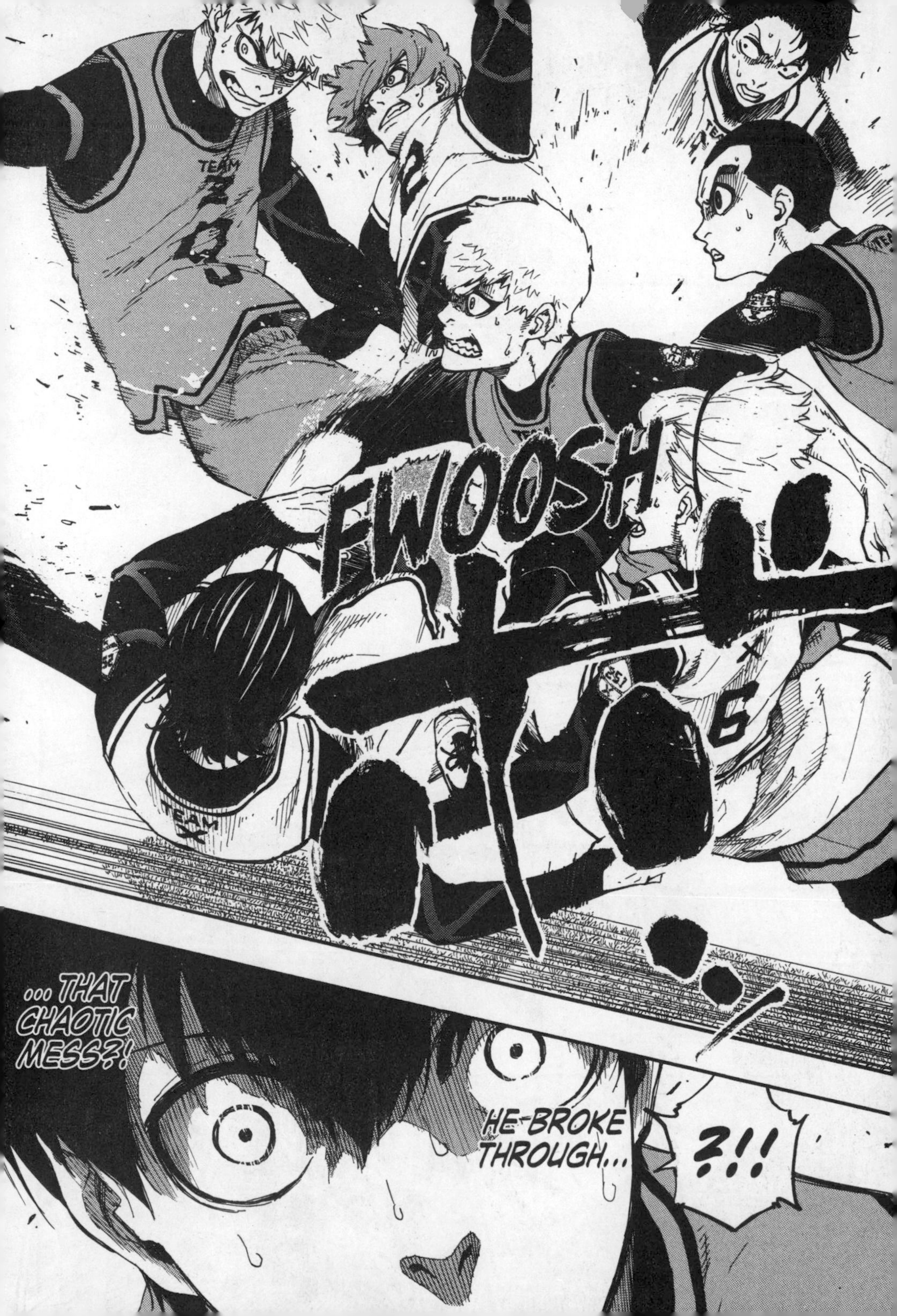
FWOOSH
?!!
HE BROKE THROUGH...
...THAT CHAOTIC MESS?!

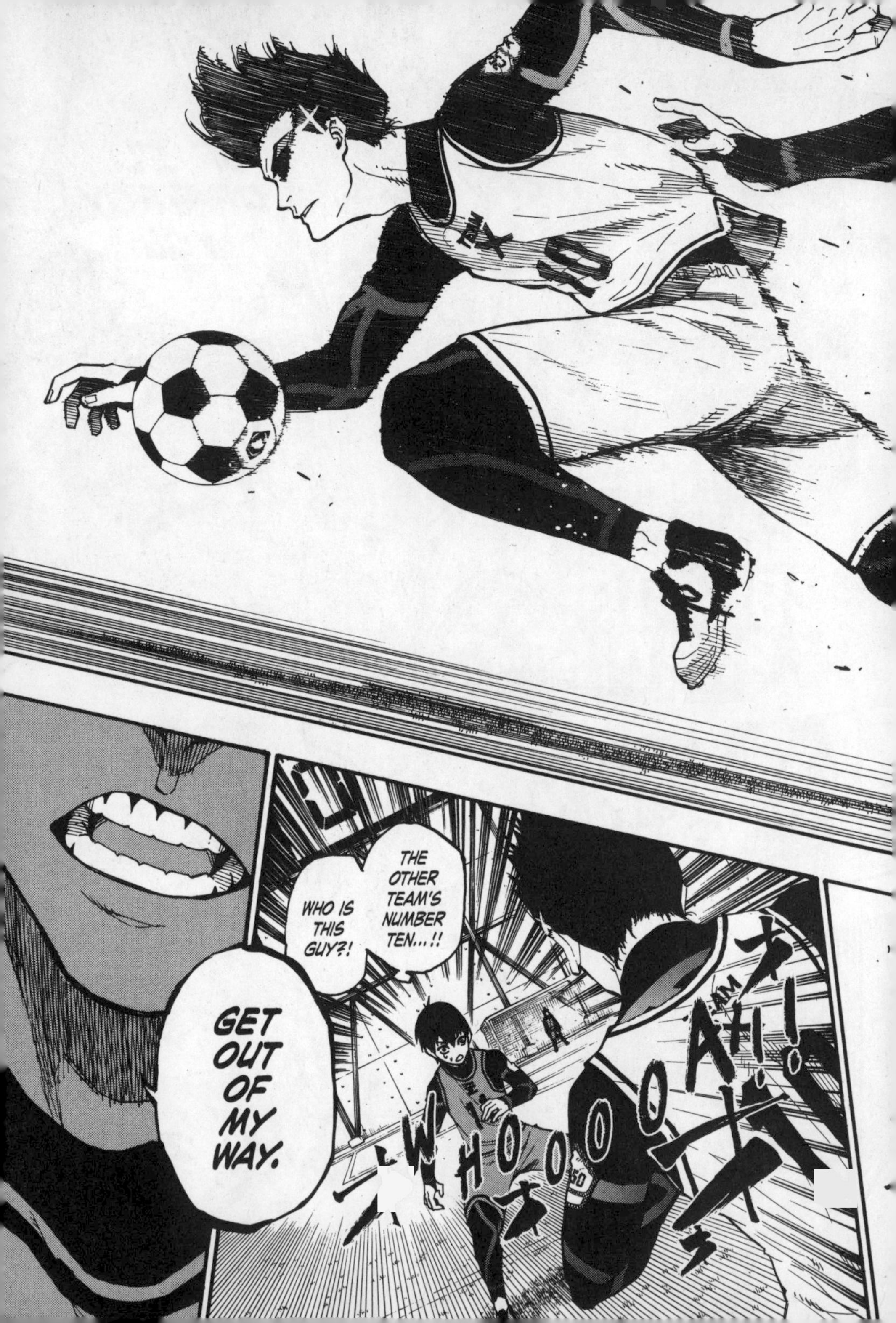
THE OTHER TEAM'S NUMBER TEN...!!
WHO IS THIS GUY?!
WHOOOOA!!
GET OUT OF MY WAY.

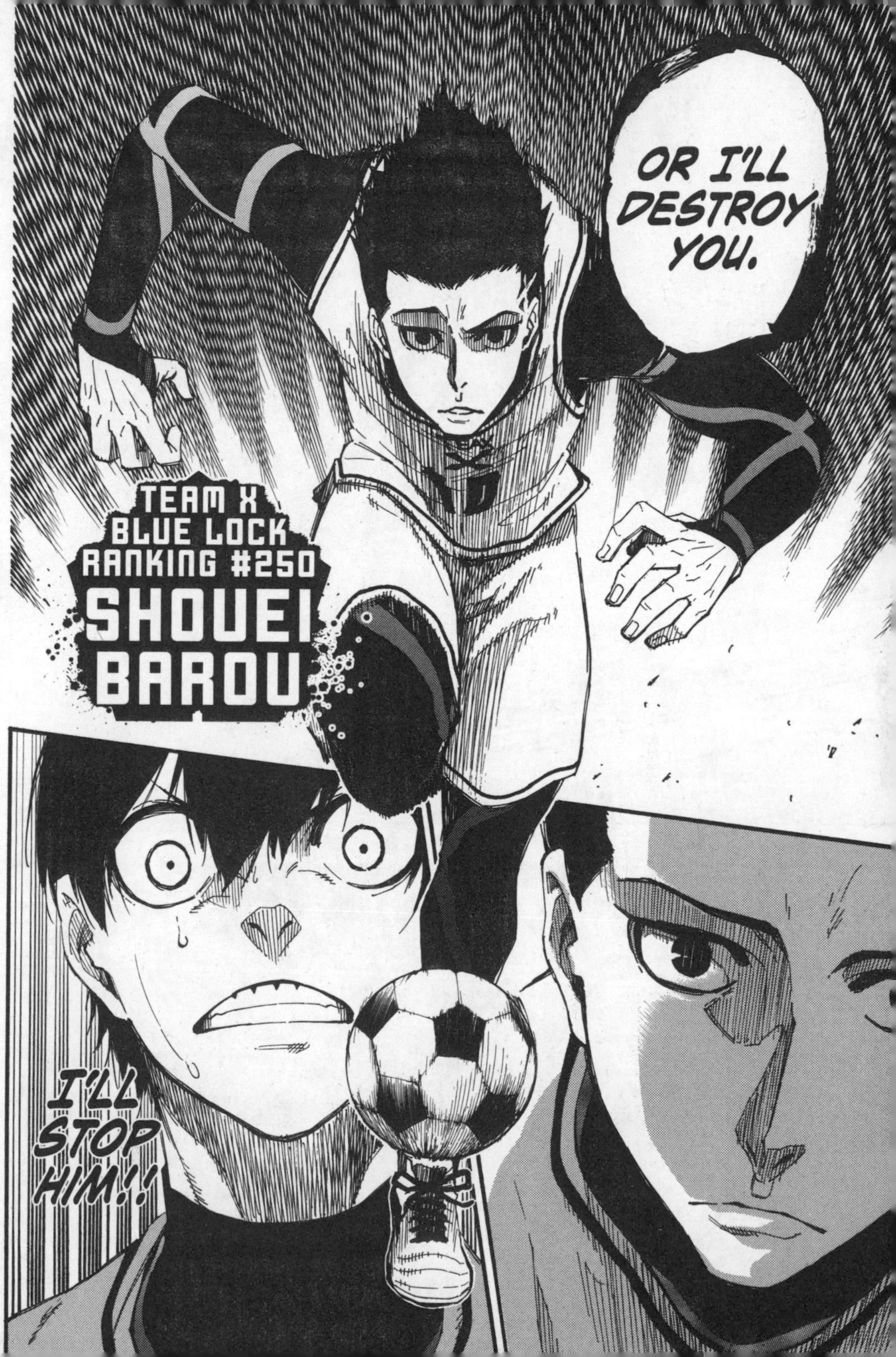
OR I'LL DESTROY YOU.
TEAM X BLUE LOCK RANKING #250
SHOUEI BAROU
I'LL STOP HIM!!

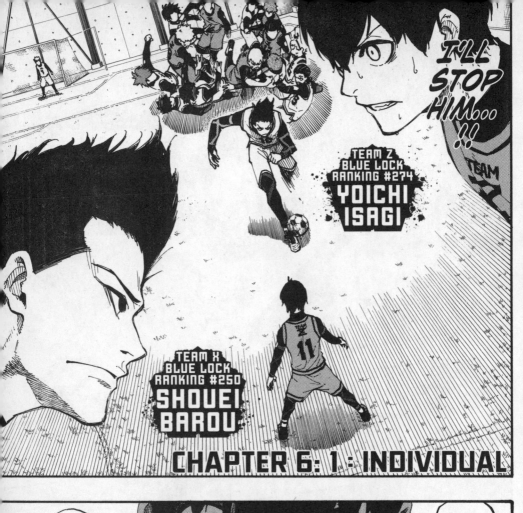

I'LL STOP HIM...!!

TEAM Z
BLUE LOCK
RANKING #274
YOICHI
ISAGI

TEAM X
BLUE LOCK
RANKING #250
SHOUEI
BAROU

CHAPTER 6: 1 · INDIVIDUAL

OR RIGHT...?!

LEFT ...?!

BRING IT...!!

HE'S GOING LEFT...!!

THERE IT IS...!

KCCH

KCCH

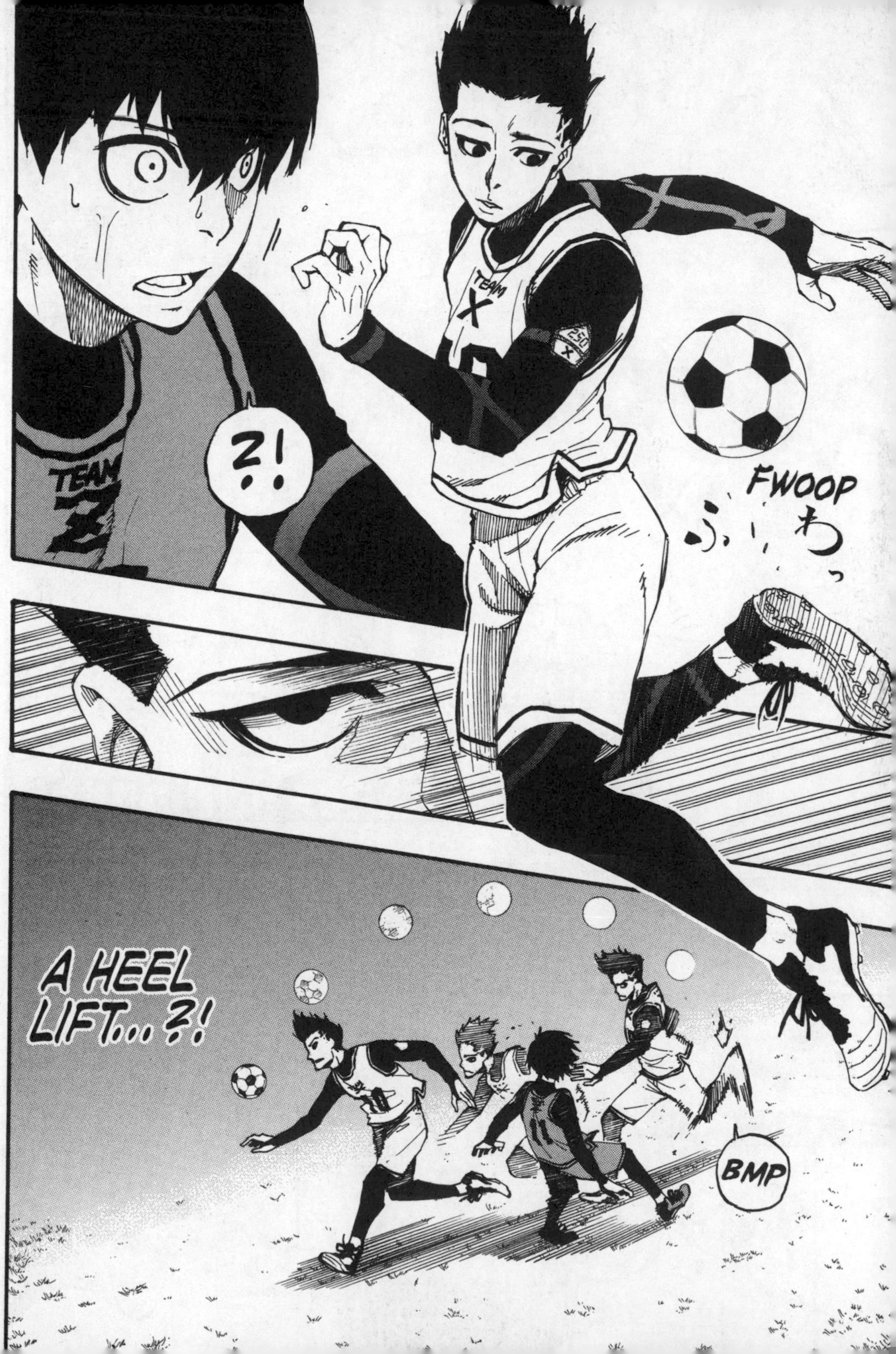
FWOOP
ふわっ
?!
BMP
A HEEL LIFT...?!

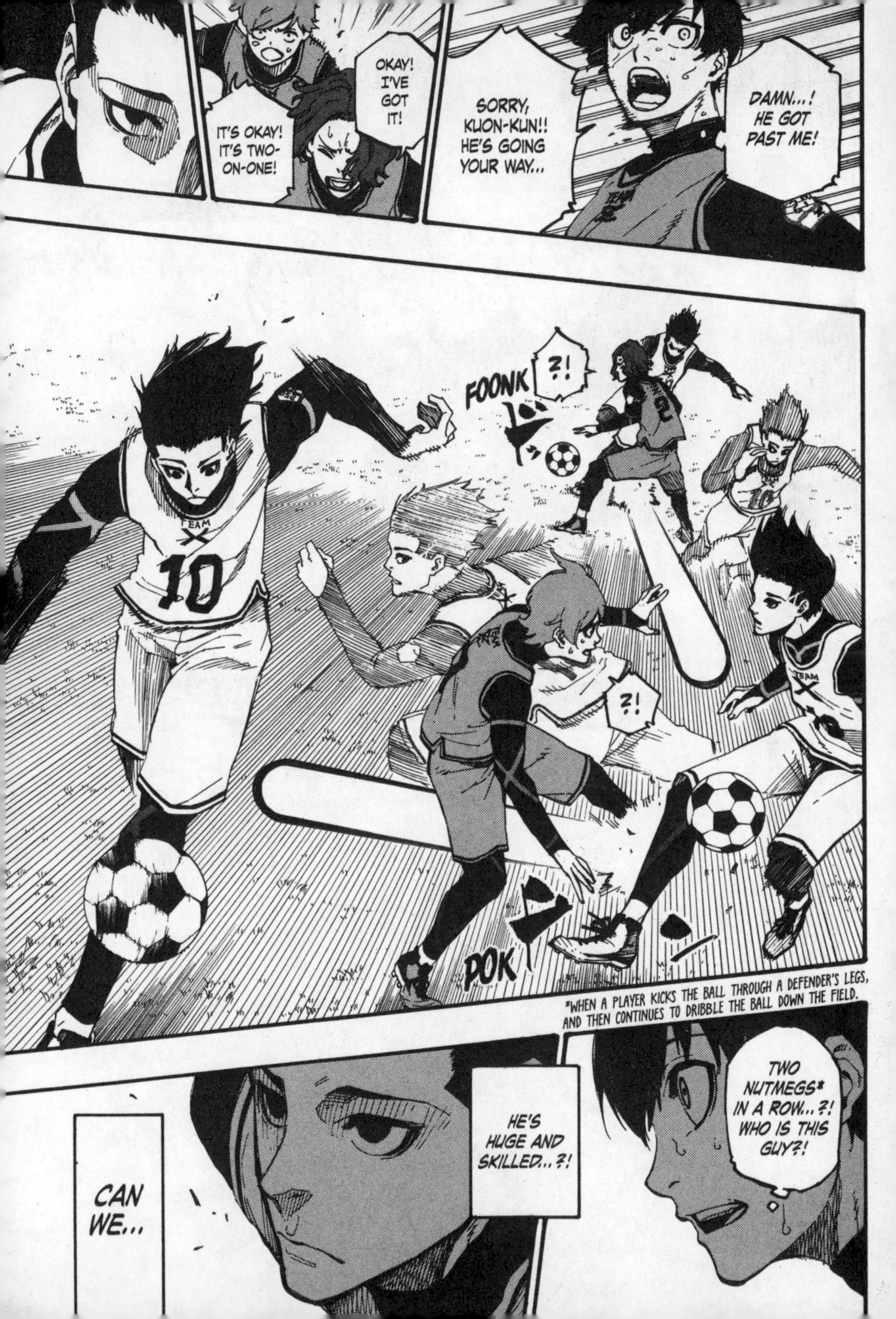
DAMN...! HE GOT PAST ME!
SORRY, KUON-KUN!! HE'S GOING YOUR WAY...
OKAY! I'VE GOT IT!
IT'S OKAY! IT'S TWO-ON-ONE!
?!
FOONK
?!
POK
*WHEN A PLAYER KICKS THE BALL THROUGH A DEFENDER'S LEGS, AND THEN CONTINUES TO DRIBBLE THE BALL DOWN THE FIELD.
TWO NUTMEGS* IN A ROW...?! WHO IS THIS GUY?!
HE'S HUGE AND SKILLED...?!
CAN WE...

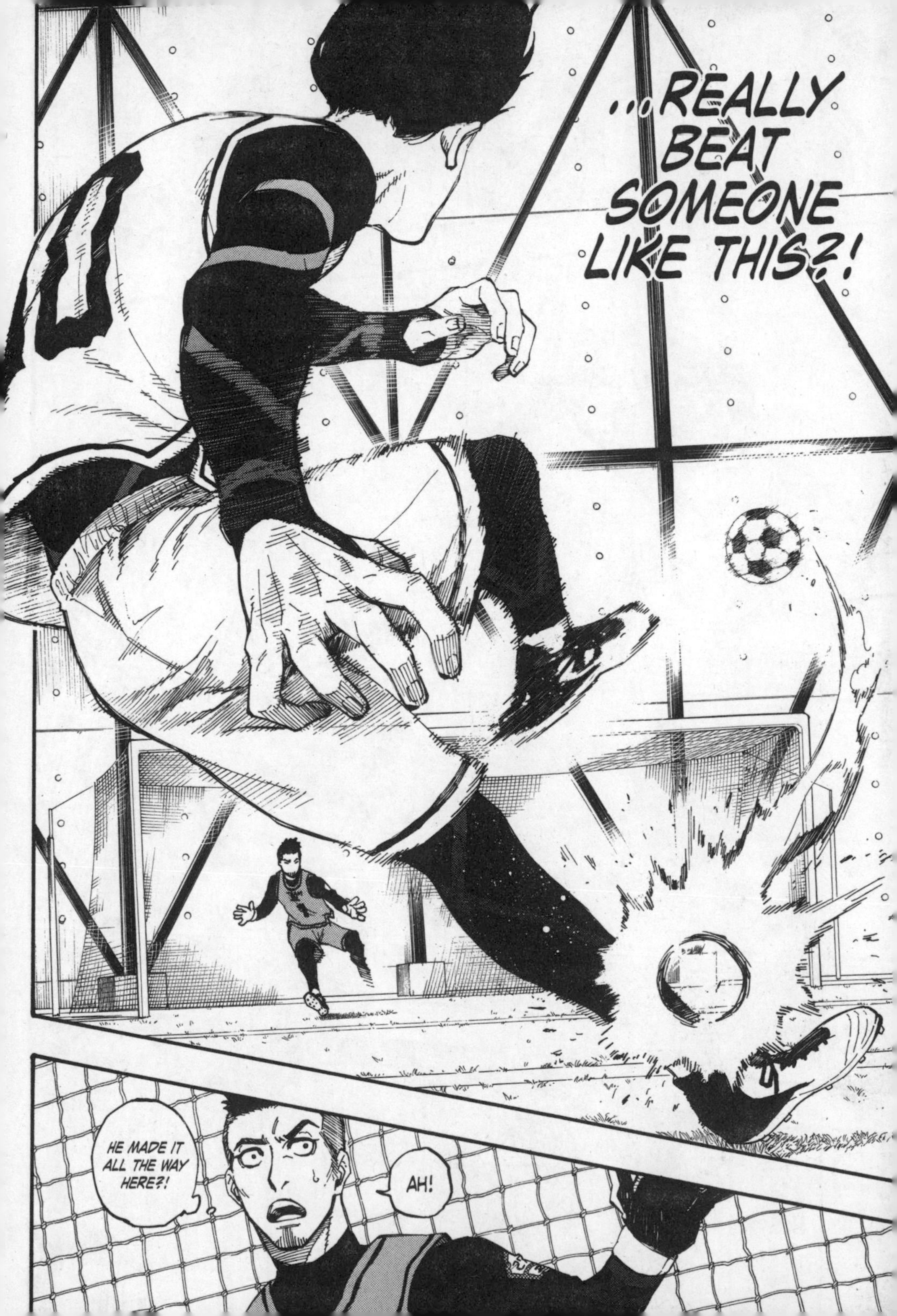
...REALLY BEAT SOMEONE LIKE THIS?!
AH!
HE MADE IT ALL THE WAY HERE?!

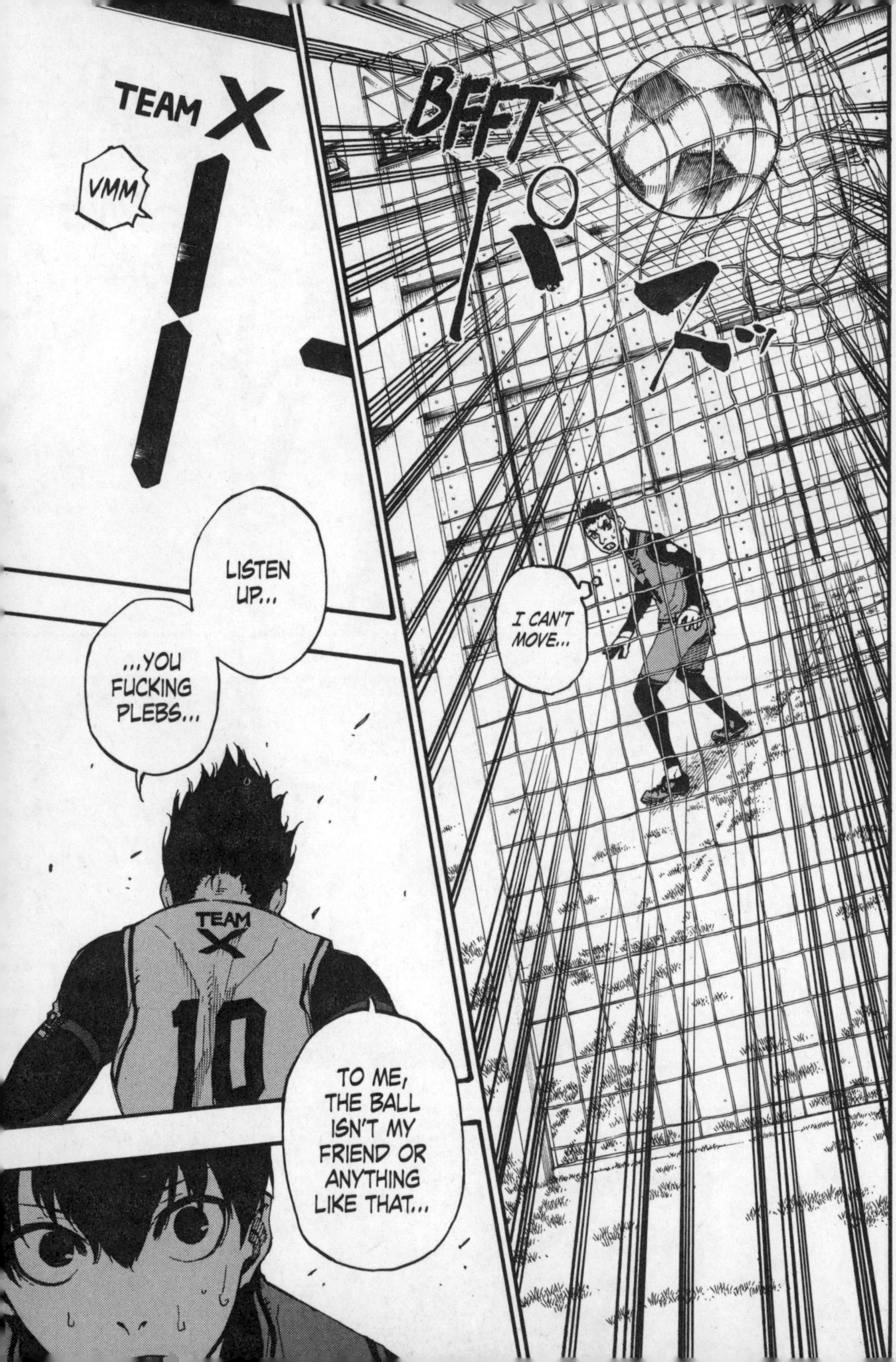
BFFT
パーッ
I CAN'T MOVE...
TEAM X
VMM
LISTEN UP...
...YOU FUCKING PLEBS...
TEAM X
10
TO ME, THE BALL ISN'T MY FRIEND OR ANYTHING LIKE THAT...

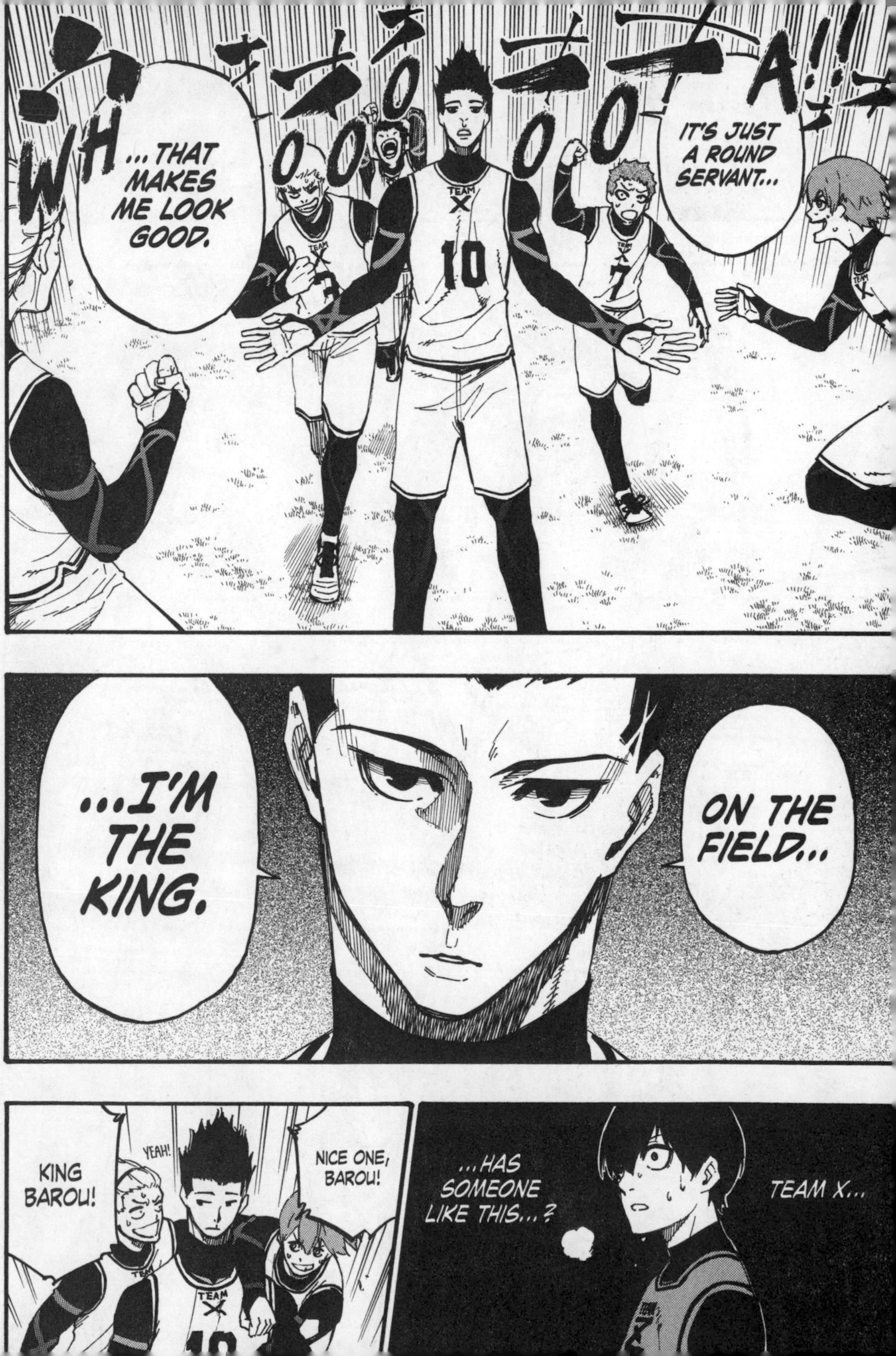
WHOOOOOA!!
IT'S JUST A ROUND SERVANT...
...THAT MAKES ME LOOK GOOD.
ON THE FIELD...
...I'M THE KING.
TEAM X...
...HAS SOMEONE LIKE THIS...?
NICE ONE, BAROU!
YEAH!
KING BAROU!

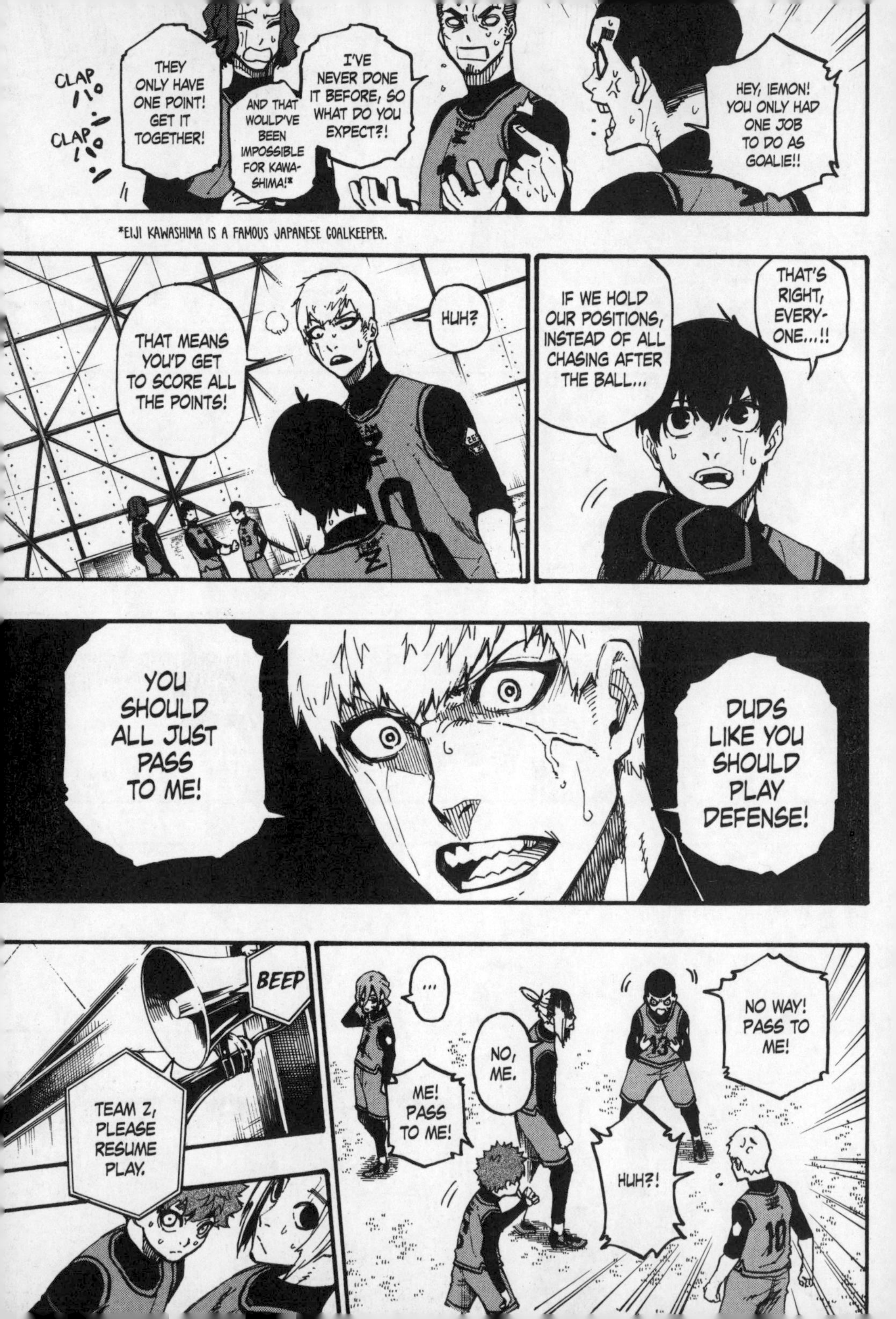
HEY, IEMON! YOU ONLY HAD ONE JOB TO DO AS GOALIE!!
I'VE NEVER DONE IT BEFORE, SO WHAT DO YOU EXPECT?!
AND THAT WOULD'VE BEEN IMPOSSIBLE FOR KAWASHIMA!*
THEY ONLY HAVE ONE POINT! GET IT TOGETHER!
CLAP
CLAP
THAT'S RIGHT, EVERYONE...!!
IF WE HOLD OUR POSITIONS, INSTEAD OF ALL CHASING AFTER THE BALL...
HUH?
THAT MEANS YOU'D GET TO SCORE ALL THE POINTS!
DUDS LIKE YOU SHOULD PLAY DEFENSE!
YOU SHOULD ALL JUST PASS TO ME!
NO WAY! PASS TO ME!
HUH?!
NO, ME.
...
ME! PASS TO ME!
BEEP
TEAM Z, PLEASE RESUME PLAY.

*EIJI KAWASHIMA IS A FAMOUS JAPANESE GOALKEEPER.

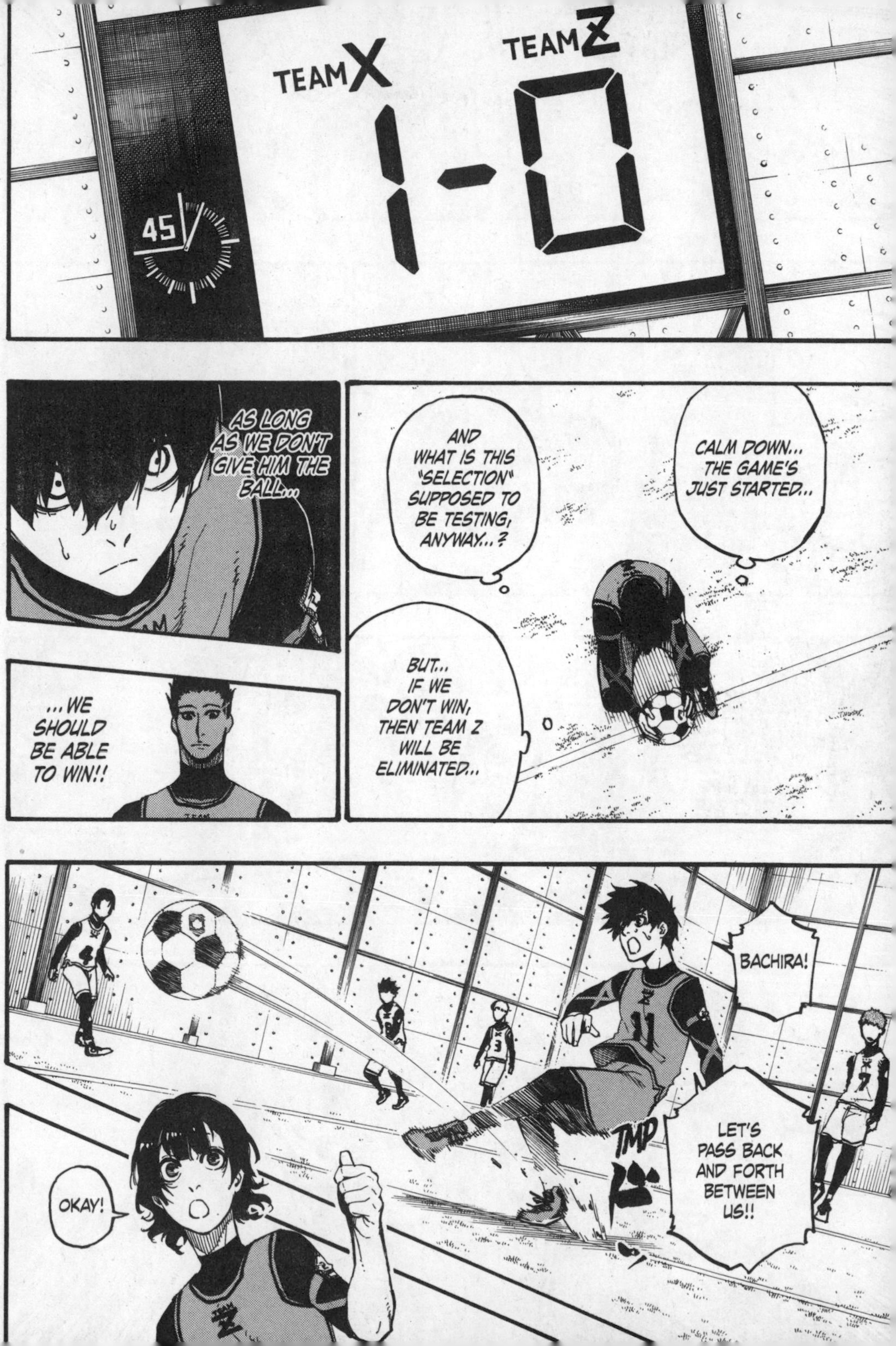
TEAM X
TEAM Z
1-0
45
CALM DOWN... THE GAME'S JUST STARTED...
AND WHAT IS THIS "SELECTION" SUPPOSED TO BE TESTING, ANYWAY...?
BUT... IF WE DON'T WIN, THEN TEAM Z WILL BE ELIMINATED...
AS LONG AS WE DON'T GIVE HIM THE BALL...
...WE SHOULD BE ABLE TO WIN!!
BACHIRA!
LET'S PASS BACK AND FORTH BETWEEN US!!
TMP
OKAY!

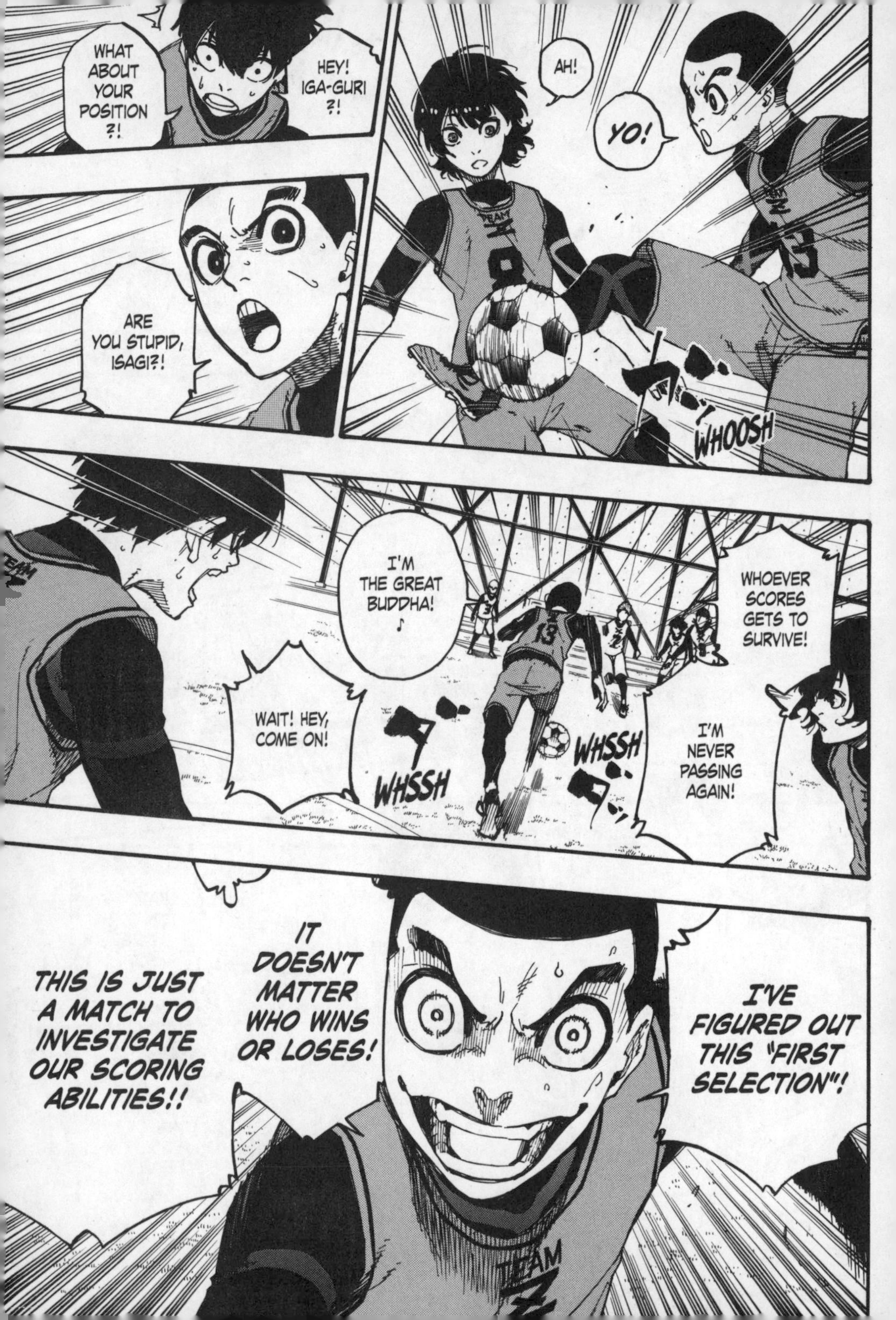
AH!
YO!
WHOOSH
HEY! IGA-GURI ?!
WHAT ABOUT YOUR POSITION ?!
ARE YOU STUPID, ISAGI?!
WHOEVER SCORES GETS TO SURVIVE!
I'M NEVER PASSING AGAIN!
WHSSH
I'M THE GREAT BUDDHA! ♪
WHSSH
WAIT! HEY, COME ON!
I'VE FIGURED OUT THIS "FIRST SELECTION"!
IT DOESN'T MATTER WHO WINS OR LOSES!
THIS IS JUST A MATCH TO INVESTIGATE OUR SCORING ABILITIES!!

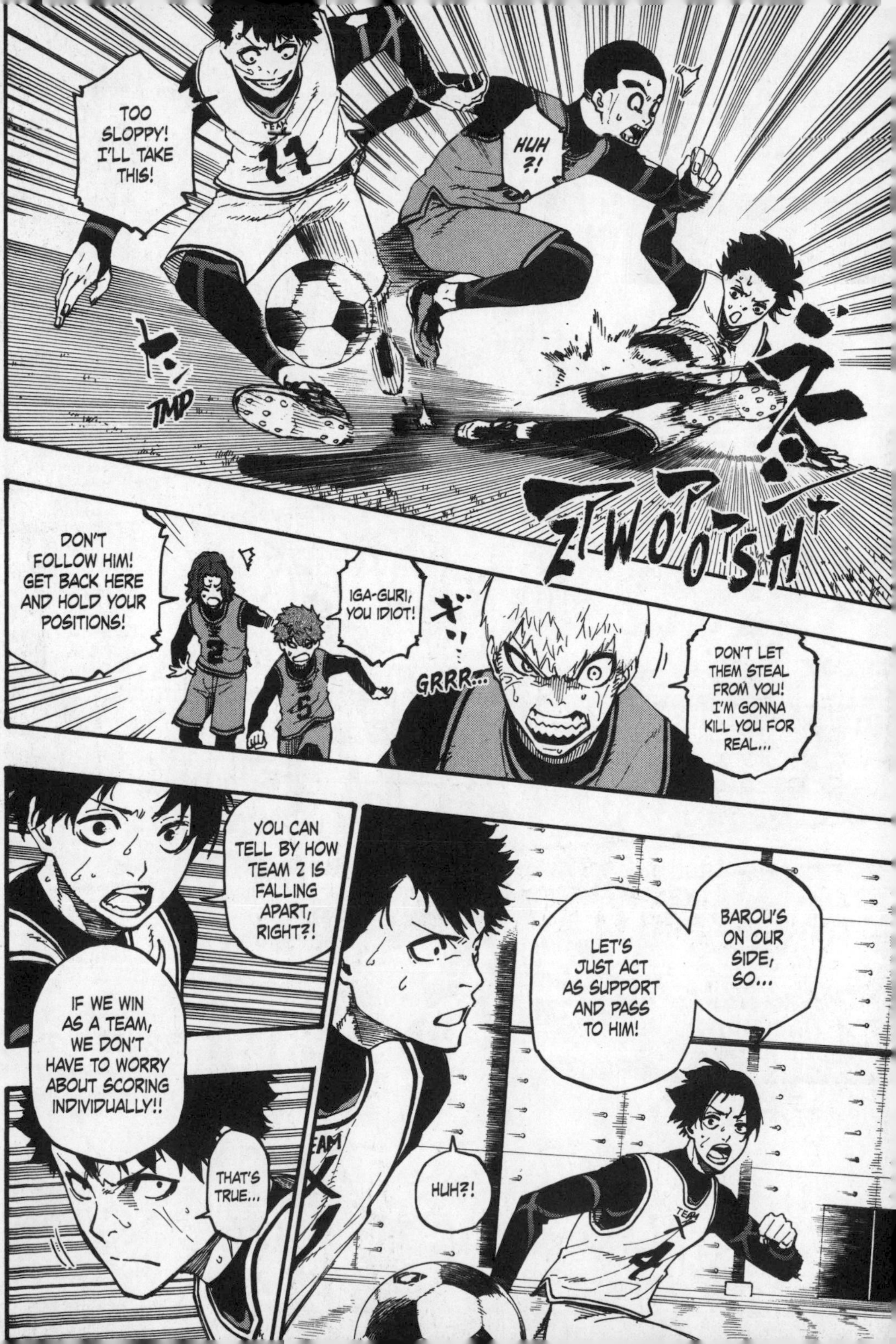
HUH?!
TOO SLOPPY! I'LL TAKE THIS!
TMP
ZWOOSH
DON'T LET THEM STEAL FROM YOU! I'M GONNA KILL YOU FOR REAL...
GRRR...
IGA-GURI, YOU IDIOT!
DON'T FOLLOW HIM! GET BACK HERE AND HOLD YOUR POSITIONS!
BAROU'S ON OUR SIDE, SO...
LET'S JUST ACT AS SUPPORT AND PASS TO HIM!
HUH?!
YOU CAN TELL BY HOW TEAM Z IS FALLING APART, RIGHT?!
IF WE WIN AS A TEAM, WE DON'T HAVE TO WORRY ABOUT SCORING INDIVIDUALLY!!
THAT'S TRUE...

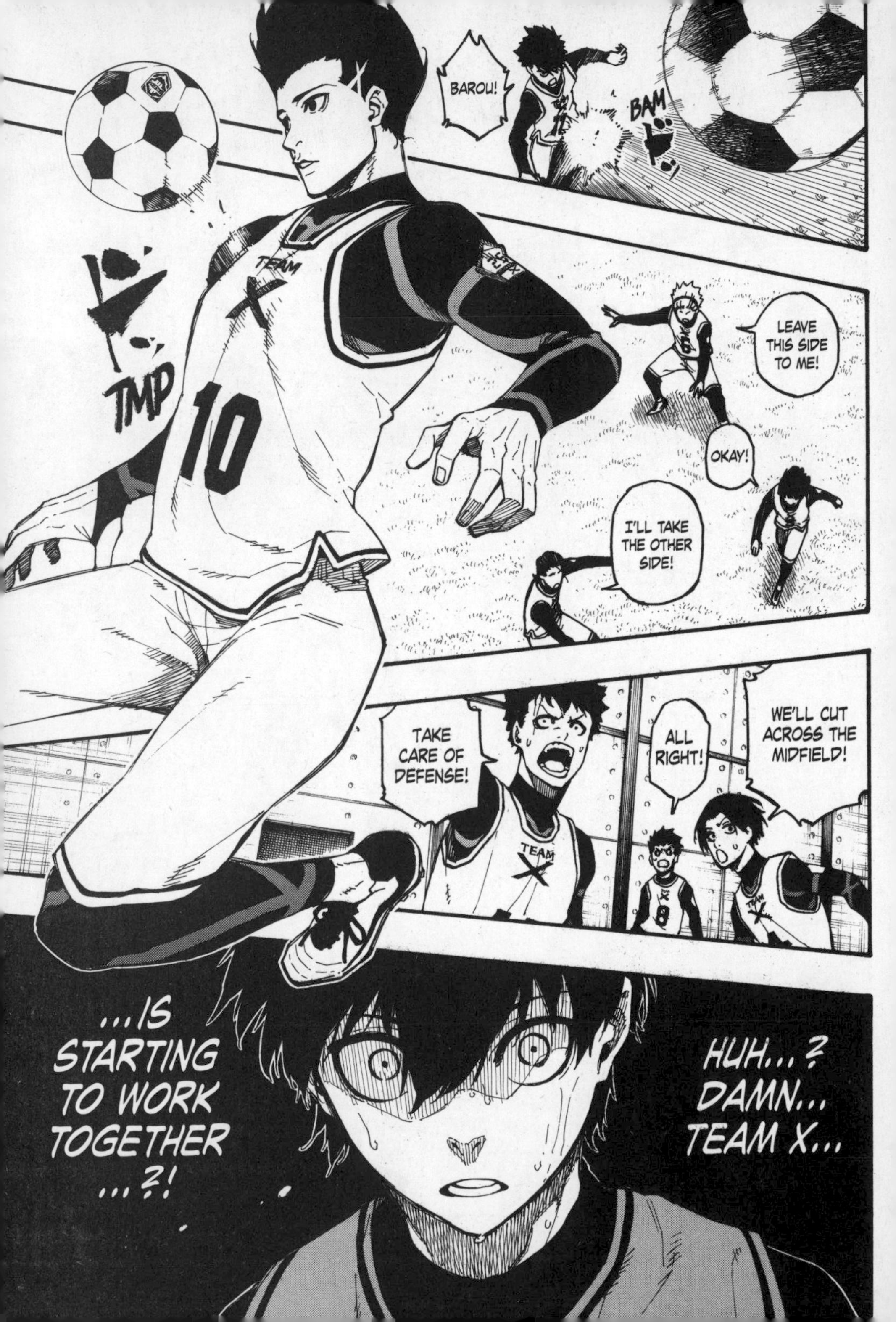
BAROU!
BAM
LEAVE THIS SIDE TO ME!
OKAY!
I'LL TAKE THE OTHER SIDE!
WE'LL CUT ACROSS THE MIDFIELD!
ALL RIGHT!
TAKE CARE OF DEFENSE!
TMP
HUH...? DAMN... TEAM X...
...IS STARTING TO WORK TOGETHER ...?!

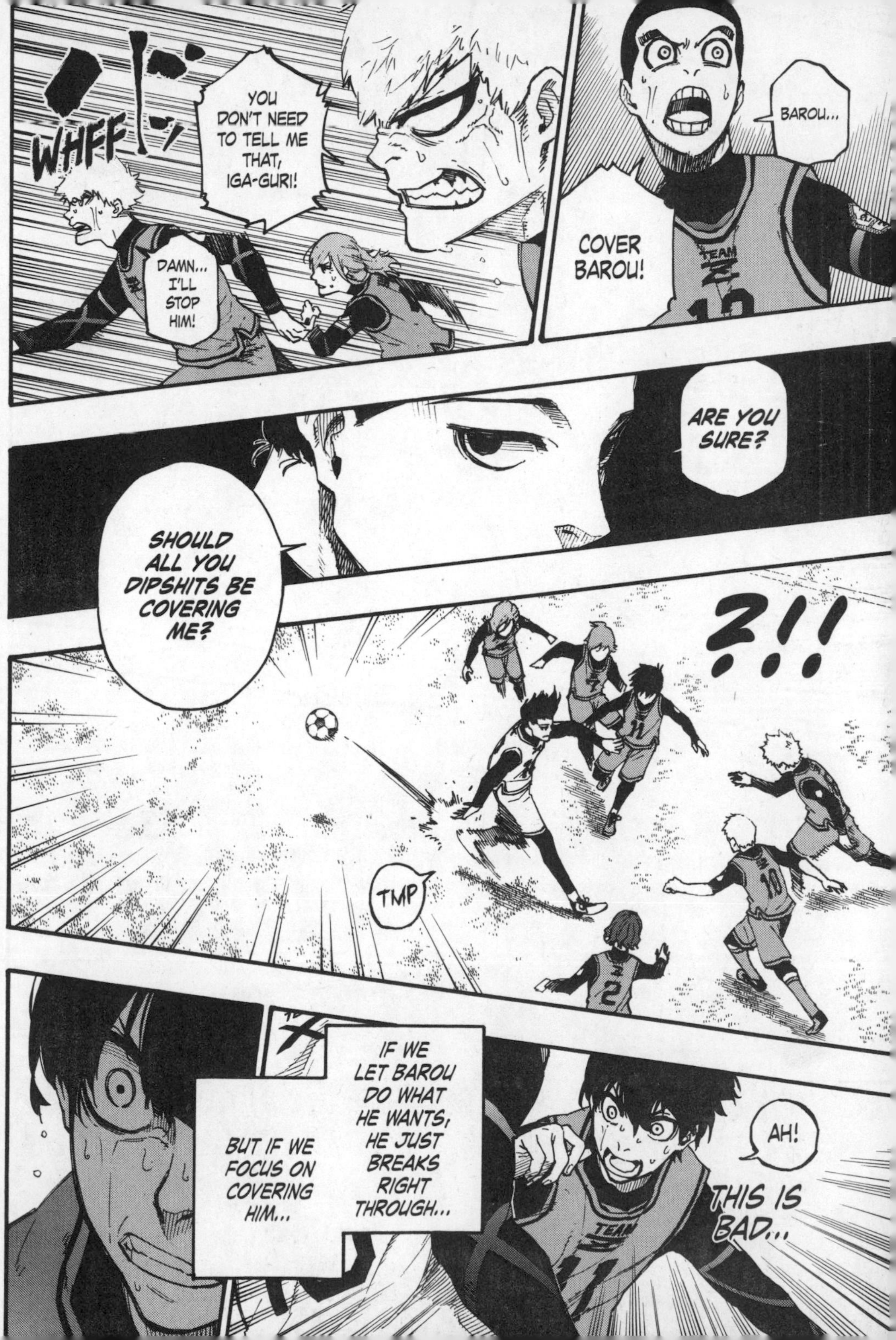

BAROU...
COVER BAROU!
YOU DON'T NEED TO TELL ME THAT, IGA-GURI!
WHFF
DAMN... I'LL STOP HIM!
ARE YOU SURE?
SHOULD ALL YOU DIPSHITS BE COVERING ME?
?!!
TMP
AH!
THIS IS BAD...
IF WE LET BAROU DO WHAT HE WANTS, HE JUST BREAKS RIGHT THROUGH...
BUT IF WE FOCUS ON COVERING HIM...

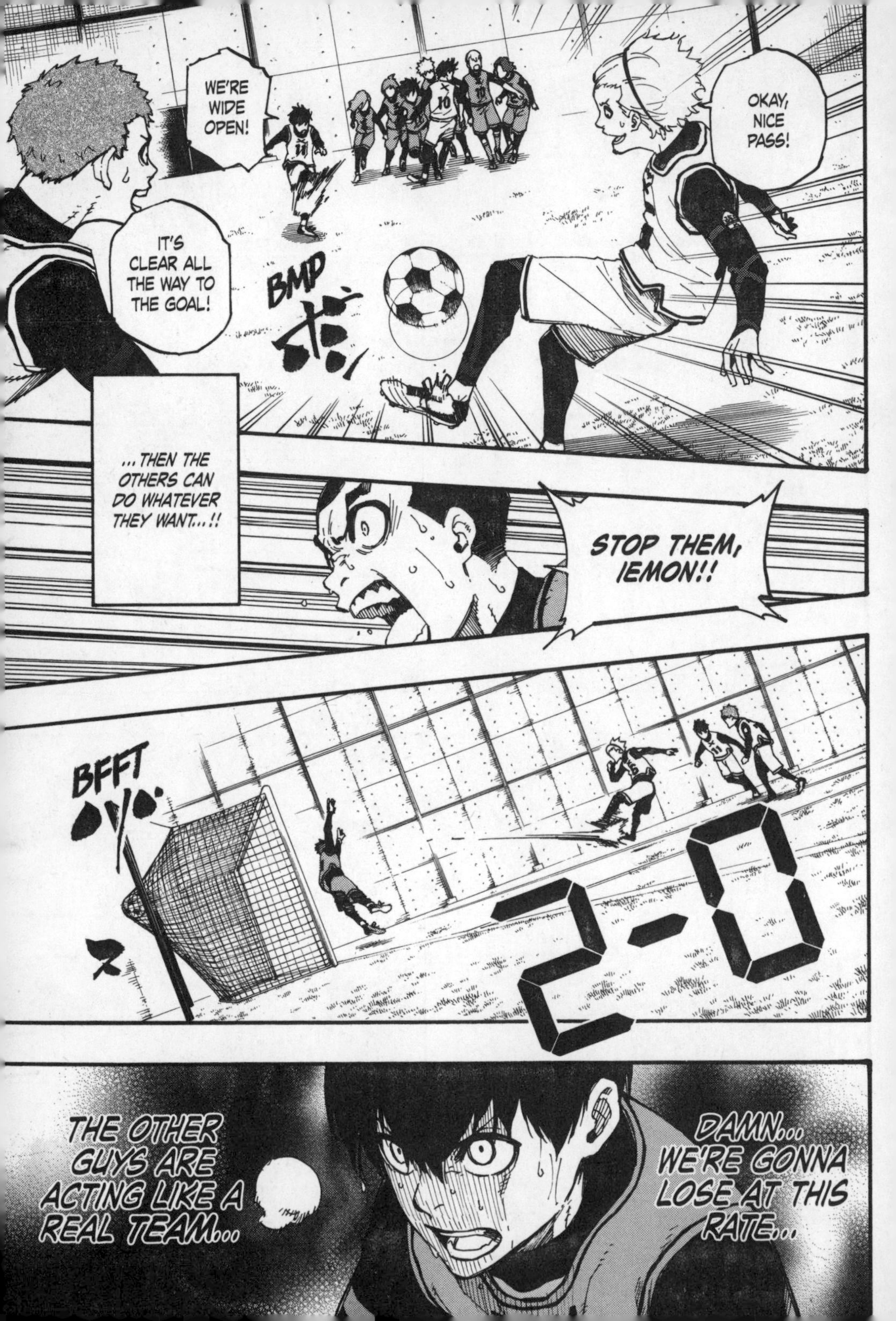
OKAY, NICE PASS!
WE'RE WIDE OPEN!
IT'S CLEAR ALL THE WAY TO THE GOAL!
BMP
...THEN THE OTHERS CAN DO WHATEVER THEY WANT...!!
STOP THEM, IEMON!!
BFFT
2-0
DAMN... WE'RE GONNA LOSE AT THIS RATE...
THE OTHER GUYS ARE ACTING LIKE A REAL TEAM...

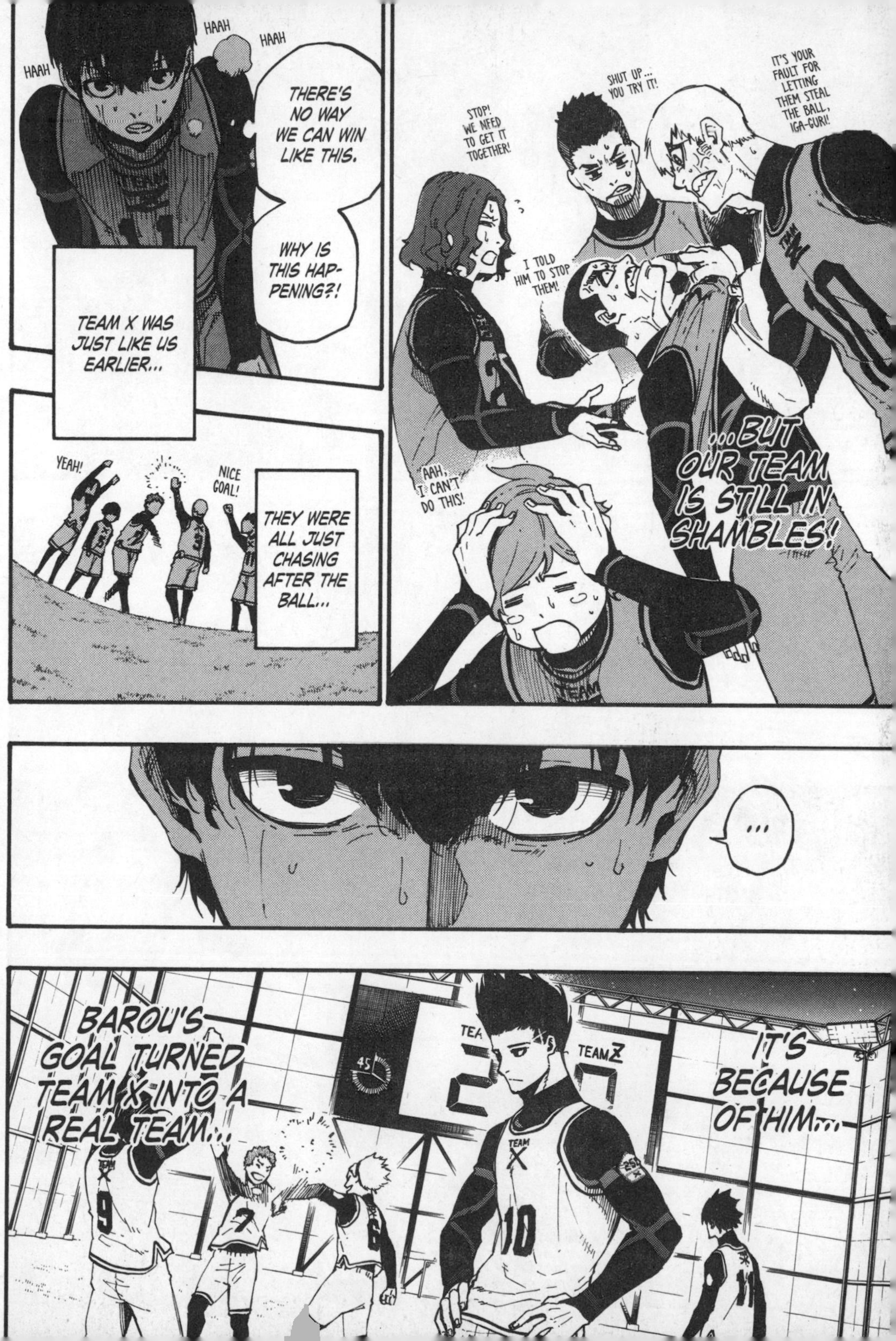
IT'S YOUR FAULT FOR LETTING THEM STEAL THE BALL, IGA-GURI!
SHUT UP... YOU TRY IT!
STOP! WE NEED TO GET IT TOGETHER!
I TOLD HIM TO STOP THEM!
...BUT OUR TEAM IS STILL IN SHAMBLES!
AAH, I CAN'T DO THIS!
HAAH
HAAH
HAAH
THERE'S NO WAY WE CAN WIN LIKE THIS.
WHY IS THIS HAPPENING?!
TEAM X WAS JUST LIKE US EARLIER...
THEY WERE ALL JUST CHASING AFTER THE BALL...
NICE GOAL!
YEAH!
...
IT'S BECAUSE OF HIM...
TEAM Z
BAROU'S GOAL TURNED TEAM X INTO A REAL TEAM...

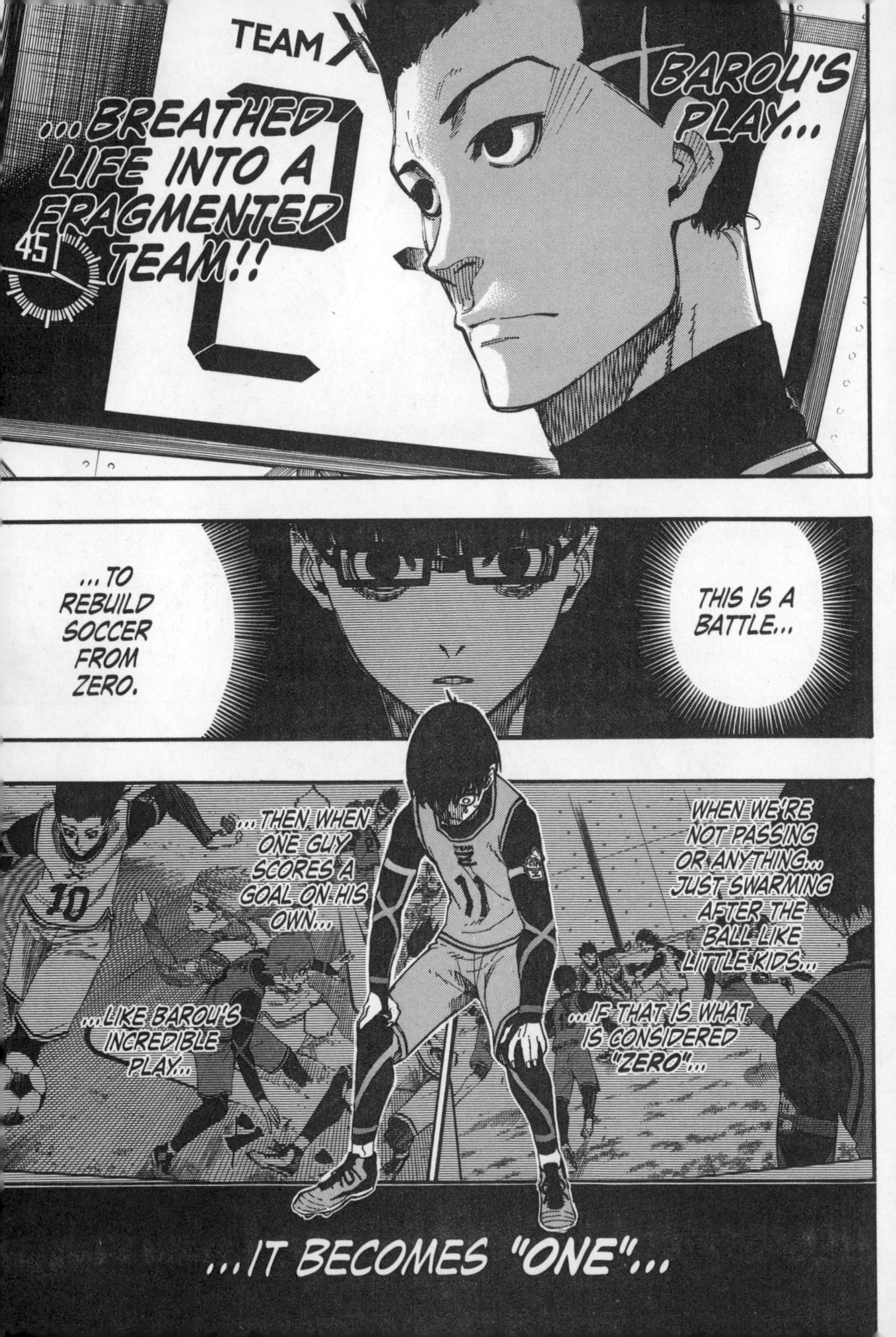
BAROU'S PLAY...
TEAM X
...BREATHED LIFE INTO A FRAGMENTED TEAM!!
45
THIS IS A BATTLE...
...TO REBUILD SOCCER FROM ZERO.
WHEN WE'RE NOT PASSING OR ANYTHING... JUST SWARMING AFTER THE BALL LIKE LITTLE KIDS...
...IF THAT IS WHAT IS CONSIDERED "ZERO"...
...THEN WHEN ONE GUY SCORES A GOAL ON HIS OWN...
...LIKE BAROU'S INCREDIBLE PLAY...
...IT BECOMES "ONE"...

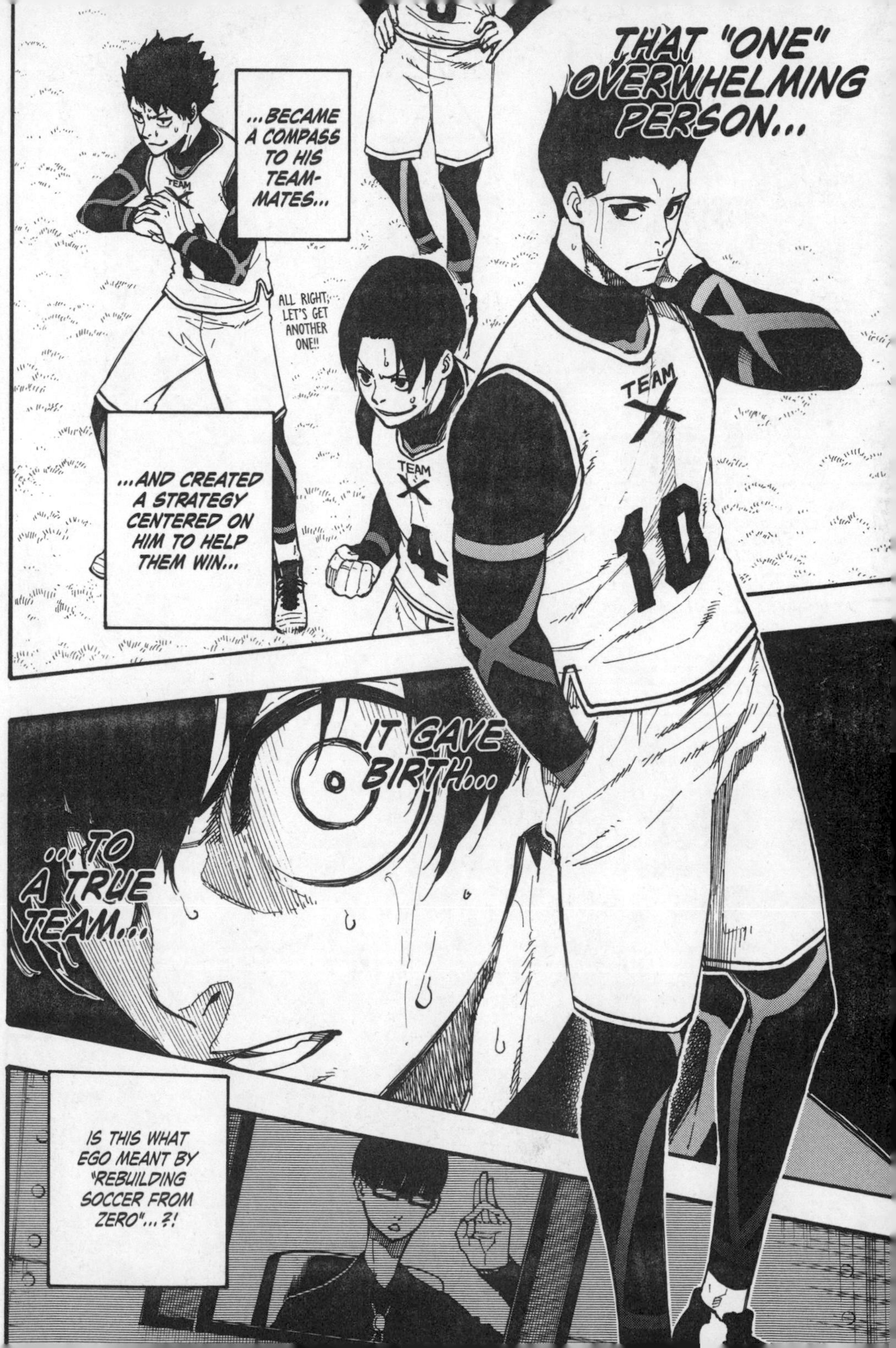
THAT "ONE" OVERWHELMING PERSON...
...BECAME A COMPASS TO HIS TEAM-MATES...
ALL RIGHT, LET'S GET ANOTHER ONE!!
...AND CREATED A STRATEGY CENTERED ON HIM TO HELP THEM WIN...
IT GAVE BIRTH...
...TO A TRUE TEAM...
IS THIS WHAT EGO MEANT BY "REBUILDING SOCCER FROM ZERO"...?!

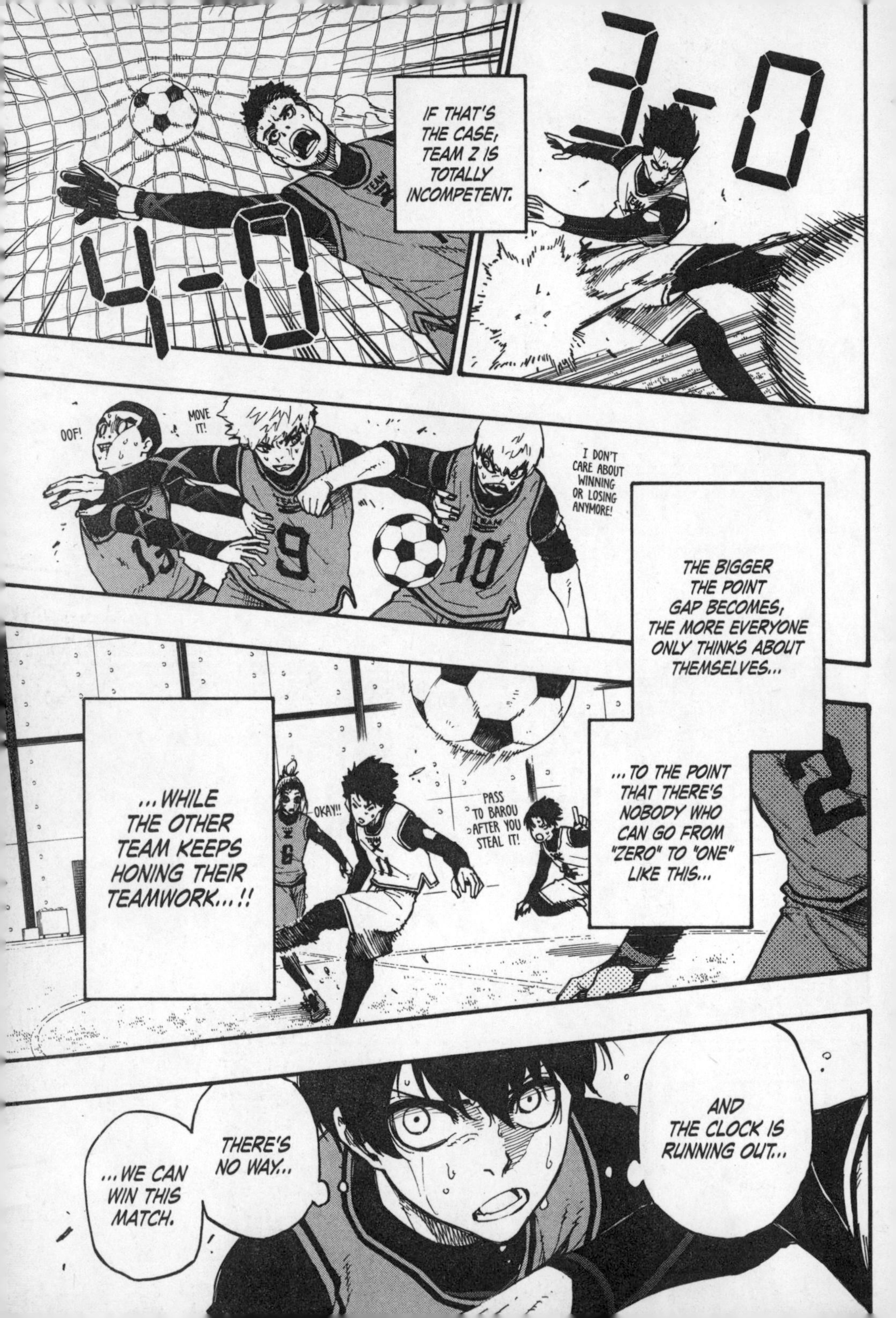
3-0
IF THAT'S THE CASE, TEAM Z IS TOTALLY INCOMPETENT.
4-0
I DON'T CARE ABOUT WINNING OR LOSING ANYMORE!
MOVE IT!
OOF!
THE BIGGER THE POINT GAP BECOMES, THE MORE EVERYONE ONLY THINKS ABOUT THEMSELVES...
...TO THE POINT THAT THERE'S NOBODY WHO CAN GO FROM "ZERO" TO "ONE" LIKE THIS...
PASS TO BAROU AFTER YOU STEAL IT!
OKAY!!
...WHILE THE OTHER TEAM KEEPS HONING THEIR TEAMWORK...!!
AND THE CLOCK IS RUNNING OUT...
THERE'S NO WAY...
...WE CAN WIN THIS MATCH.

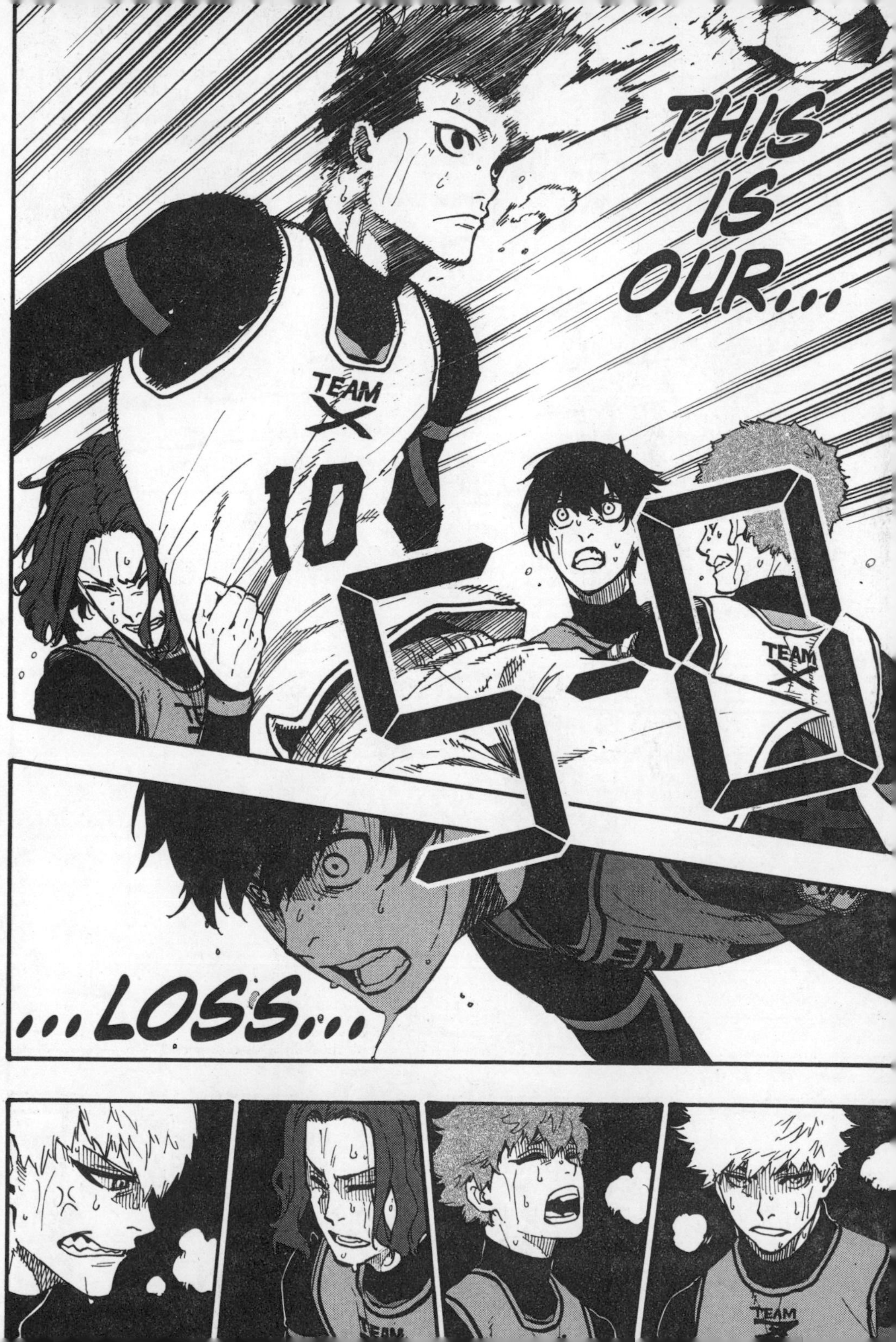
THIS IS OUR...
TEAM X
10
5-0
...LOSS...

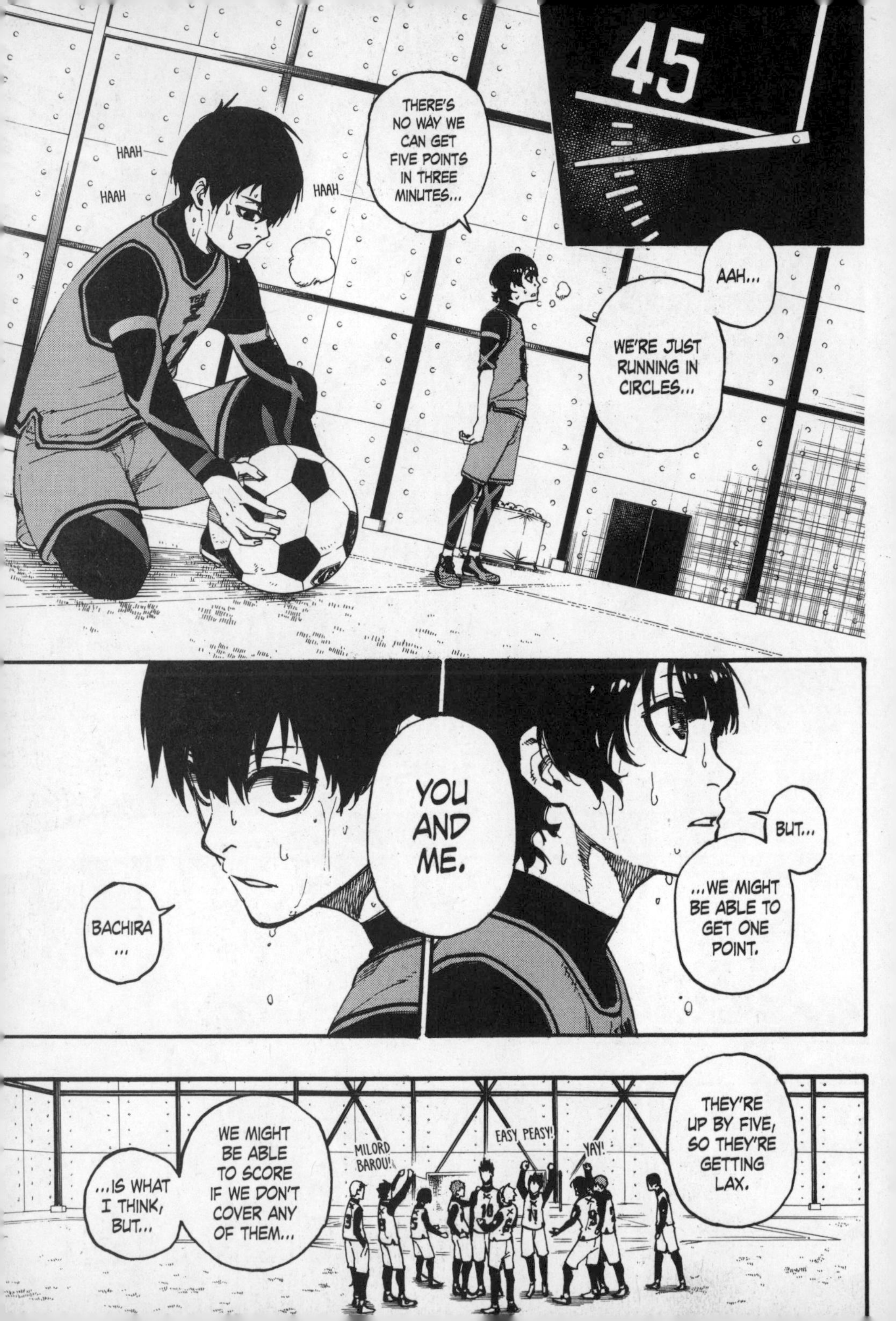
45
AAH...
WE'RE JUST RUNNING IN CIRCLES...
THERE'S NO WAY WE CAN GET FIVE POINTS IN THREE MINUTES...
HAAH
HAAH
HAAH
BUT...
...WE MIGHT BE ABLE TO GET ONE POINT.
YOU AND ME.
BACHIRA ...
THEY'RE UP BY FIVE, SO THEY'RE GETTING LAX.
YAY!
EASY PEASY!
MILORD BAROU!
WE MIGHT BE ABLE TO SCORE IF WE DON'T COVER ANY OF THEM...
...IS WHAT I THINK, BUT...

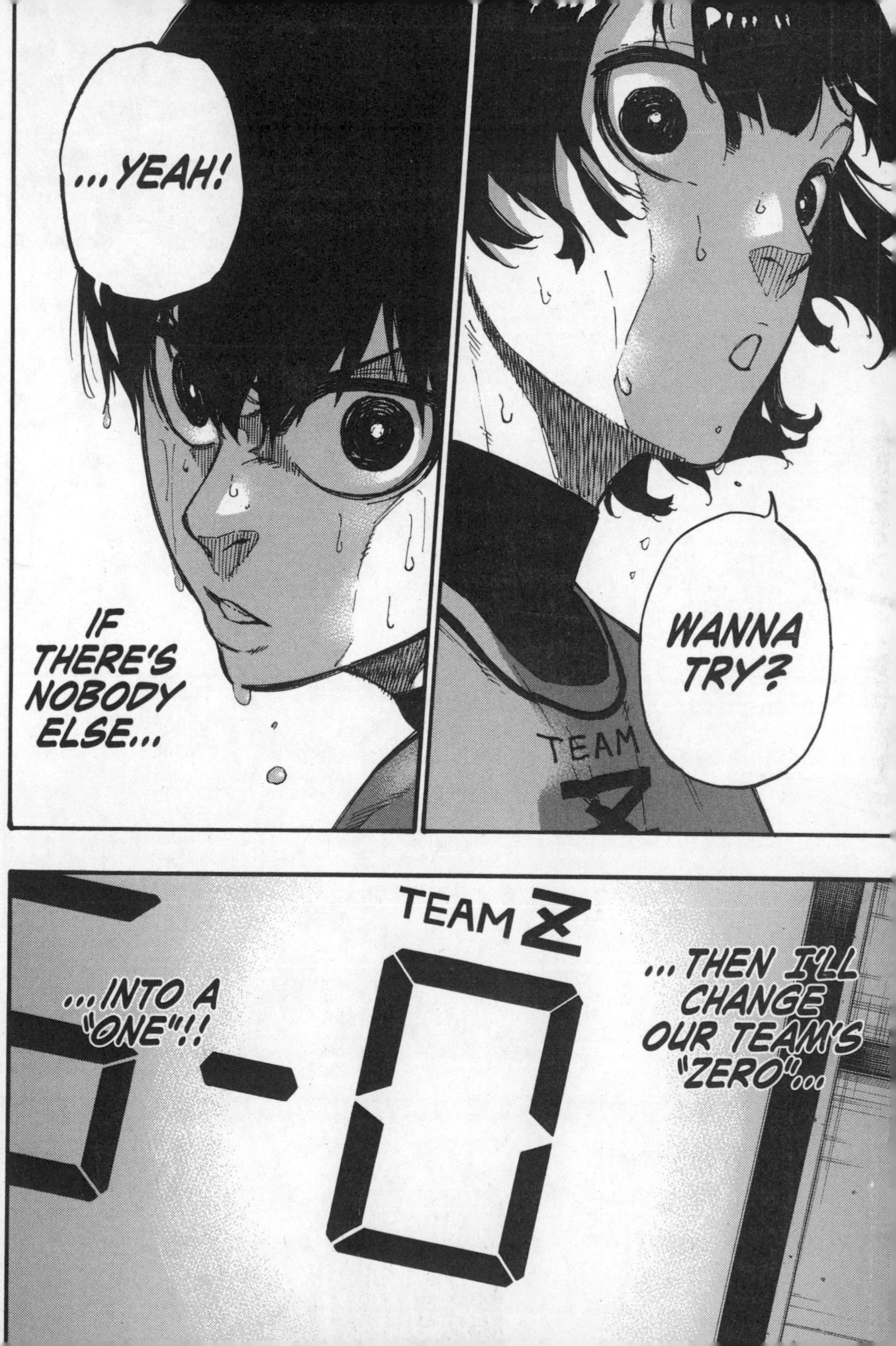
WANNA TRY?
TEAM Z
...YEAH!
IF THERE'S NOBODY ELSE...
TEAM Z
...THEN I'LL CHANGE OUR TEAM'S "ZERO"...
...INTO A "ONE"!!

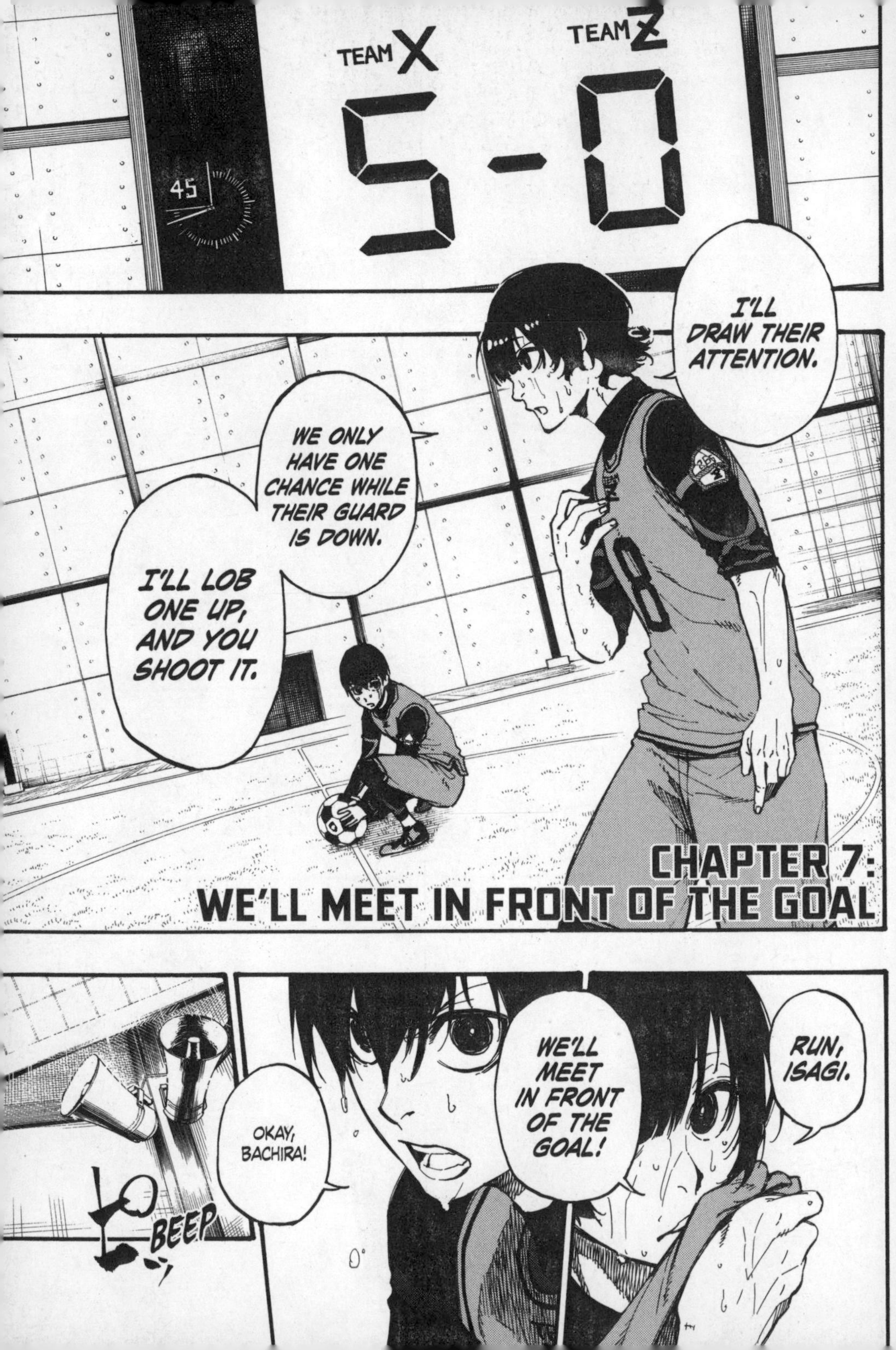
TEAM X
TEAM Z
5-0
45
I'LL DRAW THEIR ATTENTION.
WE ONLY HAVE ONE CHANCE WHILE THEIR GUARD IS DOWN.
I'LL LOB ONE UP, AND YOU SHOOT IT.
CHAPTER 7: WE'LL MEET IN FRONT OF THE GOAL
RUN, ISAGI.
WE'LL MEET IN FRONT OF THE GOAL!
OKAY, BACHIRA!
BEEP

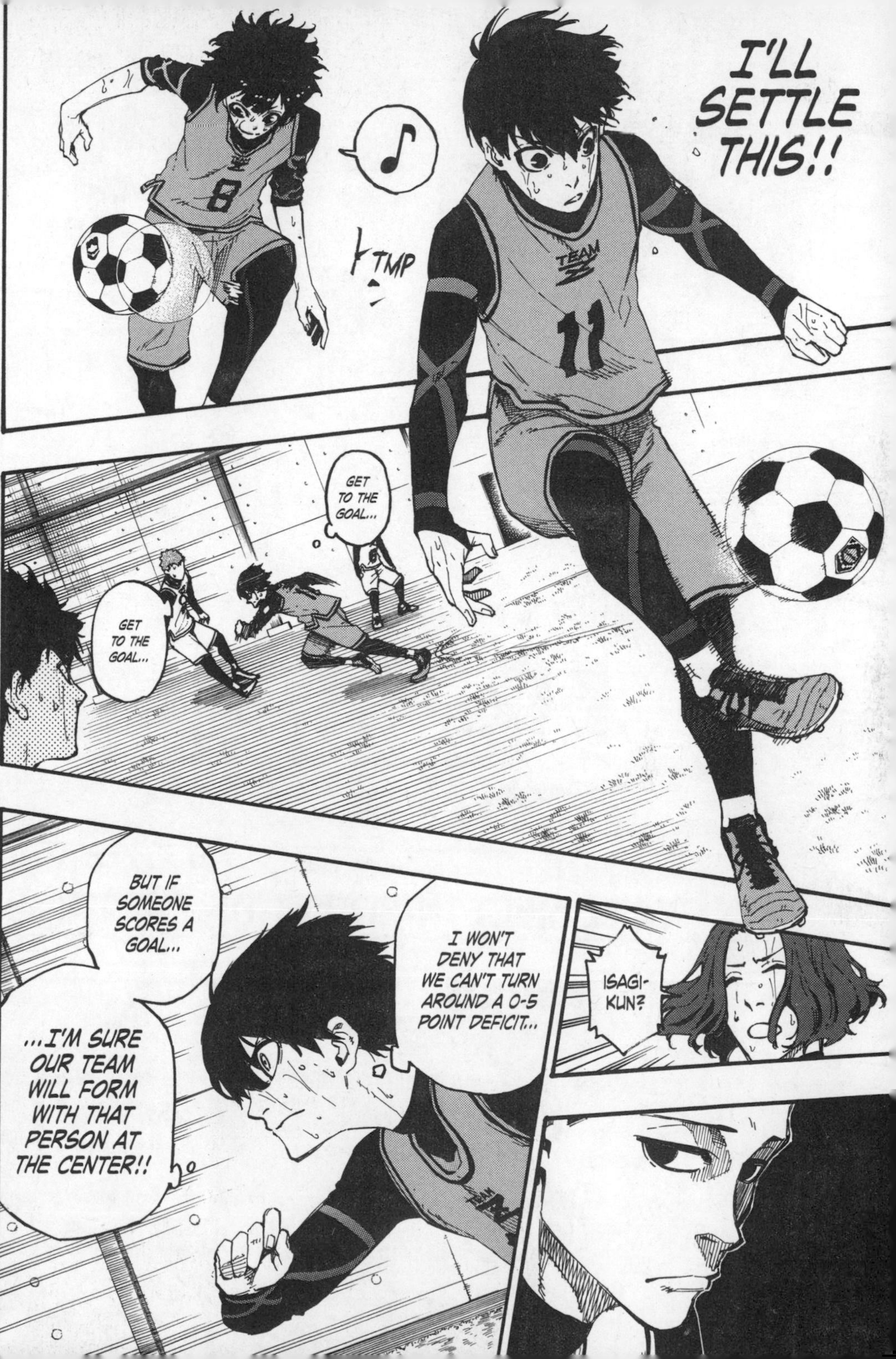
I'LL SETTLE THIS!!
♪
TMP
GET TO THE GOAL...
GET TO THE GOAL...
ISAGI-KUN?
I WON'T DENY THAT WE CAN'T TURN AROUND A 0-5 POINT DEFICIT...
BUT IF SOMEONE SCORES A GOAL...
...I'M SURE OUR TEAM WILL FORM WITH THAT PERSON AT THE CENTER!!

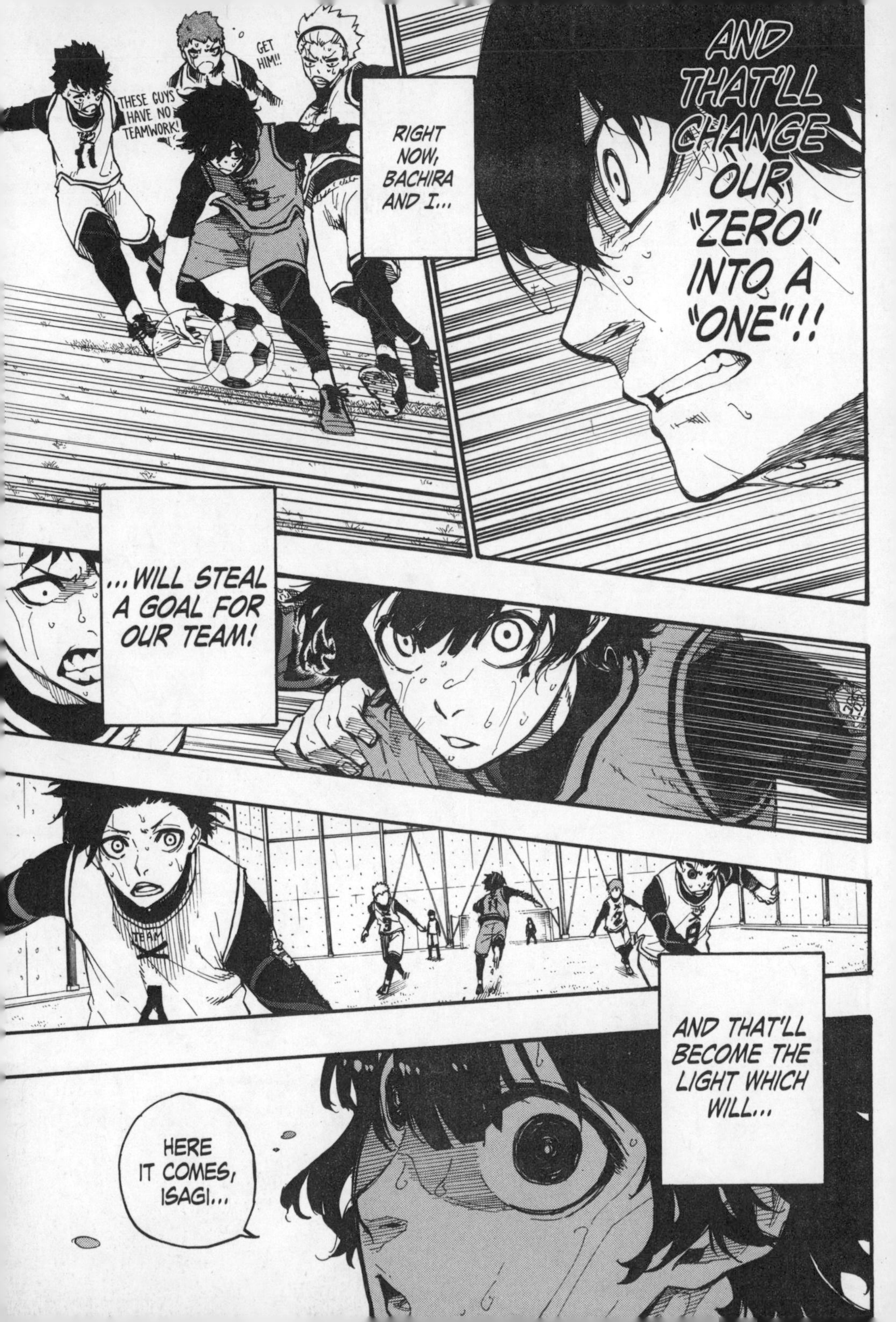
AND THAT'LL CHANGE OUR "ZERO" INTO A "ONE"!!
RIGHT NOW, BACHIRA AND I...
GET HIM!!
THESE GUYS HAVE NO TEAMWORK!
...WILL STEAL A GOAL FOR OUR TEAM!
AND THAT'LL BECOME THE LIGHT WHICH WILL...
HERE IT COMES, ISAGI...

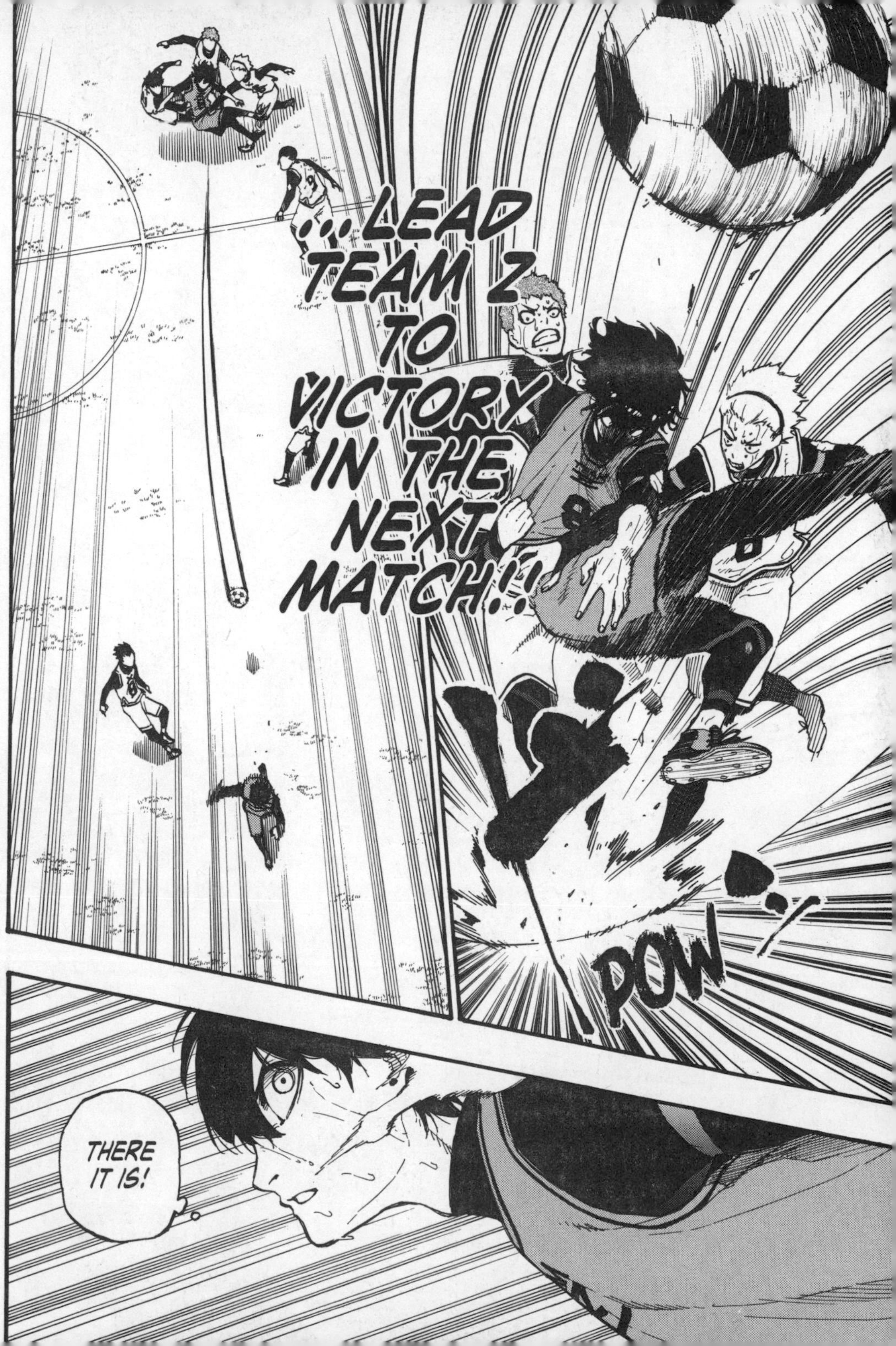
...LEAD TEAM Z TO VICTORY IN THE NEXT MATCH!!
POW
THERE IT IS!

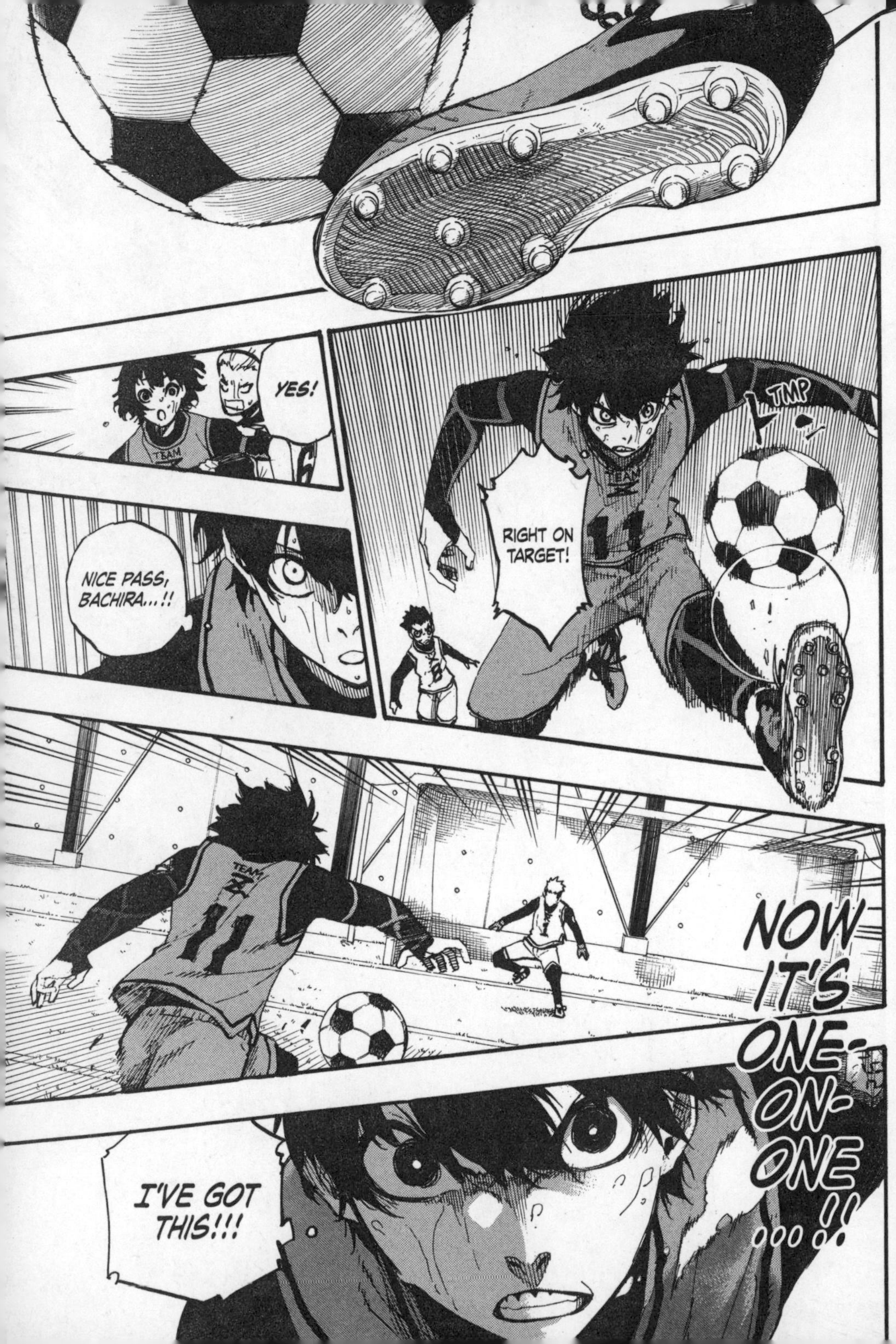
TMP
RIGHT ON TARGET!
YES!
NICE PASS, BACHIRA...!!
NOW IT'S ONE-ON-ONE...!!
I'VE GOT THIS!!!

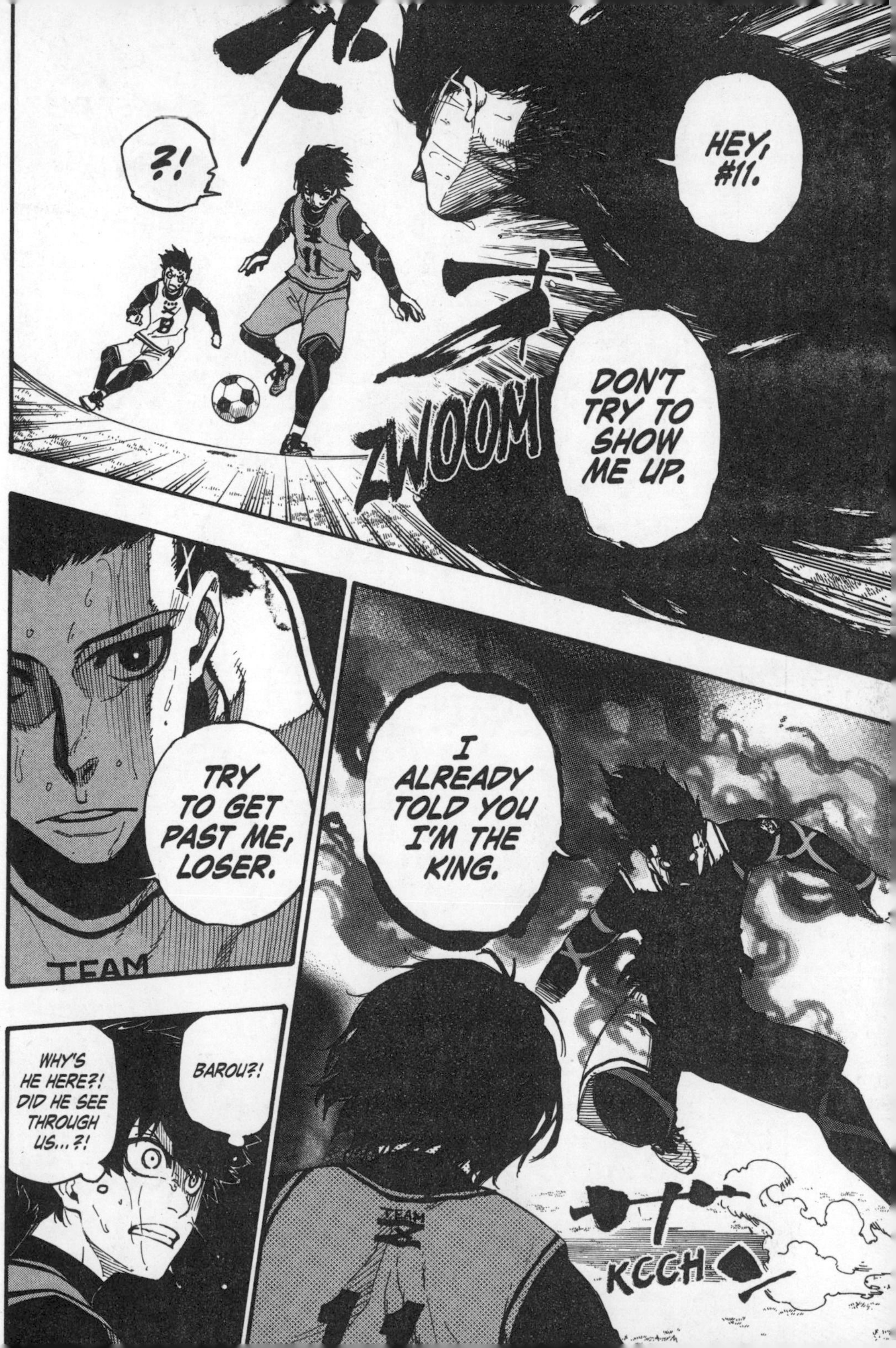
HEY, #11.
?!
ZWOOM
DON'T TRY TO SHOW ME UP.
I ALREADY TOLD YOU I'M THE KING.
KCCH
TRY TO GET PAST ME, LOSER.
TEAM
BAROU?!
WHY'S HE HERE?! DID HE SEE THROUGH US...?!

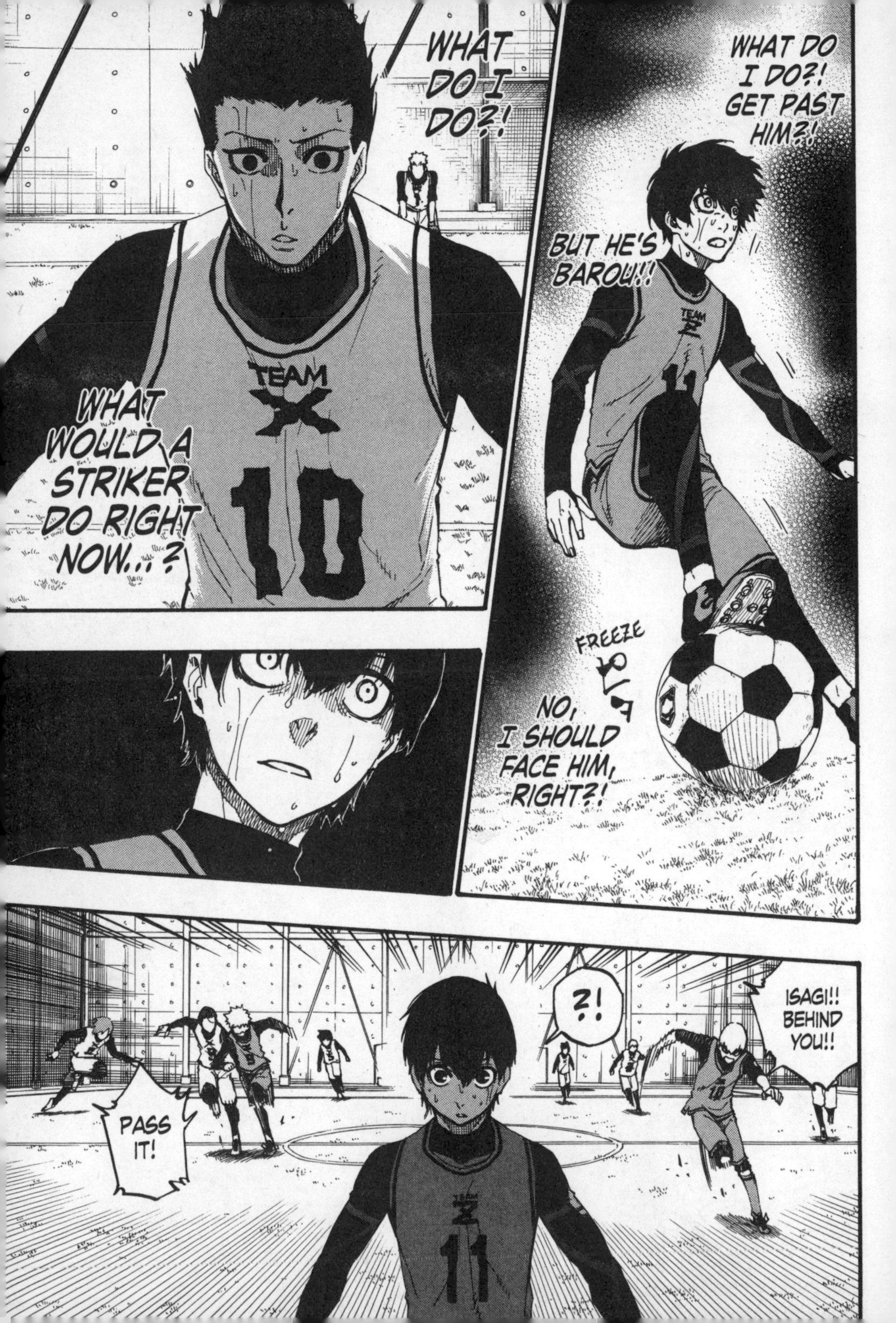
WHAT DO I DO?! GET PAST HIM?!
BUT HE'S BAROU!!
FREEZE
NO, I SHOULD FACE HIM, RIGHT?!
WHAT DO I DO?!
WHAT WOULD A STRIKER DO RIGHT NOW...?
ISAGI!! BEHIND YOU!!
?!
PASS IT!

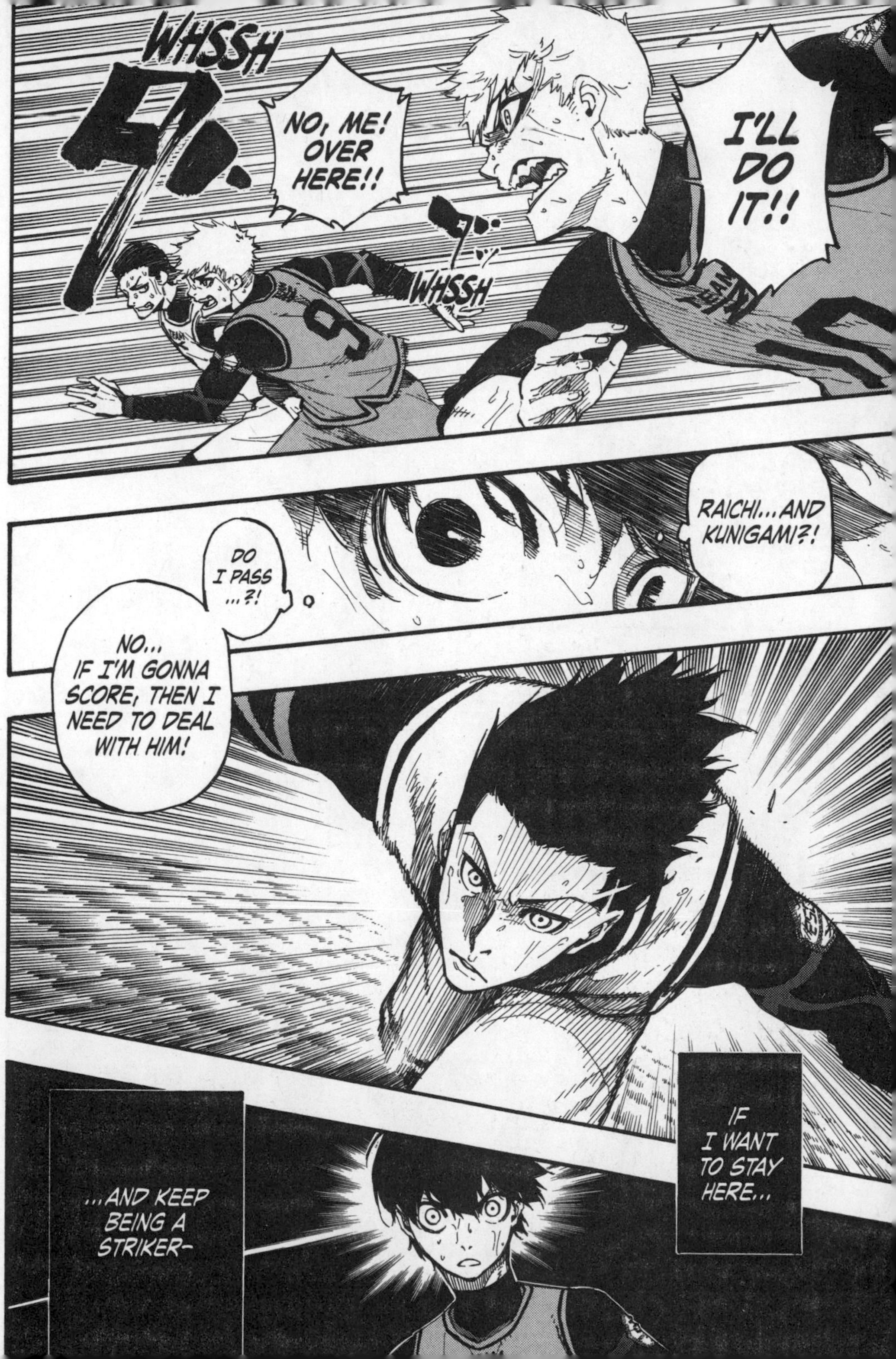
I'LL DO IT!!
NO, ME! OVER HERE!!
WHSSH
WHSSH
RAICHI...AND KUNIGAMI?!
DO I PASS ...?!
NO... IF I'M GONNA SCORE, THEN I NEED TO DEAL WITH HIM!
IF I WANT TO STAY HERE...
...AND KEEP BEING A STRIKER-

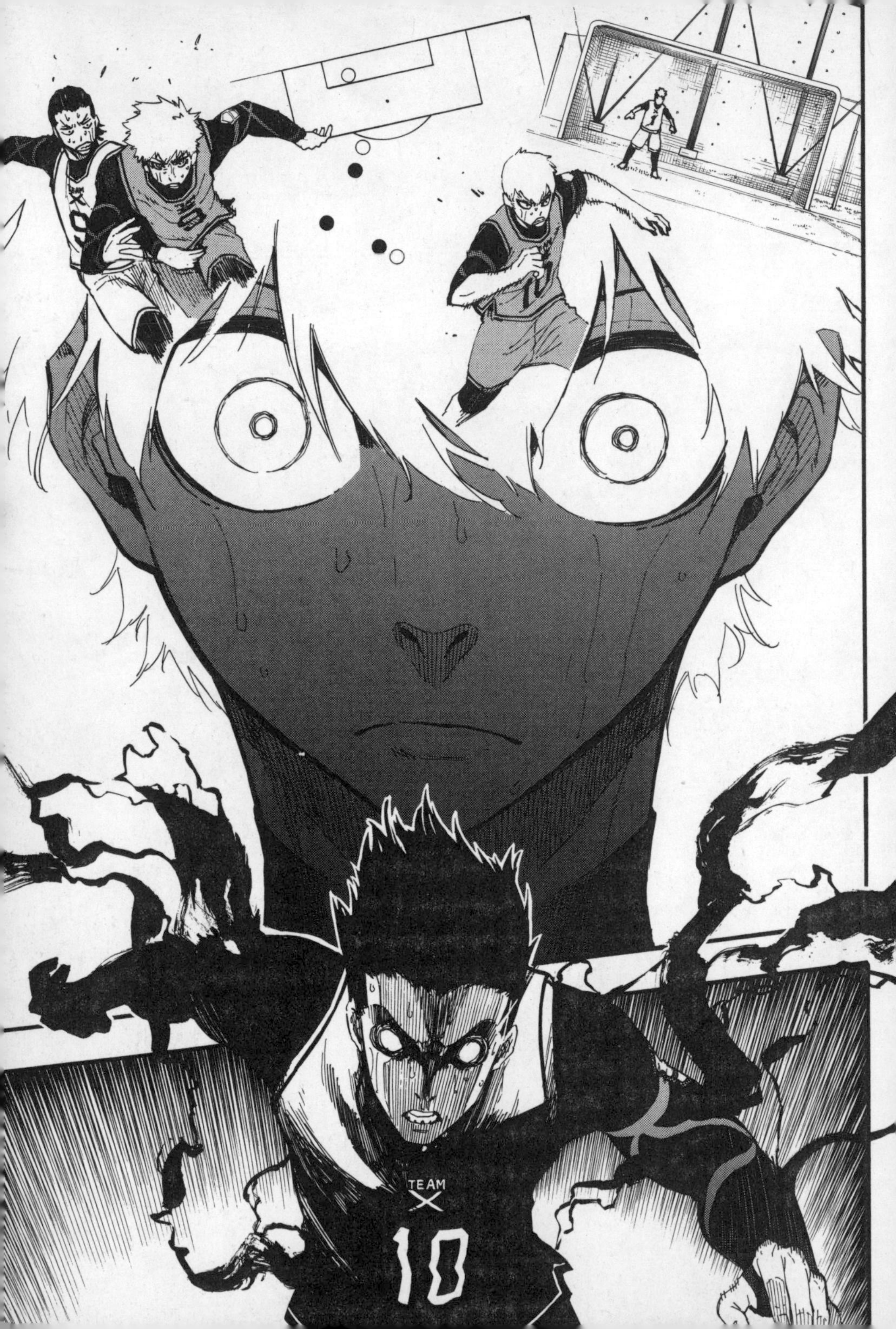
TEAM

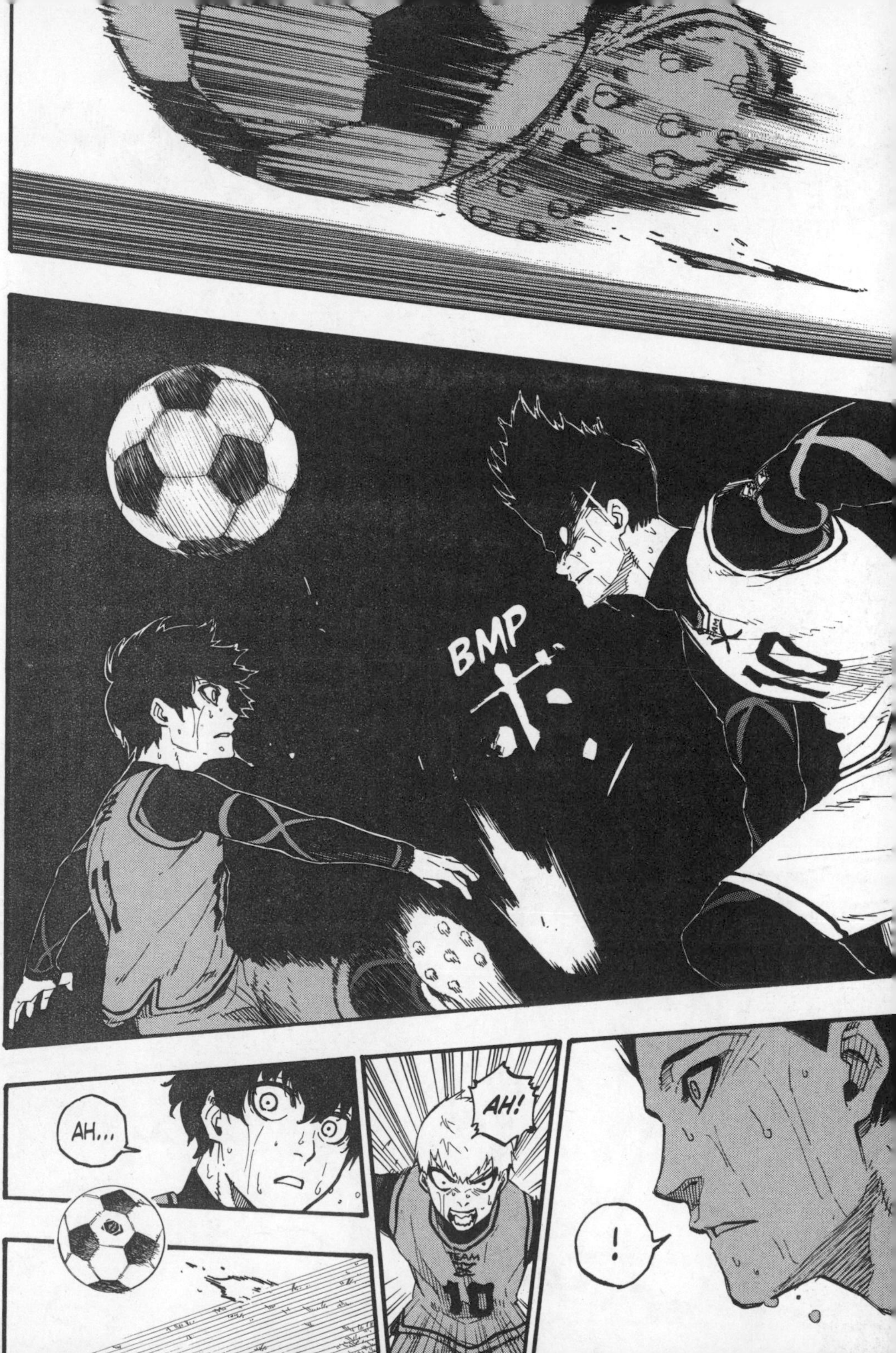
BMP
!
AH!
AH...

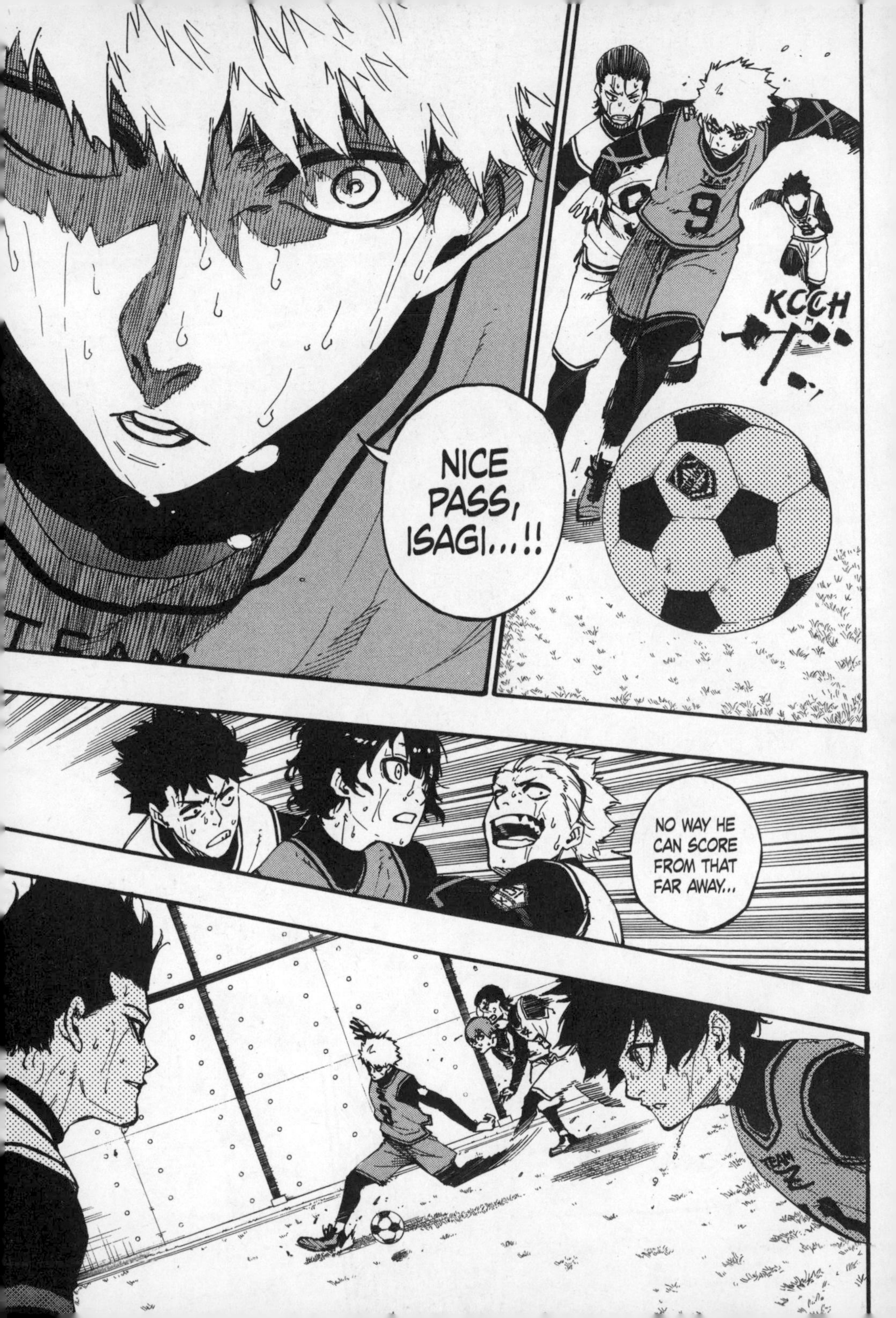
KCCH
NICE PASS, ISAGI...!!
NO WAY HE CAN SCORE FROM THAT FAR AWAY...

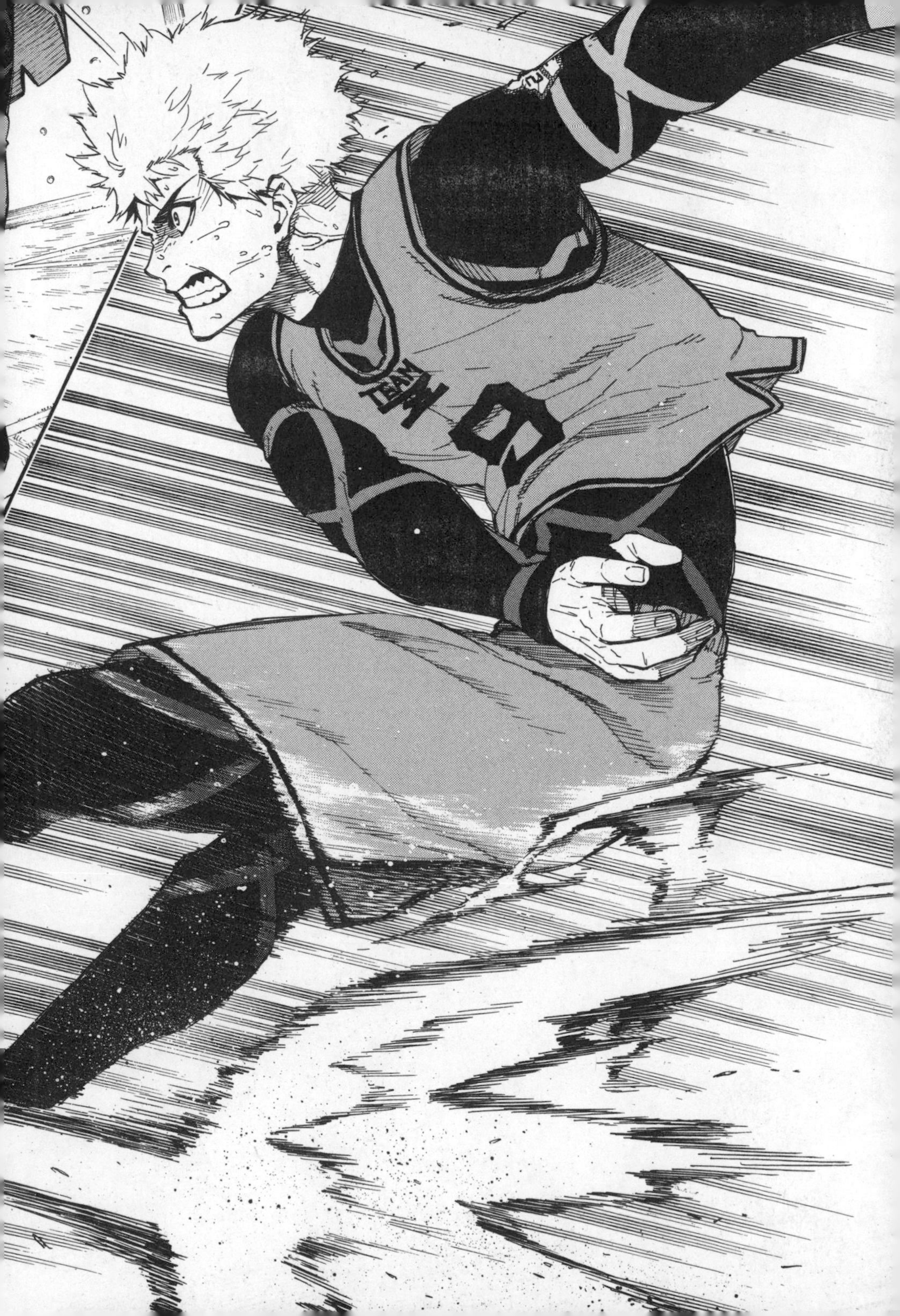

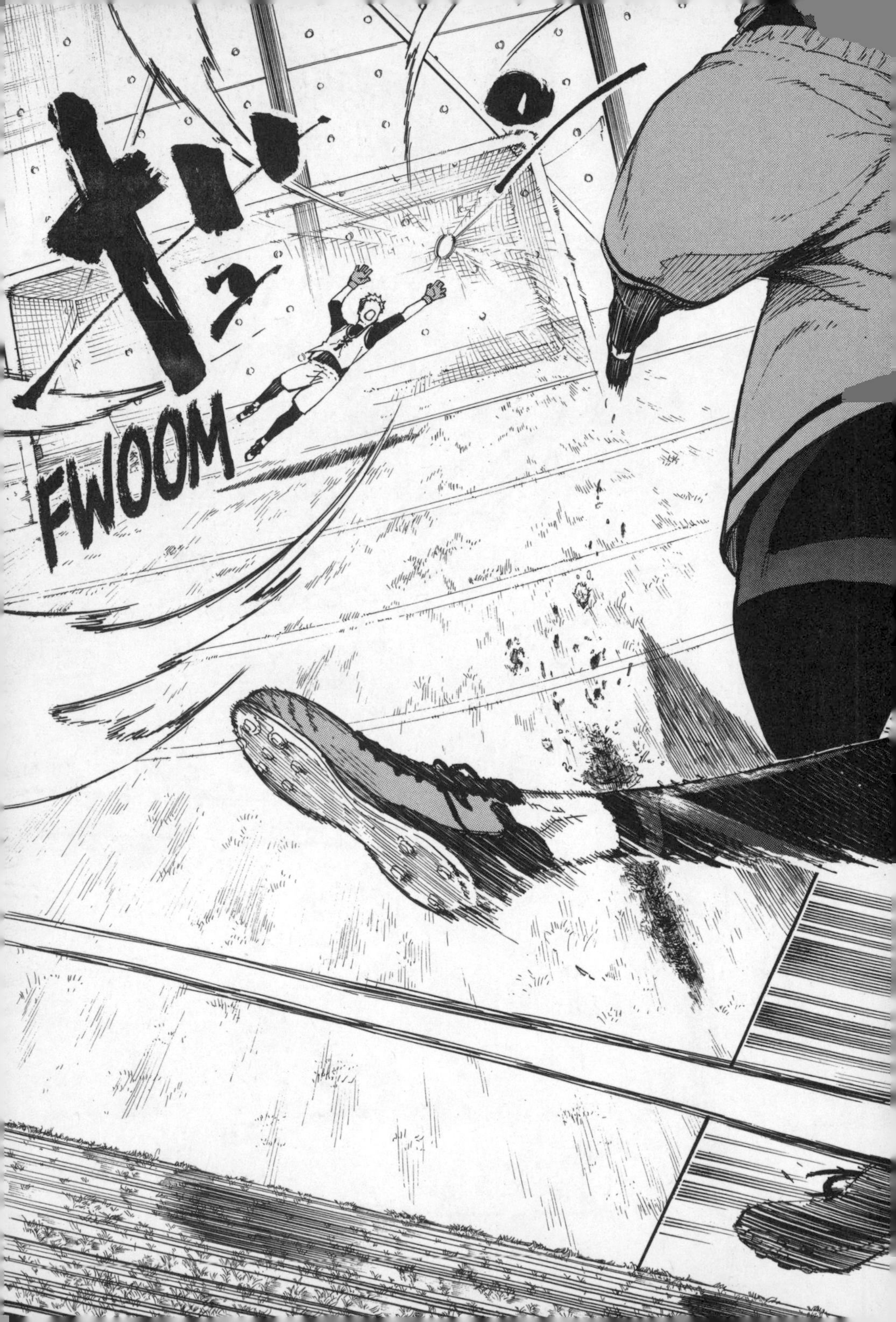
FWOOM

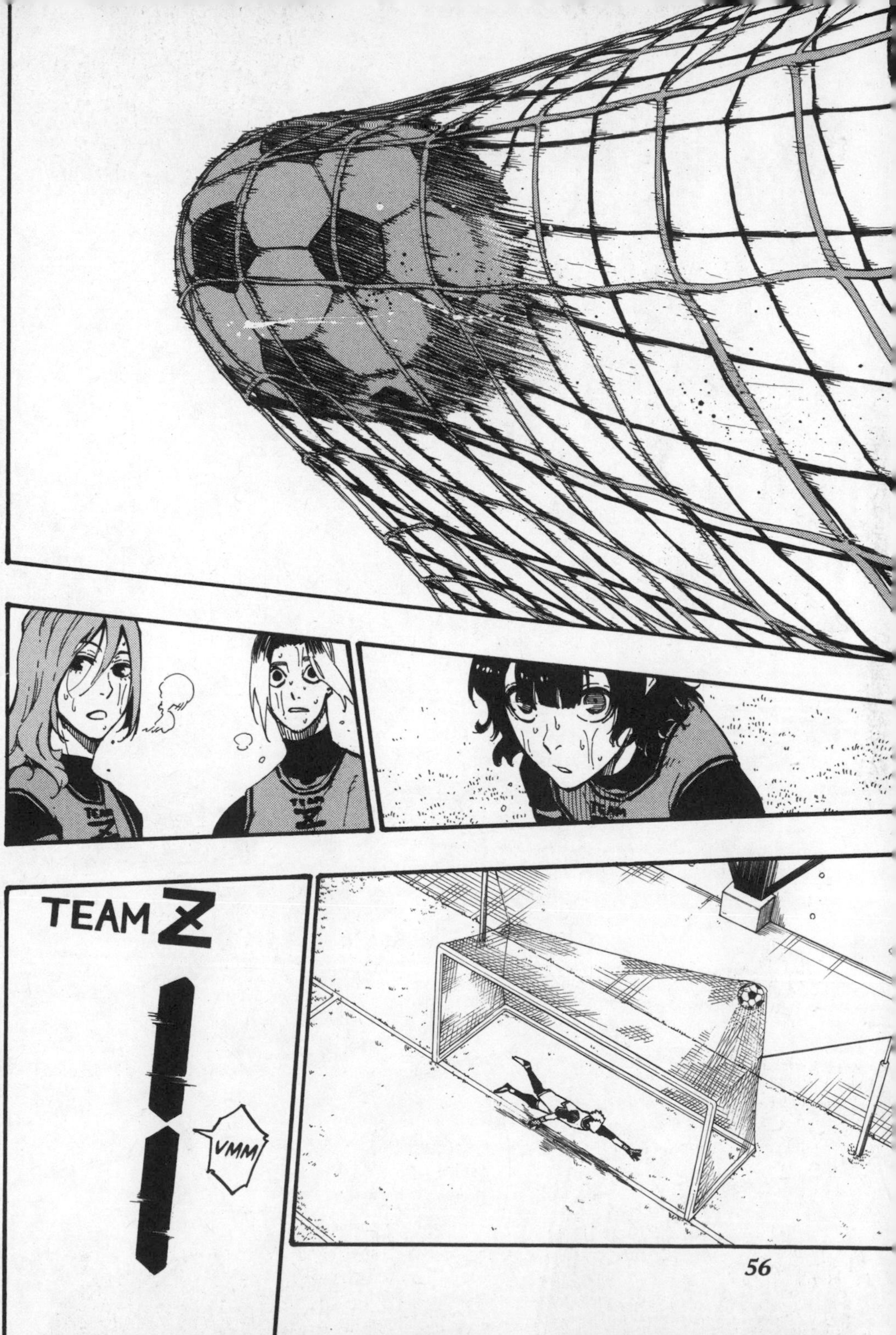
TEAM Z
VMM

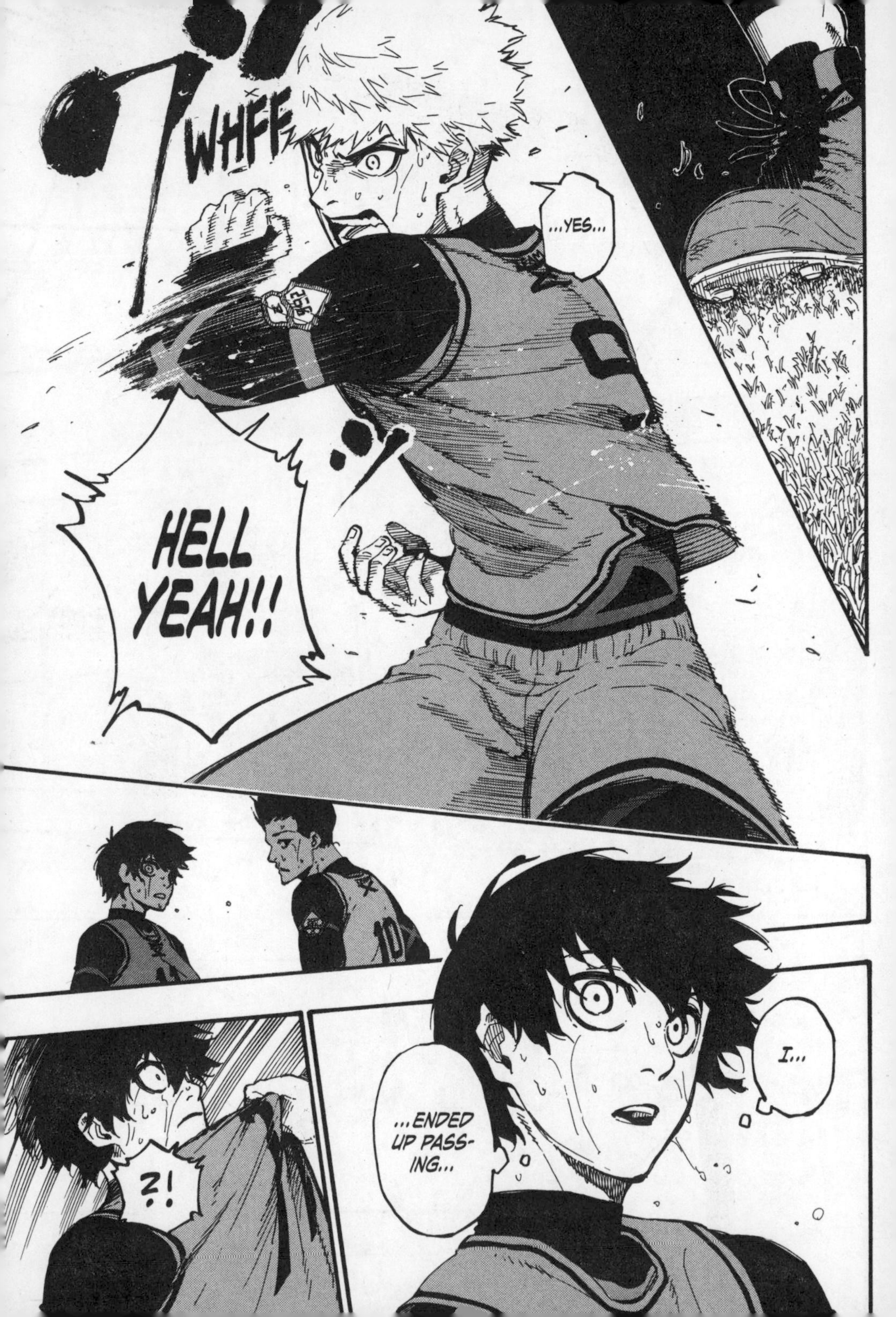
...YES...
WHFF
HELL YEAH!!
I...
...ENDED UP PASSING...
?!

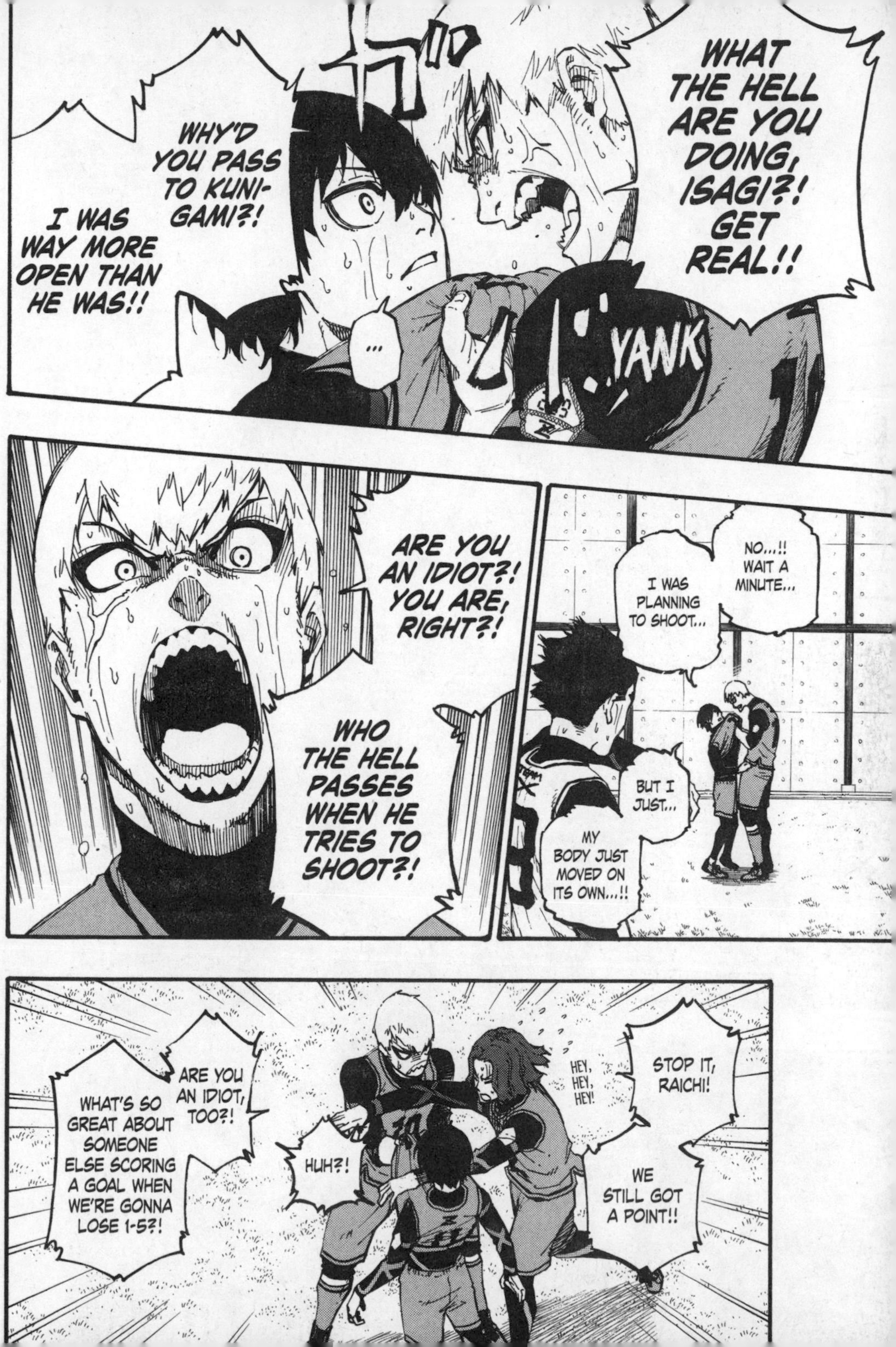
WHAT THE HELL ARE YOU DOING, ISAGI?! GET REAL!!
WHY'D YOU PASS TO KUNI-GAMI?!
I WAS WAY MORE OPEN THAN HE WAS!!
YANK
...
NO...!! WAIT A MINUTE...
I WAS PLANNING TO SHOOT...
BUT I JUST...
MY BODY JUST MOVED ON ITS OWN...!!
ARE YOU AN IDIOT?! YOU ARE, RIGHT?!
WHO THE HELL PASSES WHEN HE TRIES TO SHOOT?!
STOP IT, RAICHI!
HEY, HEY, HEY!
WE STILL GOT A POINT!!
HUH?!
ARE YOU AN IDIOT, TOO?!
WHAT'S SO GREAT ABOUT SOMEONE ELSE SCORING A GOAL WHEN WE'RE GONNA LOSE 1-5?!

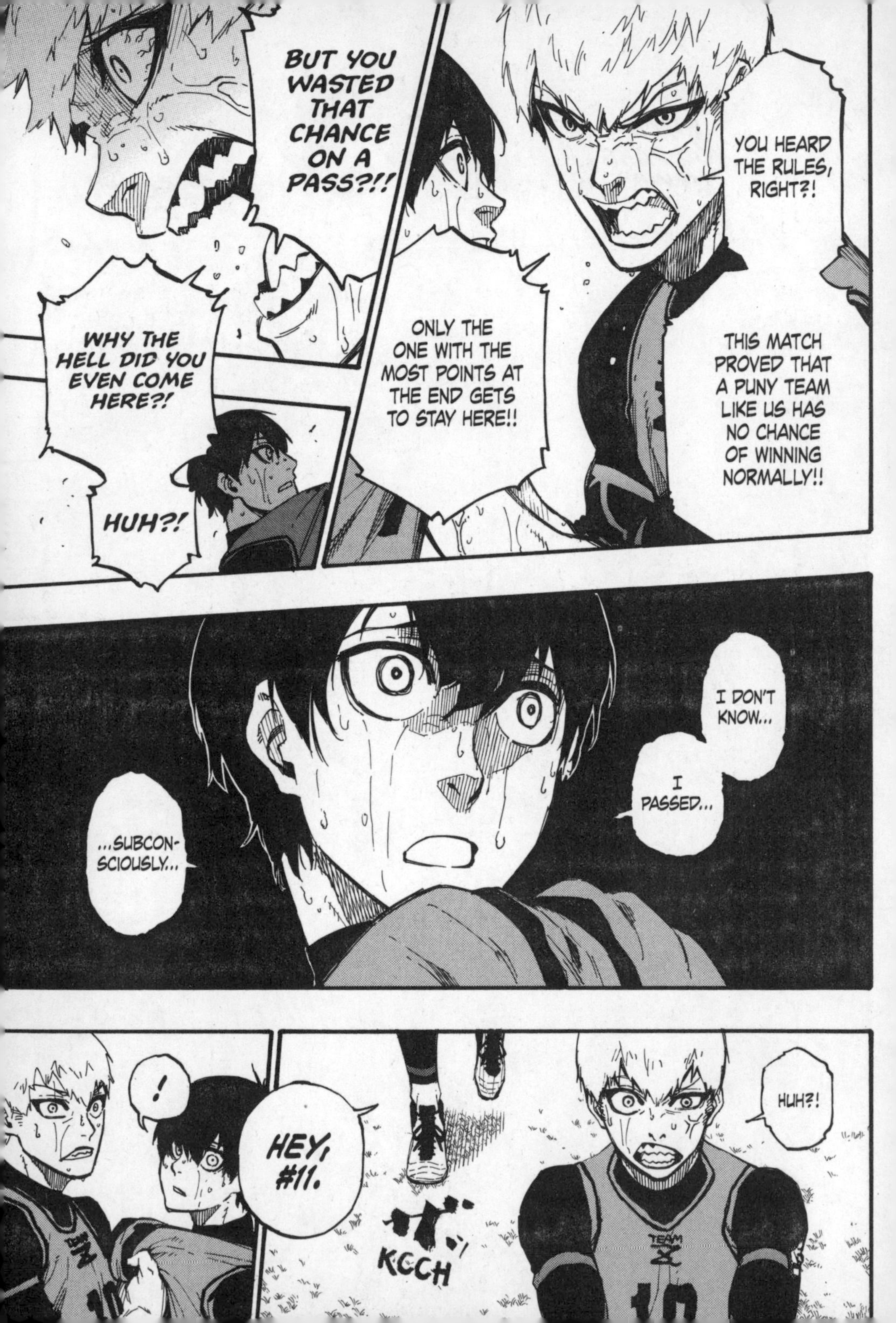

YOU HEARD THE RULES, RIGHT?!
THIS MATCH PROVED THAT A PUNY TEAM LIKE US HAS NO CHANCE OF WINNING NORMALLY!!
BUT YOU WASTED THAT CHANCE ON A PASS?!!
ONLY THE ONE WITH THE MOST POINTS AT THE END GETS TO STAY HERE!!
WHY THE HELL DID YOU EVEN COME HERE?!
HUH?!
I DON'T KNOW...
I PASSED...
...SUBCONSCIOUSLY...
HUH?!
HEY, #11.
KCCH
!

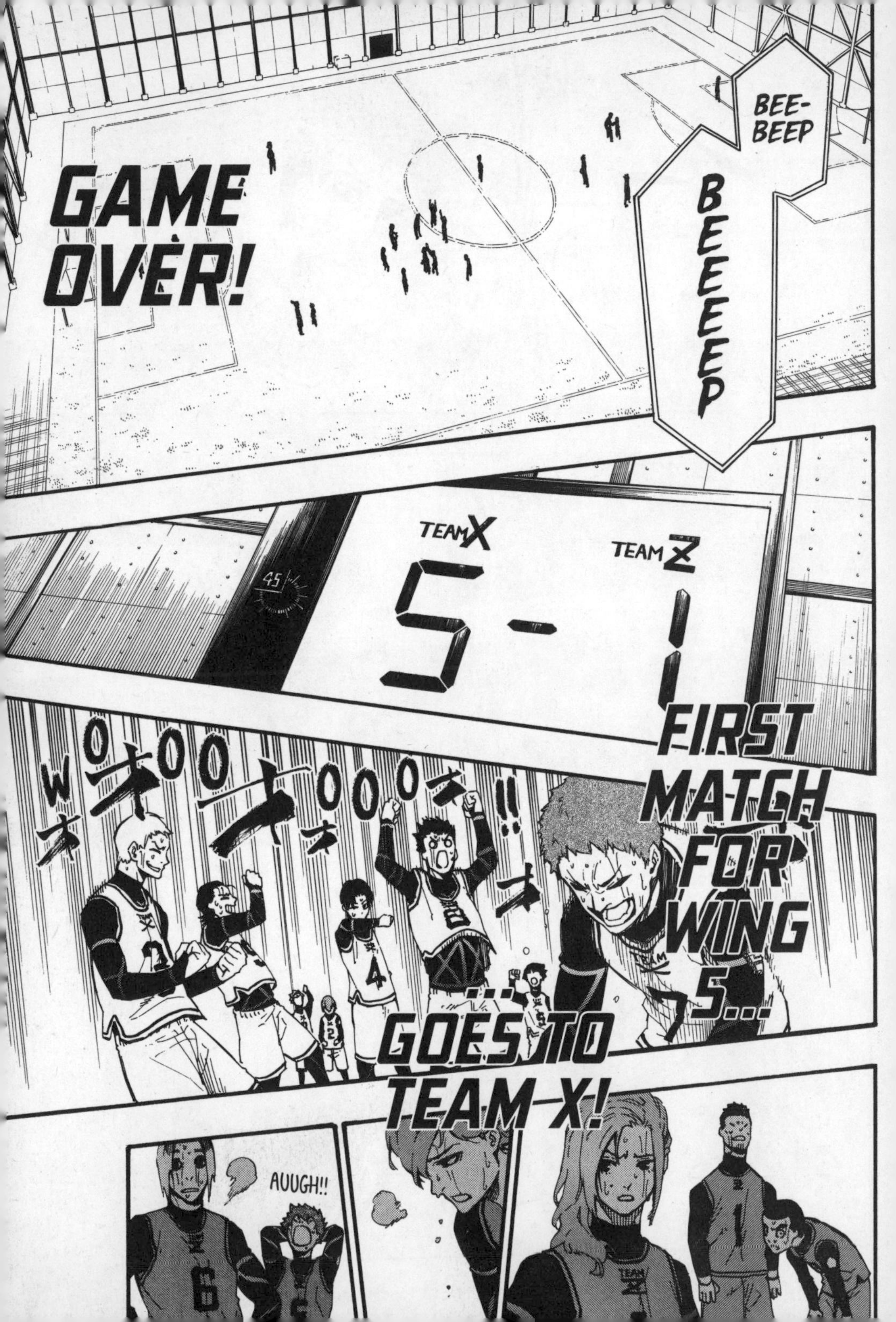
BEE-BEEP
BEEEEEP
GAME OVER!
TEAM X
TEAM Z
5-1
FIRST MATCH FOR WING 5...
WOOOOOOO!!
...GOES TO TEAM X!
AUUGH!!

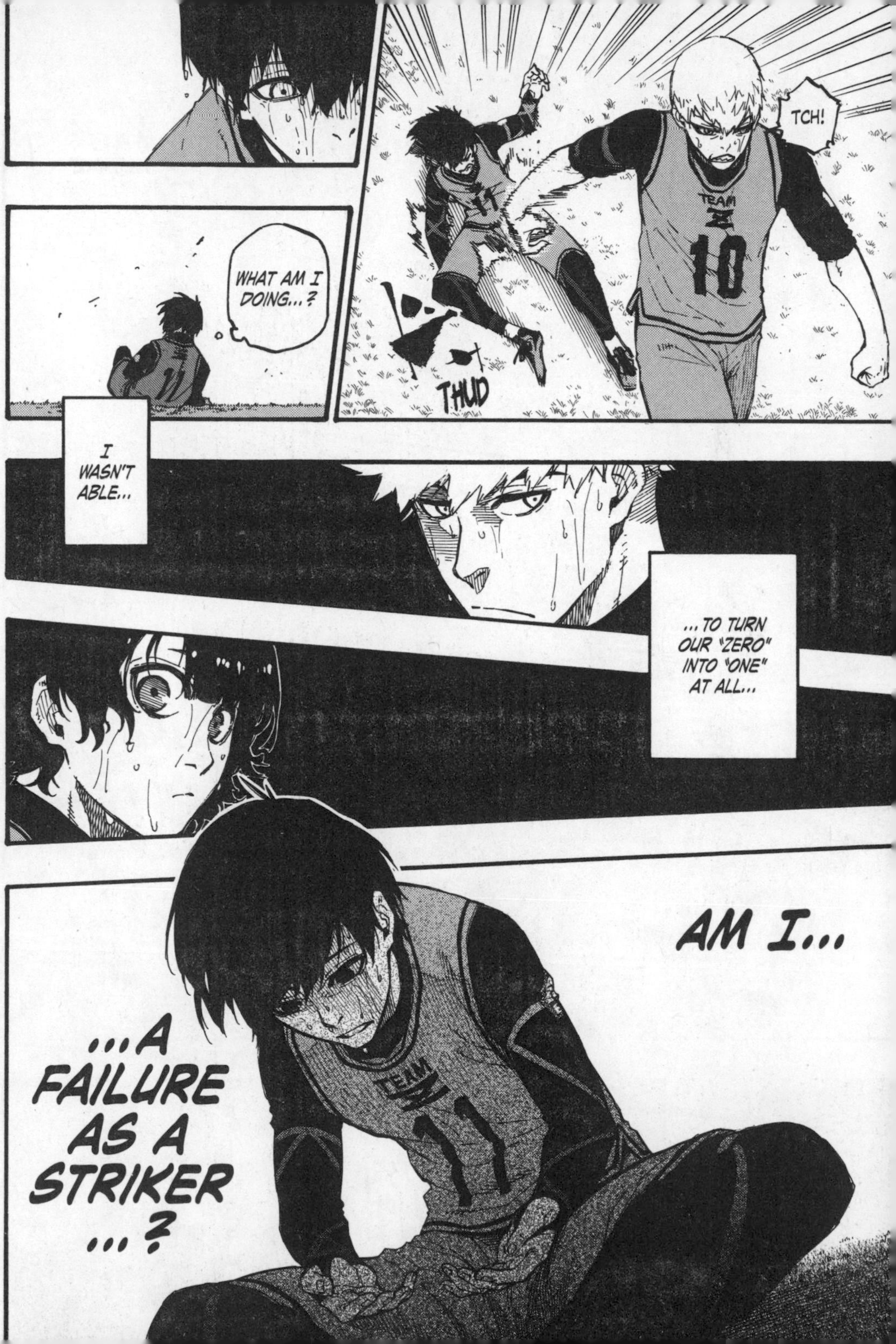

TCH!
THUD
WHAT AM I DOING...?
I WASN'T ABLE...
...TO TURN OUR "ZERO" INTO "ONE" AT ALL...
AM I...
...A FAILURE AS A STRIKER ...?

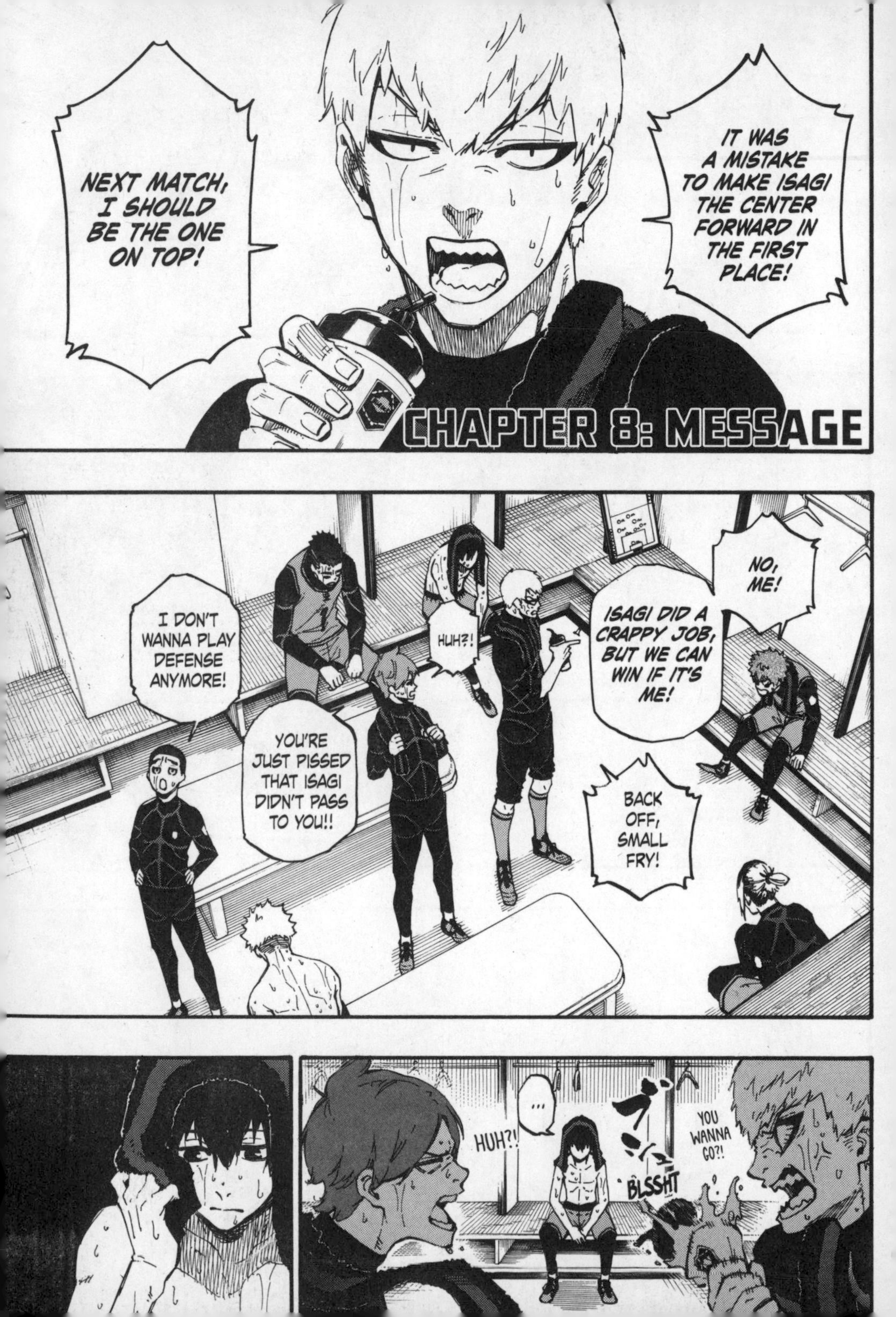
IT WAS A MISTAKE TO MAKE ISAGI THE CENTER FORWARD IN THE FIRST PLACE!
NEXT MATCH, I SHOULD BE THE ONE ON TOP!
CHAPTER 8: MESSAGE
NO, ME!
ISAGI DID A CRAPPY JOB, BUT WE CAN WIN IF IT'S ME!
BACK OFF, SMALL FRY!
HUH?!
YOU'RE JUST PISSED THAT ISAGI DIDN'T PASS TO YOU!!
I DON'T WANNA PLAY DEFENSE ANYMORE!
YOU WANNA GO?!
BLSSHT
...
HUH?!

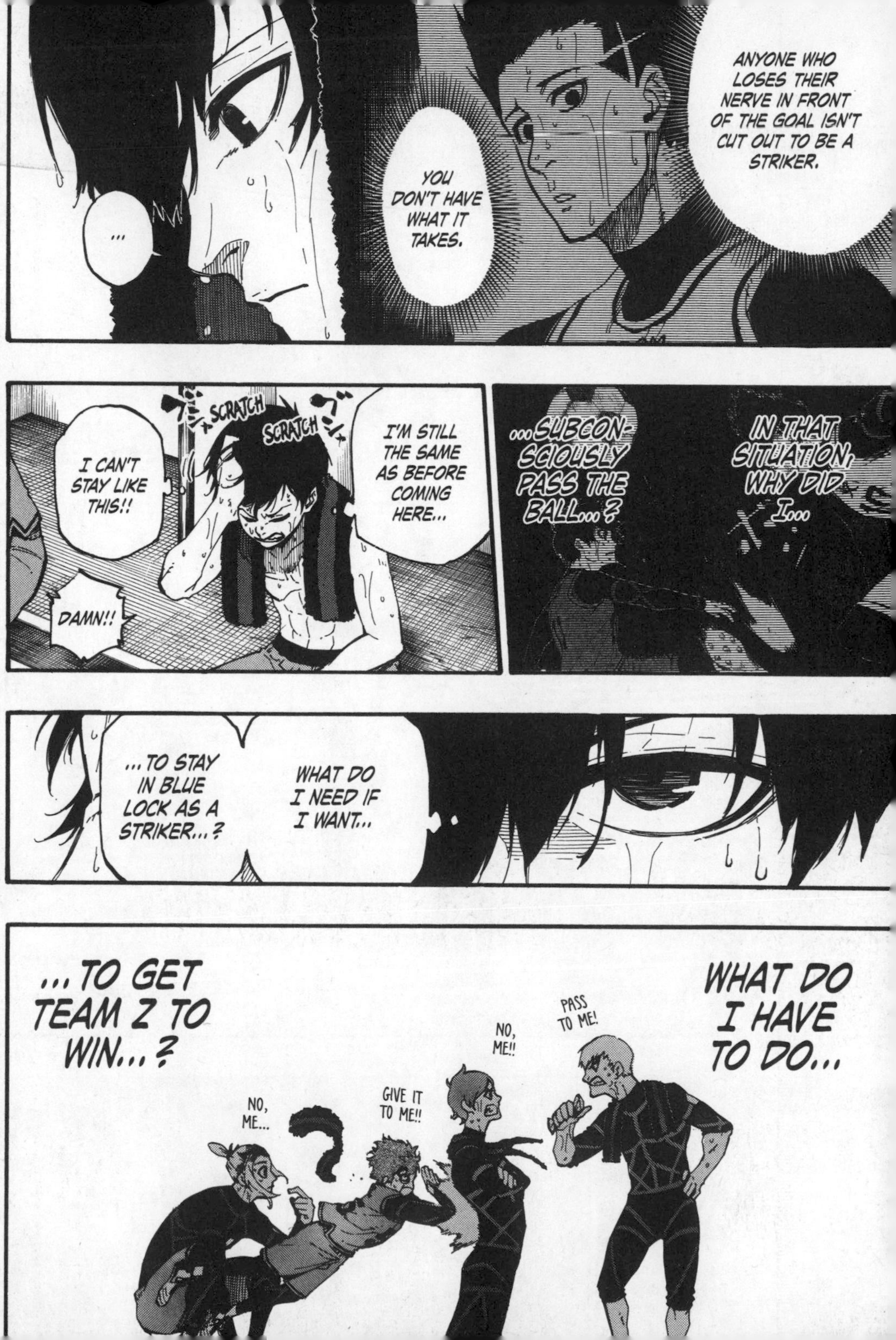

ANYONE WHO LOSES THEIR NERVE IN FRONT OF THE GOAL ISN'T CUT OUT TO BE A STRIKER.
YOU DON'T HAVE WHAT IT TAKES.
...
IN THAT SITUATION, WHY DID I...
...SUBCONSCIOUSLY PASS THE BALL...?
I'M STILL THE SAME AS BEFORE COMING HERE...
SCRATCH
SCRATCH
I CAN'T STAY LIKE THIS!!
DAMN!!
WHAT DO I NEED IF I WANT...
...TO STAY IN BLUE LOCK AS A STRIKER...?
WHAT DO I HAVE TO DO...
PASS TO ME!
NO, ME!!
GIVE IT TO ME!!
NO, ME...
...TO GET TEAM Z TO WIN...?

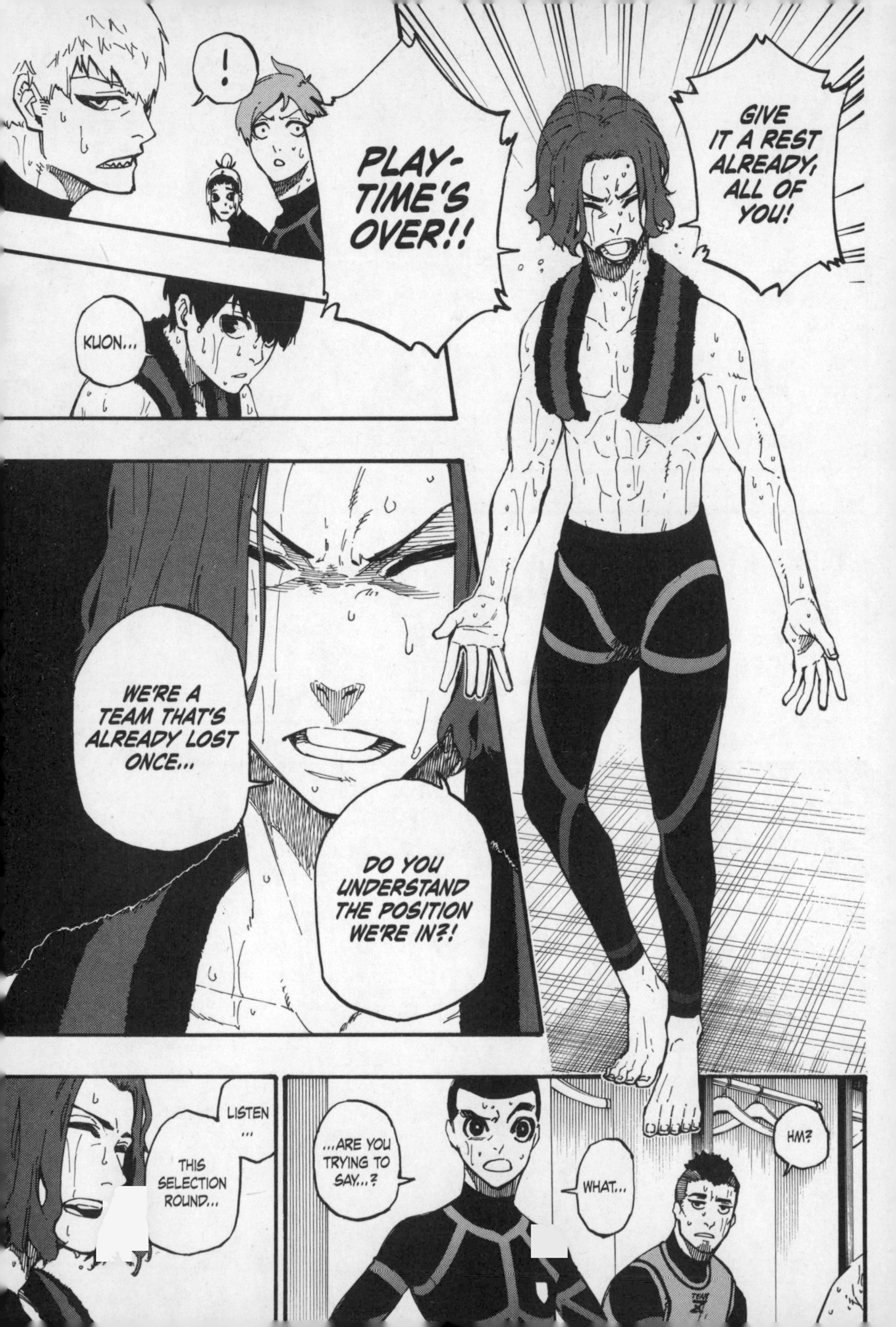
GIVE IT A REST ALREADY, ALL OF YOU!
PLAY-TIME'S OVER!!
!
KUON...
WE'RE A TEAM THAT'S ALREADY LOST ONCE...
DO YOU UNDERSTAND THE POSITION WE'RE IN?!
HM?
WHAT...
...ARE YOU TRYING TO SAY...?
LISTEN...
THIS SELECTION ROUND...

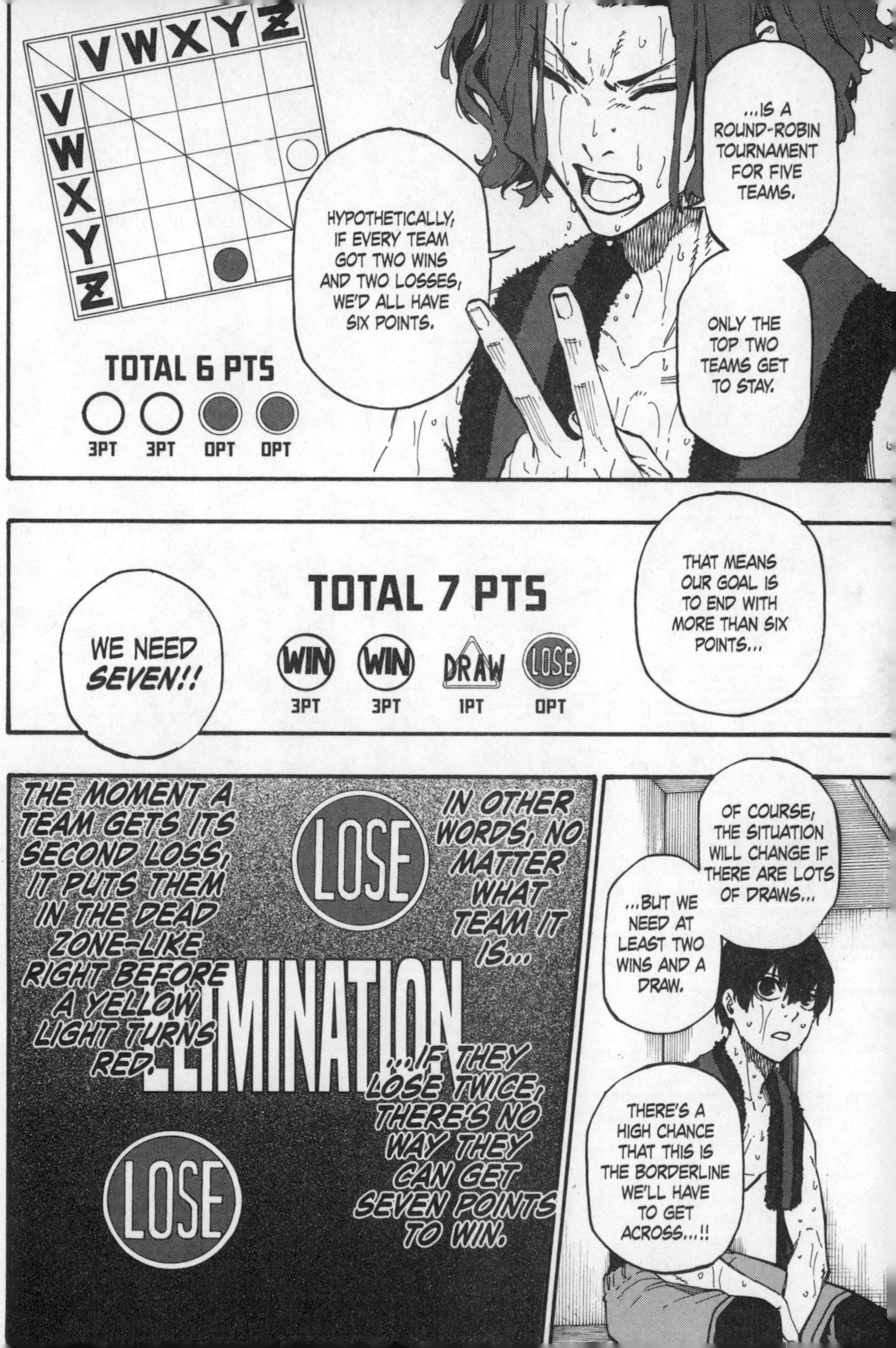
...IS A ROUND-ROBIN TOURNAMENT FOR FIVE TEAMS.
ONLY THE TOP TWO TEAMS GET TO STAY.
HYPOTHETICALLY, IF EVERY TEAM GOT TWO WINS AND TWO LOSSES, WE'D ALL HAVE SIX POINTS.
V W X Y Z
V W X Y Z
TOTAL 6 PTS
3PT 3PT 0PT 0PT
THAT MEANS OUR GOAL IS TO END WITH MORE THAN SIX POINTS...
TOTAL 7 PTS
WIN WIN DRAW LOSE
3PT 3PT 1PT 0PT
WE NEED SEVEN!!
OF COURSE, THE SITUATION WILL CHANGE IF THERE ARE LOTS OF DRAWS...
...BUT WE NEED AT LEAST TWO WINS AND A DRAW.
THERE'S A HIGH CHANCE THAT THIS IS THE BORDERLINE WE'LL HAVE TO GET ACROSS...!!
LOSE
IN OTHER WORDS, NO MATTER WHAT TEAM IT IS...
THE MOMENT A TEAM GETS ITS SECOND LOSS, IT PUTS THEM IN THE DEAD ZONE-LIKE RIGHT BEFORE A YELLOW LIGHT TURNS RED.
...IF THEY LOSE TWICE, THERE'S NO WAY THEY CAN GET SEVEN POINTS TO WIN.
LOSE

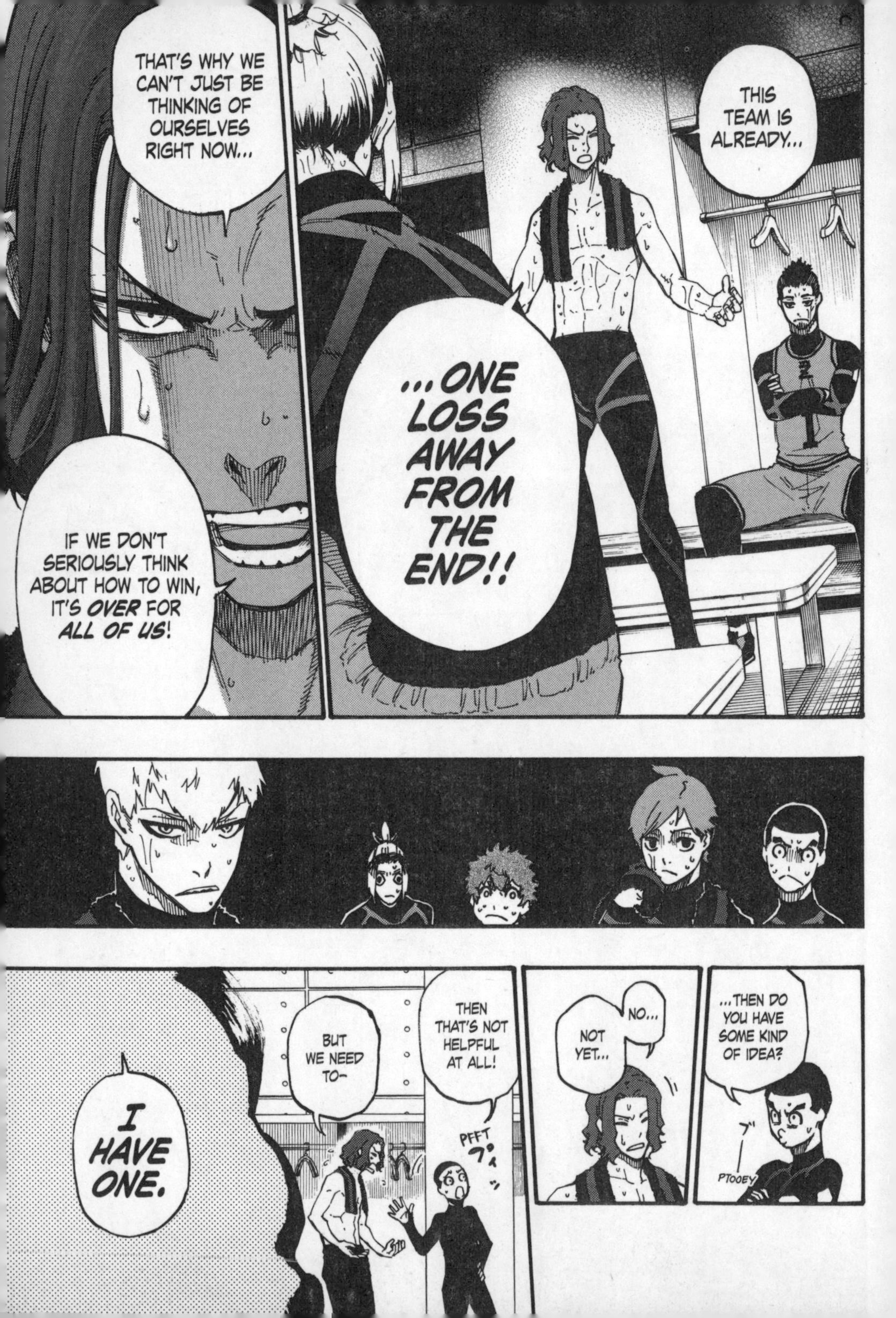
THIS TEAM IS ALREADY...
...ONE LOSS AWAY FROM THE END!!
THAT'S WHY WE CAN'T JUST BE THINKING OF OURSELVES RIGHT NOW...
IF WE DON'T SERIOUSLY THINK ABOUT HOW TO WIN, IT'S OVER FOR ALL OF US!
...THEN DO YOU HAVE SOME KIND OF IDEA?
PTOOEY
NO...
NOT YET...
THEN THAT'S NOT HELPFUL AT ALL!
PFFT
BUT WE NEED TO-
I HAVE ONE.

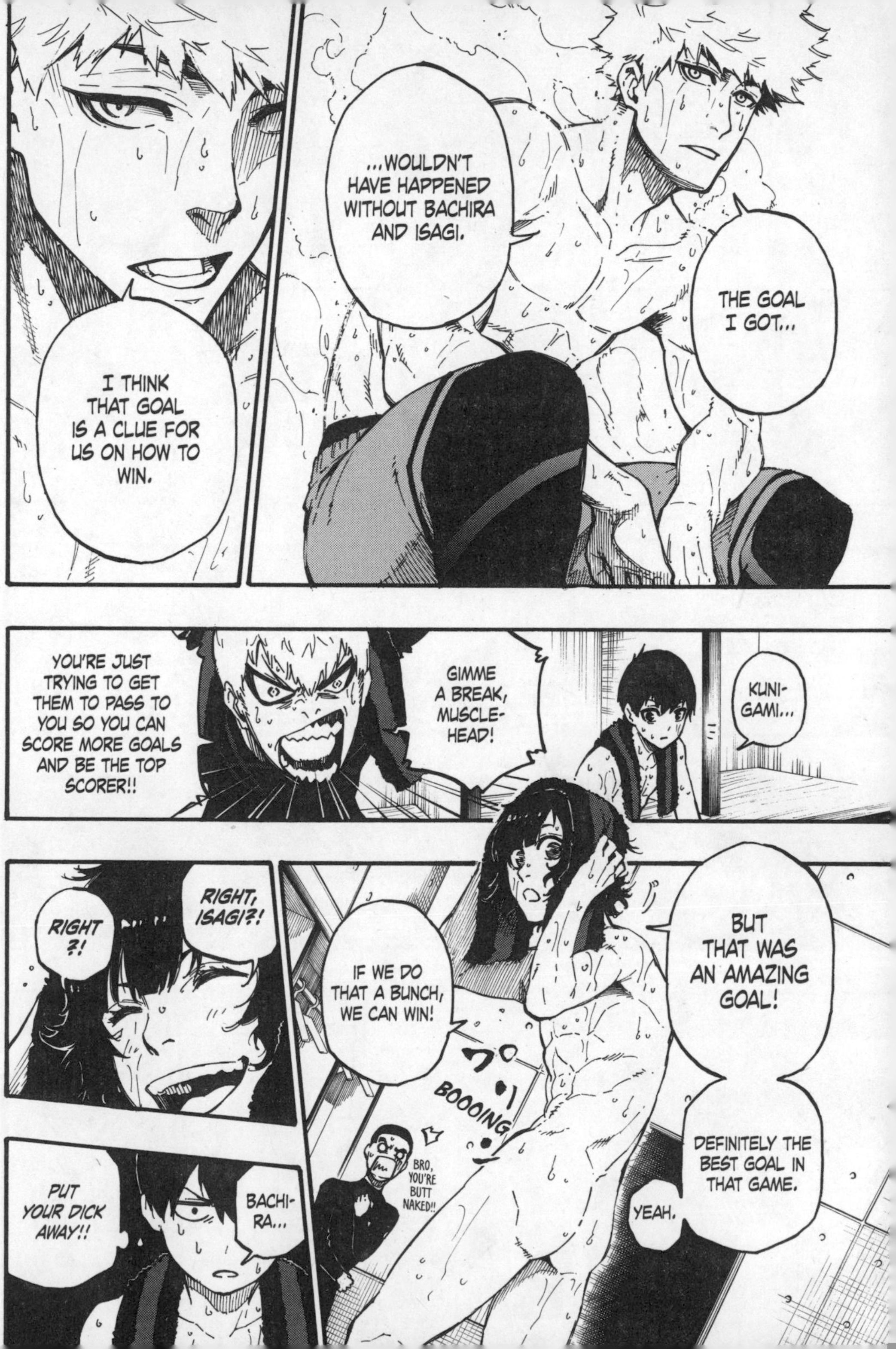
THE GOAL I GOT...
...WOULDN'T HAVE HAPPENED WITHOUT BACHIRA AND ISAGI.
I THINK THAT GOAL IS A CLUE FOR US ON HOW TO WIN.
KUNI-GAMI...
GIMME A BREAK, MUSCLE-HEAD!
YOU'RE JUST TRYING TO GET THEM TO PASS TO YOU SO YOU CAN SCORE MORE GOALS AND BE THE TOP SCORER!!
BUT THAT WAS AN AMAZING GOAL!
DEFINITELY THE BEST GOAL IN THAT GAME.
YEAH.
IF WE DO THAT A BUNCH, WE CAN WIN!
BOOOING
BRO, YOU'RE BUTT NAKED!!
RIGHT, ISAGI?!
RIGHT ?!
BACHI-RA...
PUT YOUR DICK AWAY!!

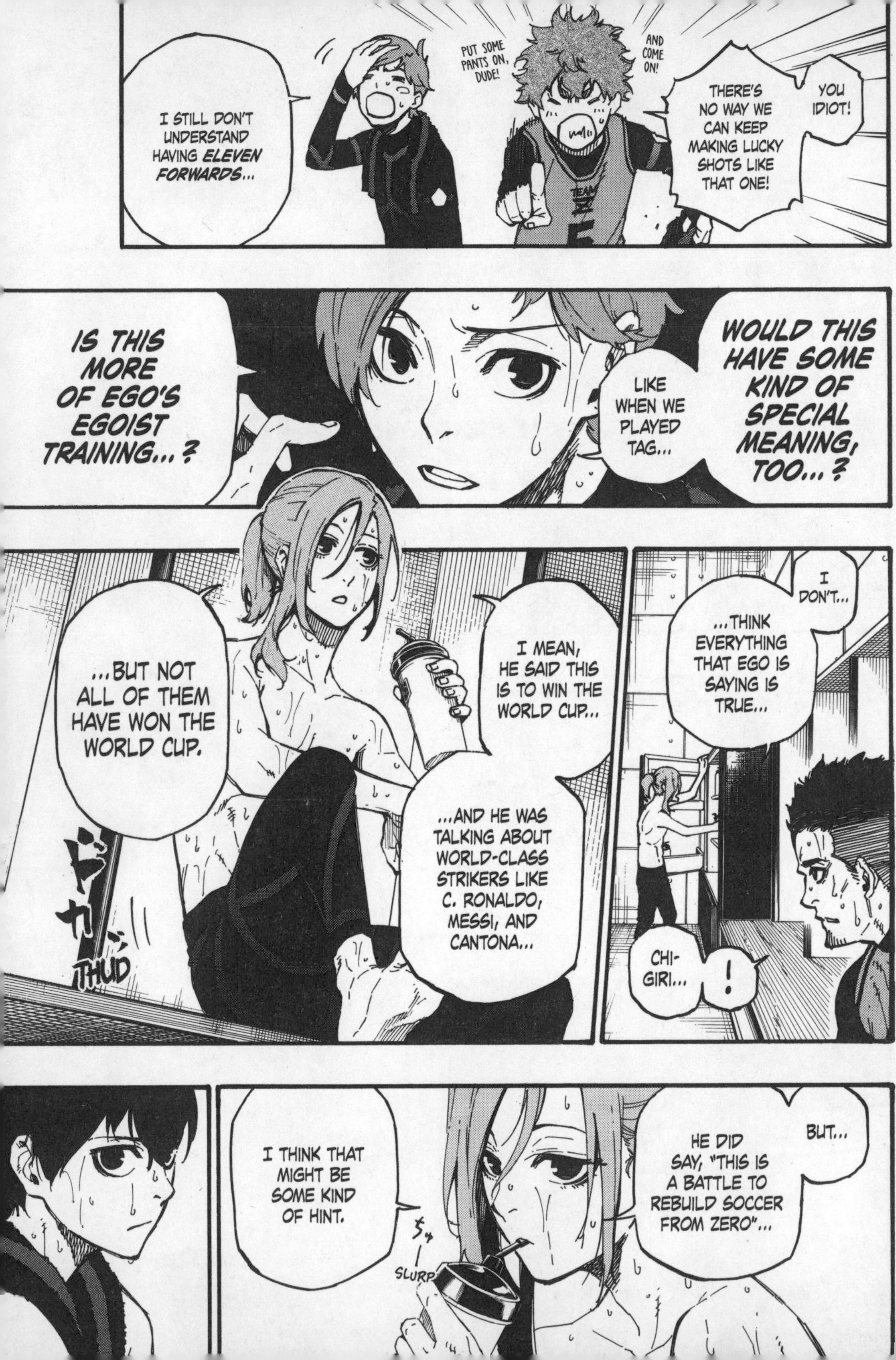
YOU IDIOT!
THERE'S NO WAY WE CAN KEEP MAKING LUCKY SHOTS LIKE THAT ONE!
AND COME ON!
PUT SOME PANTS ON, DUDE!
I STILL DON'T UNDERSTAND HAVING *ELEVEN FORWARDS*...
WOULD THIS HAVE SOME KIND OF SPECIAL MEANING, TOO...?
LIKE WHEN WE PLAYED TAG...
IS THIS MORE OF EGO'S EGOIST TRAINING...?
I DON'T...
...THINK EVERYTHING THAT EGO IS SAYING IS TRUE...
!
CHI-GIRI...
I MEAN, HE SAID THIS IS TO WIN THE WORLD CUP...
...AND HE WAS TALKING ABOUT WORLD-CLASS STRIKERS LIKE C. RONALDO, MESSI, AND CANTONA...
...BUT NOT ALL OF THEM HAVE WON THE WORLD CUP.
THUD
BUT...
HE DID SAY, "THIS IS A BATTLE TO REBUILD SOCCER FROM ZERO"...
SLURP
I THINK THAT MIGHT BE SOME KIND OF HINT.

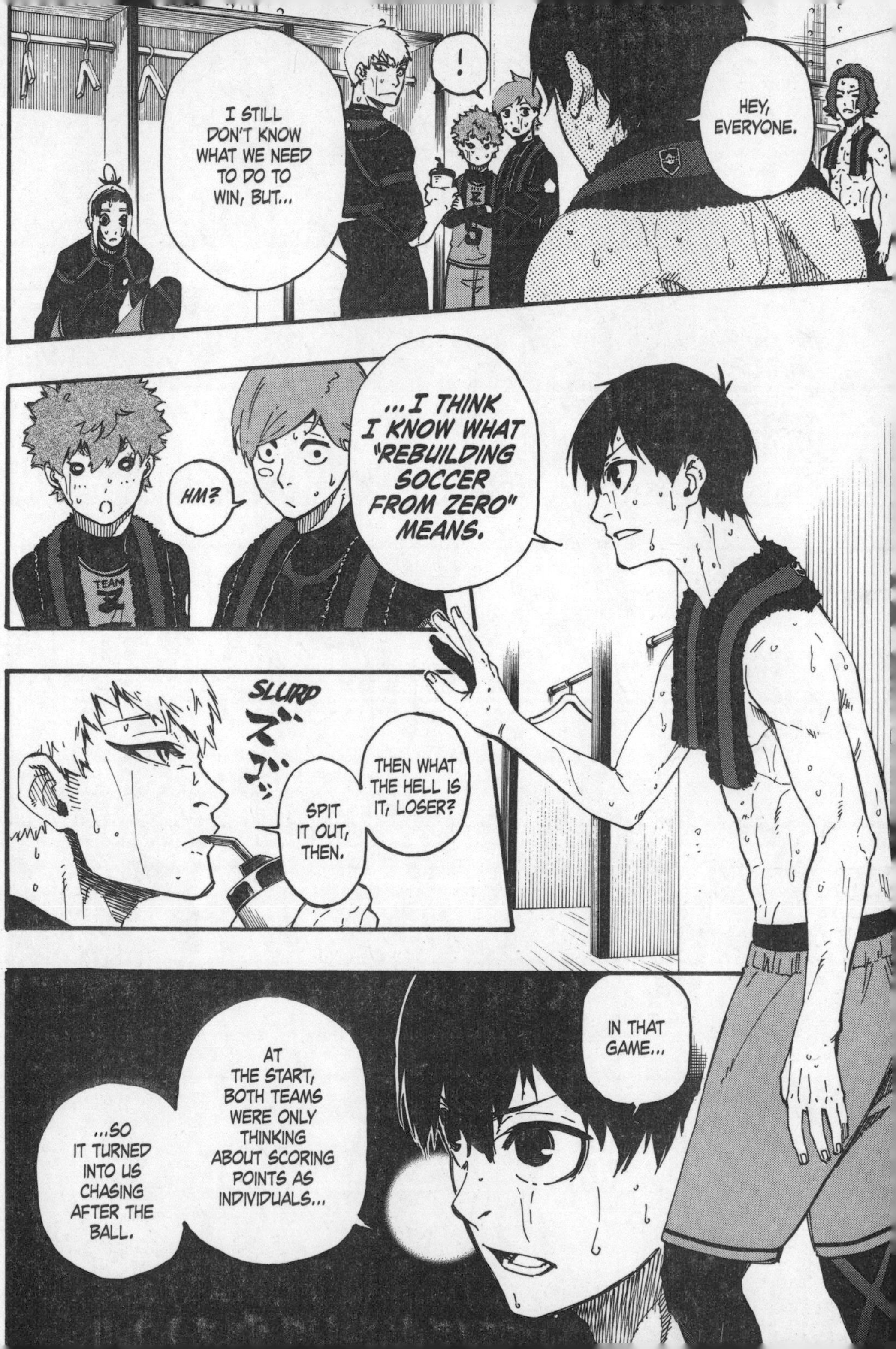
HEY, EVERYONE.
!
I STILL DON'T KNOW WHAT WE NEED TO DO TO WIN, BUT...
...I THINK I KNOW WHAT "REBUILDING SOCCER FROM ZERO" MEANS.
HM?
SLURP
THEN WHAT THE HELL IS IT, LOSER?
SPIT IT OUT, THEN.
IN THAT GAME...
AT THE START, BOTH TEAMS WERE ONLY THINKING ABOUT SCORING POINTS AS INDIVIDUALS...
...SO IT TURNED INTO US CHASING AFTER THE BALL.

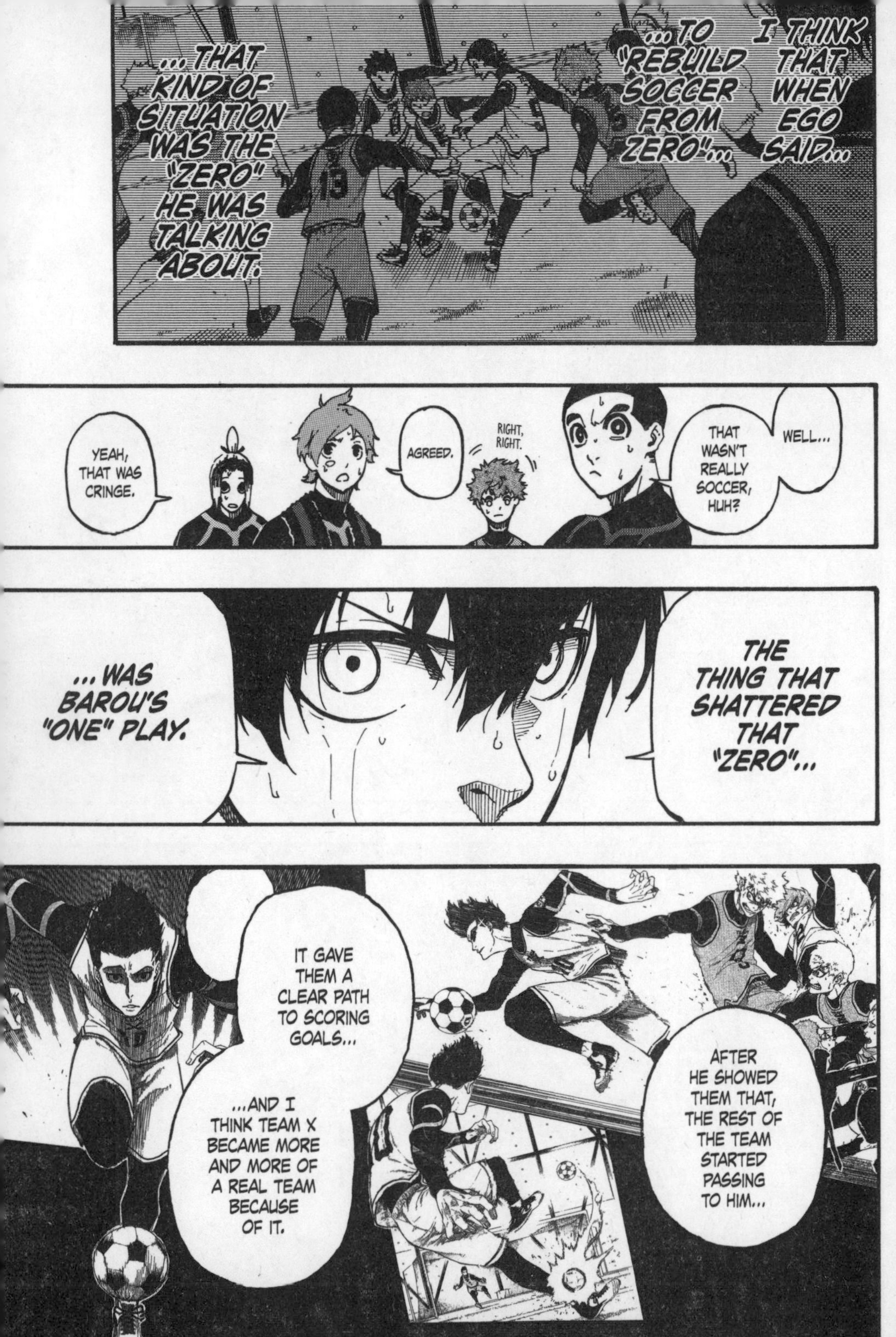
I THINK THAT WHEN EGO SAID...
...TO "REBUILD SOCCER FROM ZERO"...
...THAT KIND OF SITUATION WAS THE "ZERO" HE WAS TALKING ABOUT.
WELL...
THAT WASN'T REALLY SOCCER, HUH?
RIGHT, RIGHT.
AGREED.
YEAH, THAT WAS CRINGE.
THE THING THAT SHATTERED THAT "ZERO"...
...WAS BAROU'S "ONE" PLAY.
AFTER HE SHOWED THEM THAT, THE REST OF THE TEAM STARTED PASSING TO HIM...
IT GAVE THEM A CLEAR PATH TO SCORING GOALS...
...AND I THINK TEAM X BECAME MORE AND MORE OF A REAL TEAM BECAUSE OF IT.

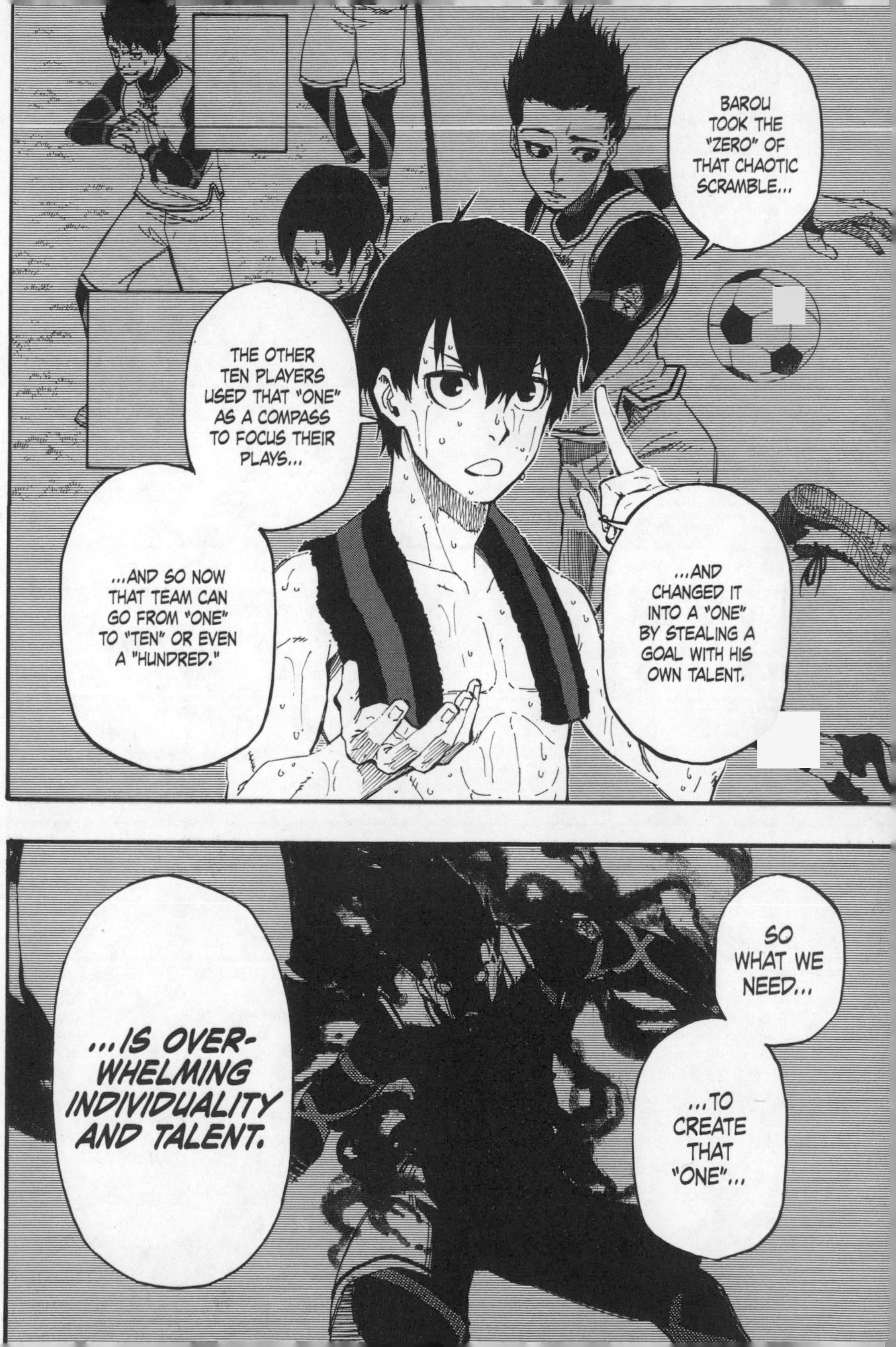
BAROU TOOK THE "ZERO" OF THAT CHAOTIC SCRAMBLE...
...AND CHANGED IT INTO A "ONE" BY STEALING A GOAL WITH HIS OWN TALENT.
THE OTHER TEN PLAYERS USED THAT "ONE" AS A COMPASS TO FOCUS THEIR PLAYS...
...AND SO NOW THAT TEAM CAN GO FROM "ONE" TO "TEN" OR EVEN A "HUNDRED."
SO WHAT WE NEED...
...TO CREATE THAT "ONE"...
...IS OVER-WHELMING INDIVIDUALITY AND TALENT.

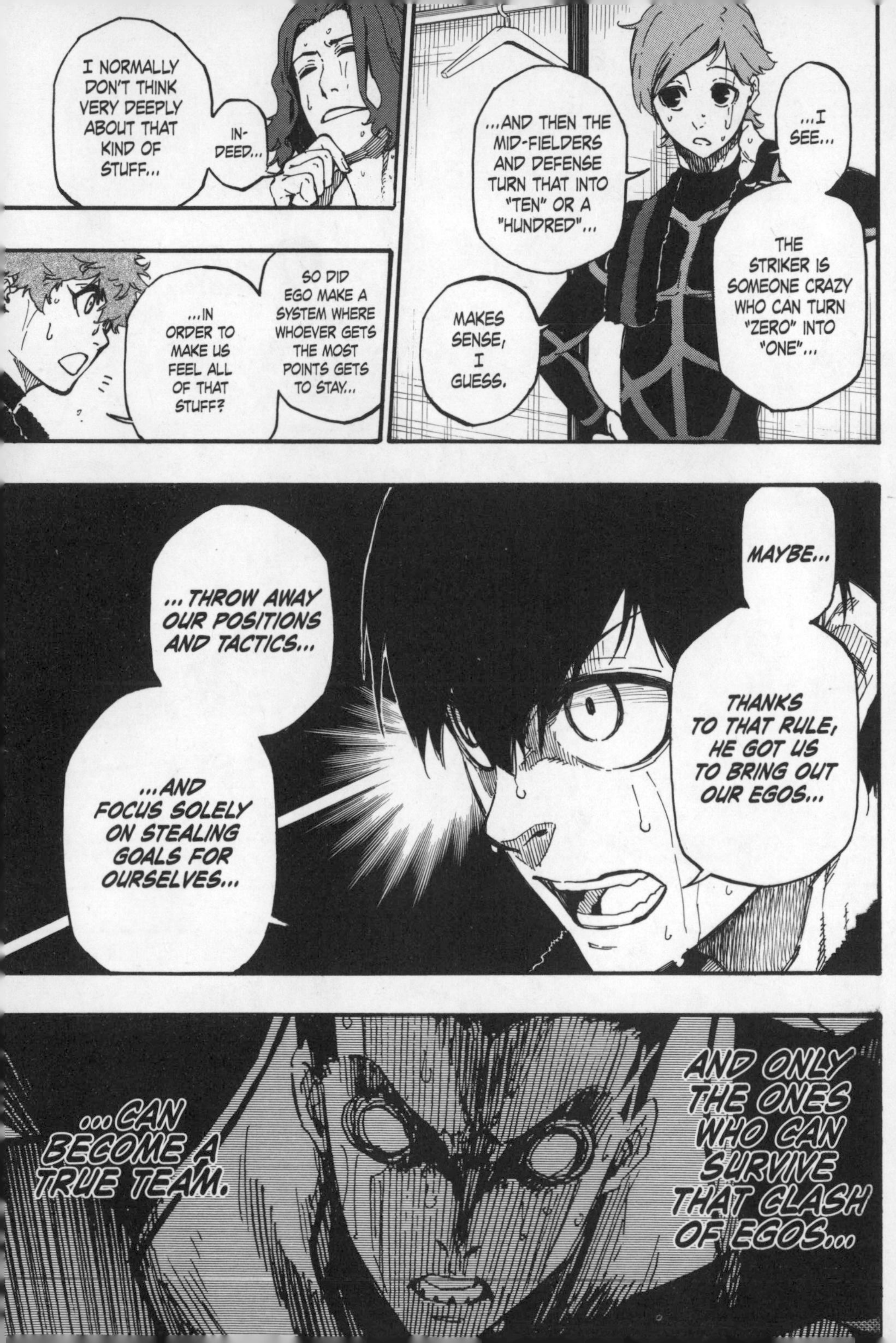
...I SEE...
THE STRIKER IS SOMEONE CRAZY WHO CAN TURN "ZERO" INTO "ONE"...
...AND THEN THE MID-FIELDERS AND DEFENSE TURN THAT INTO "TEN" OR A "HUNDRED"...
MAKES SENSE, I GUESS.
IN-DEED...
I NORMALLY DON'T THINK VERY DEEPLY ABOUT THAT KIND OF STUFF...
SO DID EGO MAKE A SYSTEM WHERE WHOEVER GETS THE MOST POINTS GETS TO STAY...
...IN ORDER TO MAKE US FEEL ALL OF THAT STUFF?
MAYBE...
THANKS TO THAT RULE, HE GOT US TO BRING OUT OUR EGOS...
...THROW AWAY OUR POSITIONS AND TACTICS...
...AND FOCUS SOLELY ON STEALING GOALS FOR OURSELVES...
AND ONLY THE ONES WHO CAN SURVIVE THAT CLASH OF EGOS...
...CAN BECOME A TRUE TEAM.

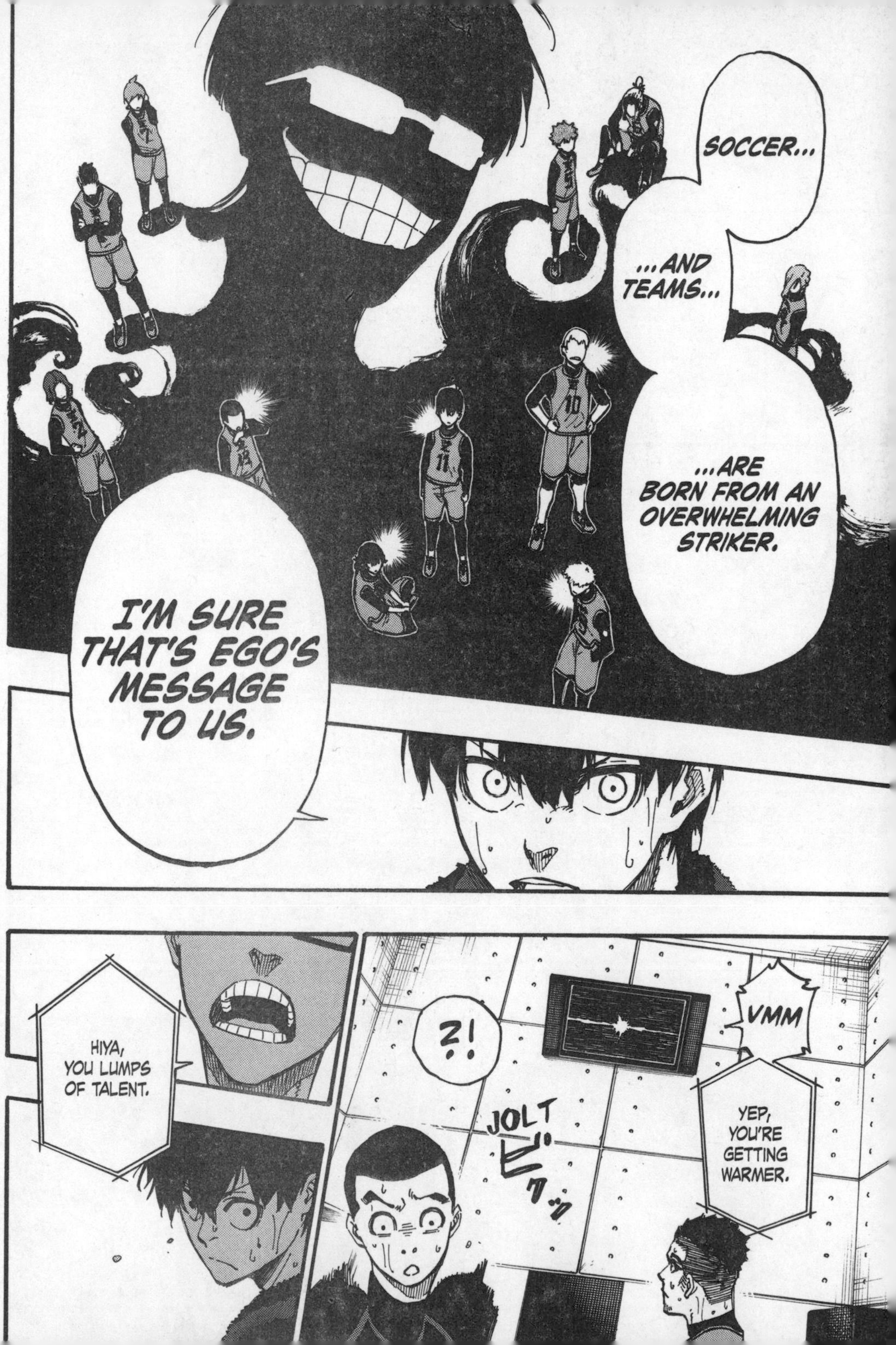
SOCCER...
...AND TEAMS...
...ARE BORN FROM AN OVERWHELMING STRIKER.
I'M SURE THAT'S EGO'S MESSAGE TO US.
VMM
?!
YEP, YOU'RE GETTING WARMER.
HIYA, YOU LUMPS OF TALENT.
JOLT

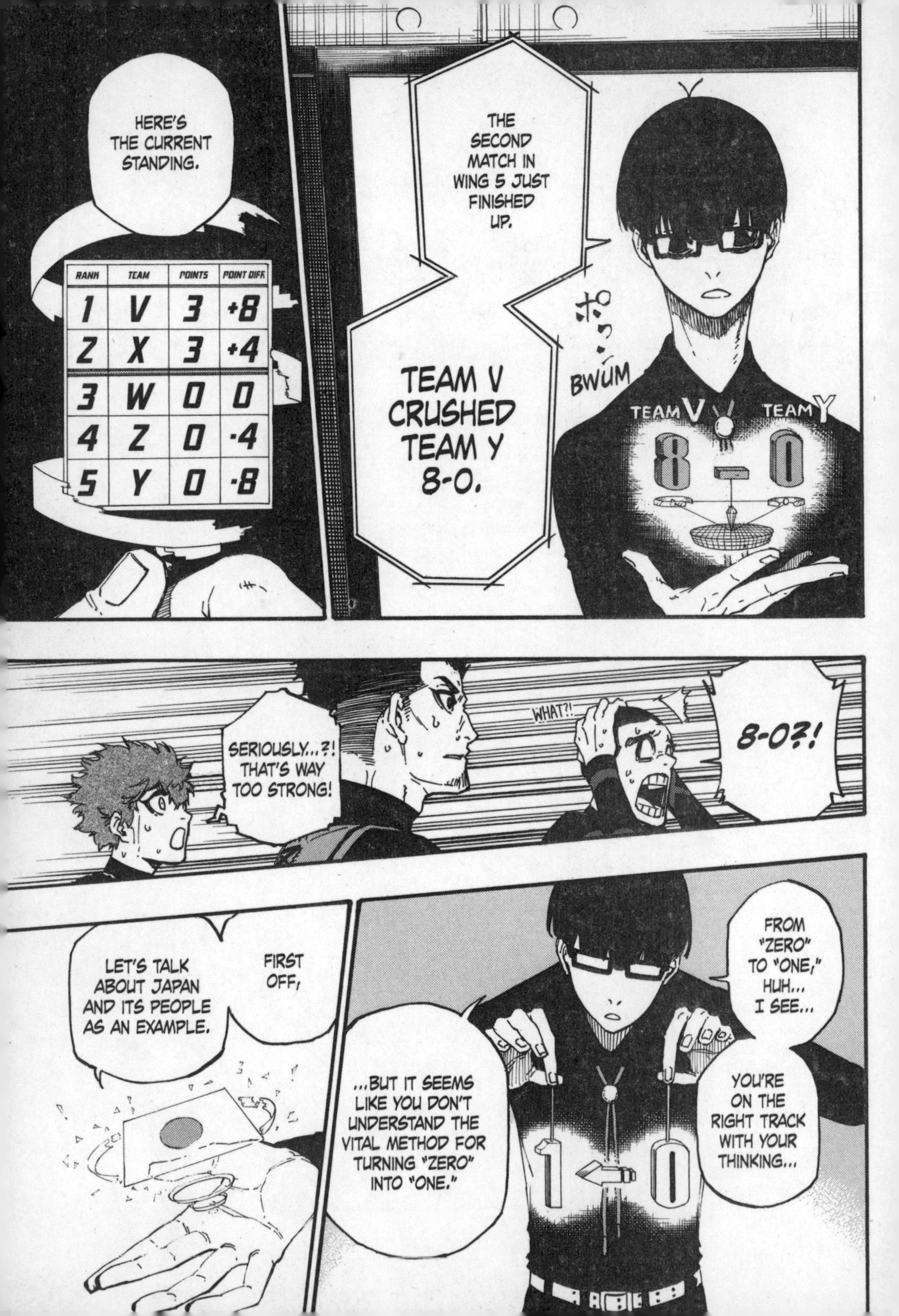
THE SECOND MATCH IN WING 5 JUST FINISHED UP.
TEAM V CRUSHED TEAM Y 8-0.
BWUM
TEAM V TEAM Y
8-0
HERE'S THE CURRENT STANDING.
RANK TEAM POINTS POINT DIFF.
1 V 3 +8
2 X 3 +4
3 W 0 0
4 Z 0 -4
5 Y 0 -8
8-0?!
WHAT?!
SERIOUSLY...?! THAT'S WAY TOO STRONG!
FROM "ZERO" TO "ONE," HUH... I SEE...
YOU'RE ON THE RIGHT TRACK WITH YOUR THINKING...
...BUT IT SEEMS LIKE YOU DON'T UNDERSTAND THE VITAL METHOD FOR TURNING "ZERO" INTO "ONE."
1-0
FIRST OFF,
LET'S TALK ABOUT JAPAN AND ITS PEOPLE AS AN EXAMPLE.

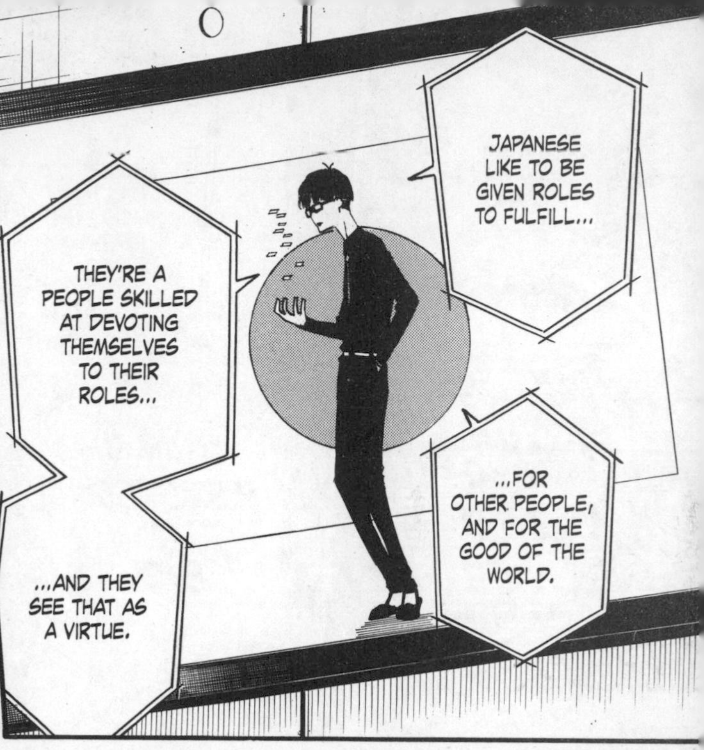
JAPANESE LIKE TO BE GIVEN ROLES TO FULFILL...
...FOR OTHER PEOPLE, AND FOR THE GOOD OF THE WORLD.
THEY'RE A PEOPLE SKILLED AT DEVOTING THEMSELVES TO THEIR ROLES...
...AND THEY SEE THAT AS A VIRTUE.
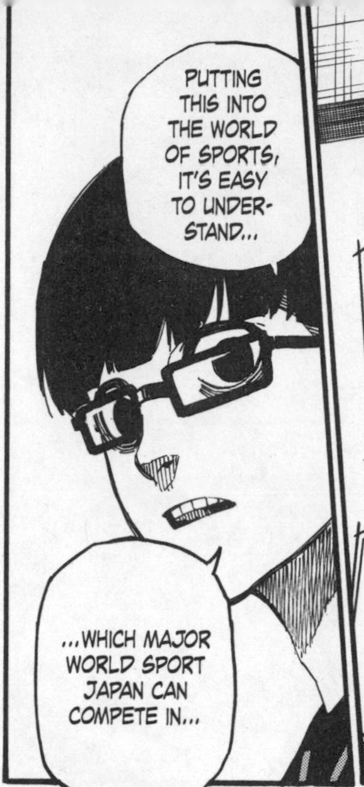
PUTTING THIS INTO THE WORLD OF SPORTS, IT'S EASY TO UNDER-STAND...
...WHICH MAJOR WORLD SPORT JAPAN CAN COMPETE IN...
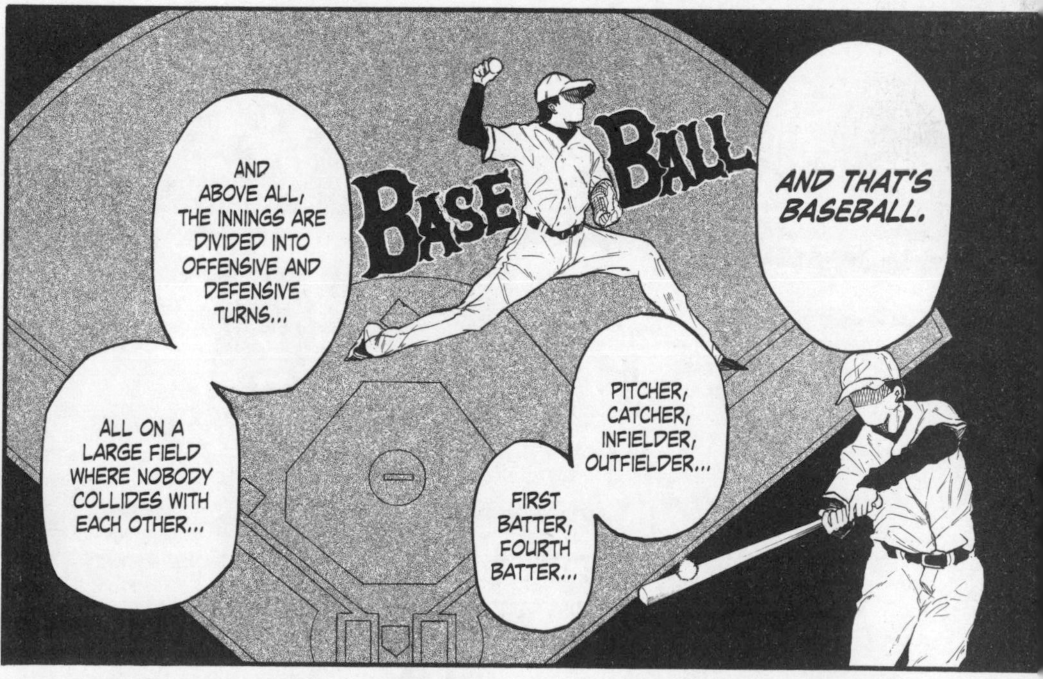
PITCHER, CATCHER, INFIELDER, OUTFIELDER...
FIRST BATTER, FOURTH BATTER...
AND ABOVE ALL, THE INNINGS ARE DIVIDED INTO OFFENSIVE AND DEFENSIVE TURNS...
ALL ON A LARGE FIELD WHERE NOBODY COLLIDES WITH EACH OTHER...
BASEBALL
AND THAT'S BASEBALL.

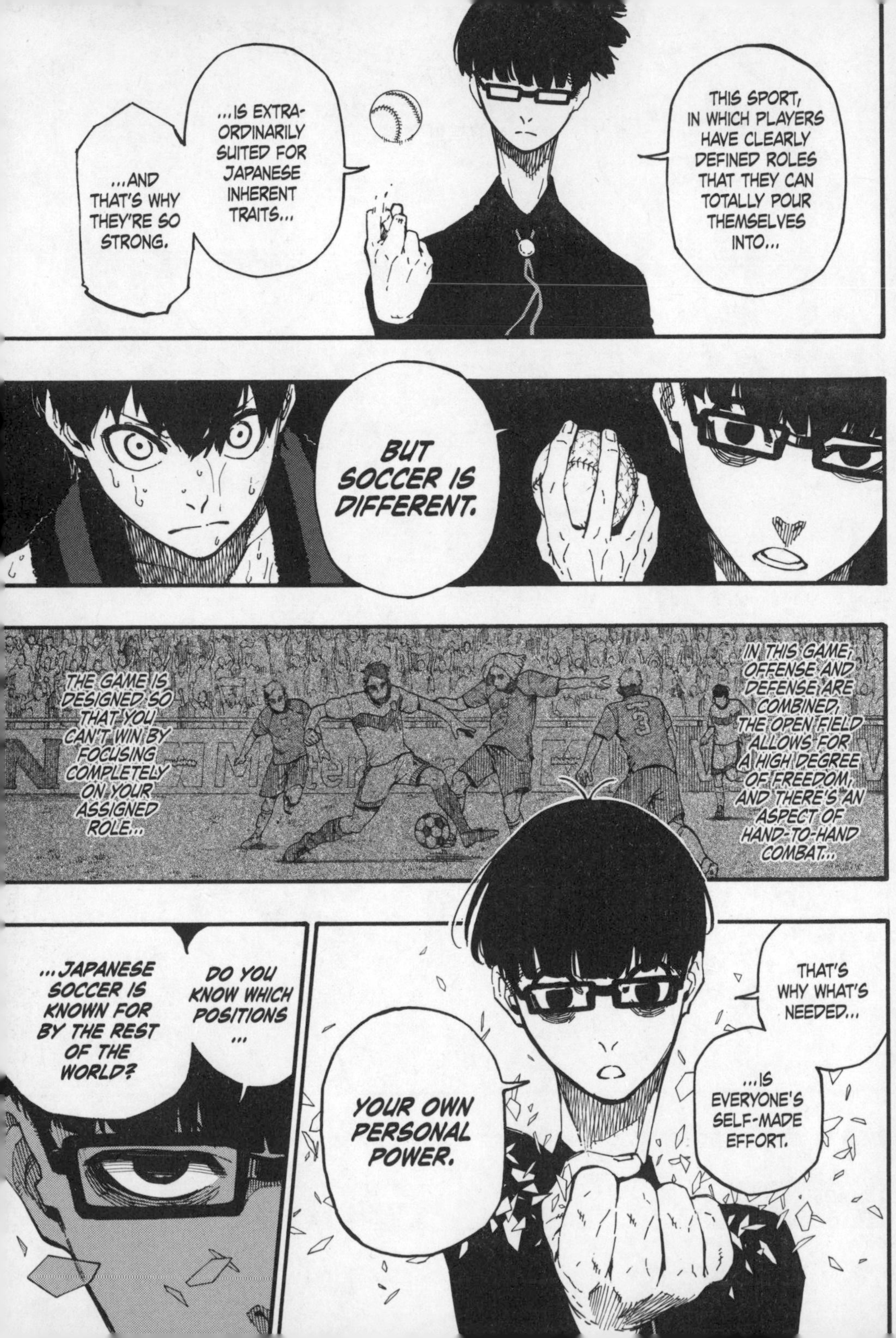
THIS SPORT, IN WHICH PLAYERS HAVE CLEARLY DEFINED ROLES THAT THEY CAN TOTALLY POUR THEMSELVES INTO...
...IS EXTRA-ORDINARILY SUITED FOR JAPANESE INHERENT TRAITS...
...AND THAT'S WHY THEY'RE SO STRONG.
BUT SOCCER IS DIFFERENT.
IN THIS GAME, OFFENSE AND DEFENSE ARE COMBINED, THE OPEN FIELD ALLOWS FOR A HIGH DEGREE OF FREEDOM, AND THERE'S AN ASPECT OF HAND-TO-HAND COMBAT...
THE GAME IS DESIGNED SO THAT YOU CAN'T WIN BY FOCUSING COMPLETELY ON YOUR ASSIGNED ROLE...
THAT'S WHY WHAT'S NEEDED...
...IS EVERYONE'S SELF-MADE EFFORT.
YOUR OWN PERSONAL POWER.
DO YOU KNOW WHICH POSITIONS ...
...JAPANESE SOCCER IS KNOWN FOR BY THE REST OF THE WORLD?

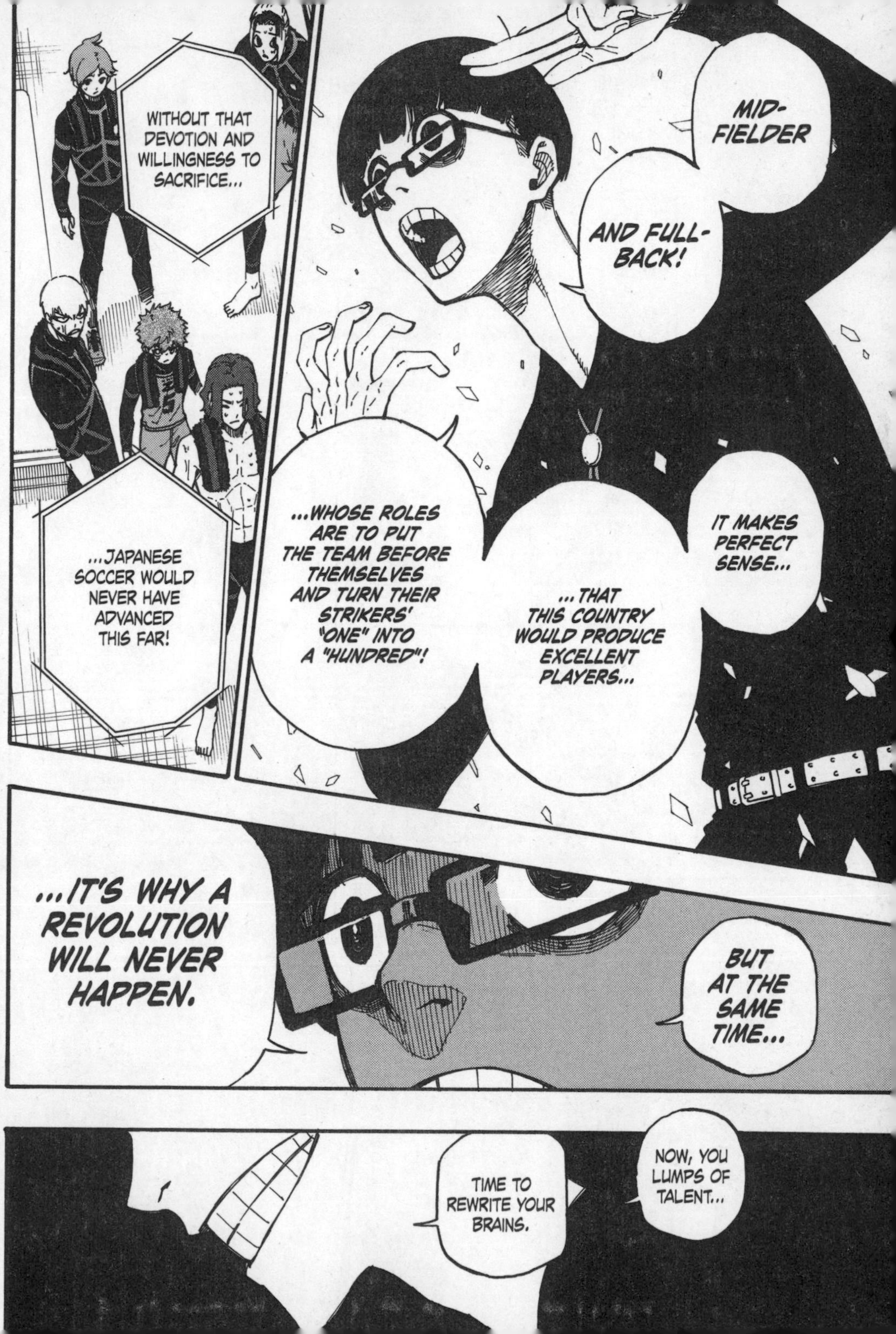
MID-FIELDER
AND FULL-BACK!
IT MAKES PERFECT SENSE...
...THAT THIS COUNTRY WOULD PRODUCE EXCELLENT PLAYERS...
...WHOSE ROLES ARE TO PUT THE TEAM BEFORE THEMSELVES AND TURN THEIR STRIKERS' "ONE" INTO A "HUNDRED"!
WITHOUT THAT DEVOTION AND WILLINGNESS TO SACRIFICE...
...JAPANESE SOCCER WOULD NEVER HAVE ADVANCED THIS FAR!
BUT AT THE SAME TIME...
...IT'S WHY A REVOLUTION WILL NEVER HAPPEN.
NOW, YOU LUMPS OF TALENT...
TIME TO REWRITE YOUR BRAINS.

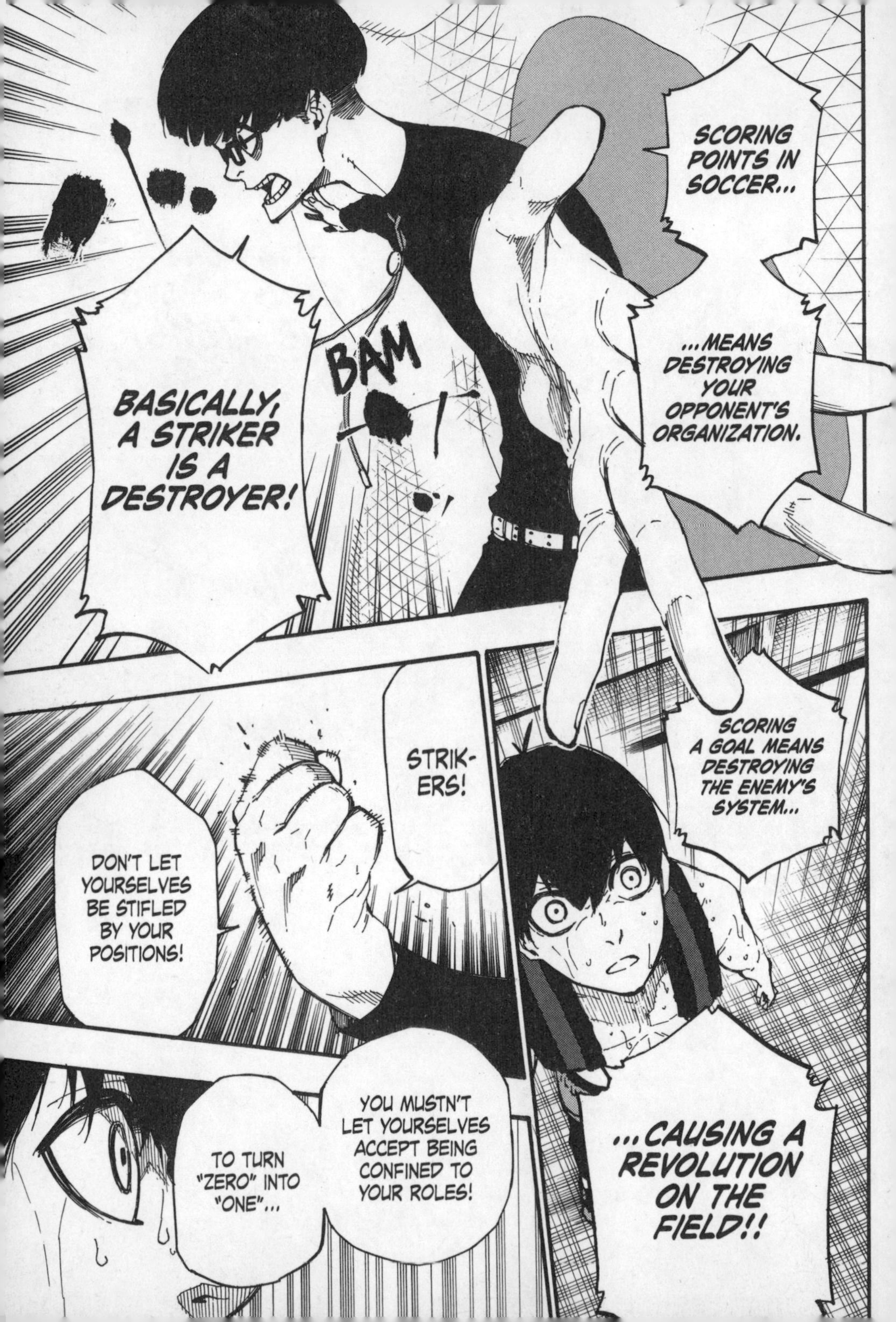
SCORING POINTS IN SOCCER...
...MEANS DESTROYING YOUR OPPONENT'S ORGANIZATION.
BAM
BASICALLY, A STRIKER IS A DESTROYER!
SCORING A GOAL MEANS DESTROYING THE ENEMY'S SYSTEM...
...CAUSING A REVOLUTION ON THE FIELD!!
STRIK-ERS!
DON'T LET YOURSELVES BE STIFLED BY YOUR POSITIONS!
YOU MUSTN'T LET YOURSELVES ACCEPT BEING CONFINED TO YOUR ROLES!
TO TURN "ZERO" INTO "ONE"...

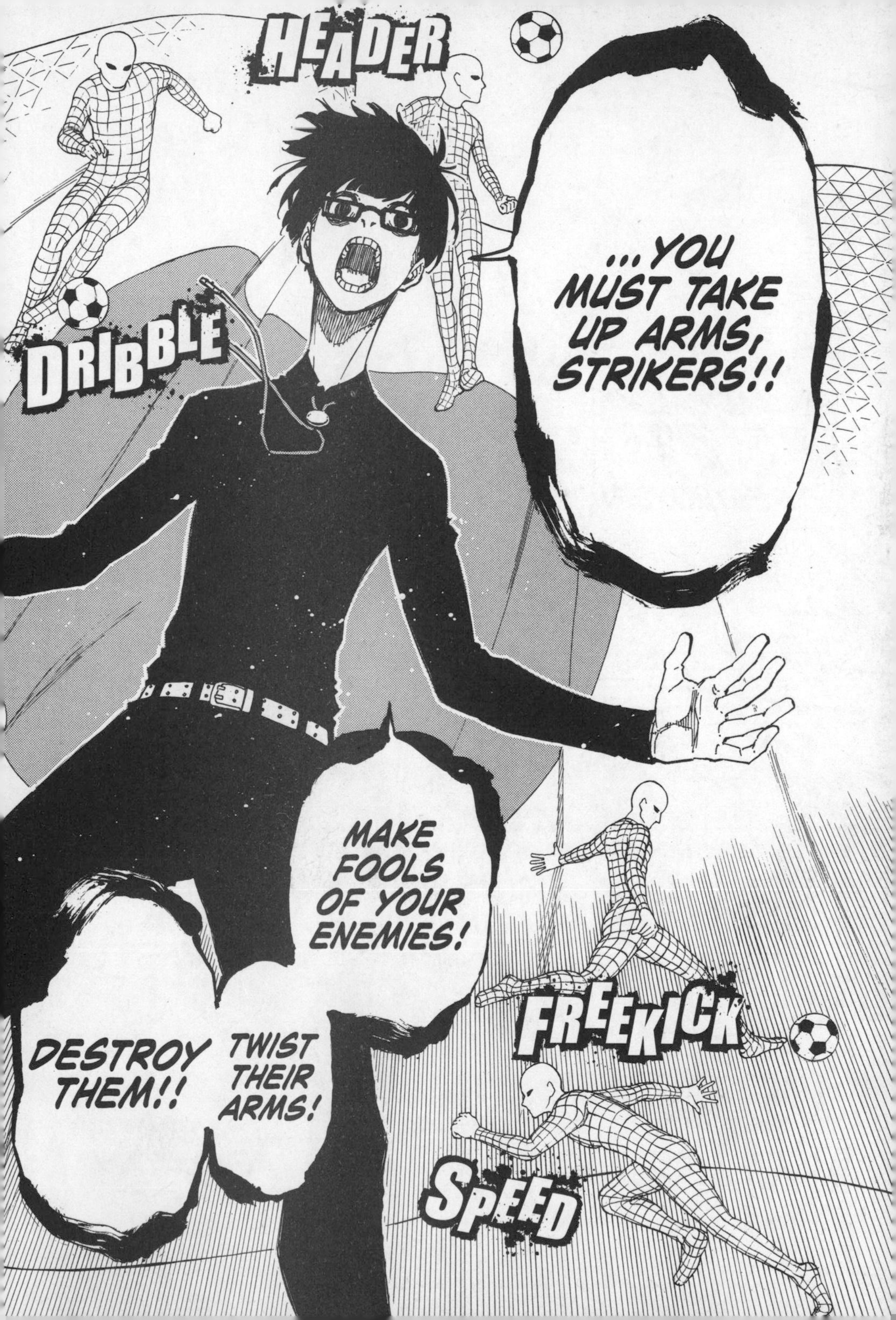
HEADER
...YOU MUST TAKE UP ARMS, STRIKERS!!
DRIBBLE
MAKE FOOLS OF YOUR ENEMIES!
TWIST THEIR ARMS!
DESTROY THEM!!
FREEKICK
SPEED

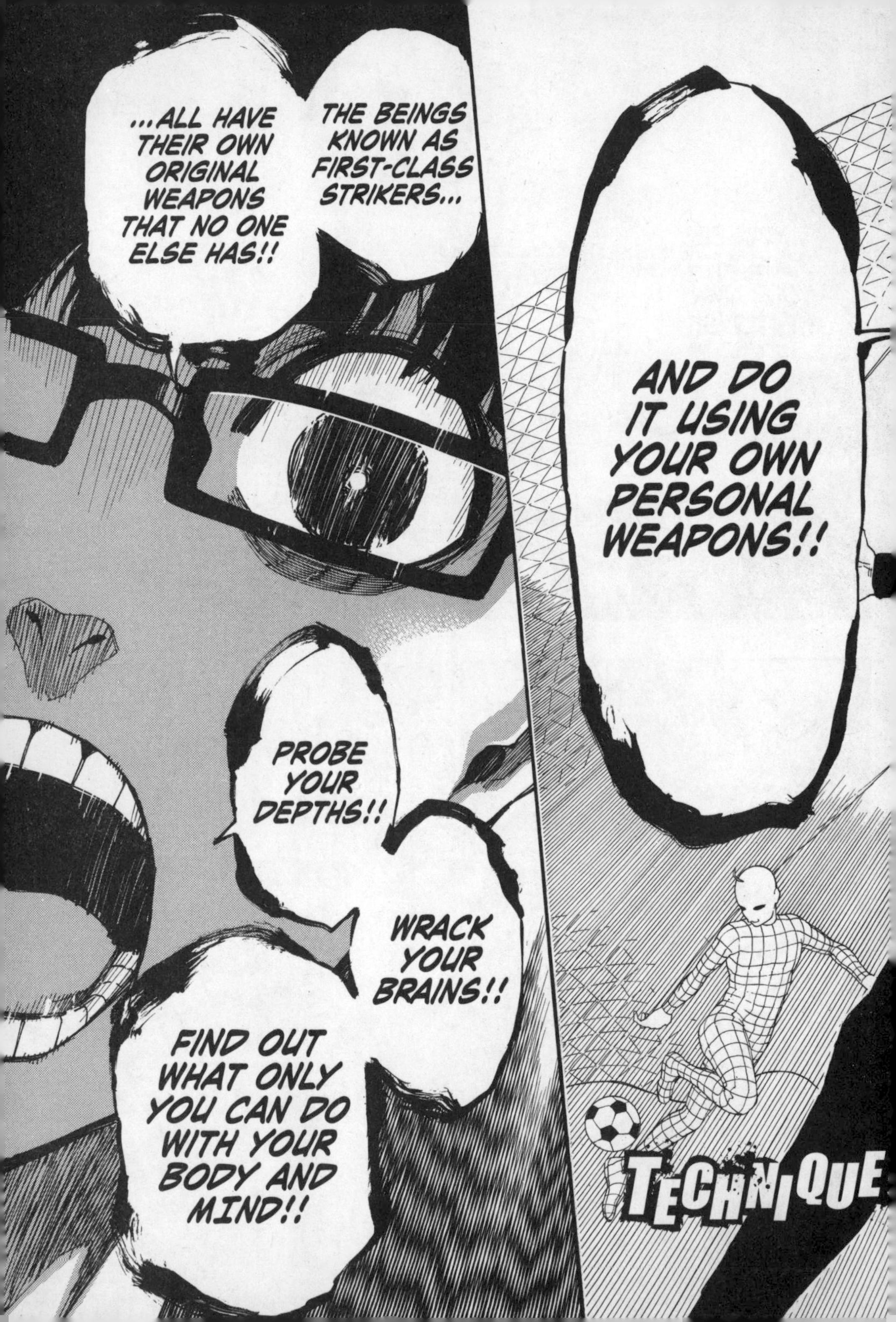
THE BEINGS KNOWN AS FIRST-CLASS STRIKERS...
...ALL HAVE THEIR OWN ORIGINAL WEAPONS THAT NO ONE ELSE HAS!!
PROBE YOUR DEPTHS!!
WRACK YOUR BRAINS!!
FIND OUT WHAT ONLY YOU CAN DO WITH YOUR BODY AND MIND!!
AND DO IT USING YOUR OWN PERSONAL WEAPONS!!
TECHNIQUE

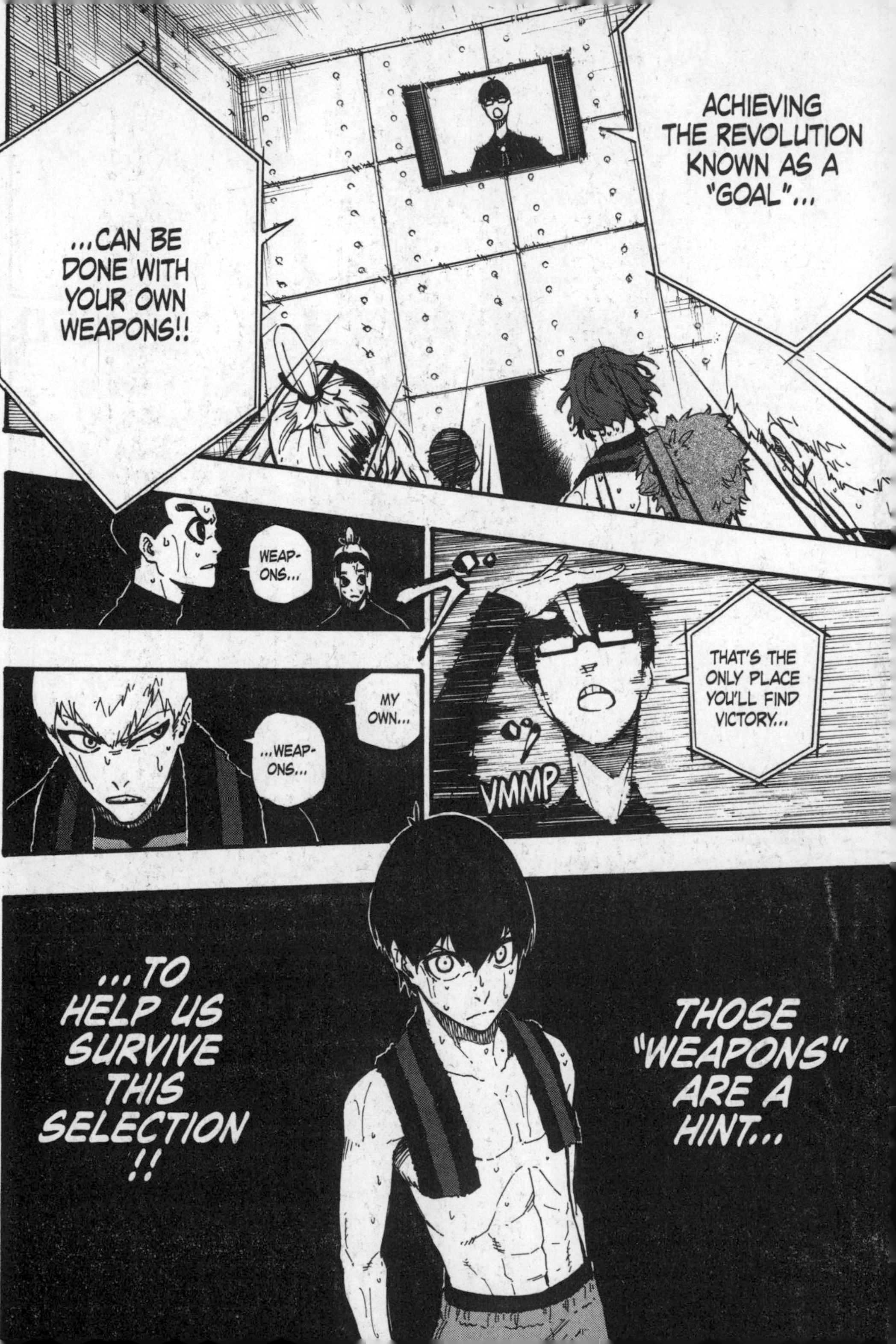
ACHIEVING THE REVOLUTION KNOWN AS A "GOAL"...
...CAN BE DONE WITH YOUR OWN WEAPONS!!
THAT'S THE ONLY PLACE YOU'LL FIND VICTORY...
VMMP
WEAP-ONS...
MY OWN...
...WEAP-ONS...
THOSE "WEAPONS" ARE A HINT...
...TO HELP US SURVIVE THIS SELECTION!!

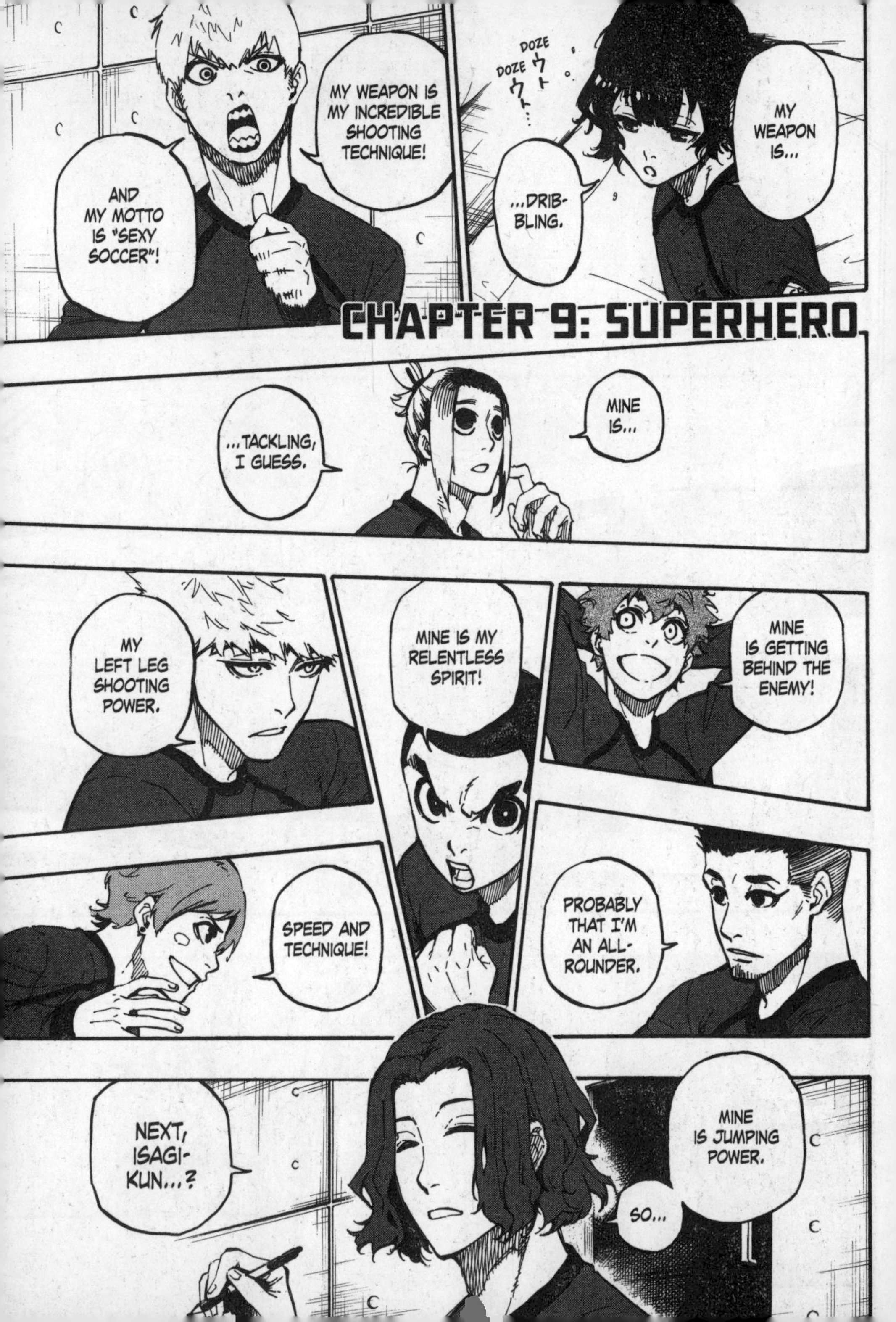
MY WEAPON IS...
DOZE DOZE
ウトウト…
...DRIBBLING.
MY WEAPON IS MY INCREDIBLE SHOOTING TECHNIQUE!
AND MY MOTTO IS "SEXY SOCCER"!
CHAPTER 9: SUPERHERO
MINE IS...
...TACKLING, I GUESS.
MINE IS GETTING BEHIND THE ENEMY!
MINE IS MY RELENTLESS SPIRIT!
MY LEFT LEG SHOOTING POWER.
PROBABLY THAT I'M AN ALL-ROUNDER.
SPEED AND TECHNIQUE!
MINE IS JUMPING POWER.
SO...
NEXT, ISAGI-KUN...?

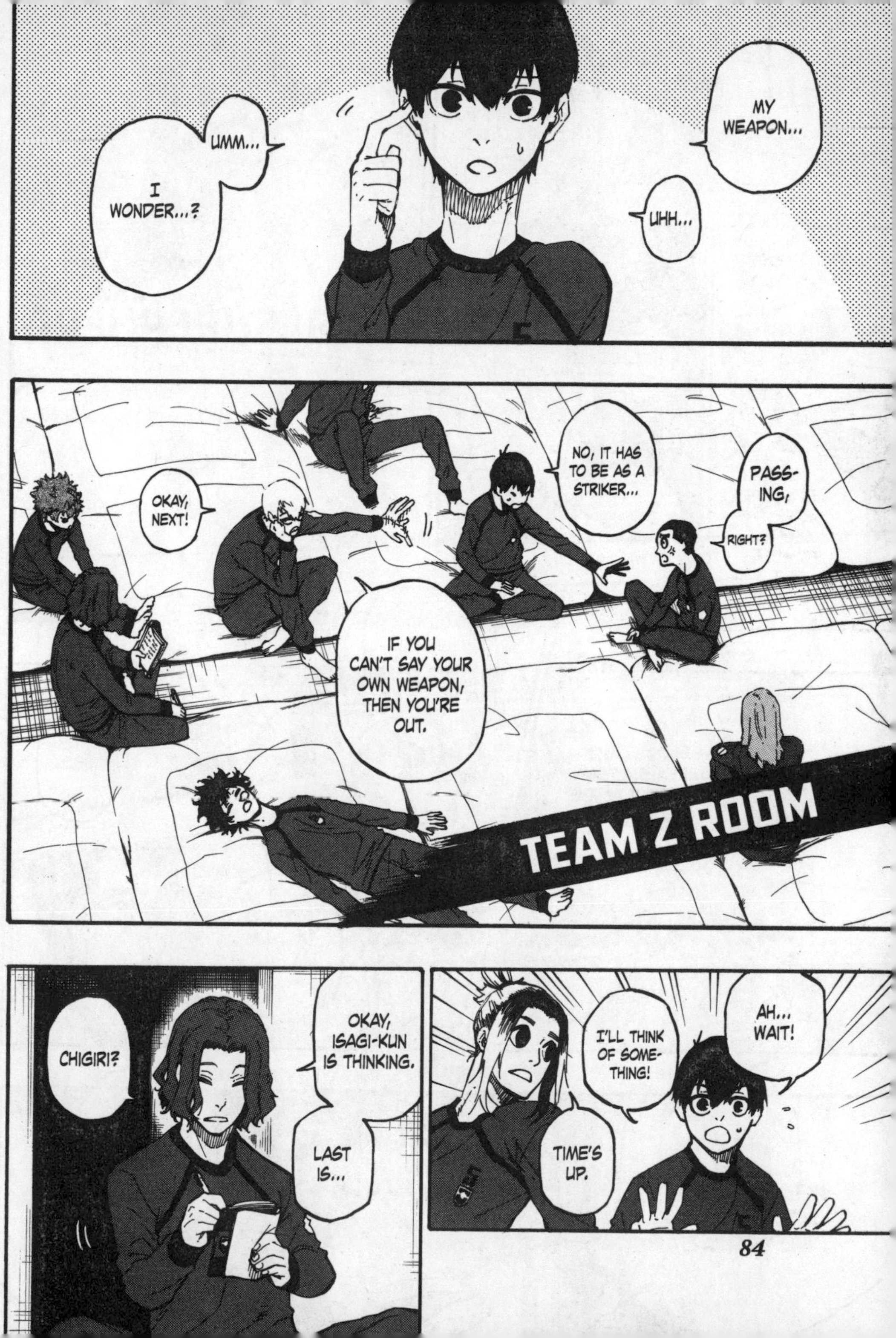
MY WEAPON...
UHH...
UMM...
I WONDER...?
PASS-ING, RIGHT?
NO, IT HAS TO BE AS A STRIKER...
OKAY, NEXT!
IF YOU CAN'T SAY YOUR OWN WEAPON, THEN YOU'RE OUT.
TEAM Z ROOM
AH... WAIT!
I'LL THINK OF SOME-THING!
TIME'S UP.
OKAY, ISAGI-KUN IS THINKING.
LAST IS...
CHIGIRI?

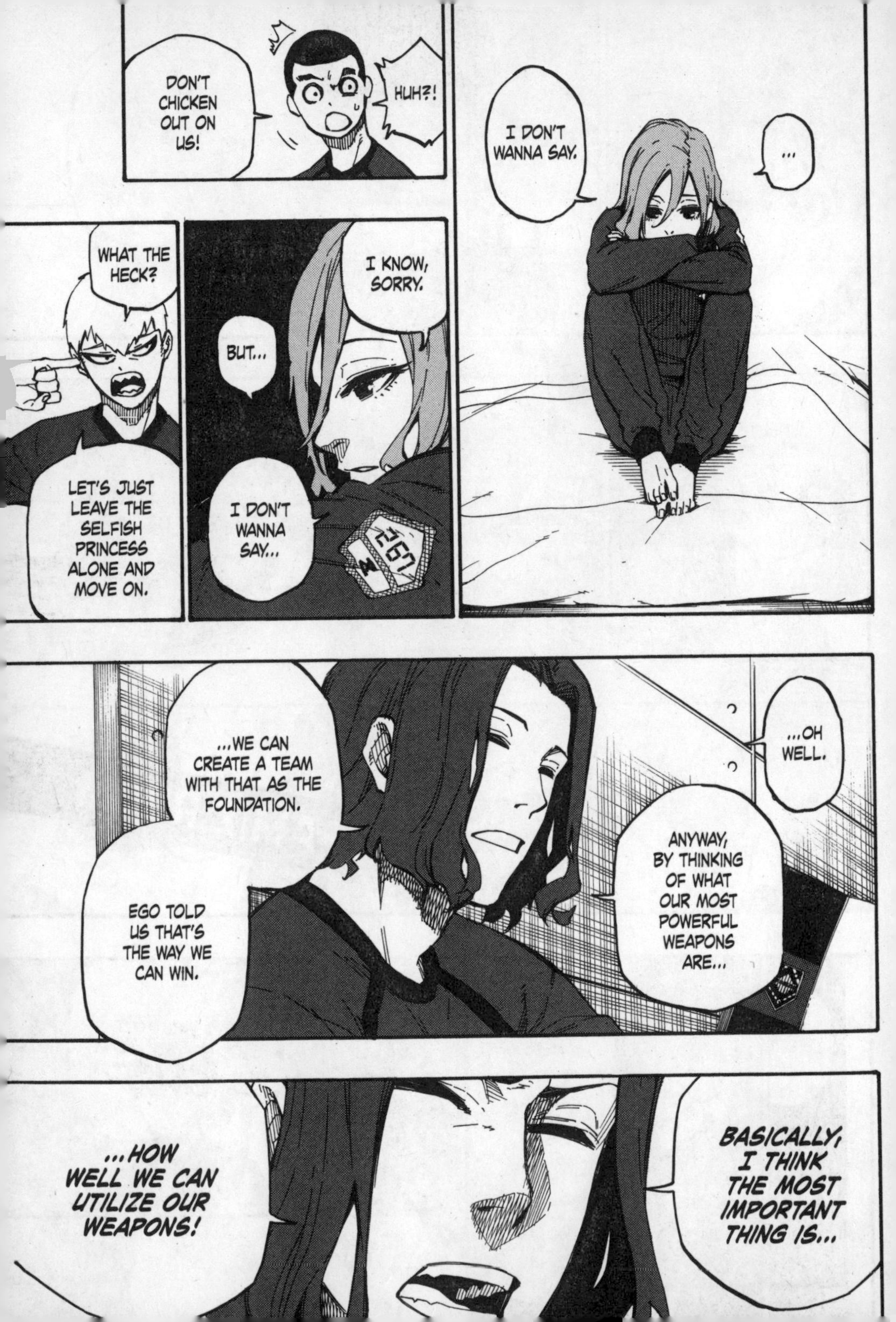
...
I DON'T WANNA SAY.
DON'T CHICKEN OUT ON US!
HUH?!
I KNOW, SORRY.
BUT...
I DON'T WANNA SAY...
WHAT THE HECK?
LET'S JUST LEAVE THE SELFISH PRINCESS ALONE AND MOVE ON.
...OH WELL.
ANYWAY, BY THINKING OF WHAT OUR MOST POWERFUL WEAPONS ARE...
...WE CAN CREATE A TEAM WITH THAT AS THE FOUNDATION.
EGO TOLD US THAT'S THE WAY WE CAN WIN.
BASICALLY, I THINK THE MOST IMPORTANT THING IS...
...HOW WELL WE CAN UTILIZE OUR WEAPONS!

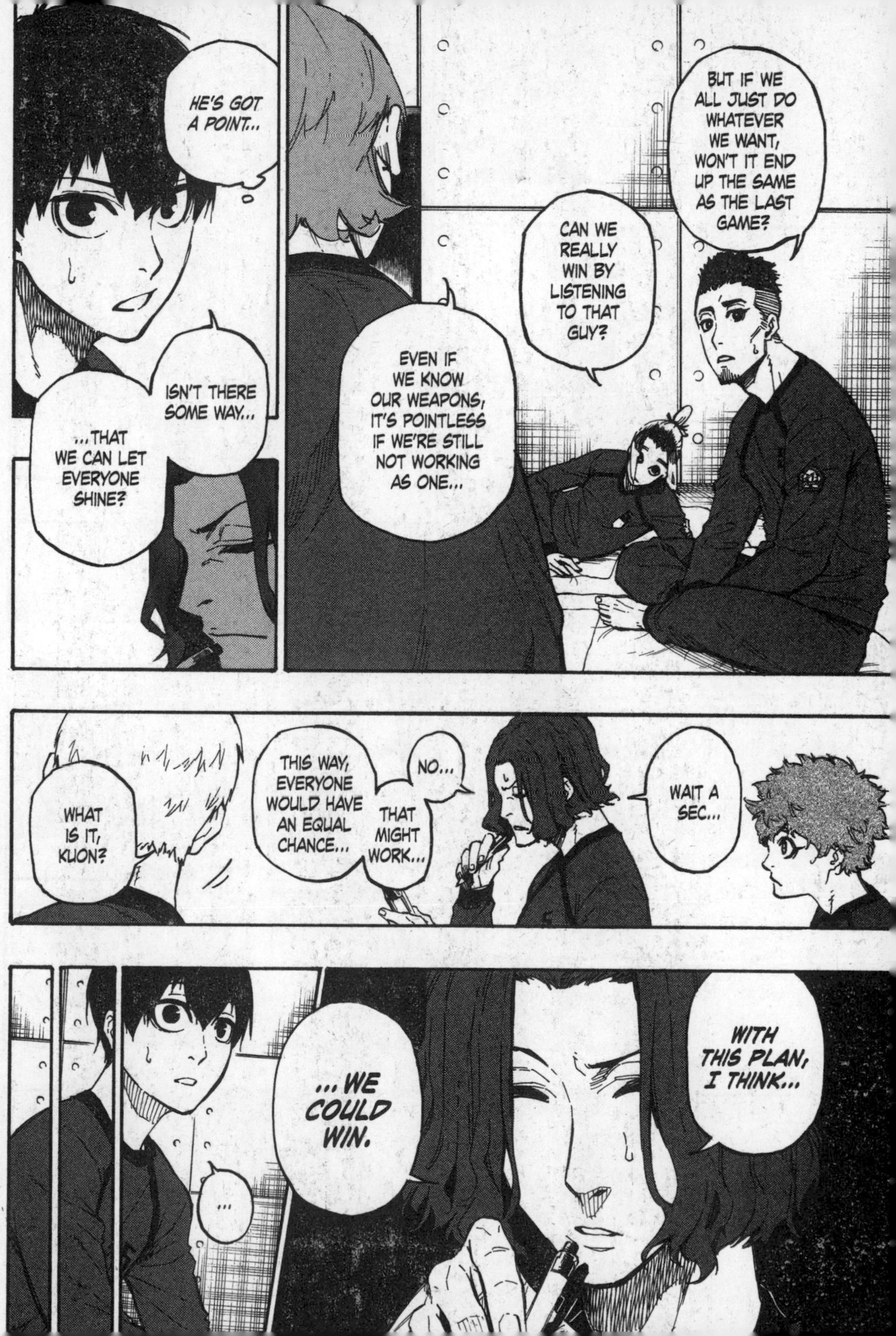
BUT IF WE ALL JUST DO WHATEVER WE WANT, WON'T IT END UP THE SAME AS THE LAST GAME?
CAN WE REALLY WIN BY LISTENING TO THAT GUY?
EVEN IF WE KNOW OUR WEAPONS, IT'S POINTLESS IF WE'RE STILL NOT WORKING AS ONE...
HE'S GOT A POINT...
ISN'T THERE SOME WAY...
...THAT WE CAN LET EVERYONE SHINE?
WAIT A SEC...
NO...
THAT MIGHT WORK...
THIS WAY, EVERYONE WOULD HAVE AN EQUAL CHANCE...
WHAT IS IT, KUON?
WITH THIS PLAN, I THINK...
...WE COULD WIN.
...

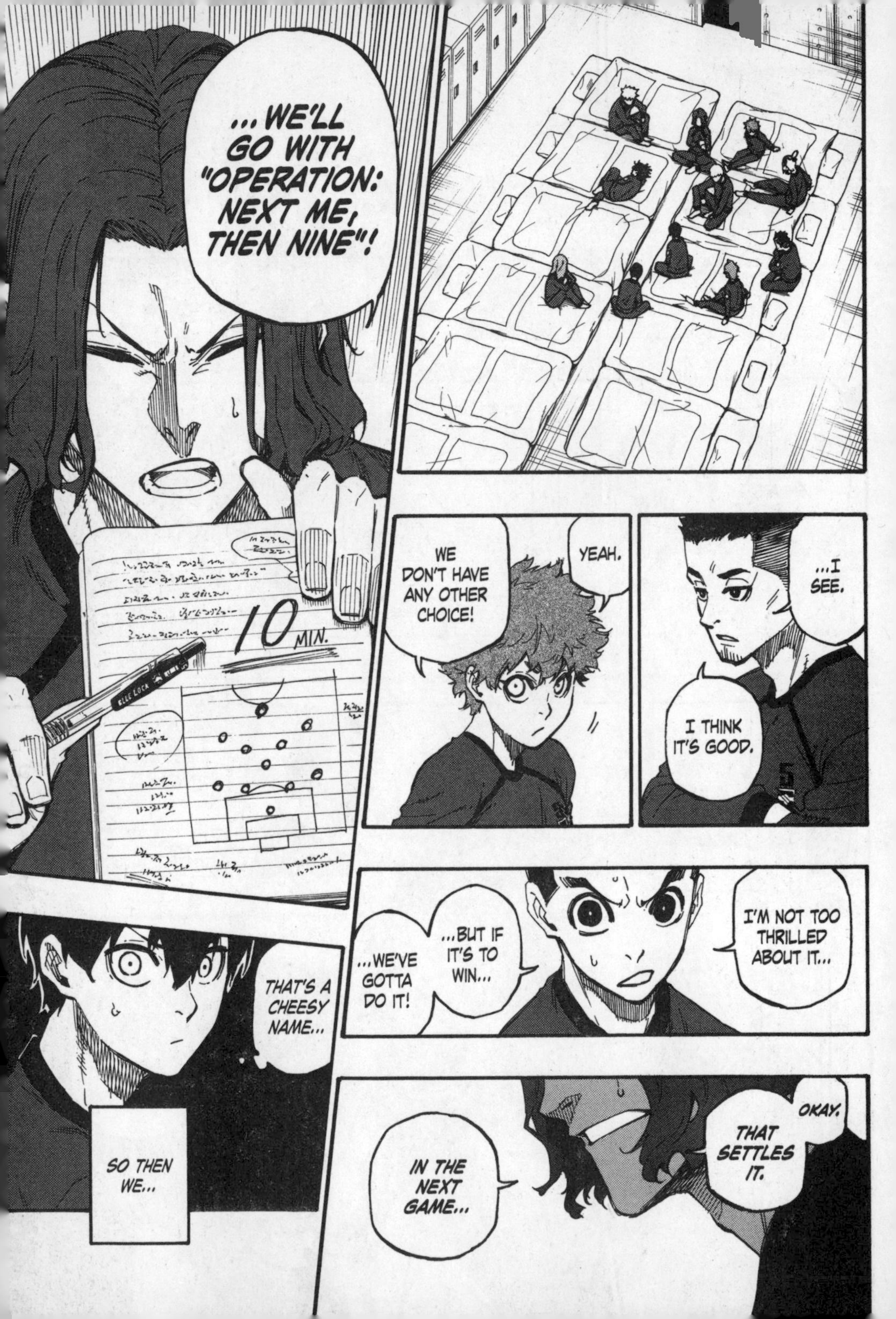
...I SEE.
I THINK IT'S GOOD.
YEAH.
WE DON'T HAVE ANY OTHER CHOICE!
...WE'LL GO WITH "OPERATION: NEXT ME, THEN NINE"!
10 MIN.
I'M NOT TOO THRILLED ABOUT IT...
...BUT IF IT'S TO WIN...
...WE'VE GOTTA DO IT!
OKAY.
THAT SETTLES IT.
IN THE NEXT GAME...
THAT'S A CHEESY NAME...
SO THEN WE...

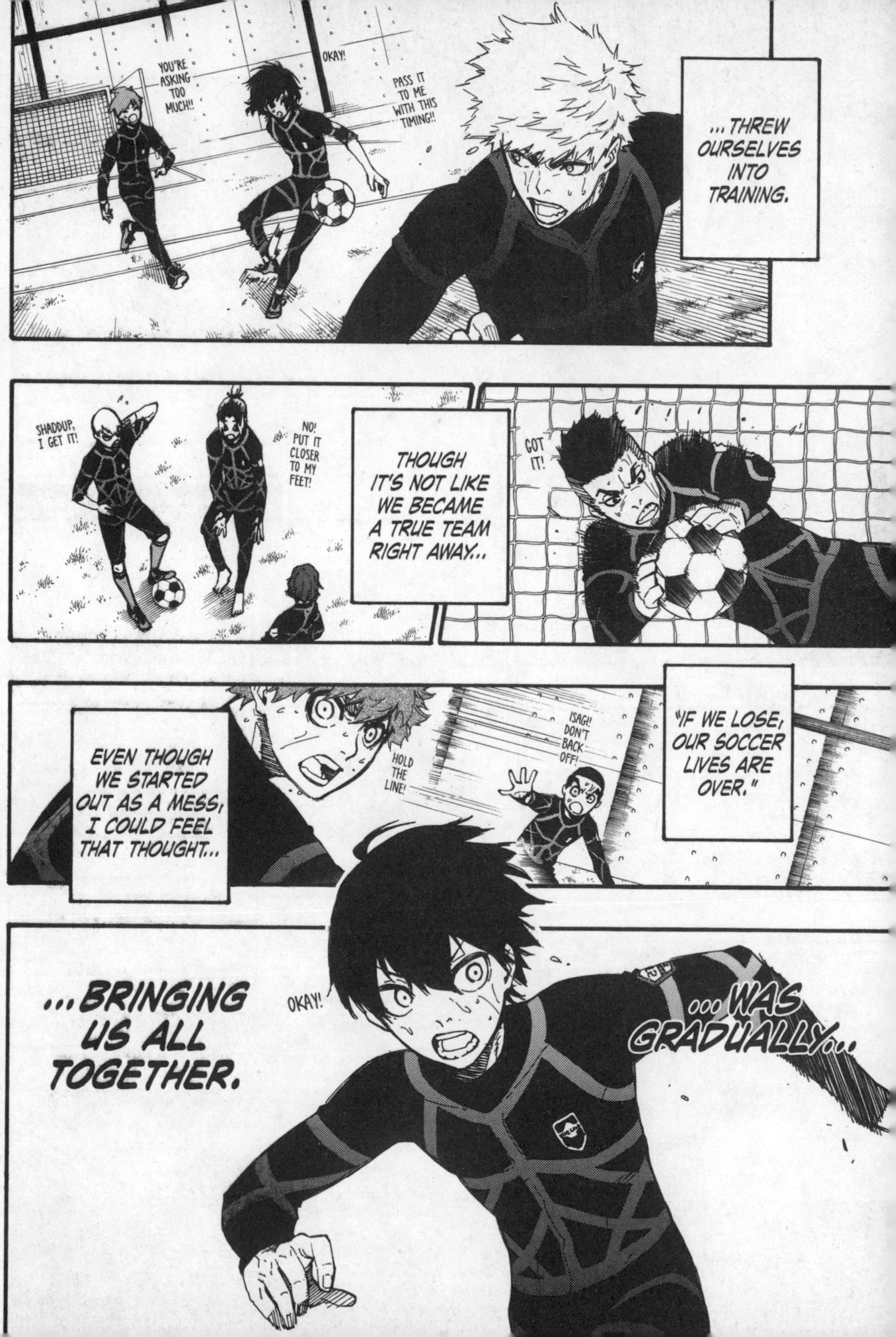
...THREW OURSELVES INTO TRAINING.
OKAY!
PASS IT TO ME WITH THIS TIMING!!
YOU'RE ASKING TOO MUCH!!
GOT IT!
THOUGH IT'S NOT LIKE WE BECAME A TRUE TEAM RIGHT AWAY...
NO! PUT IT CLOSER TO MY FEET!
SHADDUP, I GET IT!
"IF WE LOSE, OUR SOCCER LIVES ARE OVER."
ISAGI! DON'T BACK OFF!
HOLD THE LINE!
EVEN THOUGH WE STARTED OUT AS A MESS, I COULD FEEL THAT THOUGHT...
...WAS GRADUALLY...
OKAY!
...BRINGING US ALL TOGETHER.

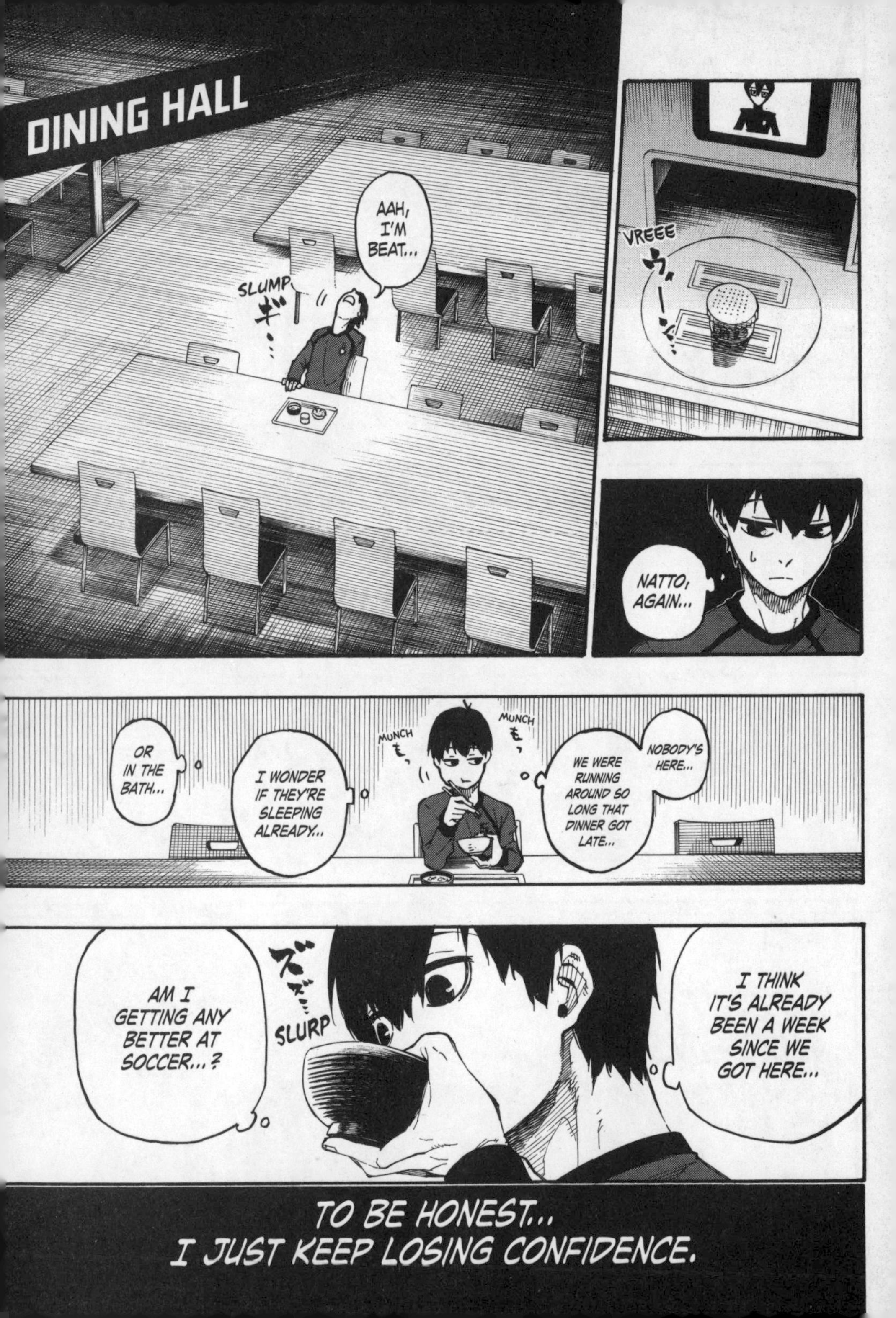
VREEE
NATTO, AGAIN...
DINING HALL
SLUMP
AAH, I'M BEAT...
NOBODY'S HERE...
WE WERE RUNNING AROUND SO LONG THAT DINNER GOT LATE...
MUNCH
MUNCH
I WONDER IF THEY'RE SLEEPING ALREADY...
OR IN THE BATH...
I THINK IT'S ALREADY BEEN A WEEK SINCE WE GOT HERE...
SLURP
AM I GETTING ANY BETTER AT SOCCER...?
TO BE HONEST...
I JUST KEEP LOSING CONFIDENCE.

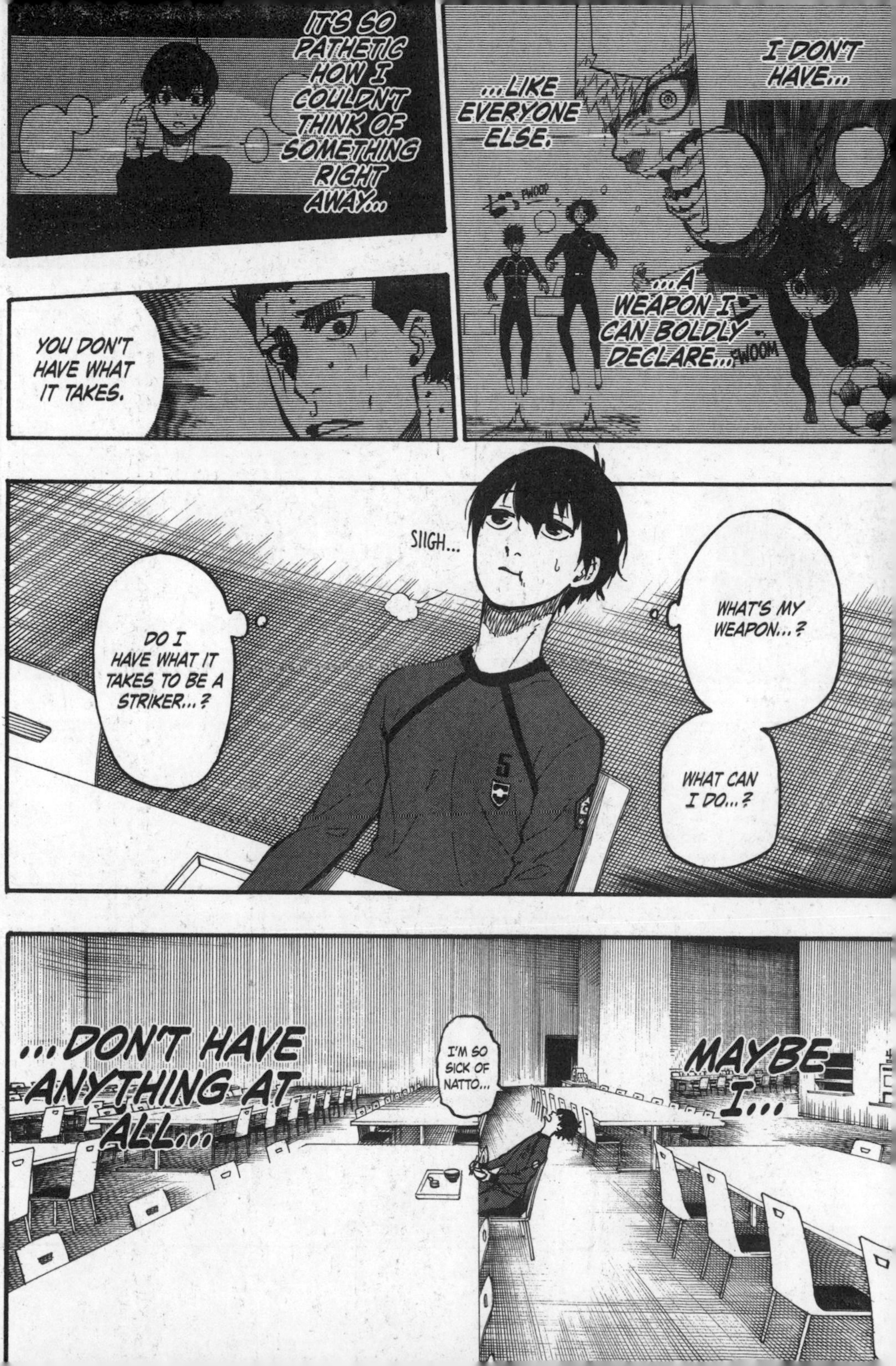
I DON'T HAVE...
...A WEAPON I CAN BOLDLY DECLARE...
WOOM
PWOOP
...LIKE EVERYONE ELSE.
IT'S SO PATHETIC HOW I COULDN'T THINK OF SOMETHING RIGHT AWAY...
YOU DON'T HAVE WHAT IT TAKES.
WHAT'S MY WEAPON...?
WHAT CAN I DO...?
SIIGH...
DO I HAVE WHAT IT TAKES TO BE A STRIKER...?
MAYBE I...
I'M SO SICK OF NATTO...
...DON'T HAVE ANYTHING AT ALL...

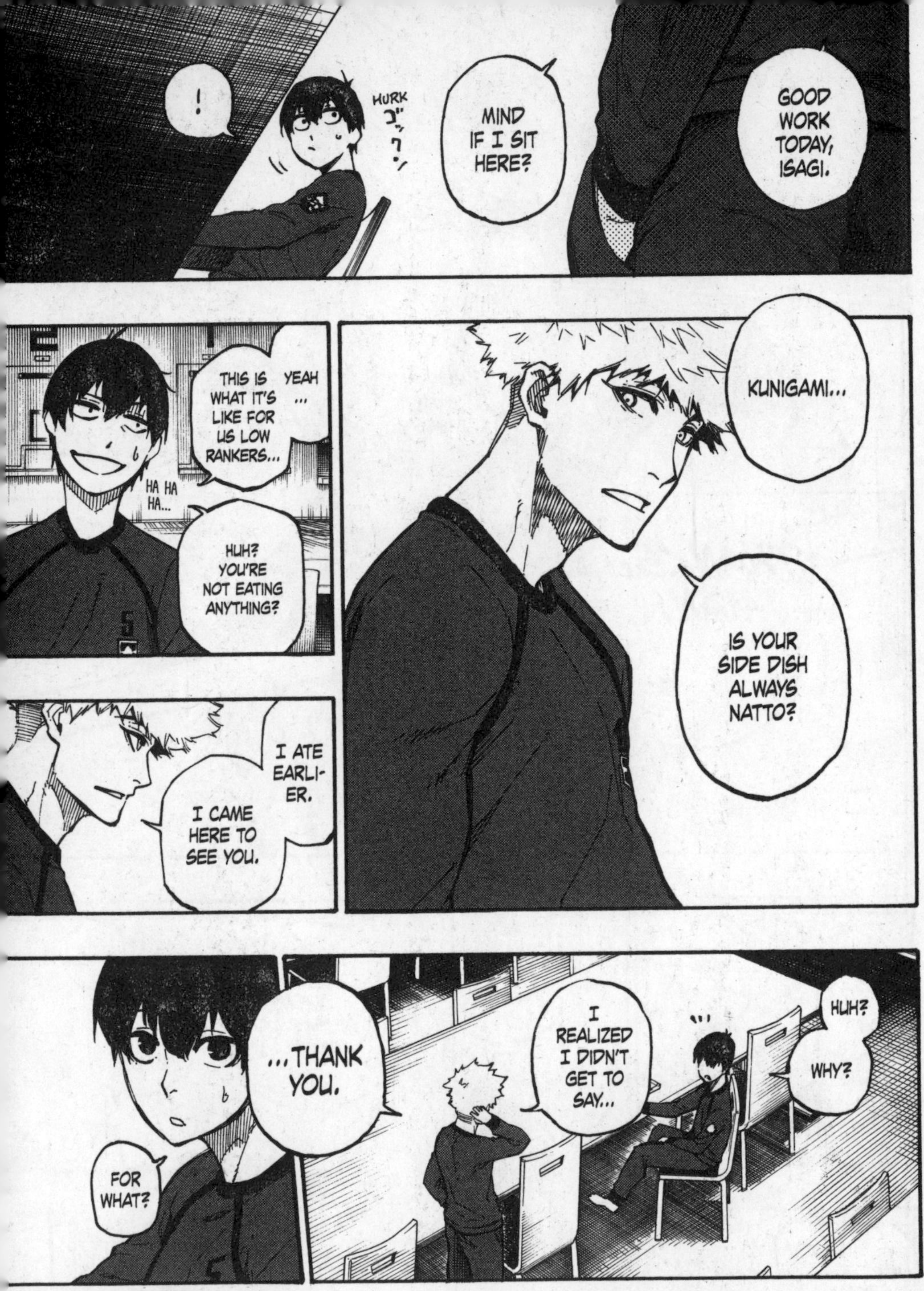
GOOD WORK TODAY, ISAGI.
MIND IF I SIT HERE?
HURK
!
KUNIGAMI...
IS YOUR SIDE DISH ALWAYS NATTO?
YEAH ...
THIS IS WHAT IT'S LIKE FOR US LOW RANKERS...
HA HA HA...
HUH? YOU'RE NOT EATING ANYTHING?
I ATE EARLI-ER.
I CAME HERE TO SEE YOU.
HUH?
WHY?
I REALIZED I DIDN'T GET TO SAY...
...THANK YOU.
FOR WHAT?

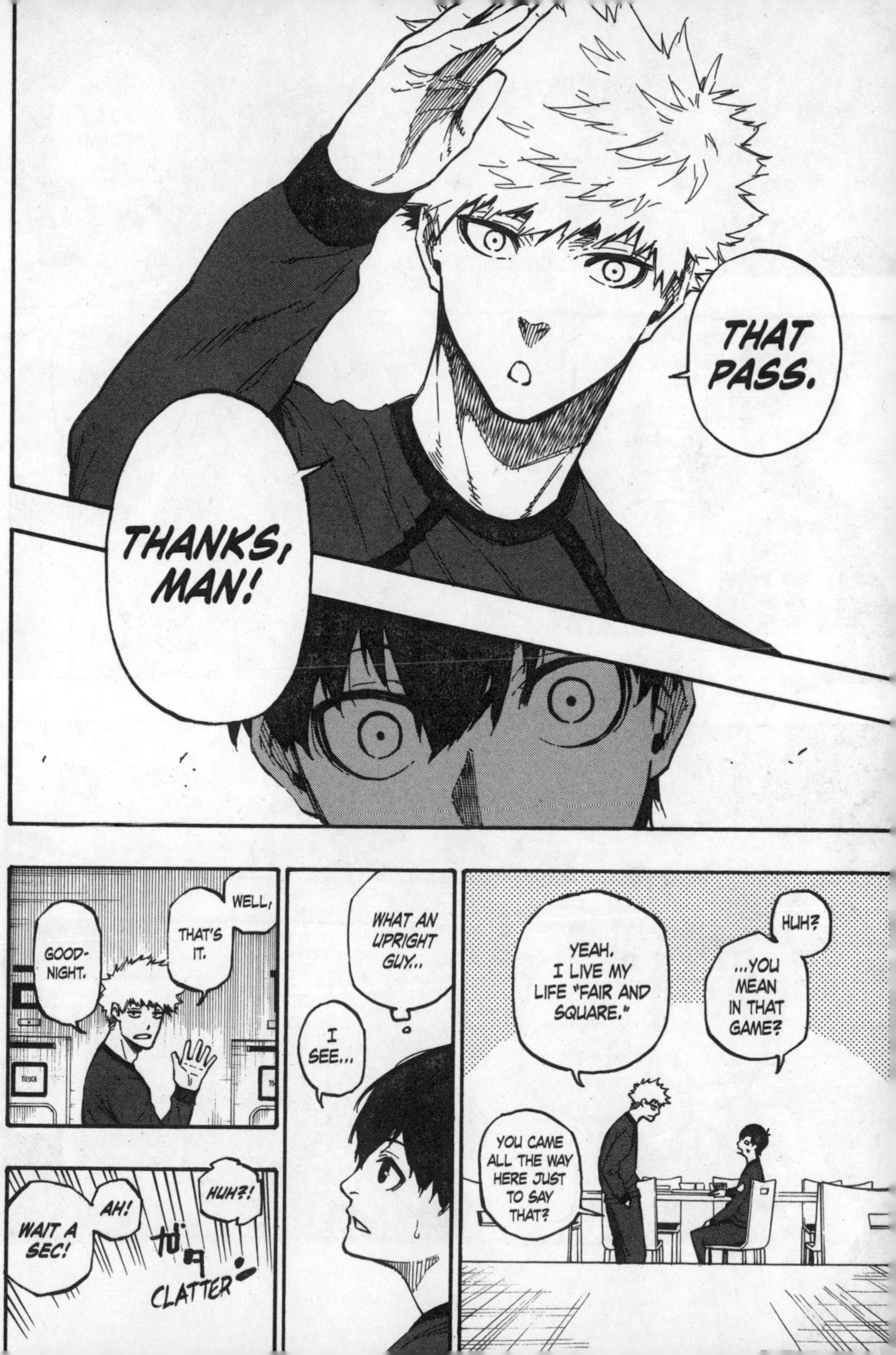
THAT PASS.
THANKS, MAN!
HUH?
...YOU MEAN IN THAT GAME?
YEAH. I LIVE MY LIFE "FAIR AND SQUARE."
YOU CAME ALL THE WAY HERE JUST TO SAY THAT?
WHAT AN UPRIGHT GUY...
I SEE...
WELL, THAT'S IT.
GOOD-NIGHT.
HUH?!
AH!
WAIT A SEC!
CLATTER

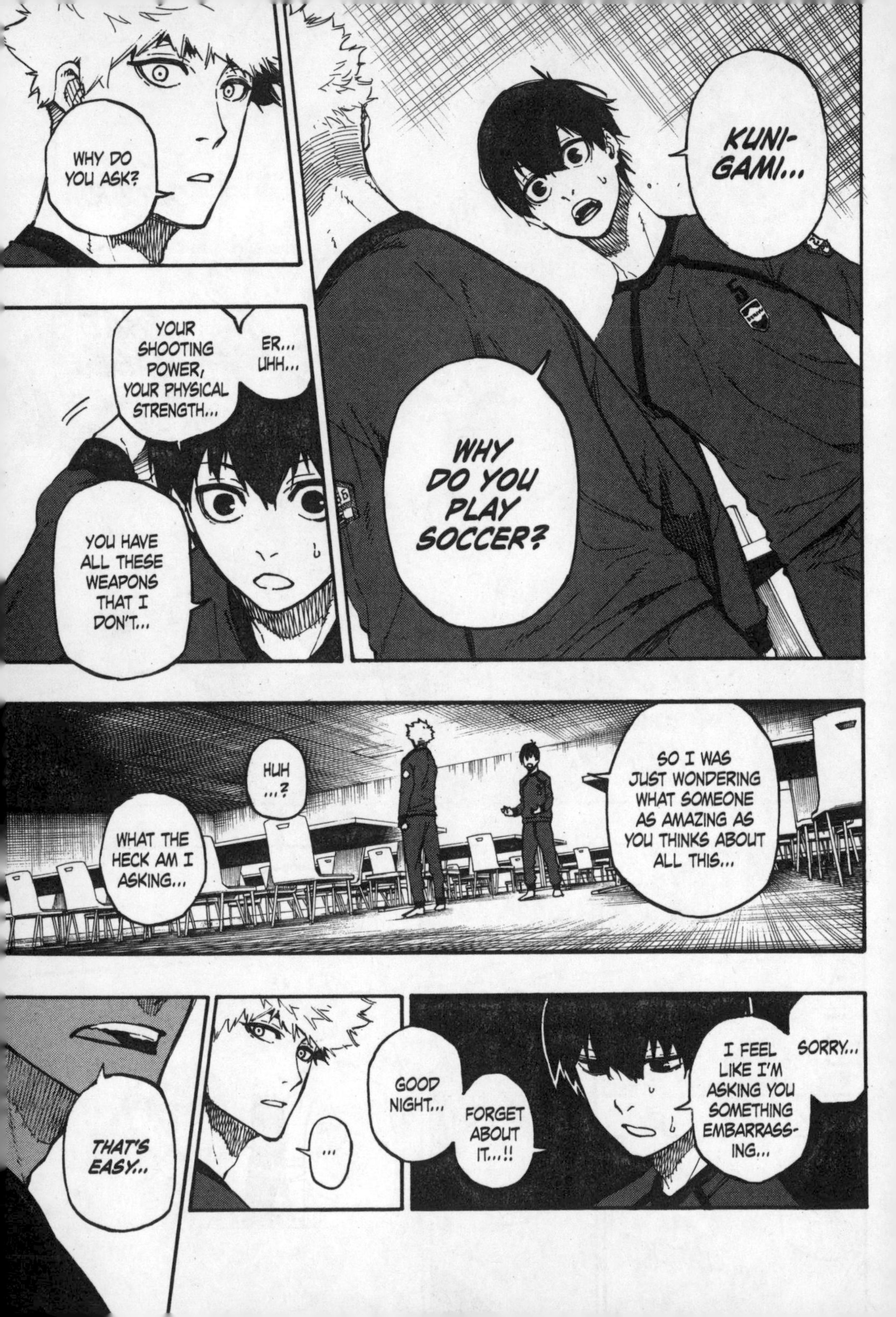
KUNI-GAMI...
WHY DO YOU PLAY SOCCER?
WHY DO YOU ASK?
ER... UHH...
YOUR SHOOTING POWER, YOUR PHYSICAL STRENGTH...
YOU HAVE ALL THESE WEAPONS THAT I DON'T...
SO I WAS JUST WONDERING WHAT SOMEONE AS AMAZING AS YOU THINKS ABOUT ALL THIS...
HUH ...?
WHAT THE HECK AM I ASKING...
SORRY...
I FEEL LIKE I'M ASKING YOU SOMETHING EMBARRASS-ING...
FORGET ABOUT IT...!!
GOOD NIGHT...
...
THAT'S EASY...

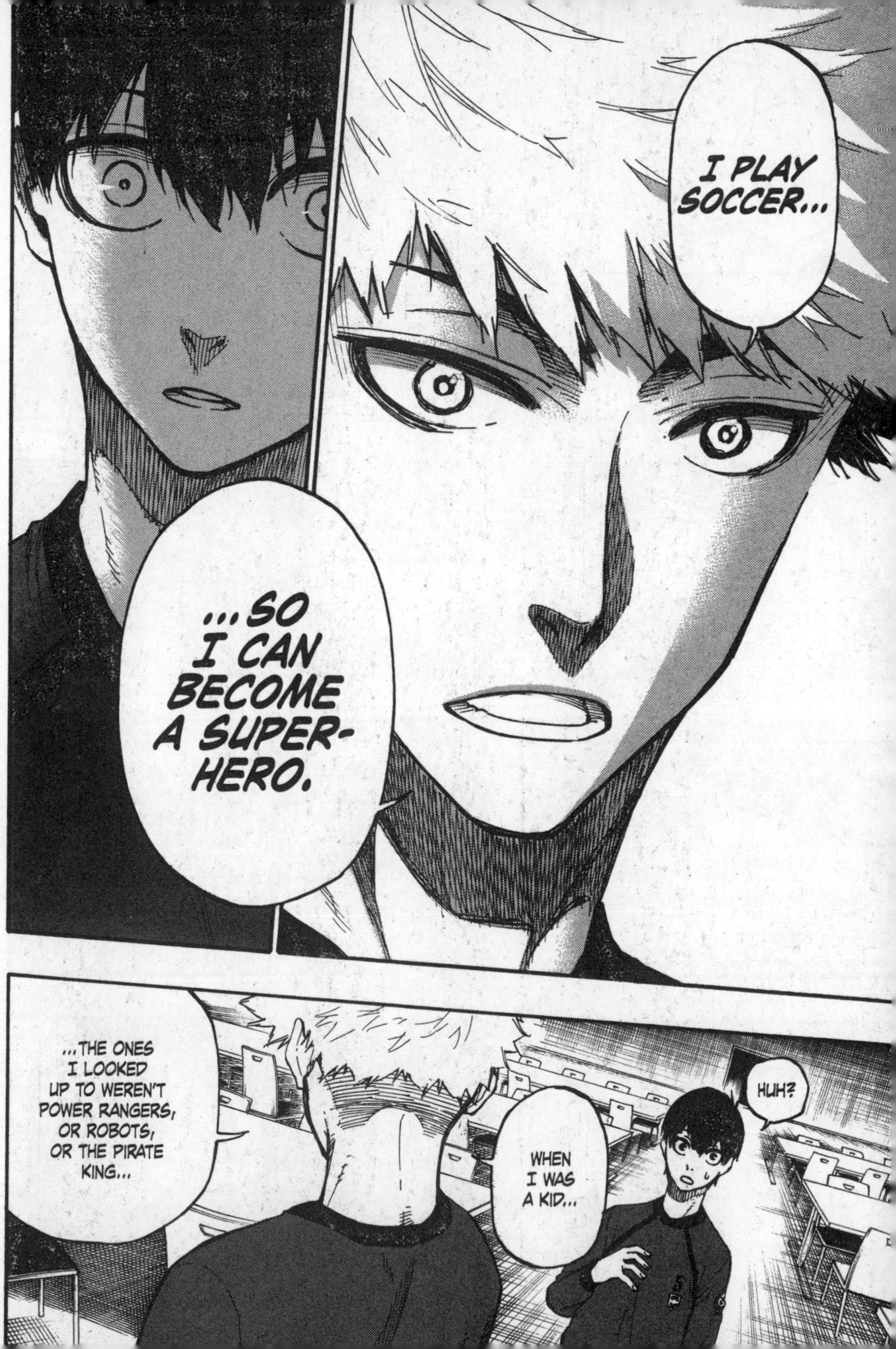
I PLAY SOCCER...
...SO I CAN BECOME A SUPER-HERO.
HUH?
WHEN I WAS A KID...
...THE ONES I LOOKED UP TO WEREN'T POWER RANGERS, OR ROBOTS, OR THE PIRATE KING...

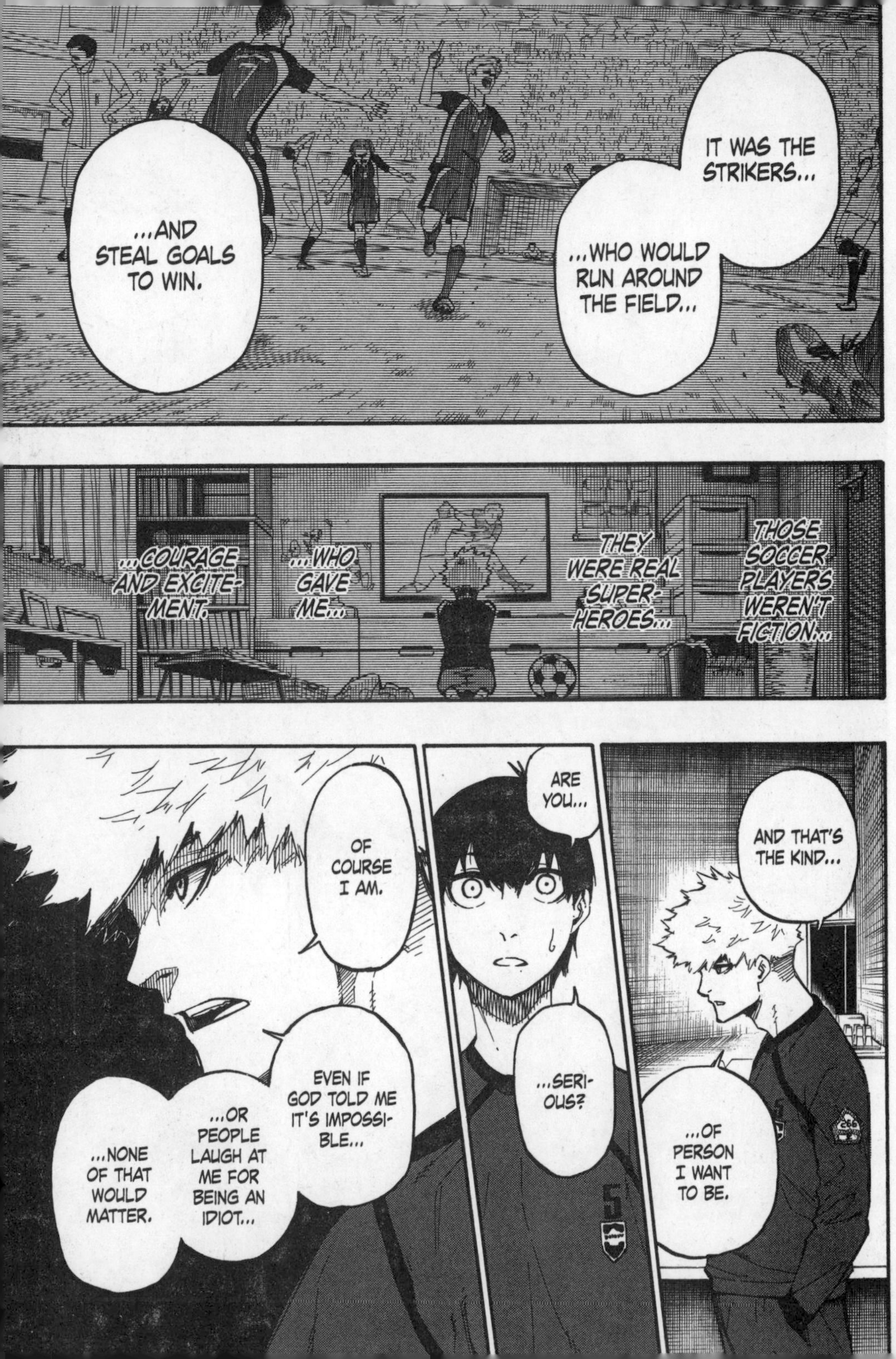
IT WAS THE STRIKERS...
...WHO WOULD RUN AROUND THE FIELD...
...AND STEAL GOALS TO WIN.
THOSE SOCCER PLAYERS WEREN'T FICTION...
THEY WERE REAL SUPER-HEROES...
...WHO GAVE ME...
...COURAGE AND EXCITE-MENT.
AND THAT'S THE KIND...
...OF PERSON I WANT TO BE.
ARE YOU...
...SERI-OUS?
OF COURSE I AM.
EVEN IF GOD TOLD ME IT'S IMPOSSI-BLE...
...OR PEOPLE LAUGH AT ME FOR BEING AN IDIOT...
...NONE OF THAT WOULD MATTER.

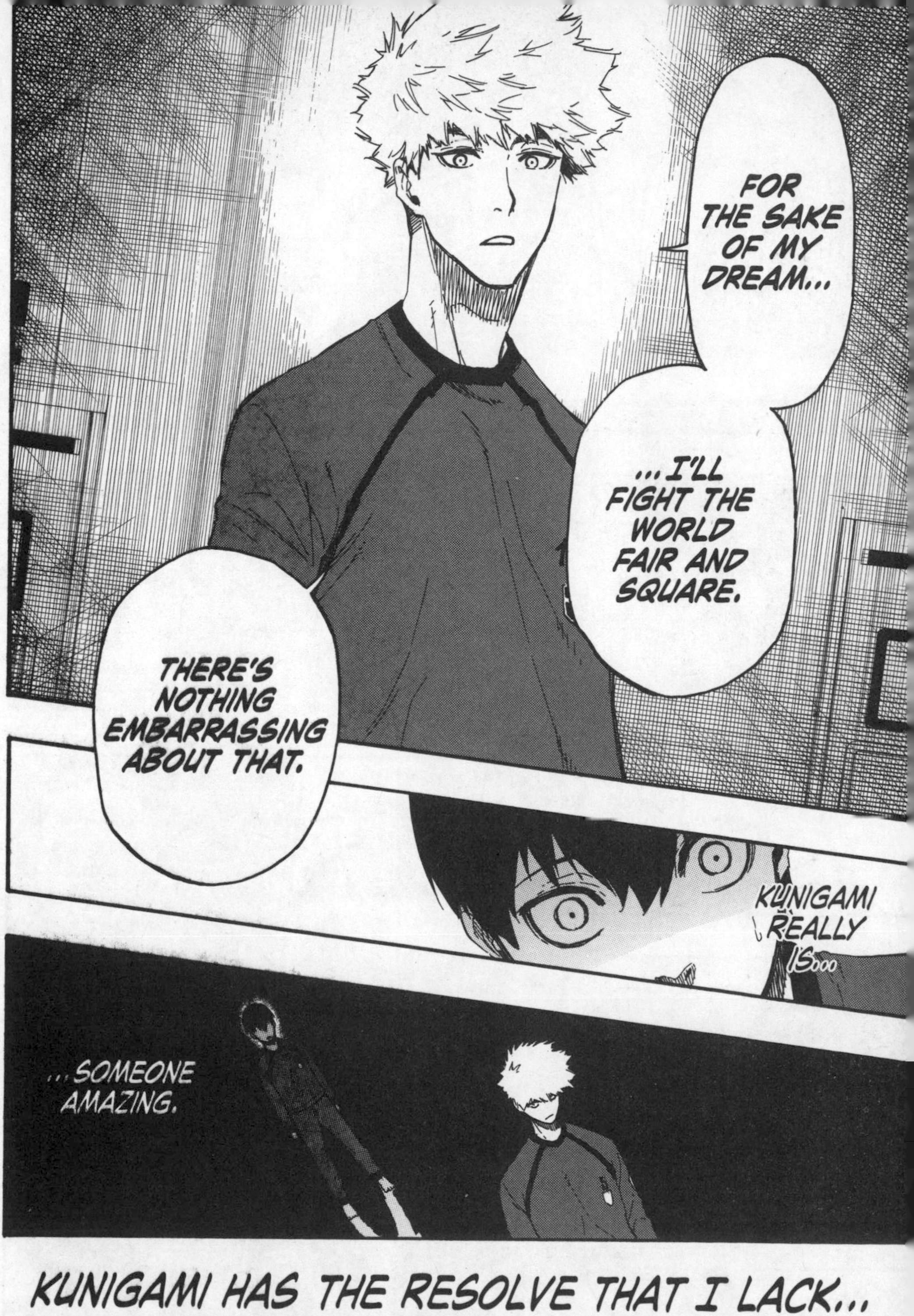
FOR THE SAKE OF MY DREAM...
...I'LL FIGHT THE WORLD FAIR AND SQUARE.
THERE'S NOTHING EMBARRASSING ABOUT THAT.
KUNIGAMI REALLY IS...
...SOMEONE AMAZING.

KUNIGAMI HAS THE RESOLVE THAT I LACK...

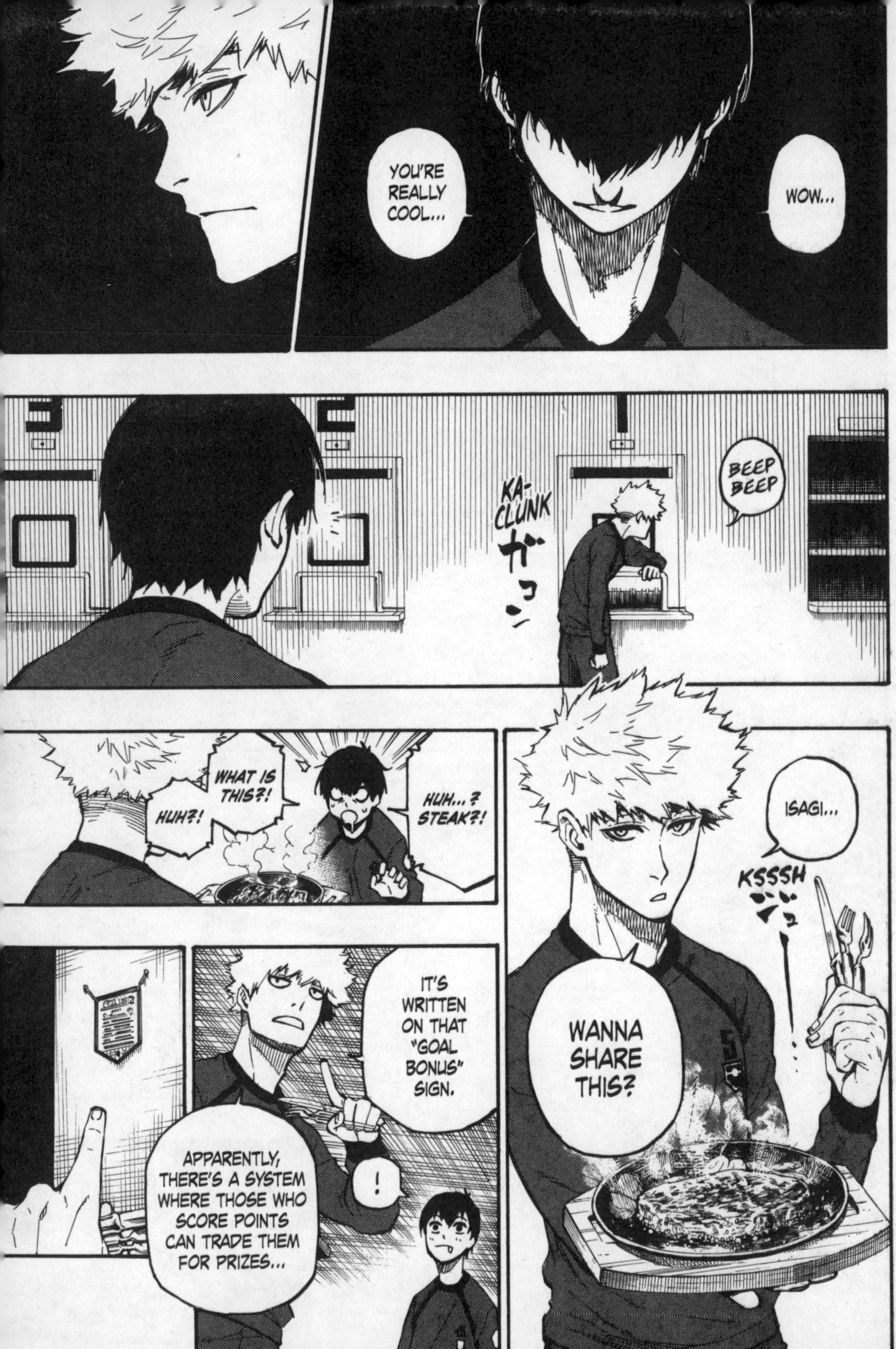
WOW...
YOU'RE REALLY COOL...
BEEP BEEP
KA-CLUNK
ガコン
ISAGI...
KSSSH
ジュ
WANNA SHARE THIS?
HUH...? STEAK?!
WHAT IS THIS?!
HUH?!
IT'S WRITTEN ON THAT "GOAL BONUS" SIGN.
!
APPARENTLY, THERE'S A SYSTEM WHERE THOSE WHO SCORE POINTS CAN TRADE THEM FOR PRIZES...

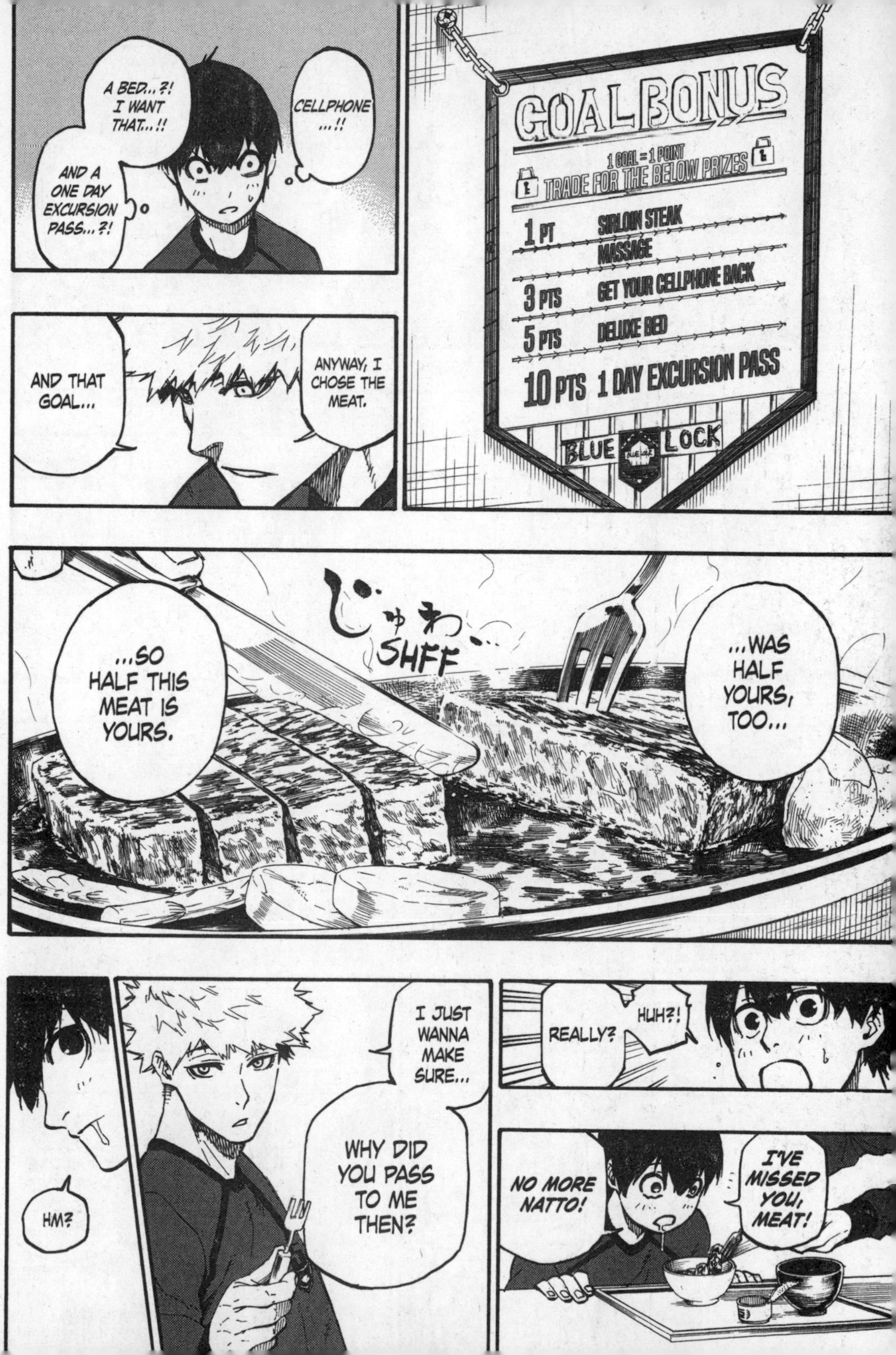
GOAL BONUS
1 GOAL = 1 POINT
TRADE FOR THE BELOW PRIZES
1 PT SIRLOIN STEAK
MASSAGE
3 PTS GET YOUR CELLPHONE BACK
5 PTS DELUXE BED
10 PTS 1 DAY EXCURSION PASS
BLUE LOCK
CELLPHONE ...!!
A BED...?! I WANT THAT...!!
AND A ONE DAY EXCURSION PASS...?!
ANYWAY, I CHOSE THE MEAT.
AND THAT GOAL...
...WAS HALF YOURS, TOO...
じゅわ…
SHFF
...SO HALF THIS MEAT IS YOURS.
HUH?!
REALLY?
I'VE MISSED YOU, MEAT!
NO MORE NATTO!
I JUST WANNA MAKE SURE...
WHY DID YOU PASS TO ME THEN?
HM?

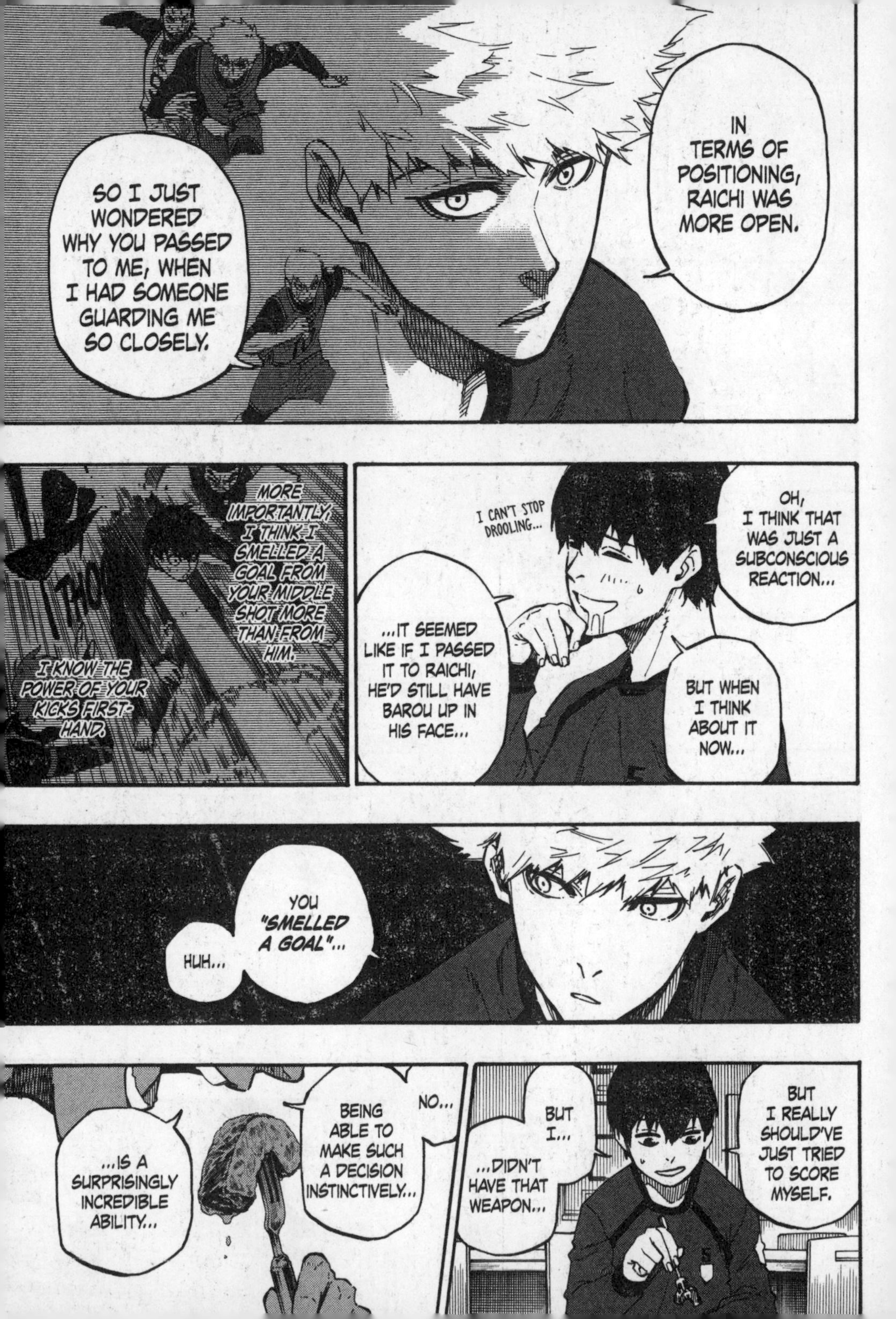
IN TERMS OF POSITIONING, RAICHI WAS MORE OPEN.
SO I JUST WONDERED WHY YOU PASSED TO ME, WHEN I HAD SOMEONE GUARDING ME SO CLOSELY.
OH, I THINK THAT WAS JUST A SUBCONSCIOUS REACTION...
I CAN'T STOP DROOLING...
BUT WHEN I THINK ABOUT IT NOW...
...IT SEEMED LIKE IF I PASSED IT TO RAICHI, HE'D STILL HAVE BAROU UP IN HIS FACE...
MORE IMPORTANTLY, I THINK I SMELLED A GOAL FROM YOUR MIDDLE SHOT MORE THAN FROM HIM.
I KNOW THE POWER OF YOUR KICKS FIRST-HAND.
YOU "SMELLED A GOAL"...
HUH...
BUT I REALLY SHOULD'VE JUST TRIED TO SCORE MYSELF.
BUT I...
...DIDN'T HAVE THAT WEAPON...
NO...
BEING ABLE TO MAKE SUCH A DECISION INSTINCTIVELY...
...IS A SURPRISINGLY INCREDIBLE ABILITY...

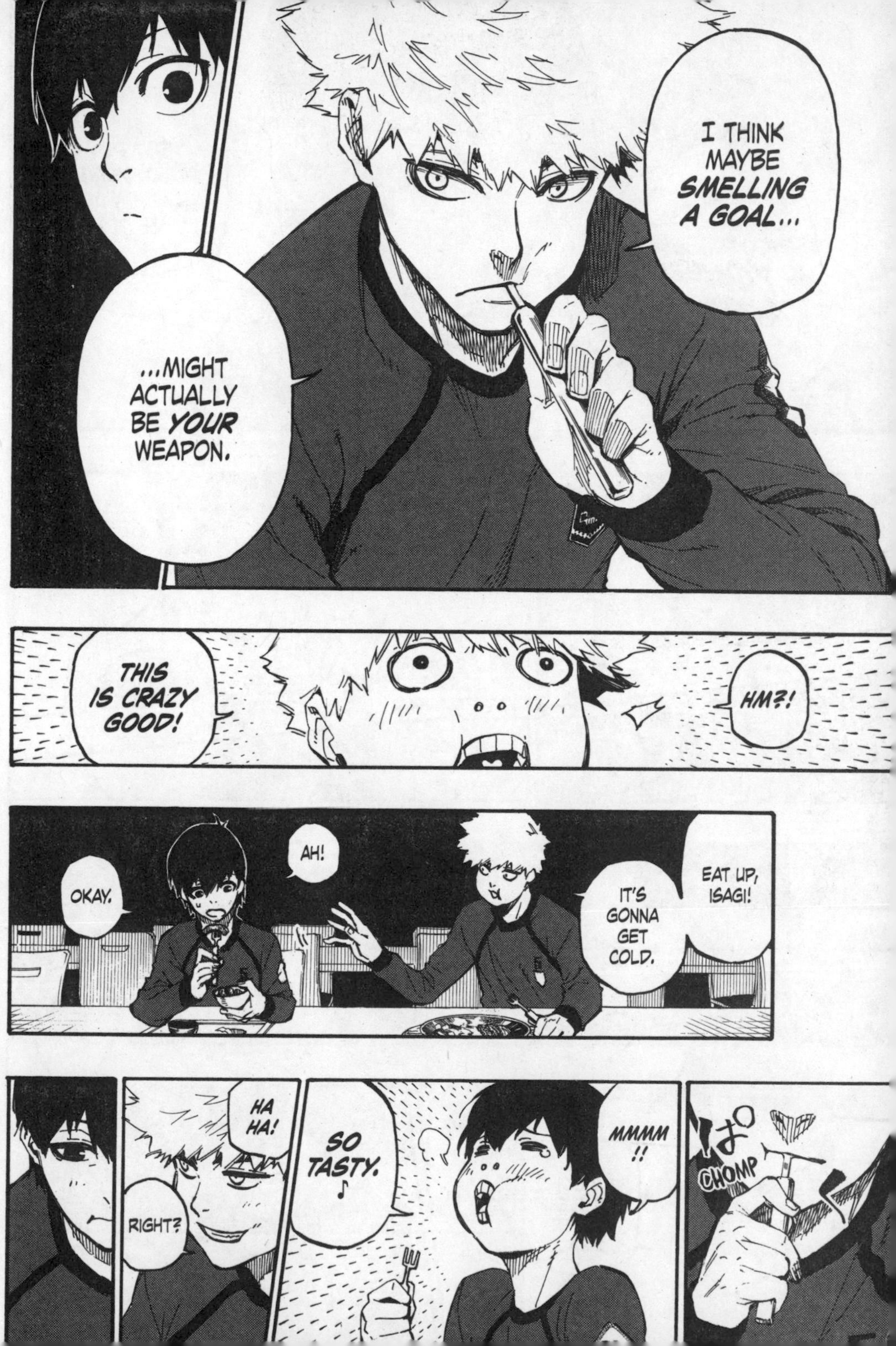
I THINK MAYBE SMELLING A GOAL...
...MIGHT ACTUALLY BE YOUR WEAPON.
HM?!
THIS IS CRAZY GOOD!
EAT UP, ISAGI!
IT'S GONNA GET COLD.
AH!
OKAY.
ぱ
CHOMP
MMMM !!
SO TASTY. ♪
HA HA!
RIGHT?

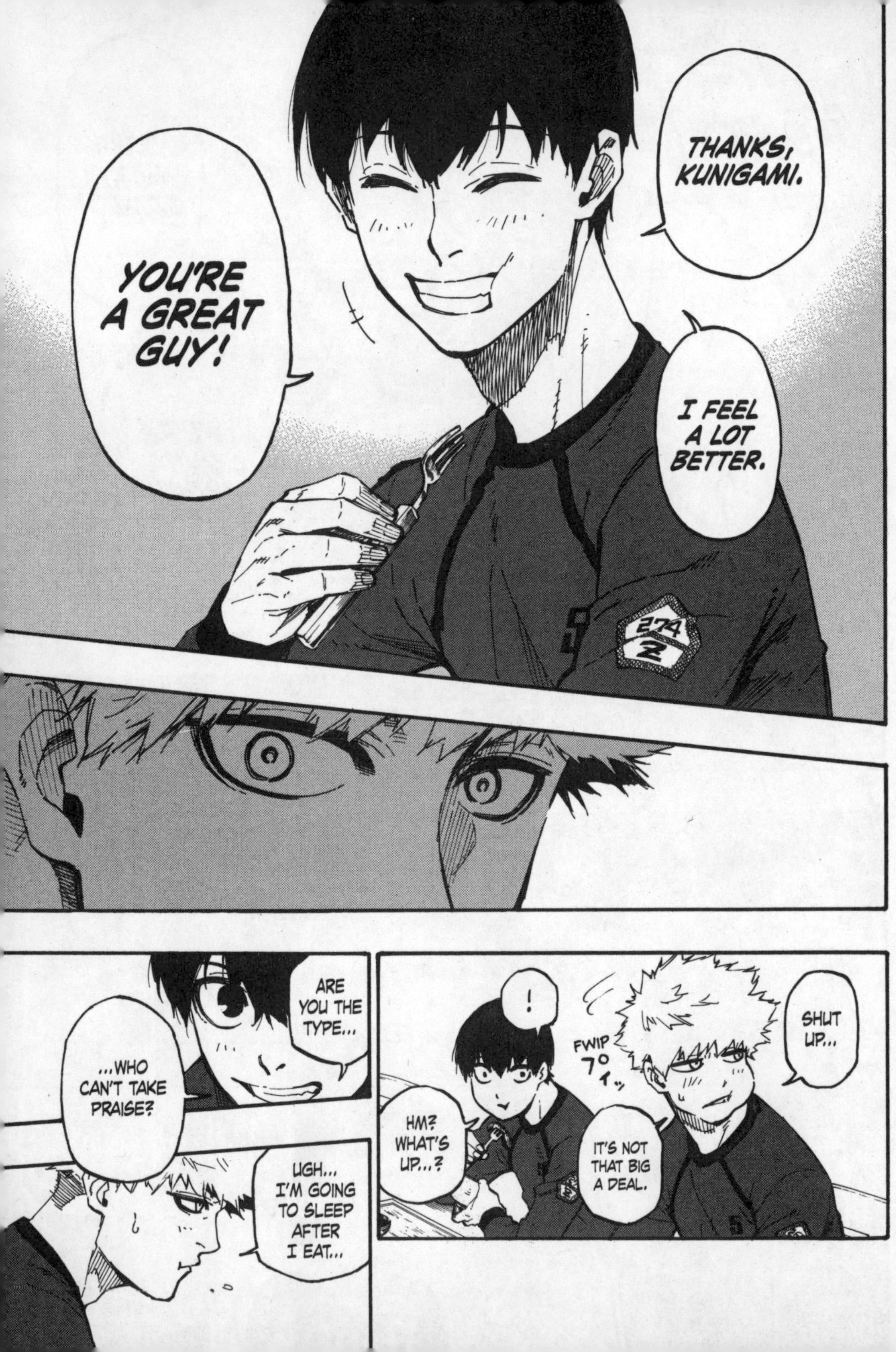
THANKS, KUNIGAMI.
I FEEL A LOT BETTER.
YOU'RE A GREAT GUY!
SHUT UP...
!
FWIP
プイッ
IT'S NOT THAT BIG A DEAL.
HM? WHAT'S UP...?
ARE YOU THE TYPE...
...WHO CAN'T TAKE PRAISE?
UGH... I'M GOING TO SLEEP AFTER I EAT...

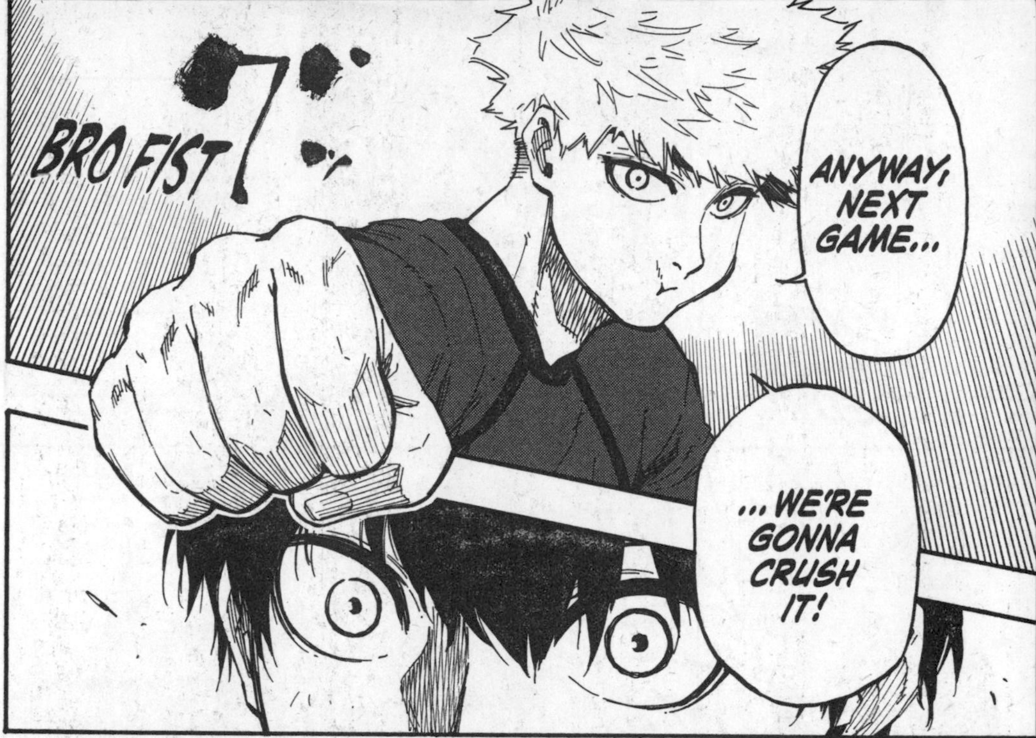
ANYWAY, NEXT GAME...
BRO FIST
...WE'RE GONNA CRUSH IT!
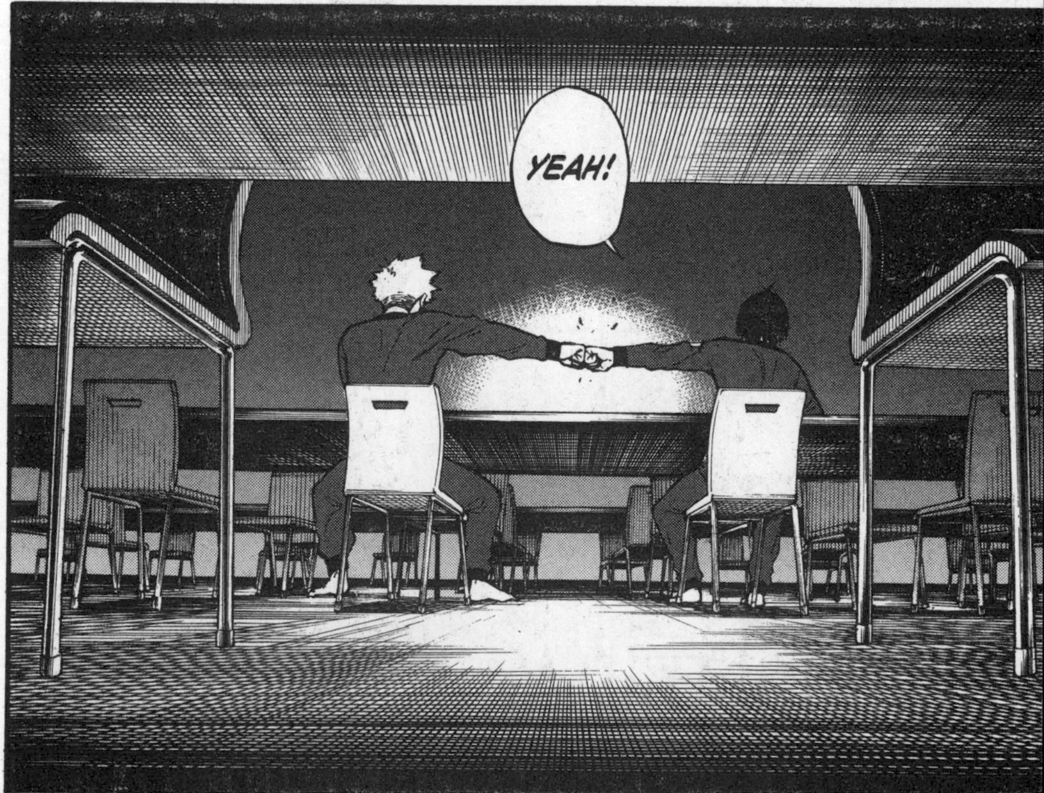
YEAH!

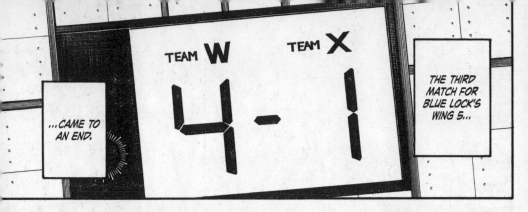

THE THIRD MATCH FOR BLUE LOCK'S WING 5...
TEAM W
TEAM X
4-1
...CAME TO AN END.
TEAM | POINTS | POINT DIFF.
1 V 3 +8
2 W 3 +3
3 X 3 +1
4 Z 0 -4
5 Y 0 -8
LOOKS LIKE BAROU-KUN'S TEAM X LOST!
V W X Y Z
8-0
4-1
1-4
5-1
0-8
1-5
CHAPTER 10:
OPERATION: NEXT ME, THEN NINE
AND FOR THE FOURTH MATCH...
THEY'RE HERE.
YEAH.
IT'S TEAM Z VERSUS...

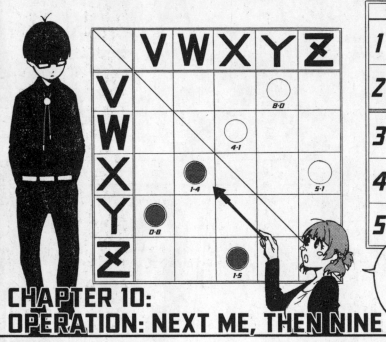

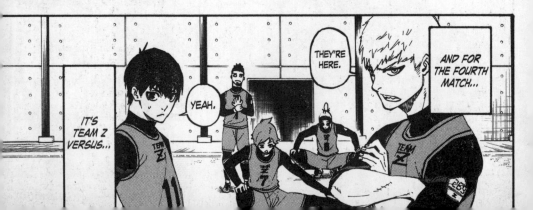

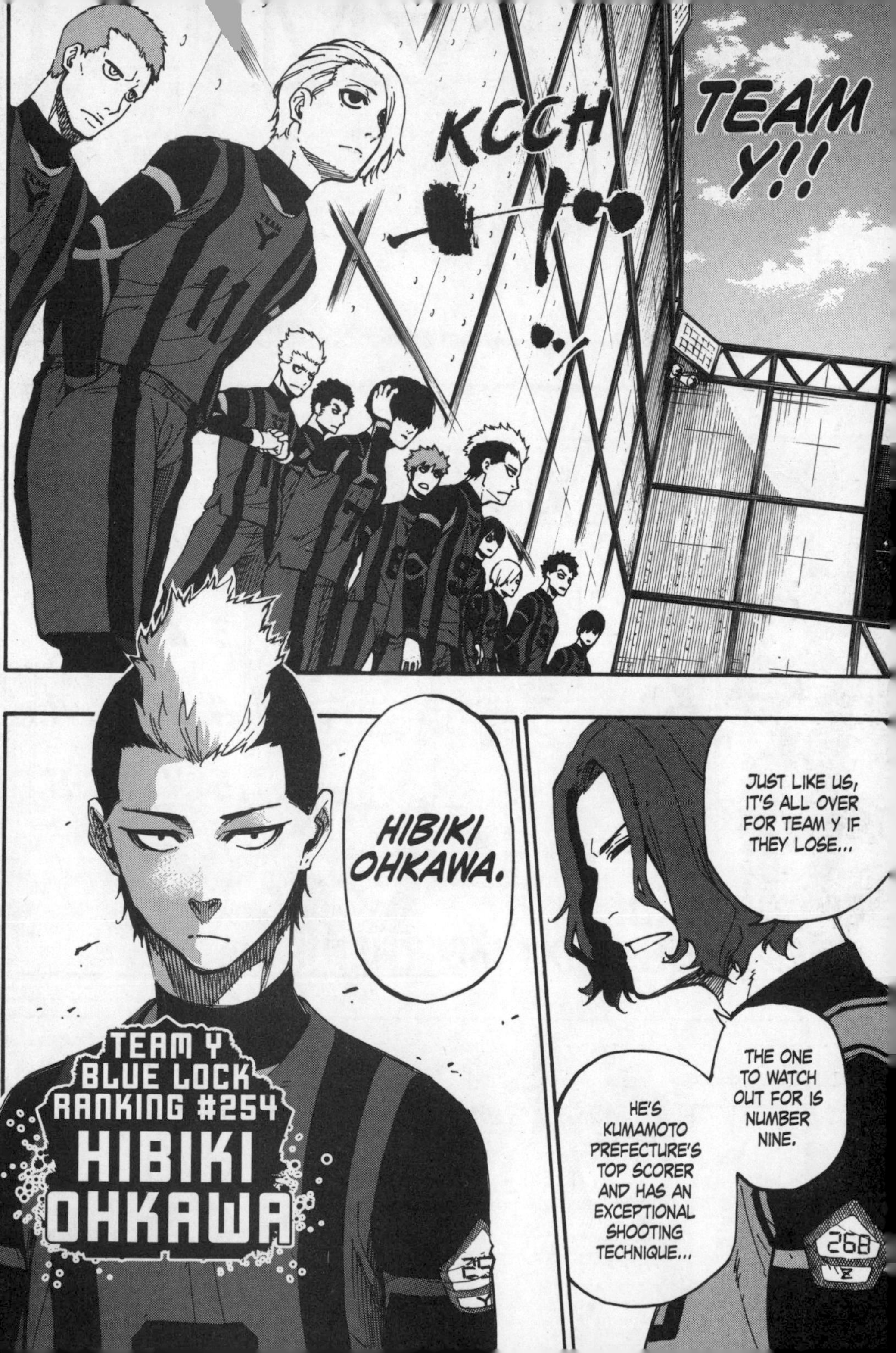
TEAM Y!!
KCCH
JUST LIKE US, IT'S ALL OVER FOR TEAM Y IF THEY LOSE...
THE ONE TO WATCH OUT FOR IS NUMBER NINE.
HE'S KUMAMOTO PREFECTURE'S TOP SCORER AND HAS AN EXCEPTIONAL SHOOTING TECHNIQUE...
268
Z
HIBIKI OHKAWA.
TEAM Y BLUE LOCK RANKING #254
HIBIKI OHKAWA

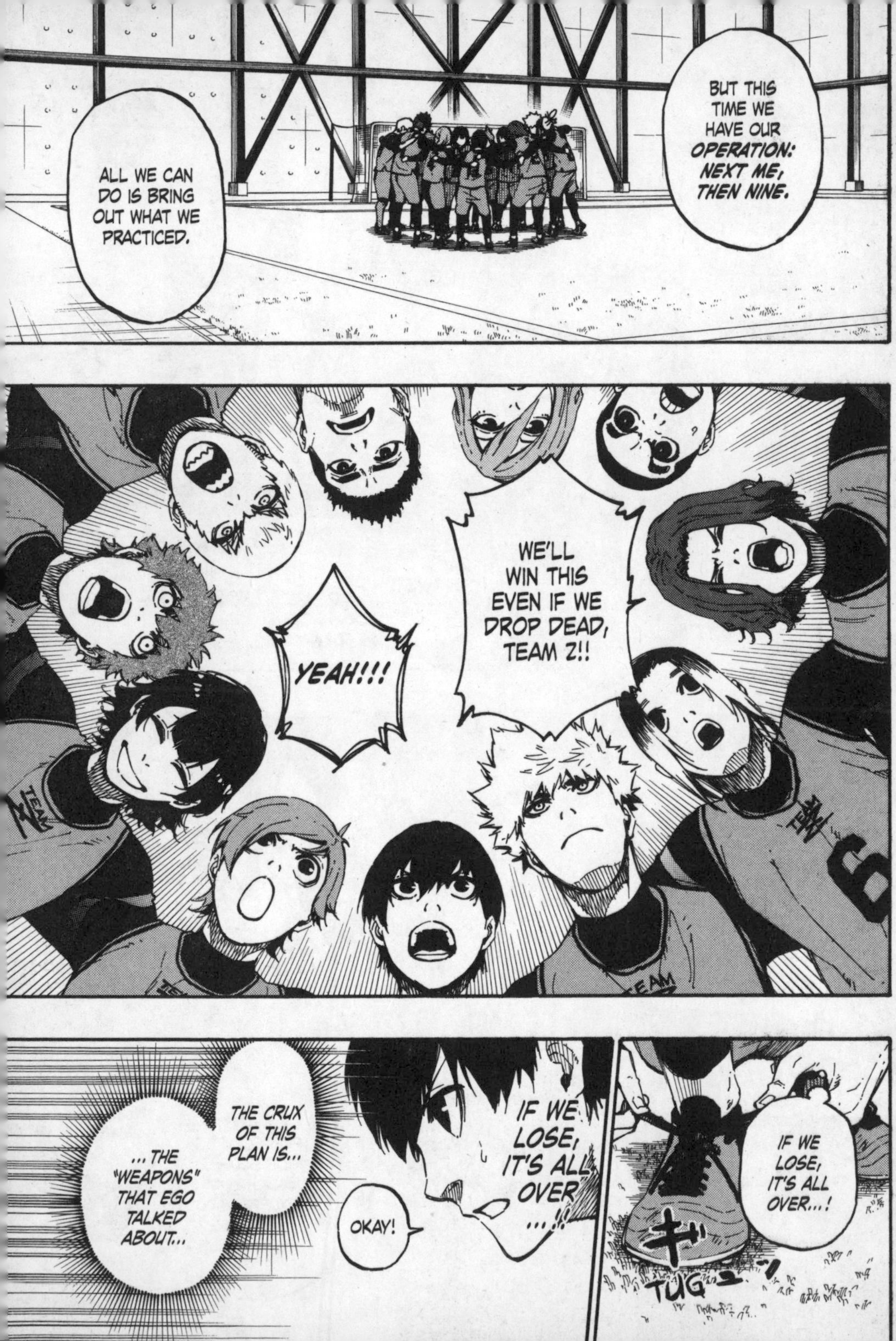

BUT THIS TIME WE HAVE OUR OPERATION: NEXT ME, THEN NINE.
ALL WE CAN DO IS BRING OUT WHAT WE PRACTICED.
WE'LL WIN THIS EVEN IF WE DROP DEAD, TEAM Z!!
YEAH!!!
IF WE LOSE, IT'S ALL OVER...!
ギ
TUG
IF WE LOSE, IT'S ALL OVER...!!
THE CRUX OF THIS PLAN IS...
...THE "WEAPONS" THAT EGO TALKED ABOUT...
OKAY!

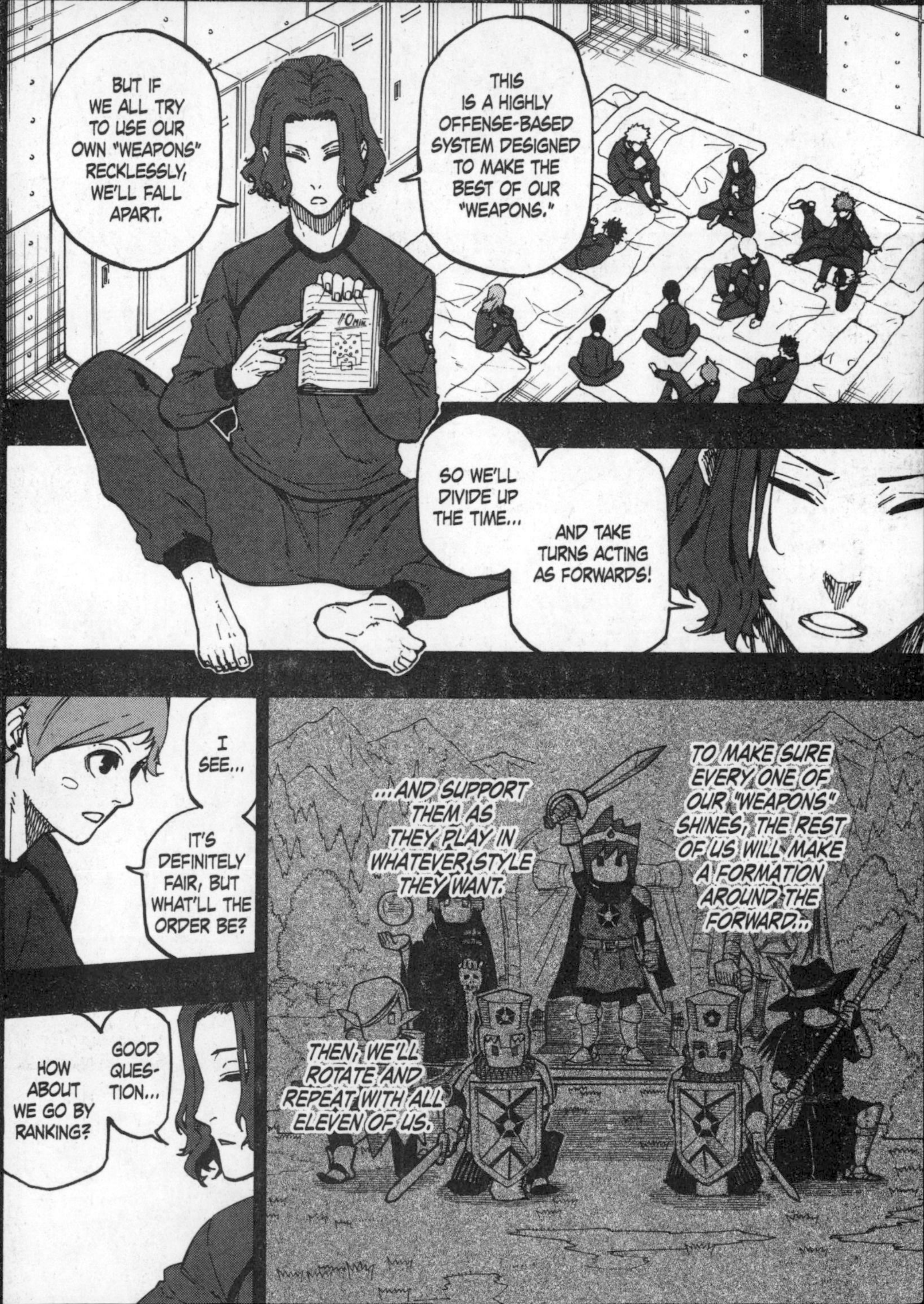
THIS IS A HIGHLY OFFENSE-BASED SYSTEM DESIGNED TO MAKE THE BEST OF OUR "WEAPONS."
BUT IF WE ALL TRY TO USE OUR OWN "WEAPONS" RECKLESSLY, WE'LL FALL APART.
SO WE'LL DIVIDE UP THE TIME...
AND TAKE TURNS ACTING AS FORWARDS!
TO MAKE SURE EVERY ONE OF OUR "WEAPONS" SHINES, THE REST OF US WILL MAKE A FORMATION AROUND THE FORWARD...
...AND SUPPORT THEM AS THEY PLAY IN WHATEVER STYLE THEY WANT.
THEN, WE'LL ROTATE AND REPEAT WITH ALL ELEVEN OF US.
I SEE...
IT'S DEFINITELY FAIR, BUT WHAT'LL THE ORDER BE?
GOOD QUESTION...
HOW ABOUT WE GO BY RANKING?

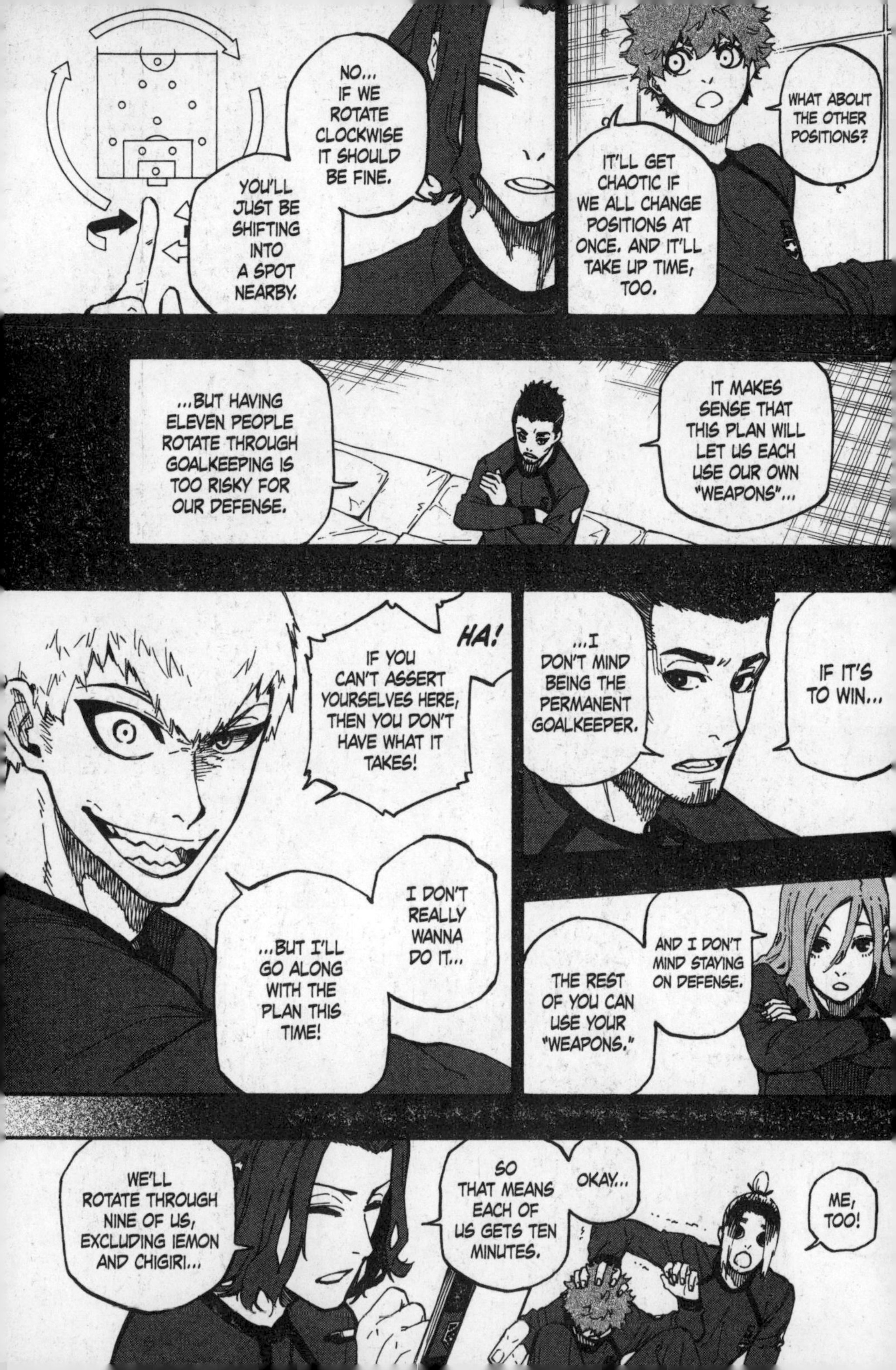
WHAT ABOUT THE OTHER POSITIONS?
IT'LL GET CHAOTIC IF WE ALL CHANGE POSITIONS AT ONCE. AND IT'LL TAKE UP TIME, TOO.
NO... IF WE ROTATE CLOCKWISE IT SHOULD BE FINE.
YOU'LL JUST BE SHIFTING INTO A SPOT NEARBY.
IT MAKES SENSE THAT THIS PLAN WILL LET US EACH USE OUR OWN "WEAPONS"...
...BUT HAVING ELEVEN PEOPLE ROTATE THROUGH GOALKEEPING IS TOO RISKY FOR OUR DEFENSE.
IF IT'S TO WIN...
...I DON'T MIND BEING THE PERMANENT GOALKEEPER.
AND I DON'T MIND STAYING ON DEFENSE.
THE REST OF YOU CAN USE YOUR "WEAPONS."
HA!
IF YOU CAN'T ASSERT YOURSELVES HERE, THEN YOU DON'T HAVE WHAT IT TAKES!
I DON'T REALLY WANNA DO IT...
...BUT I'LL GO ALONG WITH THE PLAN THIS TIME!
ME, TOO!
OKAY...
SO THAT MEANS EACH OF US GETS TEN MINUTES.
WE'LL ROTATE THROUGH NINE OF US, EXCLUDING IEMON AND CHIGIRI...

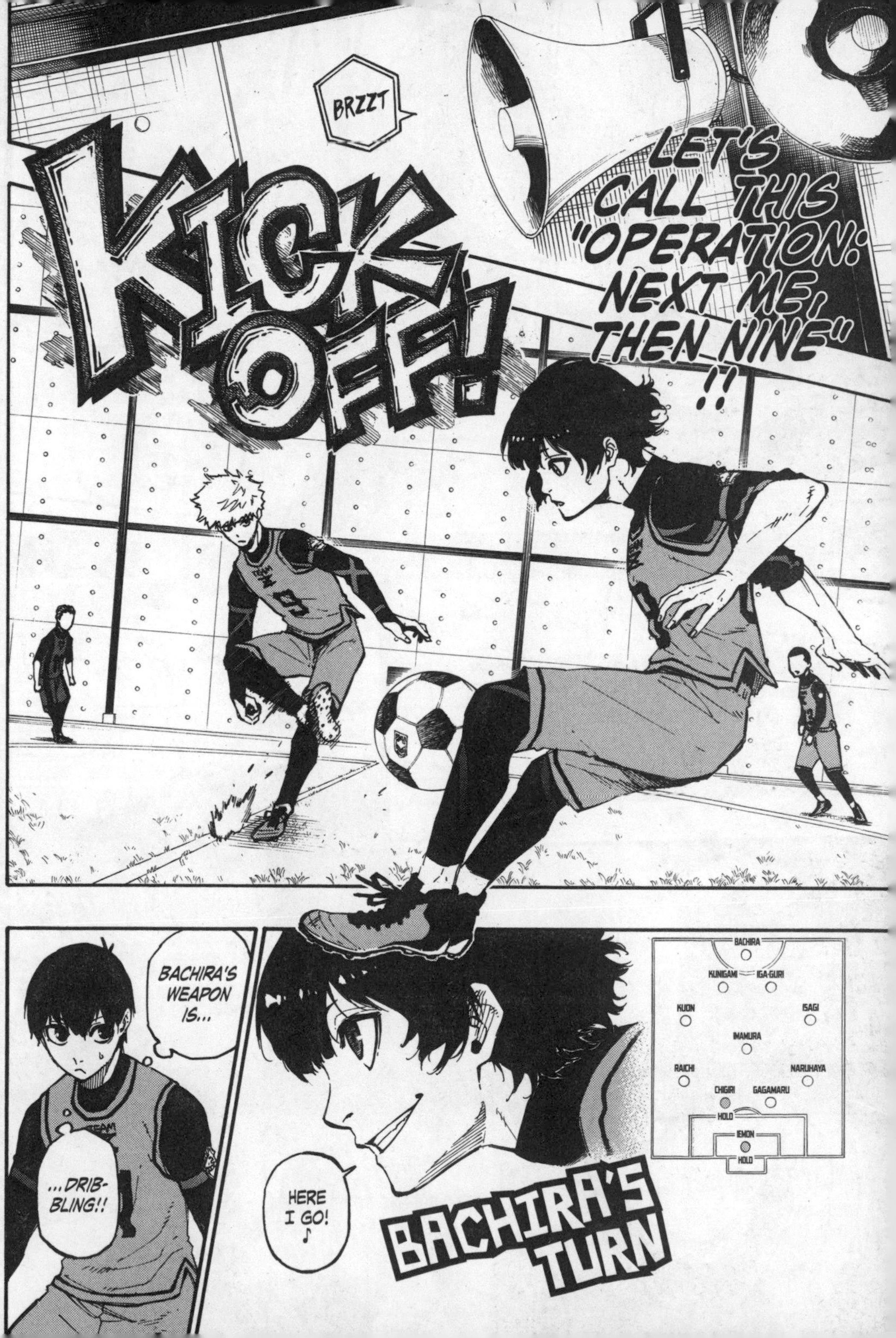
BRZZT
LET'S CALL THIS "OPERATION: NEXT ME, THEN NINE"!!
KICK OFF!
BACHIRA
KUNIGAMI
IGA-GURI
KUON
ISAGI
IMAMURA
RAICHI
NARUHAYA
CHIGIRI
GAGAMARU
HOLD
IEMON
HOLD
HERE I GO! ♪
BACHIRA'S TURN
BACHIRA'S WEAPON IS...
...DRIB-BLING!!

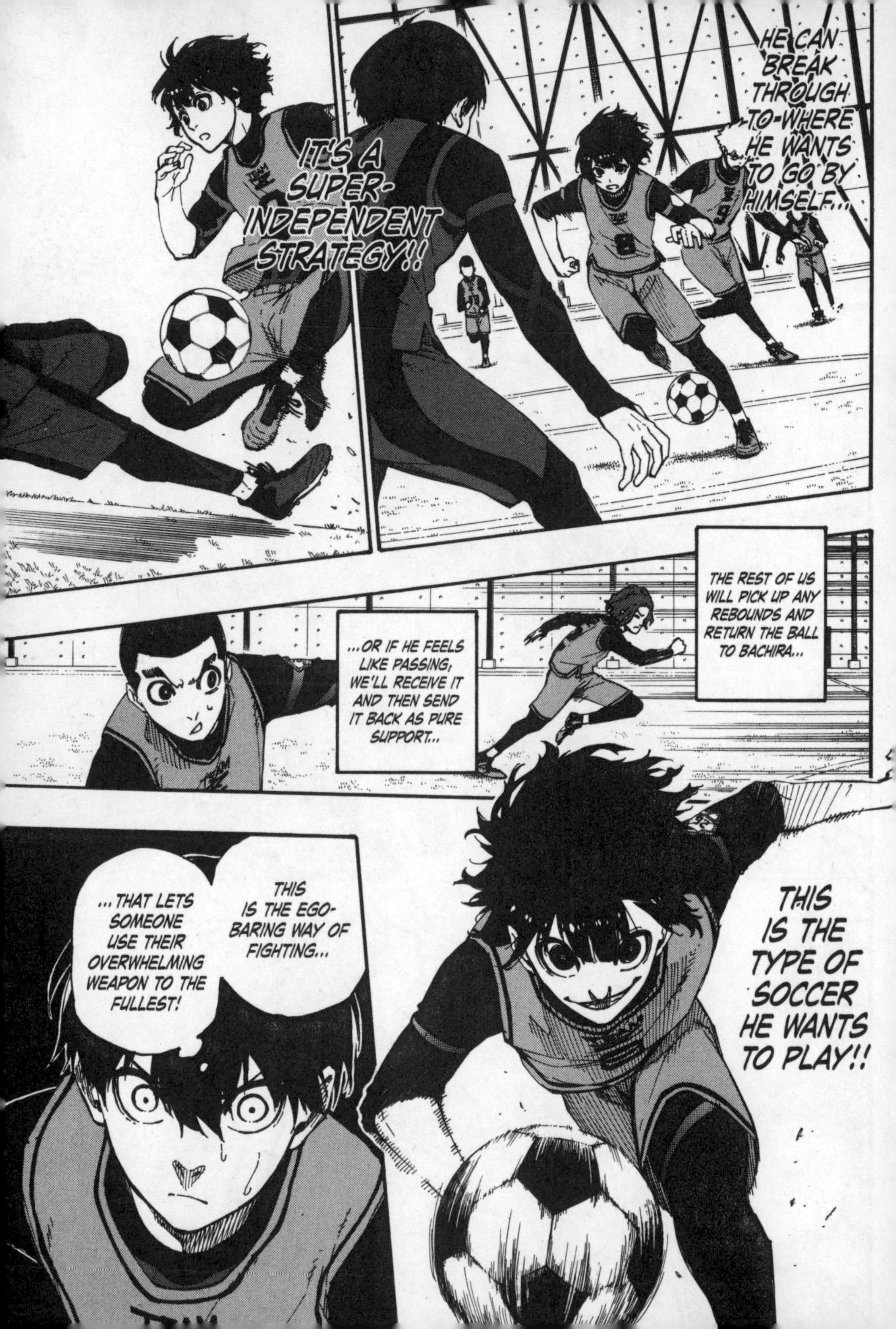
HE CAN BREAK THROUGH TO WHERE HE WANTS TO GO BY HIMSELF...
IT'S A SUPER-INDEPENDENT STRATEGY!!
THE REST OF US WILL PICK UP ANY REBOUNDS AND RETURN THE BALL TO BACHIRA...
...OR IF HE FEELS LIKE PASSING, WE'LL RECEIVE IT AND THEN SEND IT BACK AS PURE SUPPORT...
THIS IS THE TYPE OF SOCCER HE WANTS TO PLAY!!
THIS IS THE EGO-BARING WAY OF FIGHTING...
...THAT LETS SOMEONE USE THEIR OVERWHELMING WEAPON TO THE FULLEST!

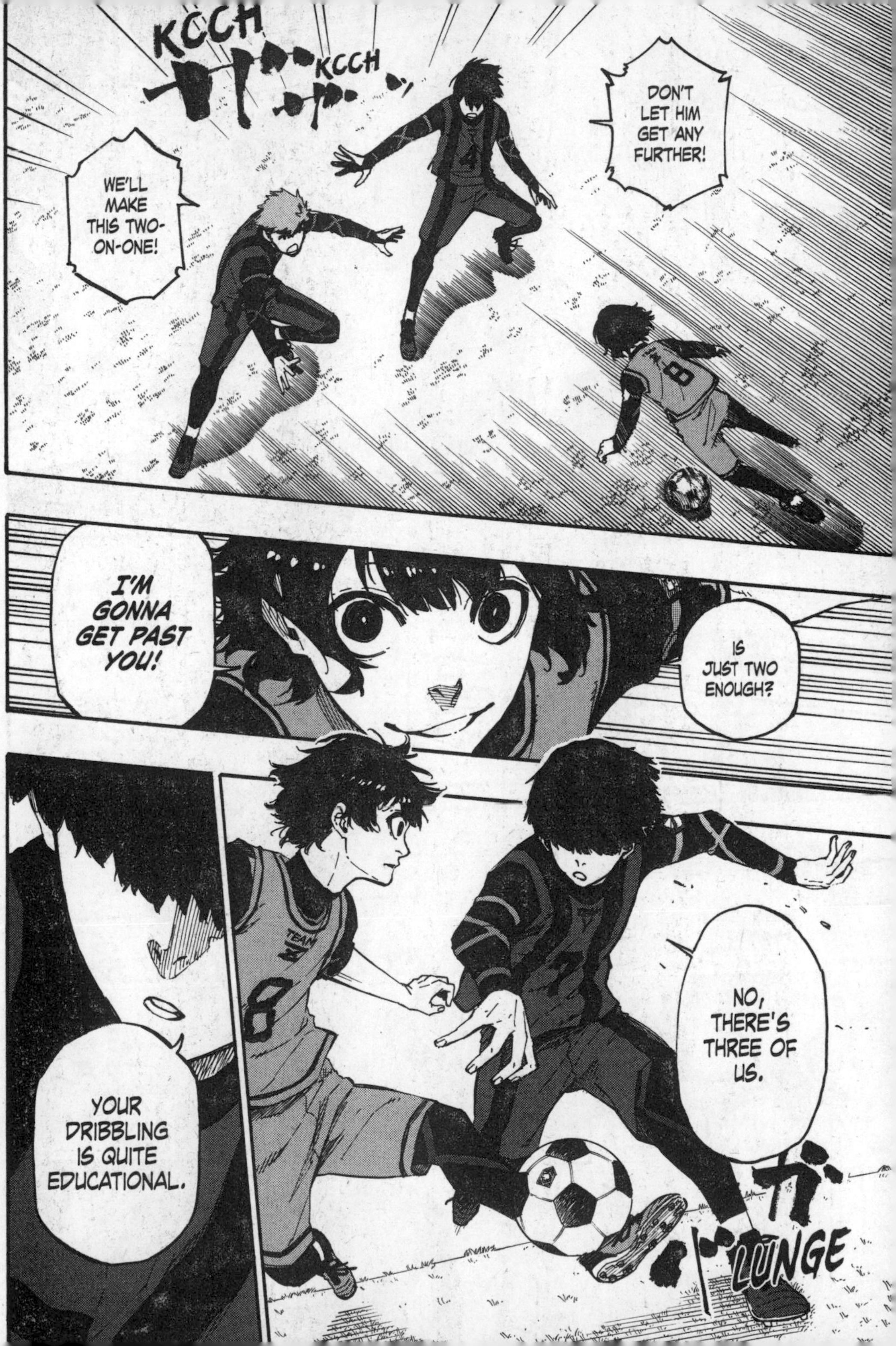
DON'T LET HIM GET ANY FURTHER!
KCCH
KCCH
WE'LL MAKE THIS TWO-ON-ONE!
I'M GONNA GET PAST YOU!
IS JUST TWO ENOUGH?
NO, THERE'S THREE OF US.
LUNGE
YOUR DRIBBLING IS QUITE EDUCATIONAL.

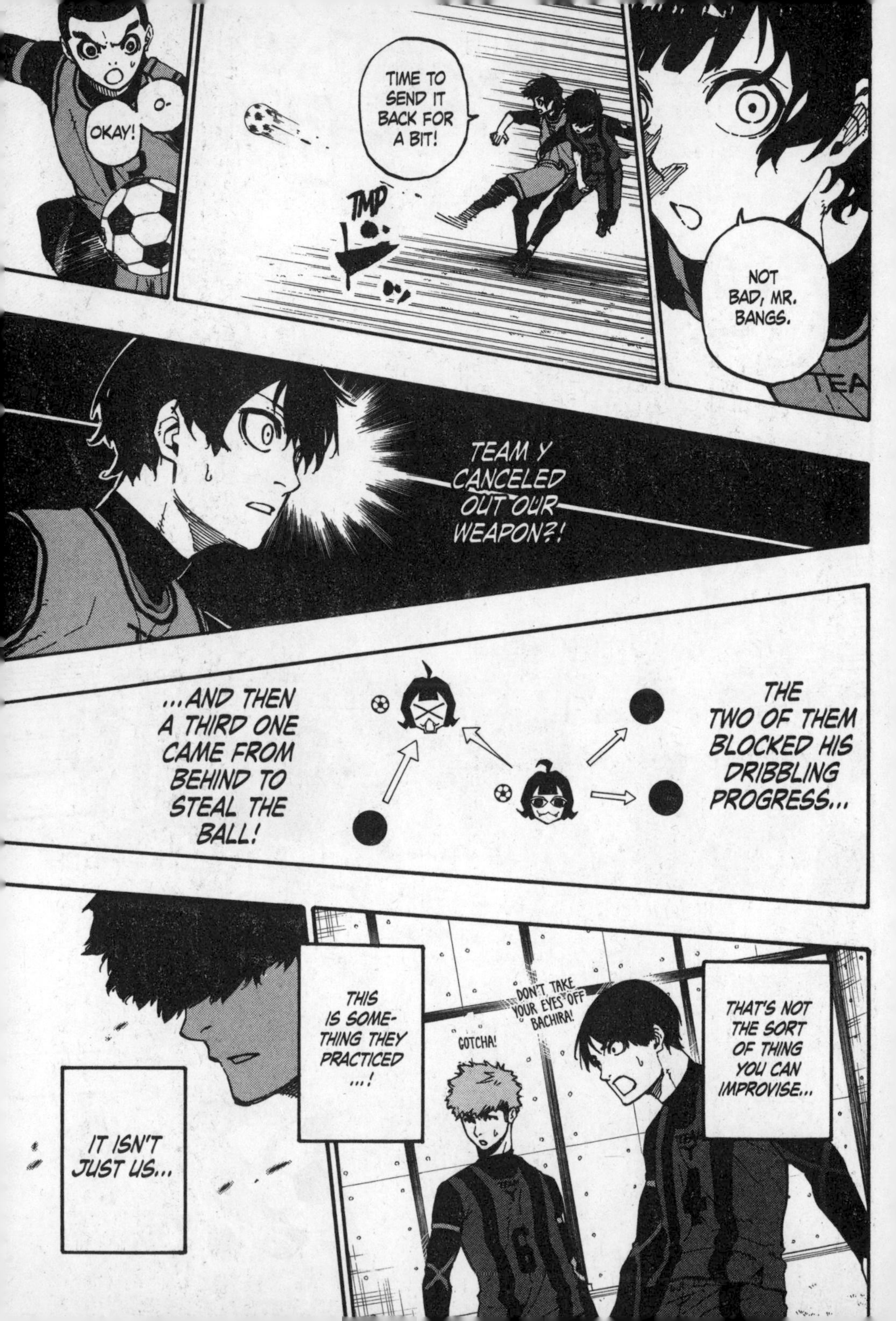
NOT BAD, MR. BANGS.
TIME TO SEND IT BACK FOR A BIT!
TMP
O- OKAY!
TEAM Y CANCELED OUT OUR WEAPON?!
THE TWO OF THEM BLOCKED HIS DRIBBLING PROGRESS...
...AND THEN A THIRD ONE CAME FROM BEHIND TO STEAL THE BALL!
THAT'S NOT THE SORT OF THING YOU CAN IMPROVISE...
DON'T TAKE YOUR EYES OFF BACHIRA!
GOTCHA!
THIS IS SOME-THING THEY PRACTICED ...!
IT ISN'T JUST US...

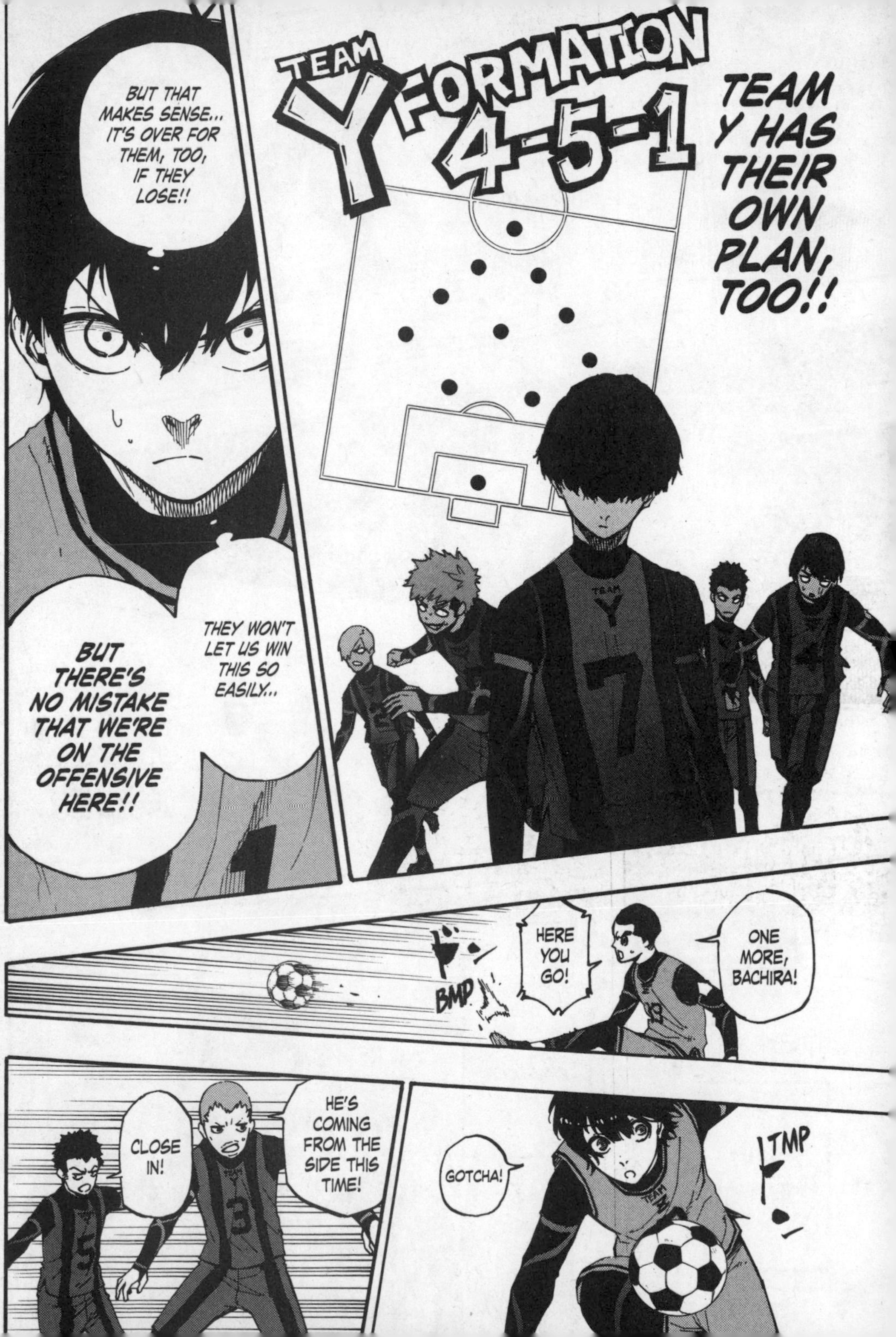
TEAM Y FORMATION 4-5-1
TEAM Y HAS THEIR OWN PLAN, TOO!!
BUT THAT MAKES SENSE... IT'S OVER FOR THEM, TOO, IF THEY LOSE!!
THEY WON'T LET US WIN THIS SO EASILY...
BUT THERE'S NO MISTAKE THAT WE'RE ON THE OFFENSIVE HERE!!
ONE MORE, BACHIRA!
HERE YOU GO!
BMP
TMP
GOTCHA!
HE'S COMING FROM THE SIDE THIS TIME!
CLOSE IN!

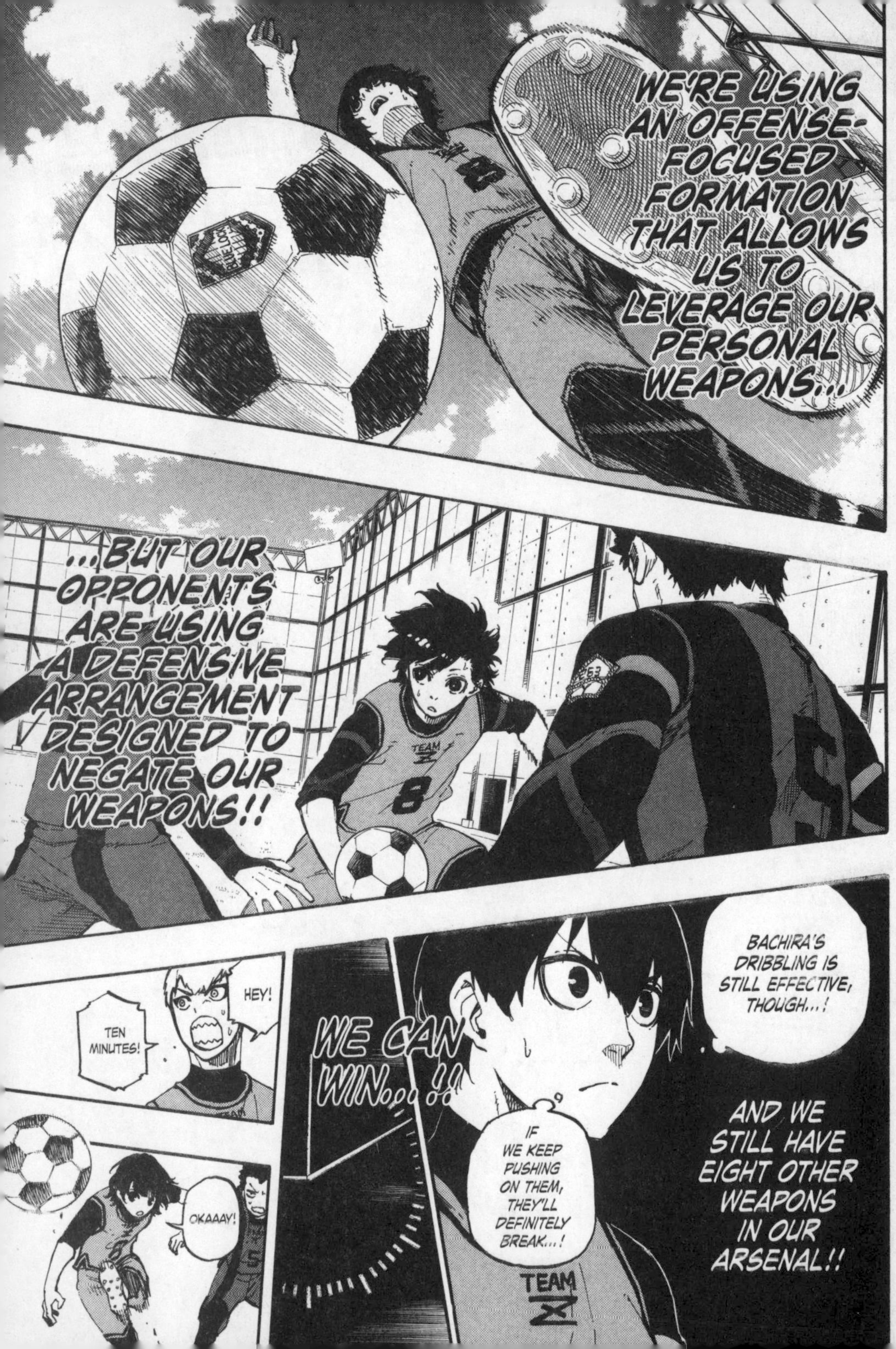
WE'RE USING AN OFFENSE-FOCUSED FORMATION THAT ALLOWS US TO LEVERAGE OUR PERSONAL WEAPONS...
...BUT OUR OPPONENTS ARE USING A DEFENSIVE ARRANGEMENT DESIGNED TO NEGATE OUR WEAPONS!!
BACHIRA'S DRIBBLING IS STILL EFFECTIVE, THOUGH...!
AND WE STILL HAVE EIGHT OTHER WEAPONS IN OUR ARSENAL!!
IF WE KEEP PUSHING ON THEM, THEY'LL DEFINITELY BREAK...!
WE CAN WIN...!!
TEAM Z
HEY!
TEN MINUTES!
OKAAAY!

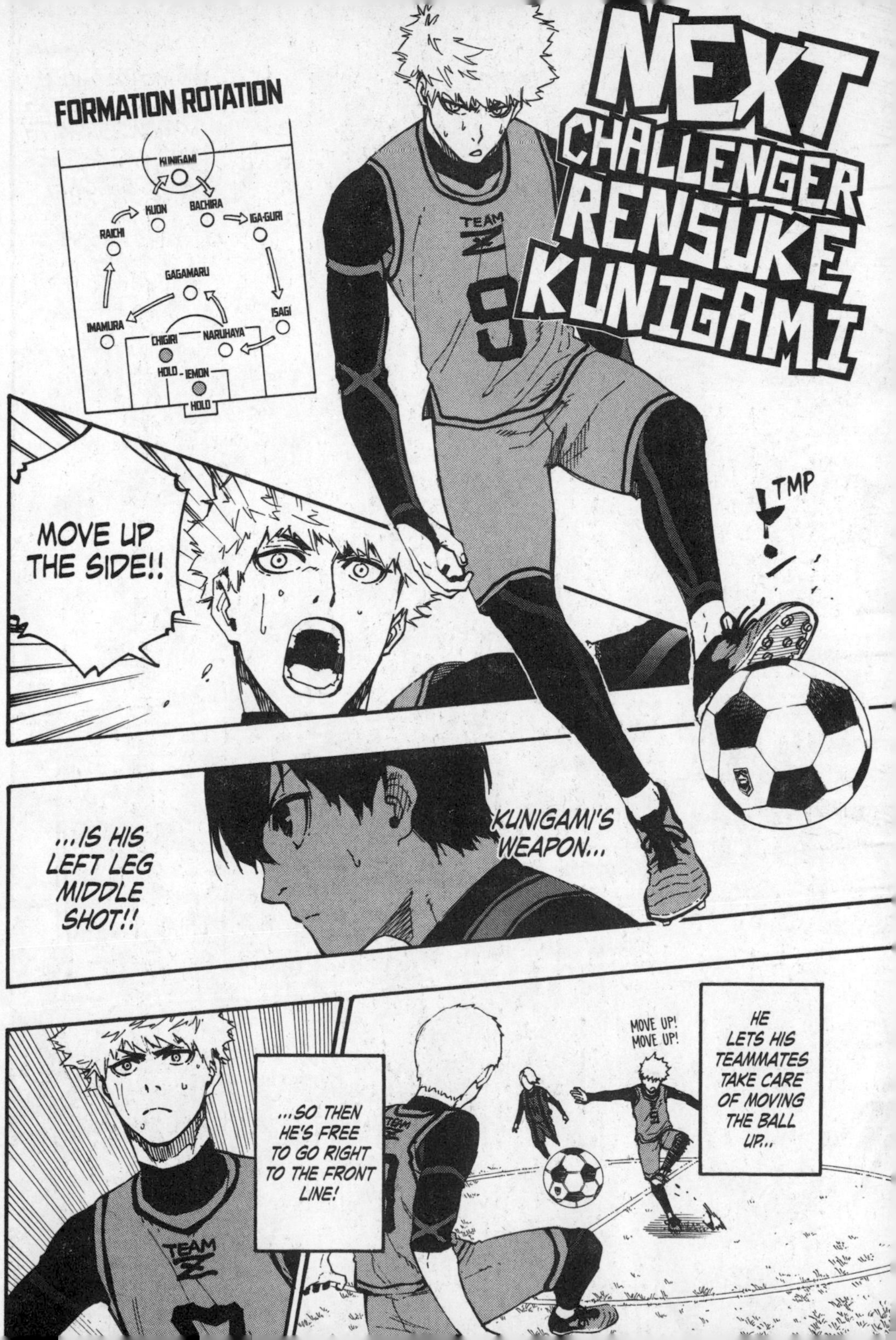
NEXT CHALLENGER RENSUKE KUNIGAMI
FORMATION ROTATION
KUNIGAMI
KUON
BACHIRA
RAICHI
IGA-GURI
GAGAMARU
IMAMURA
ISAGI
CHIGIRI
NARUHAYA
HOLD - IEMON
HOLD
TMP
MOVE UP THE SIDE!!
KUNIGAMI'S WEAPON...
...IS HIS LEFT LEG MIDDLE SHOT!!
HE LETS HIS TEAMMATES TAKE CARE OF MOVING THE BALL UP...
MOVE UP! MOVE UP!
...SO THEN HE'S FREE TO GO RIGHT TO THE FRONT LINE!

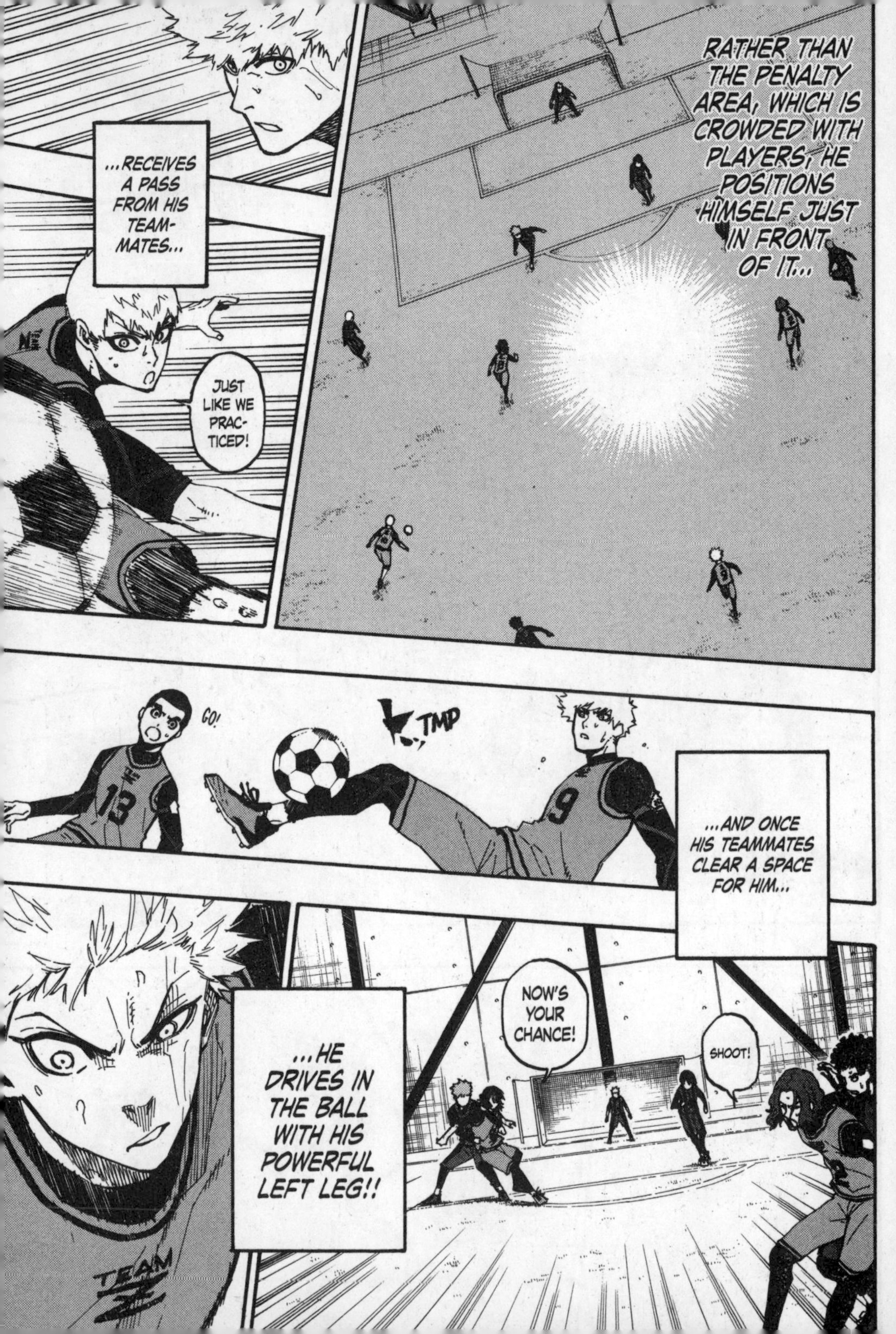
RATHER THAN THE PENALTY AREA, WHICH IS CROWDED WITH PLAYERS, HE POSITIONS HIMSELF JUST IN FRONT OF IT...
...RECEIVES A PASS FROM HIS TEAM-MATES...
JUST LIKE WE PRAC-TICED!
...AND ONCE HIS TEAMMATES CLEAR A SPACE FOR HIM...
TMP
GO!
SHOOT!
NOW'S YOUR CHANCE!
...HE DRIVES IN THE BALL WITH HIS POWERFUL LEFT LEG!!

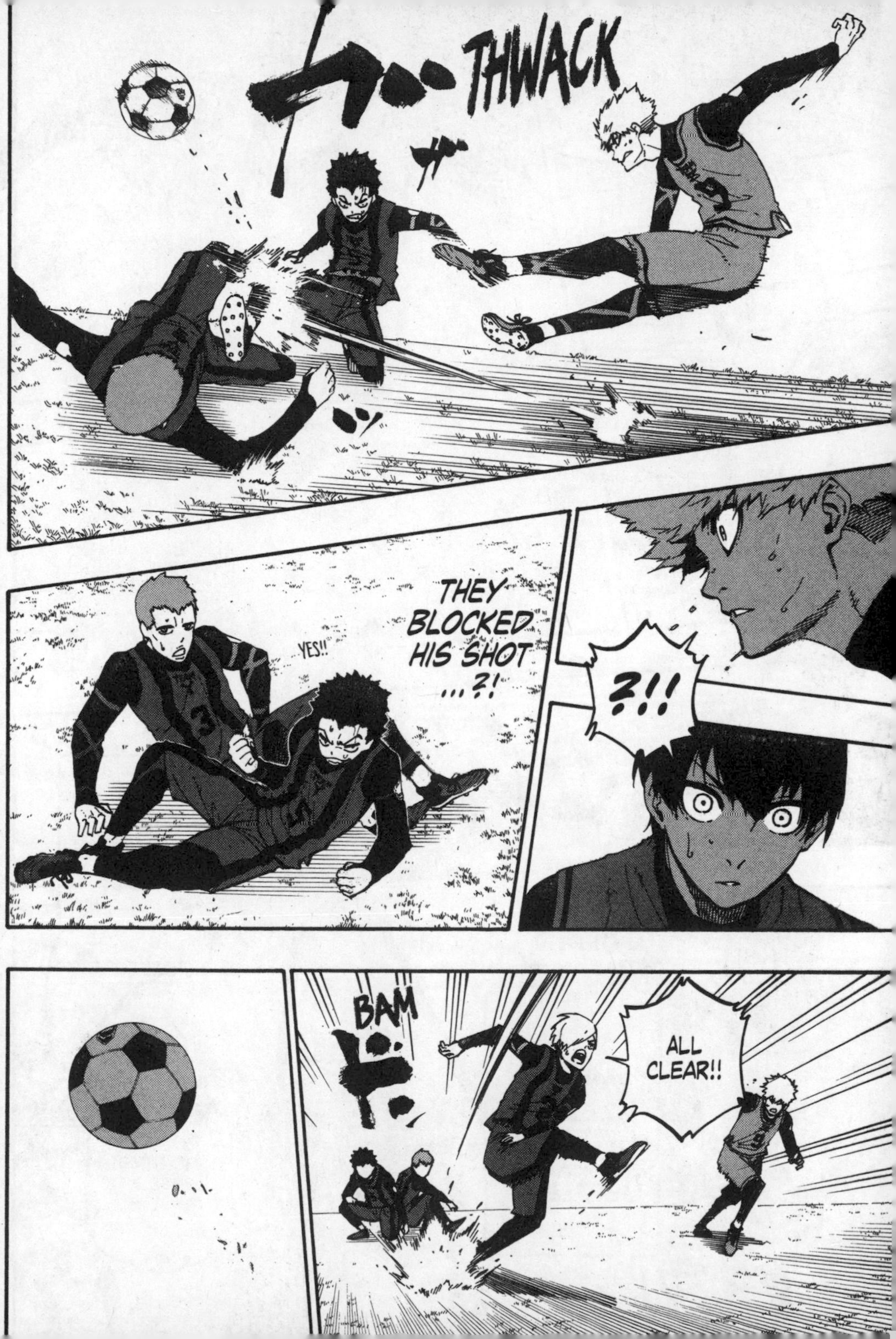
THWACK
?!!
THEY BLOCKED HIS SHOT ...?!
YES!!
ALL CLEAR!!
BAM

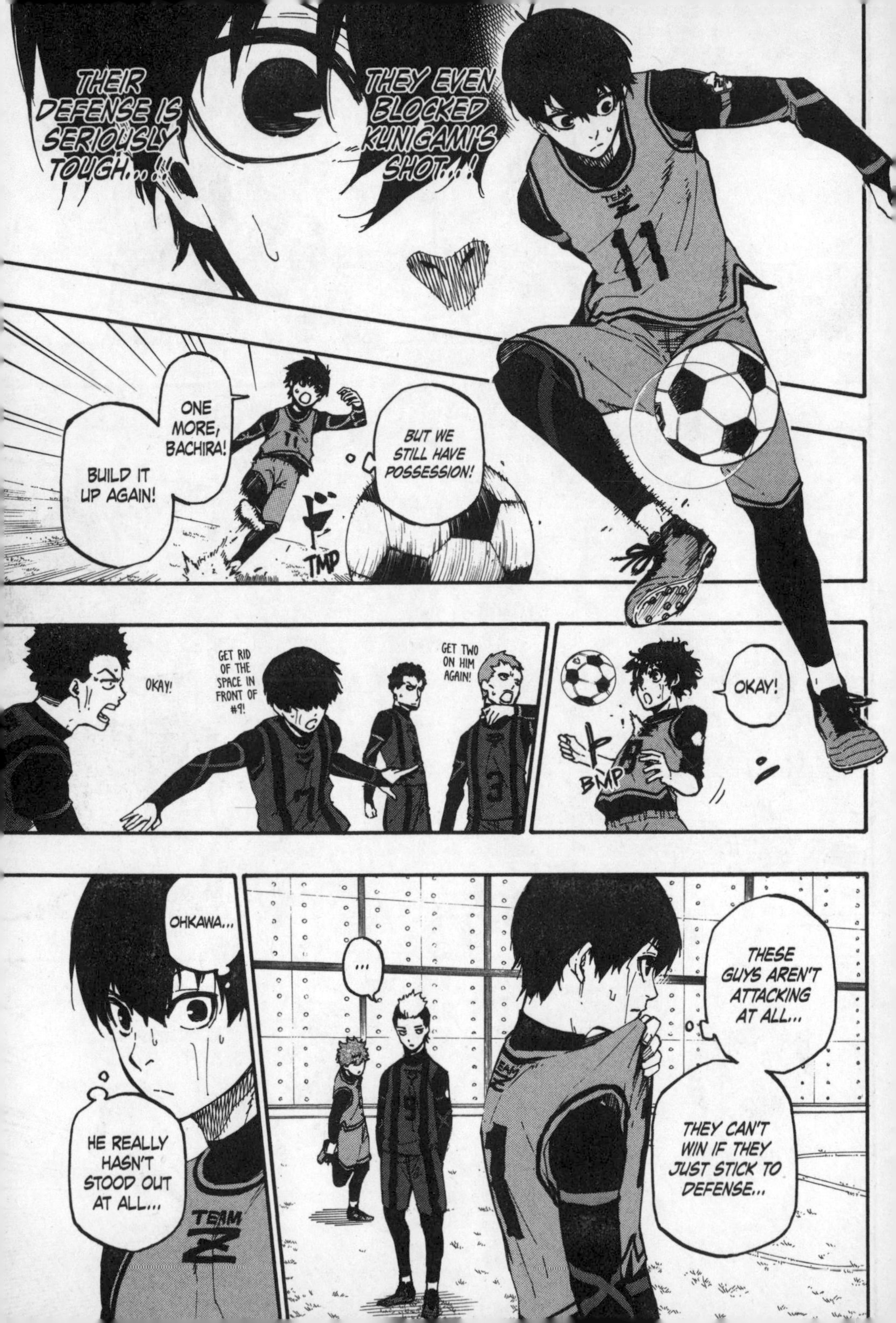

THEY EVEN BLOCKED KUNIGAMI'S SHOT...!
THEIR DEFENSE IS SERIOUSLY TOUGH...!!
BUT WE STILL HAVE POSSESSION!
ONE MORE, BACHIRA!
BUILD IT UP AGAIN!
TMP
OKAY!
BMP
GET TWO ON HIM AGAIN!
GET RID OF THE SPACE IN FRONT OF #9!
OKAY!
THESE GUYS AREN'T ATTACKING AT ALL...
THEY CAN'T WIN IF THEY JUST STICK TO DEFENSE...
...
OHKAWA...
HE REALLY HASN'T STOOD OUT AT ALL...

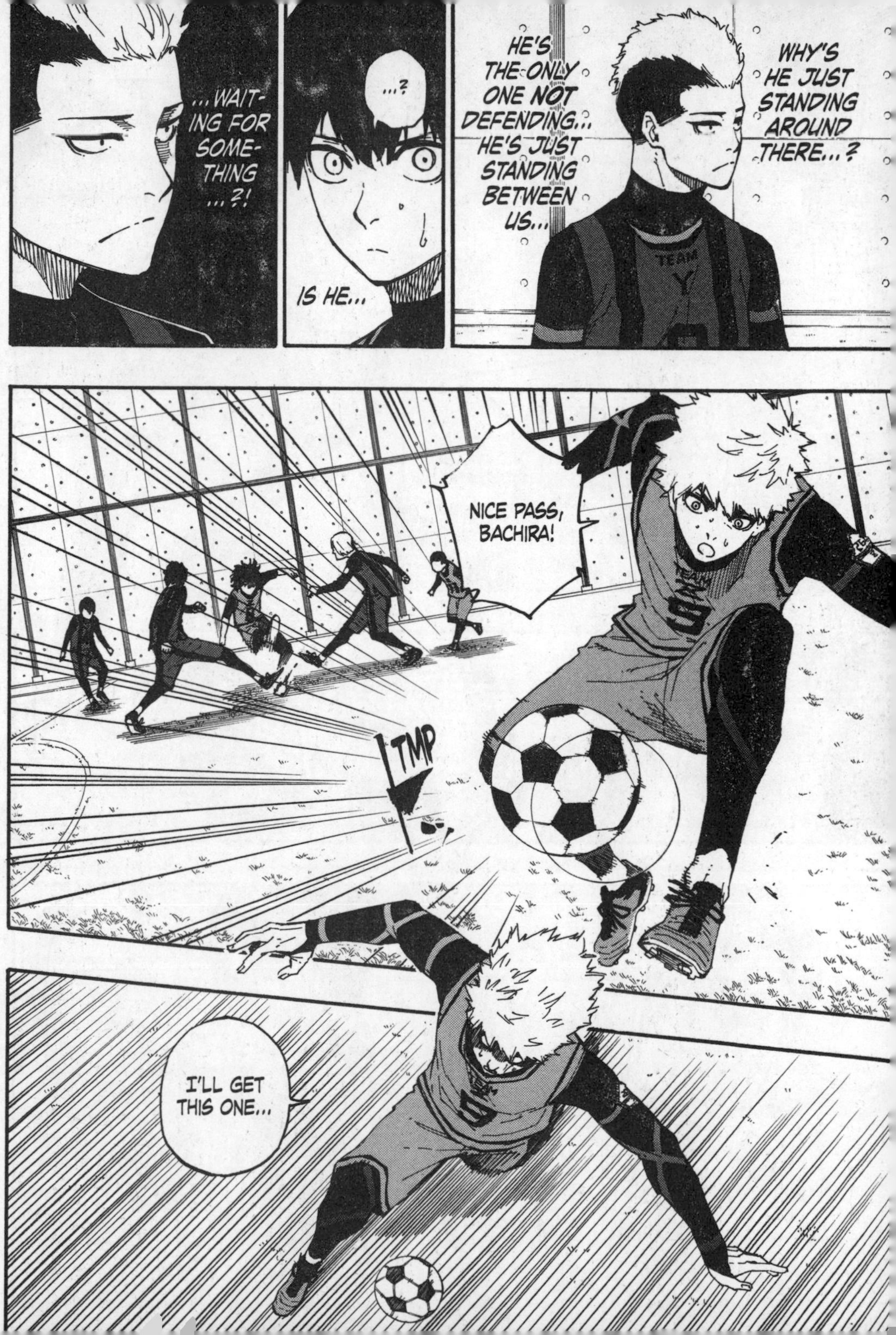
WHY'S HE JUST STANDING AROUND THERE...?
HE'S THE ONLY ONE NOT DEFENDING... HE'S JUST STANDING BETWEEN US...
...?
IS HE...
...WAITING FOR SOMETHING...?!
NICE PASS, BACHIRA!
TMP
I'LL GET THIS ONE...

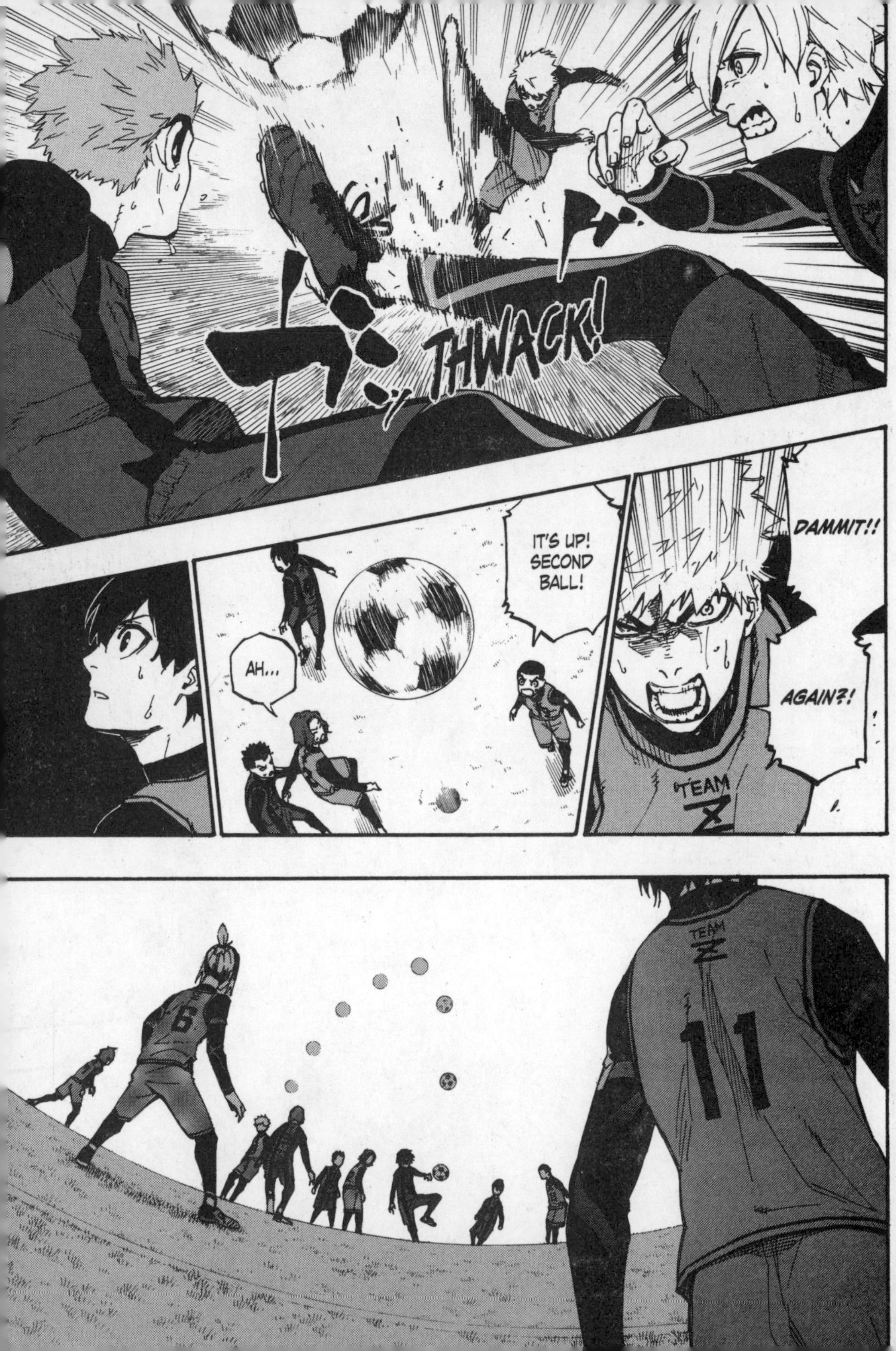
THWACK!
DAMMIT!!
AGAIN?!
IT'S UP! SECOND BALL!
AH...

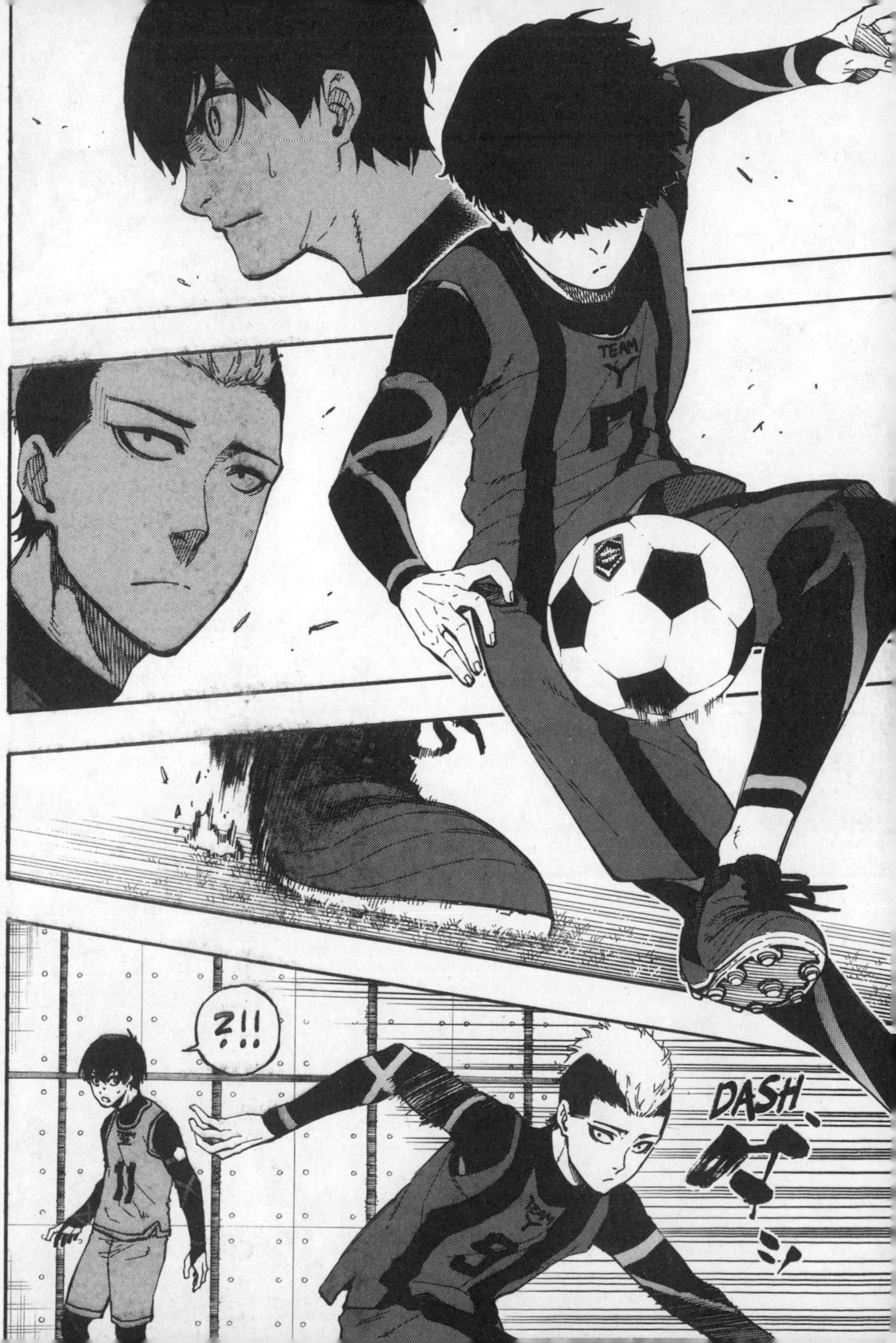
?!!
DASH

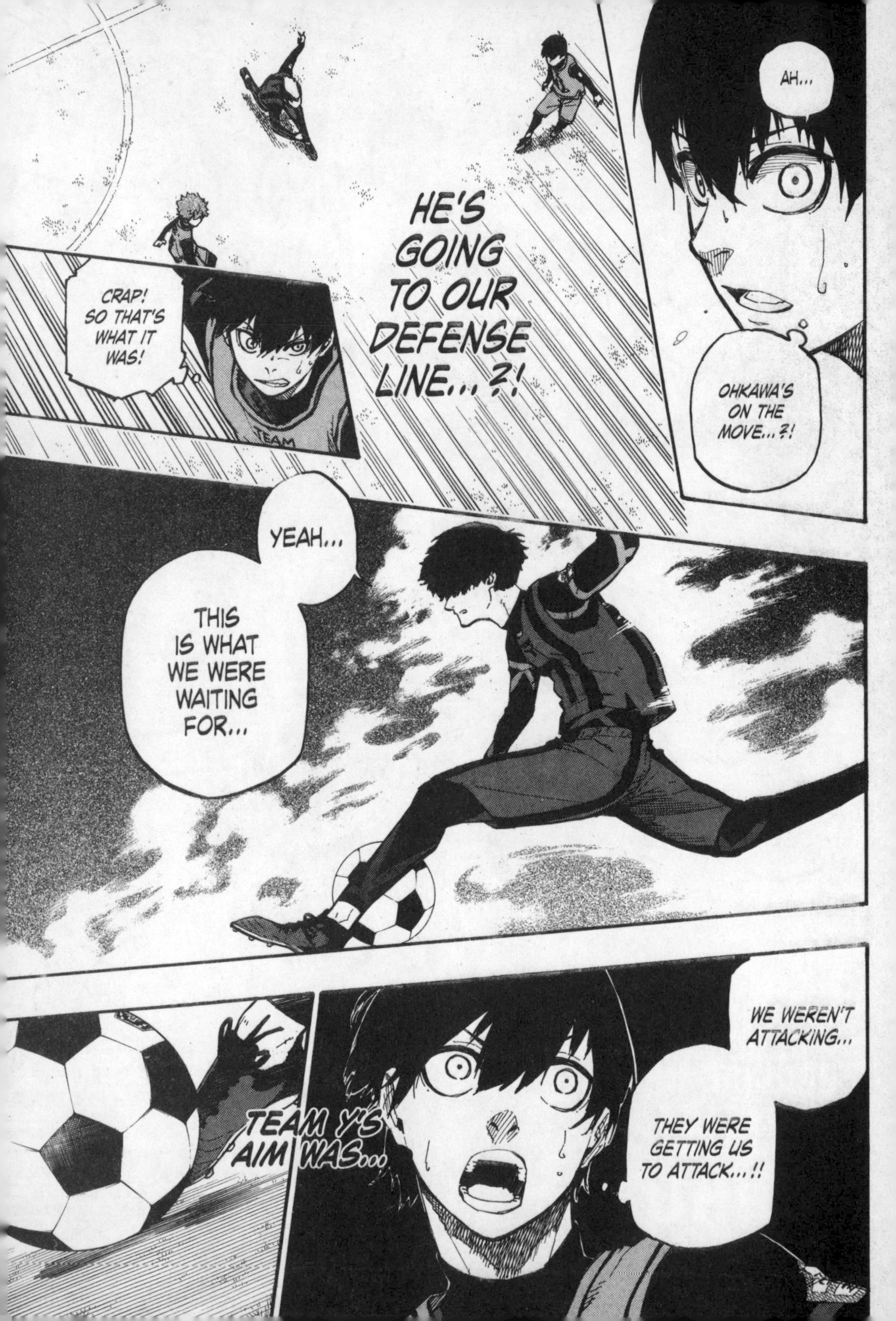
AH...
OHKAWA'S ON THE MOVE...?!
HE'S GOING TO OUR DEFENSE LINE...?!
CRAP! SO THAT'S WHAT IT WAS!
TEAM
YEAH...
THIS IS WHAT WE WERE WAITING FOR...
WE WEREN'T ATTACKING...
TEAM Y'S AIM WAS...
THEY WERE GETTING US TO ATTACK...!!

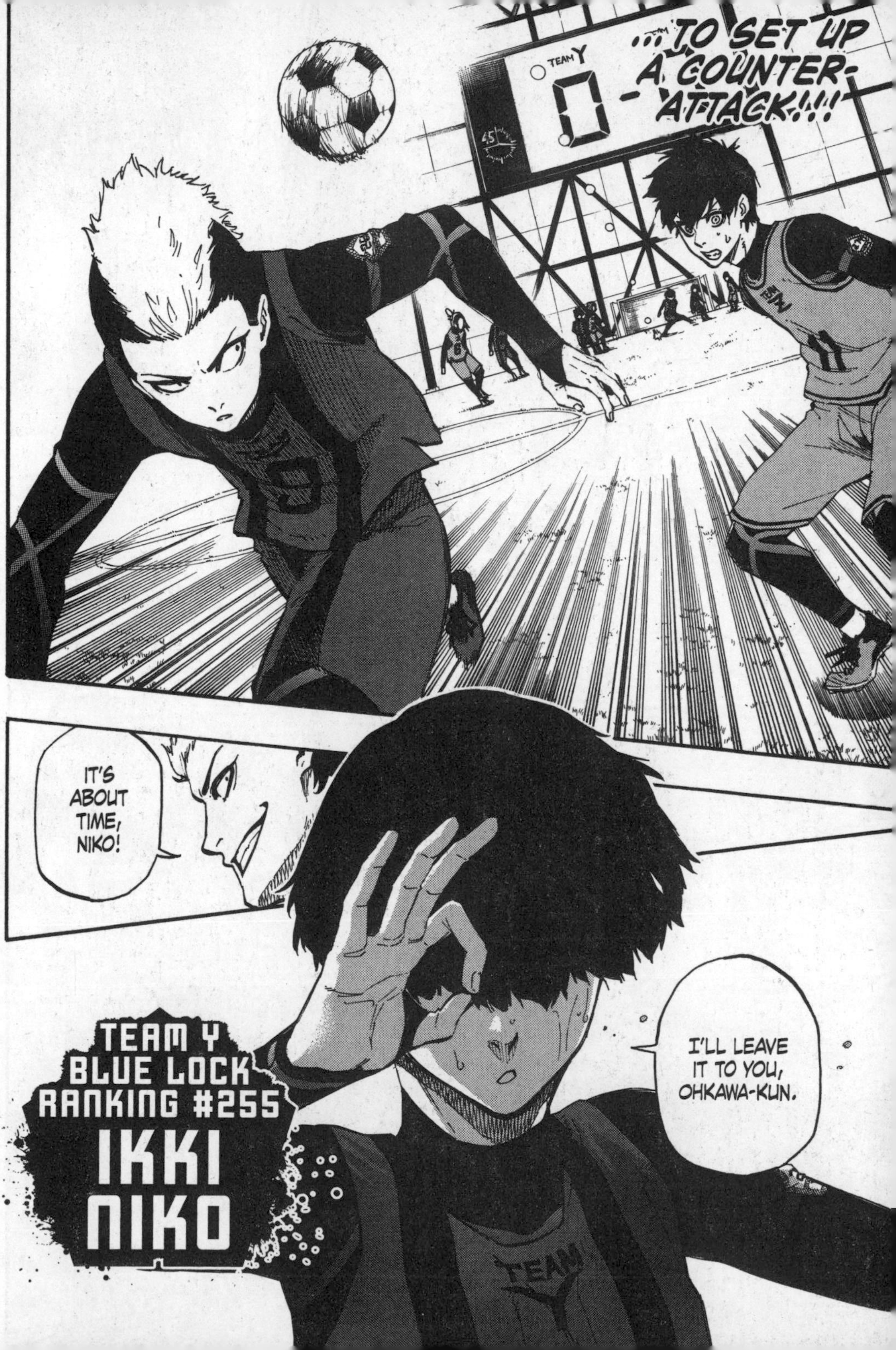
...TO SET UP A COUNTER-ATTACK!!!
TEAM Y
0 -
IT'S ABOUT TIME, NIKO!
I'LL LEAVE IT TO YOU, OHKAWA-KUN.
TEAM Y
BLUE LOCK
RANKING #255
IKKI
NIKO
TEAM

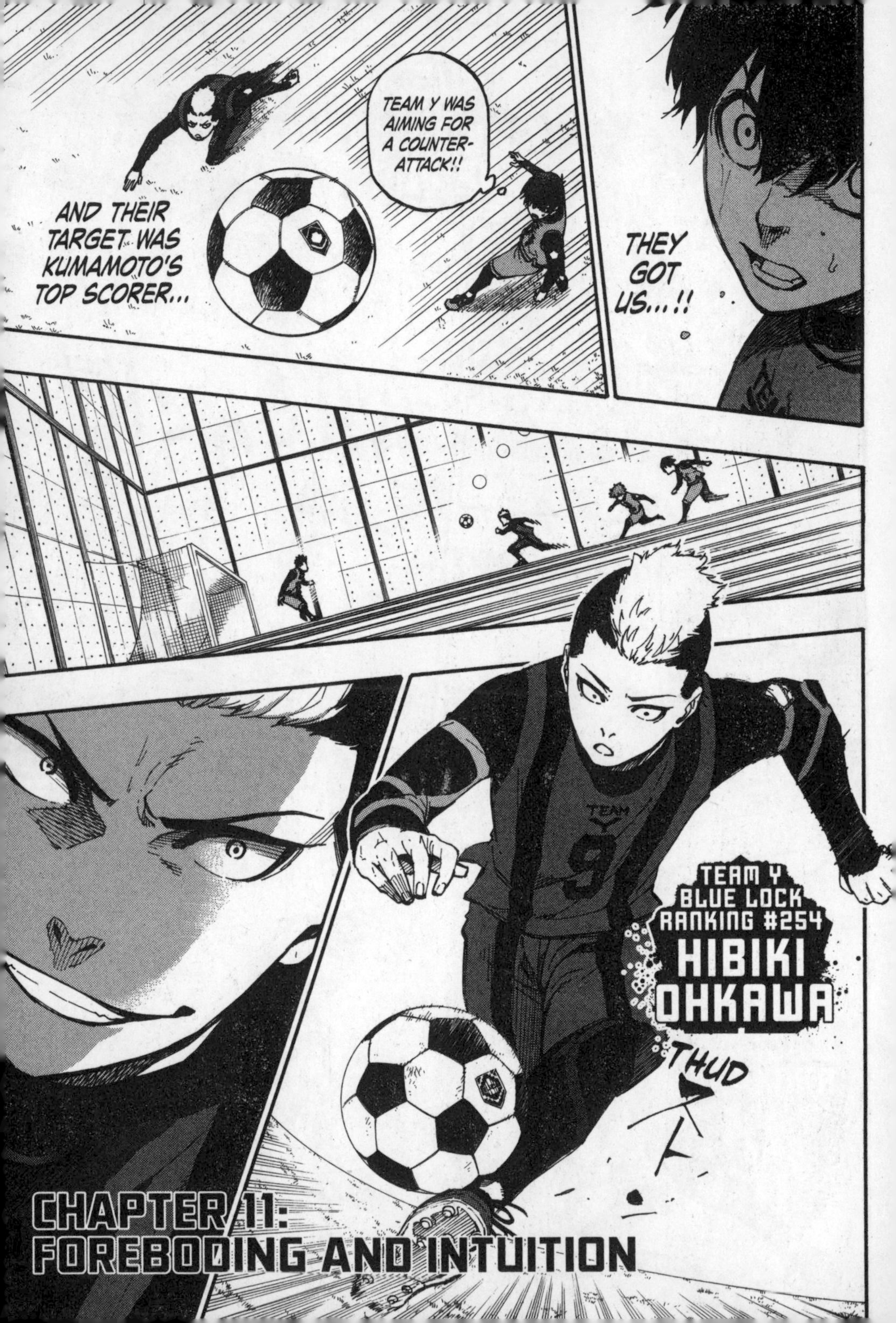
THEY GOT US...!!
TEAM Y WAS AIMING FOR A COUNTER-ATTACK!!
AND THEIR TARGET WAS KUMAMOTO'S TOP SCORER...
TEAM Y BLUE LOCK RANKING #254
HIBIKI OHKAWA
THUD
CHAPTER 11:
FOREBODING AND INTUITION

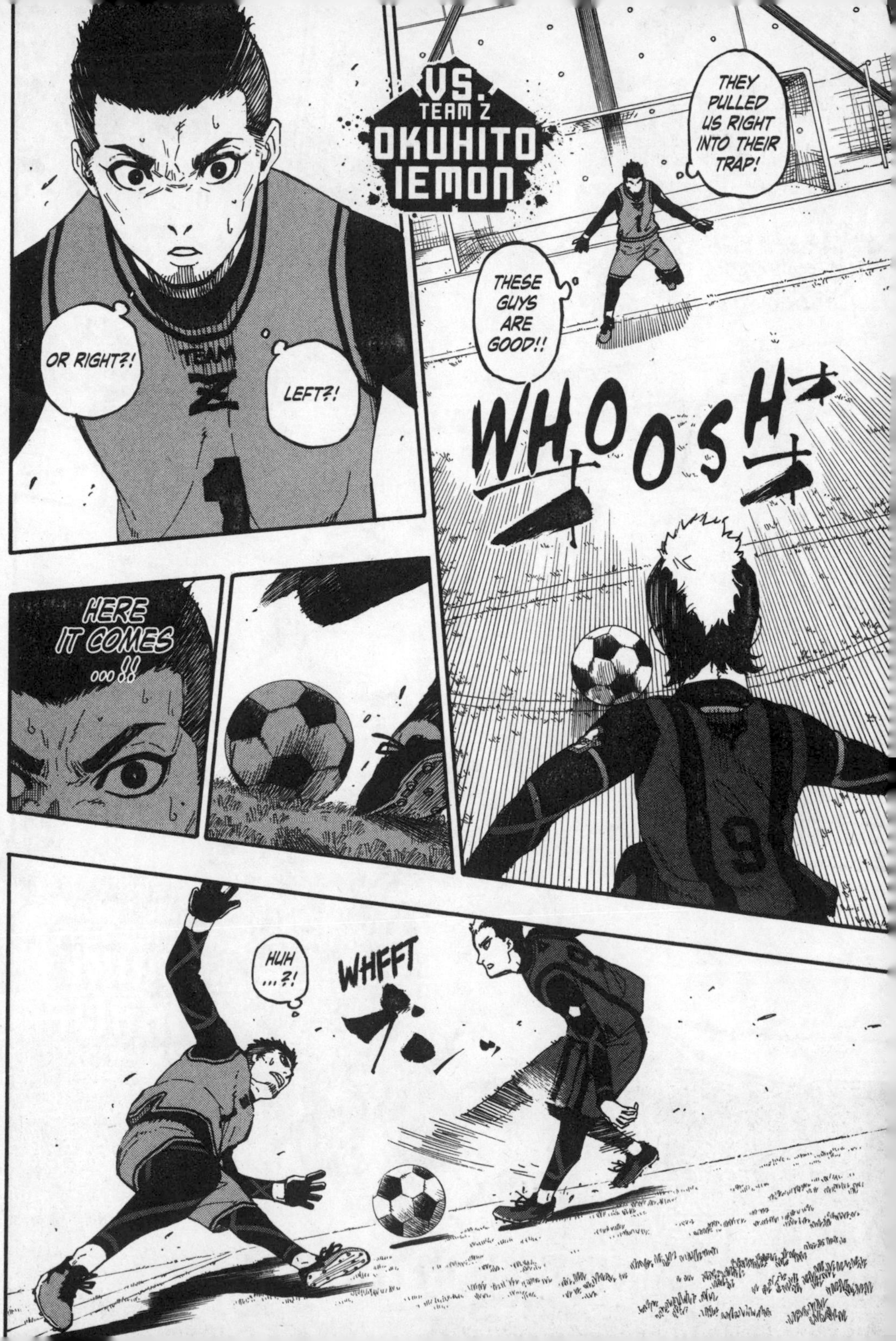
THEY PULLED US RIGHT INTO THEIR TRAP!
VS. TEAM Z OKUHITO IEMON
THESE GUYS ARE GOOD!!
WHOOSH
LEFT?!
OR RIGHT?!
HERE IT COMES ...!!
WHFFT
HUH ...?!

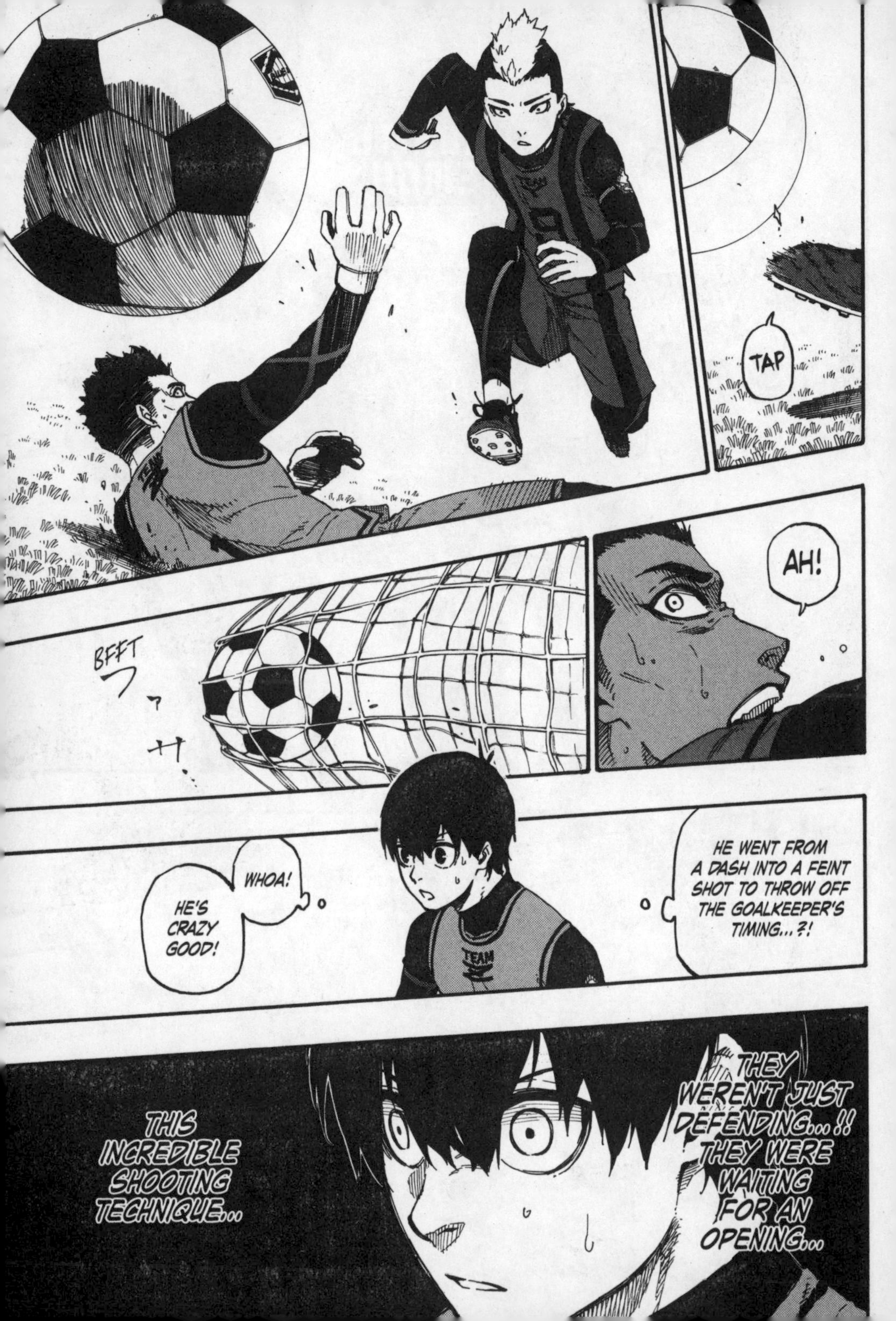
TAP
AH!
BFFT
HE WENT FROM A DASH INTO A FEINT SHOT TO THROW OFF THE GOALKEEPER'S TIMING...?!
WHOA! HE'S CRAZY GOOD!
THEY WEREN'T JUST DEFENDING...!! THEY WERE WAITING FOR AN OPENING...
THIS INCREDIBLE SHOOTING TECHNIQUE...

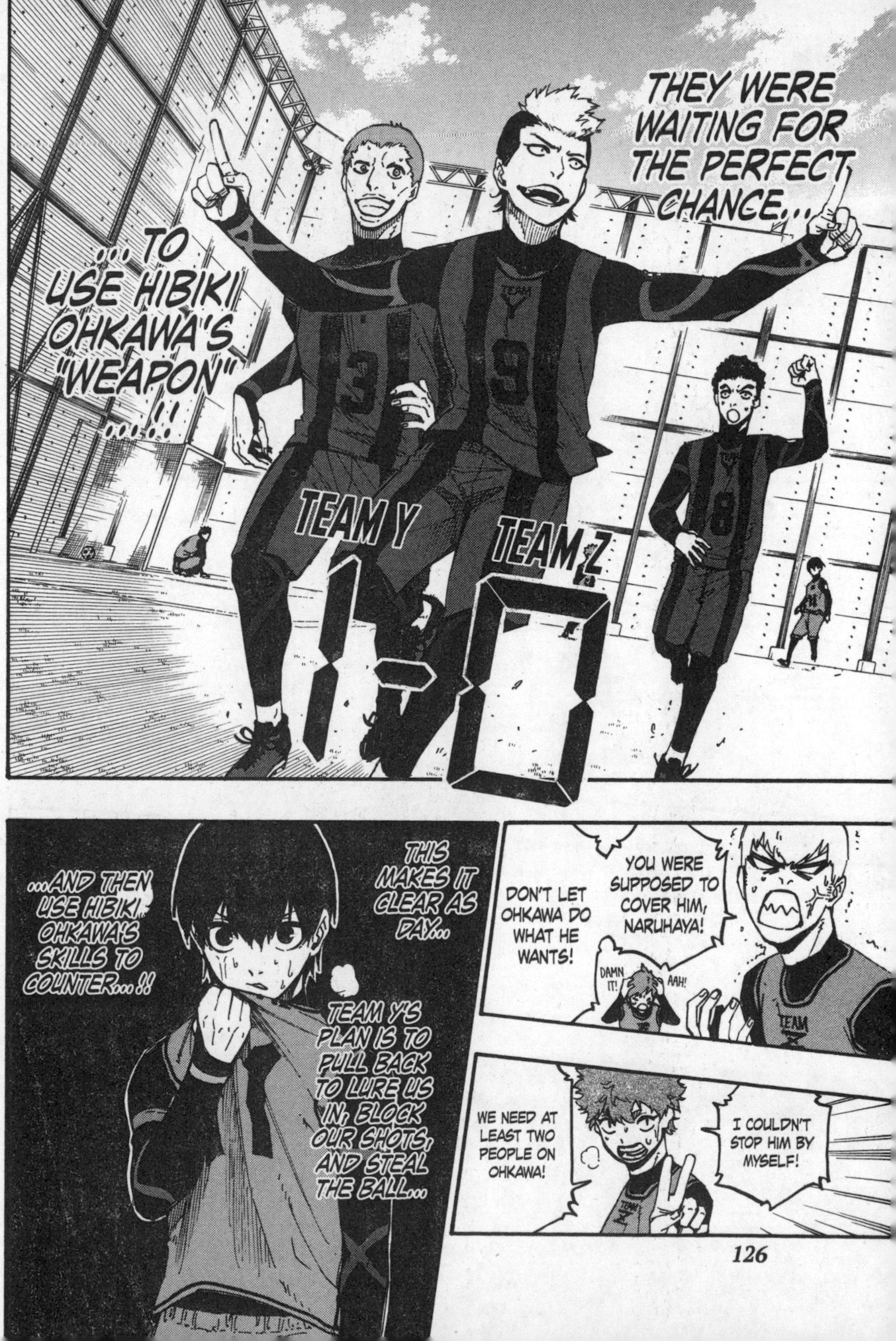
THEY WERE WAITING FOR THE PERFECT CHANCE...
...TO USE HIBIKI OHKAWA'S "WEAPON"...!!
TEAM Y
TEAM Z
1-0
YOU WERE SUPPOSED TO COVER HIM, NARUHAYA!
DON'T LET OHKAWA DO WHAT HE WANTS!
AAH!
DAMN IT!
I COULDN'T STOP HIM BY MYSELF!
WE NEED AT LEAST TWO PEOPLE ON OHKAWA!
THIS MAKES IT CLEAR AS DAY...
TEAM Y'S PLAN IS TO PULL BACK TO LURE US IN, BLOCK OUR SHOTS, AND STEAL THE BALL...
...AND THEN USE HIBIKI OHKAWA'S SKILLS TO COUNTER...!!

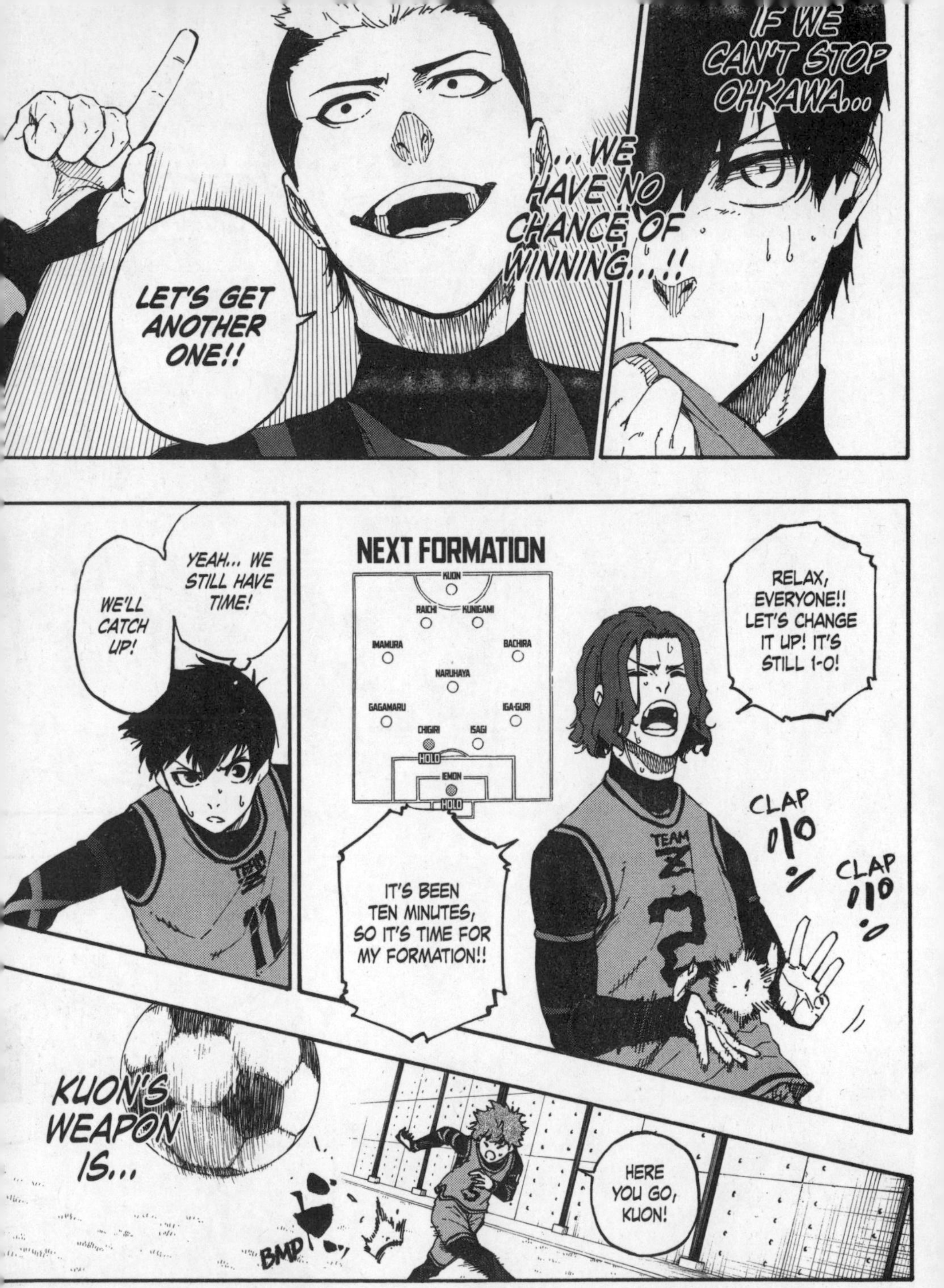
IF WE CAN'T STOP OHKAWA...
...WE HAVE NO CHANCE OF WINNING...!!
LET'S GET ANOTHER ONE!!
NEXT FORMATION
KUON
RAICHI
KUNIGAMI
IMAMURA
BACHIRA
NARUHAYA
GAGAMARU
IGA-GURI
CHIGIRI
ISAGI
HOLD
IEMON
HOLD
RELAX, EVERYONE!! LET'S CHANGE IT UP! IT'S STILL 1-0!
CLAP
CLAP
IT'S BEEN TEN MINUTES, SO IT'S TIME FOR MY FORMATION!!
YEAH... WE STILL HAVE TIME!
WE'LL CATCH UP!
HERE YOU GO, KUON!
BMP
KUON'S WEAPON IS...

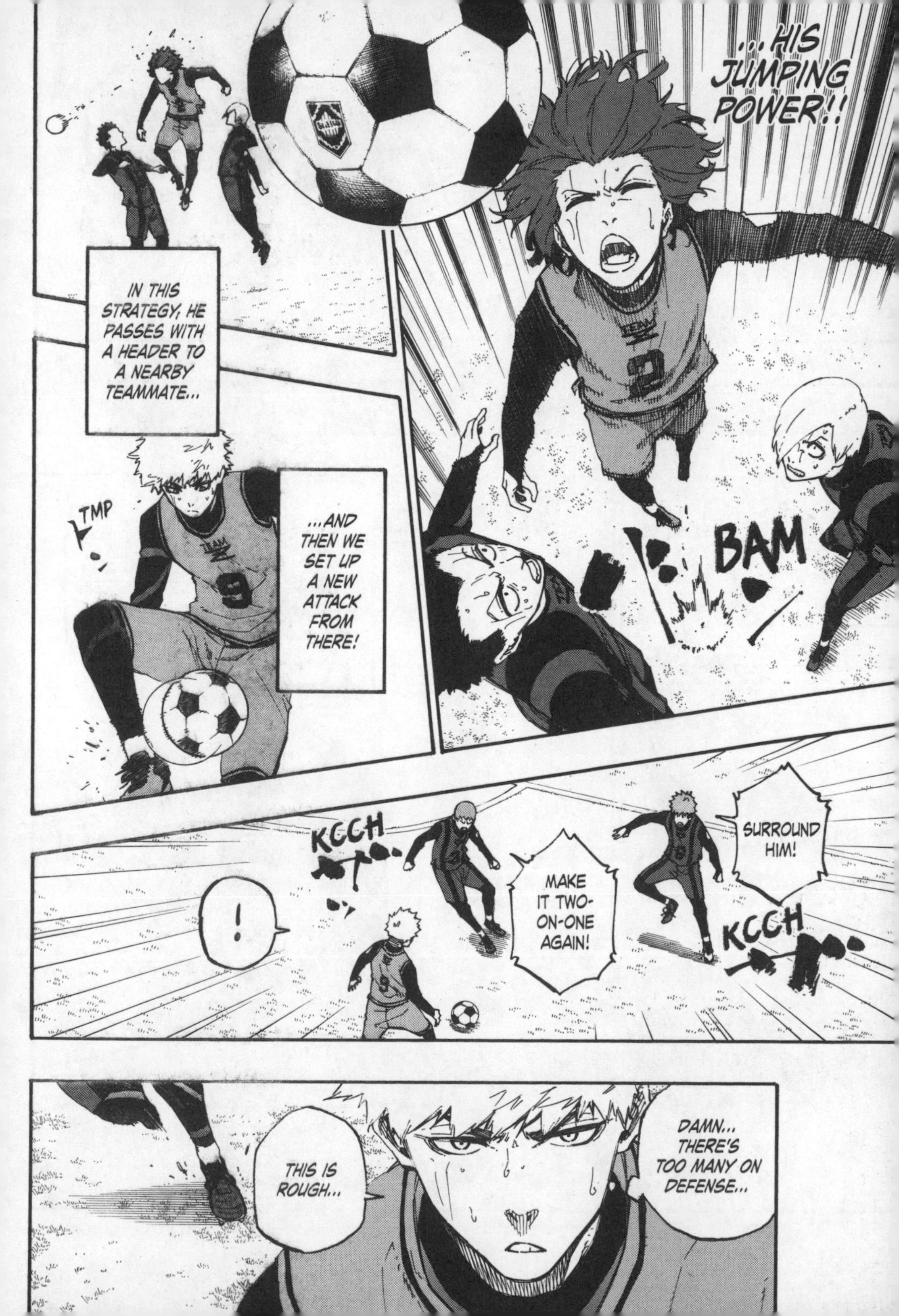

...HIS JUMPING POWER!!
BAM
IN THIS STRATEGY, HE PASSES WITH A HEADER TO A NEARBY TEAMMATE...
TMP
...AND THEN WE SET UP A NEW ATTACK FROM THERE!
SURROUND HIM!
KCCH
MAKE IT TWO-ON-ONE AGAIN!
KCCH
!
DAMN... THERE'S TOO MANY ON DEFENSE...
THIS IS ROUGH...

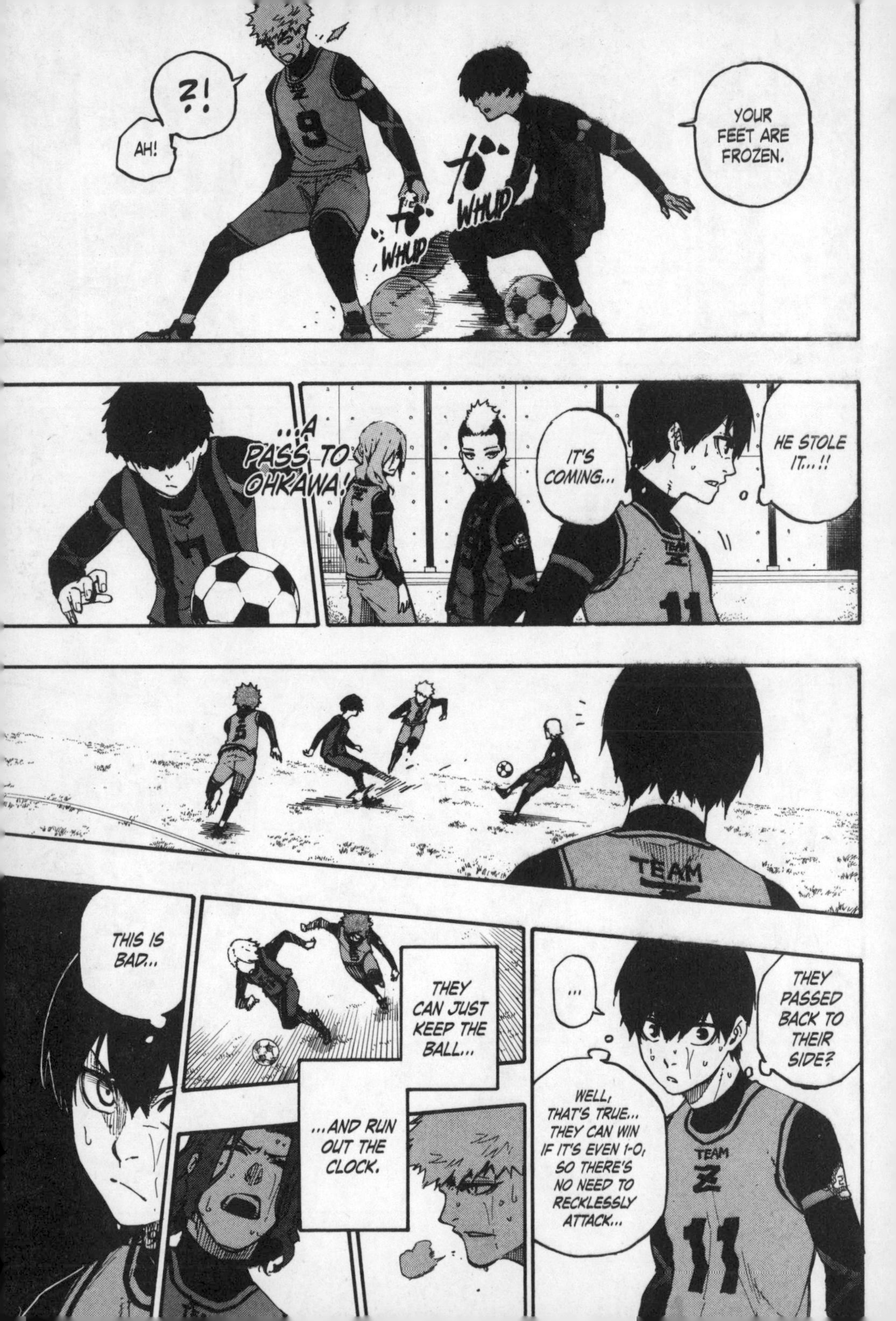
YOUR FEET ARE FROZEN.
?!
AH!
WHUP
WHUP
HE STOLE IT...!!
IT'S COMING...
...A PASS TO OHKAWA!
THEY PASSED BACK TO THEIR SIDE?
...
WELL, THAT'S TRUE... THEY CAN WIN IF IT'S EVEN 1-0, SO THERE'S NO NEED TO RECKLESSLY ATTACK...
THEY CAN JUST KEEP THE BALL...
...AND RUN OUT THE CLOCK.
THIS IS BAD...

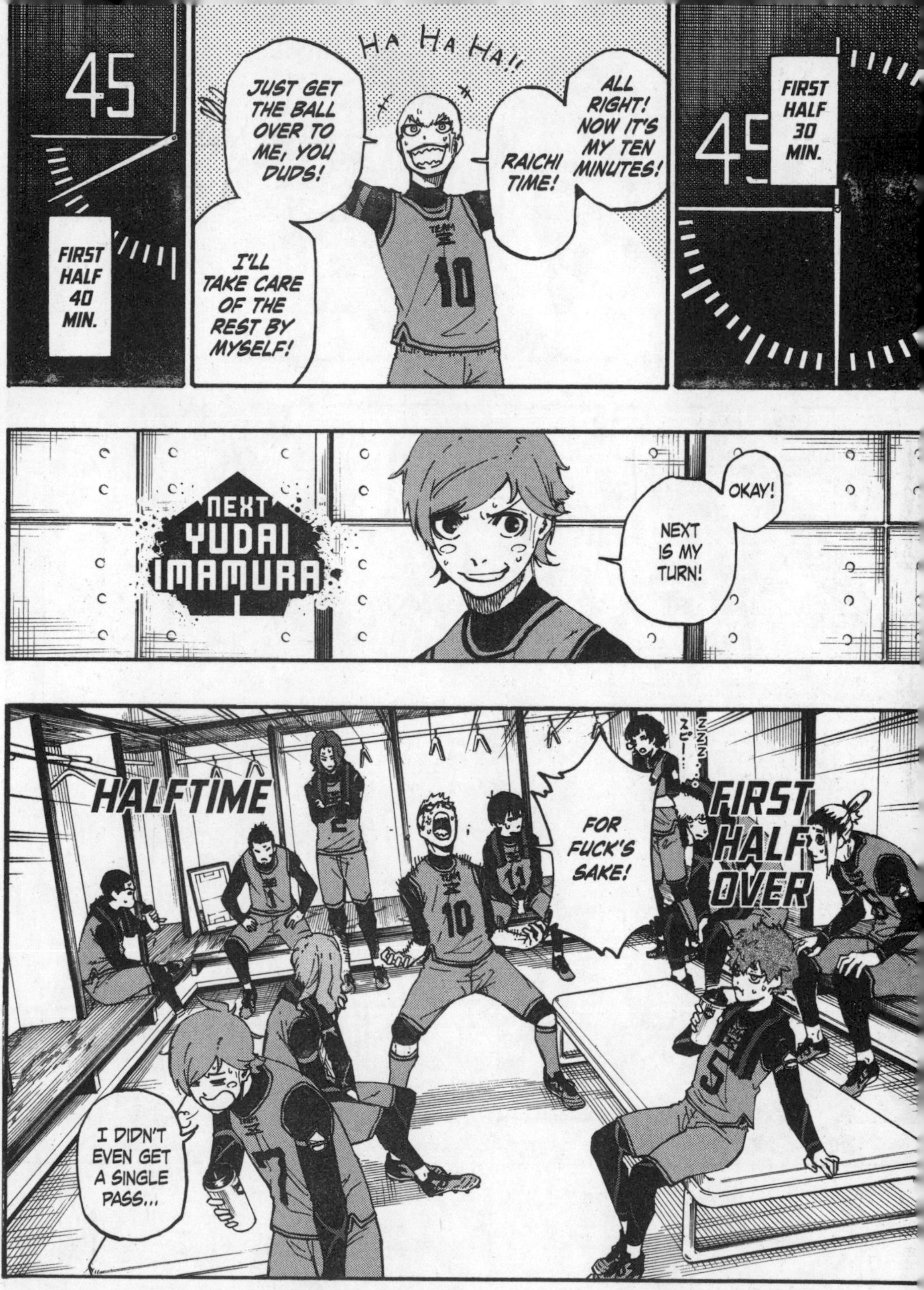
FIRST HALF 30 MIN.
45
HA HA HA!!
ALL RIGHT! NOW IT'S MY TEN MINUTES!
RAICHI TIME!
JUST GET THE BALL OVER TO ME, YOU DUDS!
I'LL TAKE CARE OF THE REST BY MYSELF!
45
FIRST HALF 40 MIN.
OKAY!
NEXT IS MY TURN!
NEXT YUDAI IMAMURA
FIRST HALF OVER
ZZZ
FOR FUCK'S SAKE!
HALFTIME
I DIDN'T EVEN GET A SINGLE PASS...

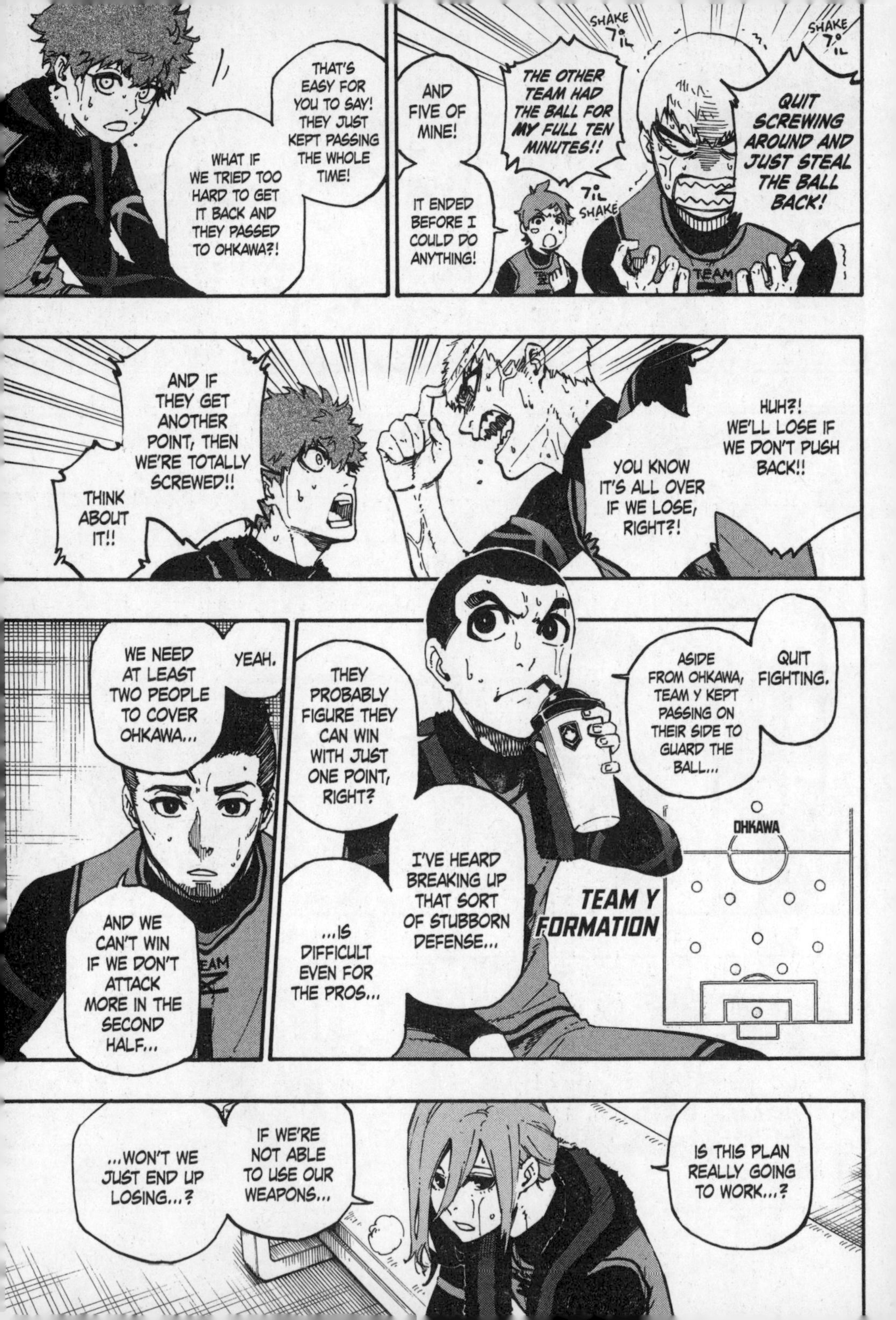
SHAKE
SHAKE
QUIT SCREWING AROUND AND JUST STEAL THE BALL BACK!
THE OTHER TEAM HAD THE BALL FOR MY FULL TEN MINUTES!!
SHAKE
AND FIVE OF MINE!
IT ENDED BEFORE I COULD DO ANYTHING!
THAT'S EASY FOR YOU TO SAY! THEY JUST KEPT PASSING THE WHOLE TIME!
WHAT IF WE TRIED TOO HARD TO GET IT BACK AND THEY PASSED TO OHKAWA?!
HUH?! WE'LL LOSE IF WE DON'T PUSH BACK!!
YOU KNOW IT'S ALL OVER IF WE LOSE, RIGHT?!
AND IF THEY GET ANOTHER POINT, THEN WE'RE TOTALLY SCREWED!!
THINK ABOUT IT!!
QUIT FIGHTING.
ASIDE FROM OHKAWA, TEAM Y KEPT PASSING ON THEIR SIDE TO GUARD THE BALL...
THEY PROBABLY FIGURE THEY CAN WIN WITH JUST ONE POINT, RIGHT?
OHKAWA
TEAM Y FORMATION
I'VE HEARD BREAKING UP THAT SORT OF STUBBORN DEFENSE...
...IS DIFFICULT EVEN FOR THE PROS...
YEAH.
WE NEED AT LEAST TWO PEOPLE TO COVER OHKAWA...
AND WE CAN'T WIN IF WE DON'T ATTACK MORE IN THE SECOND HALF...
IS THIS PLAN REALLY GOING TO WORK...?
IF WE'RE NOT ABLE TO USE OUR WEAPONS...
...WON'T WE JUST END UP LOSING...?

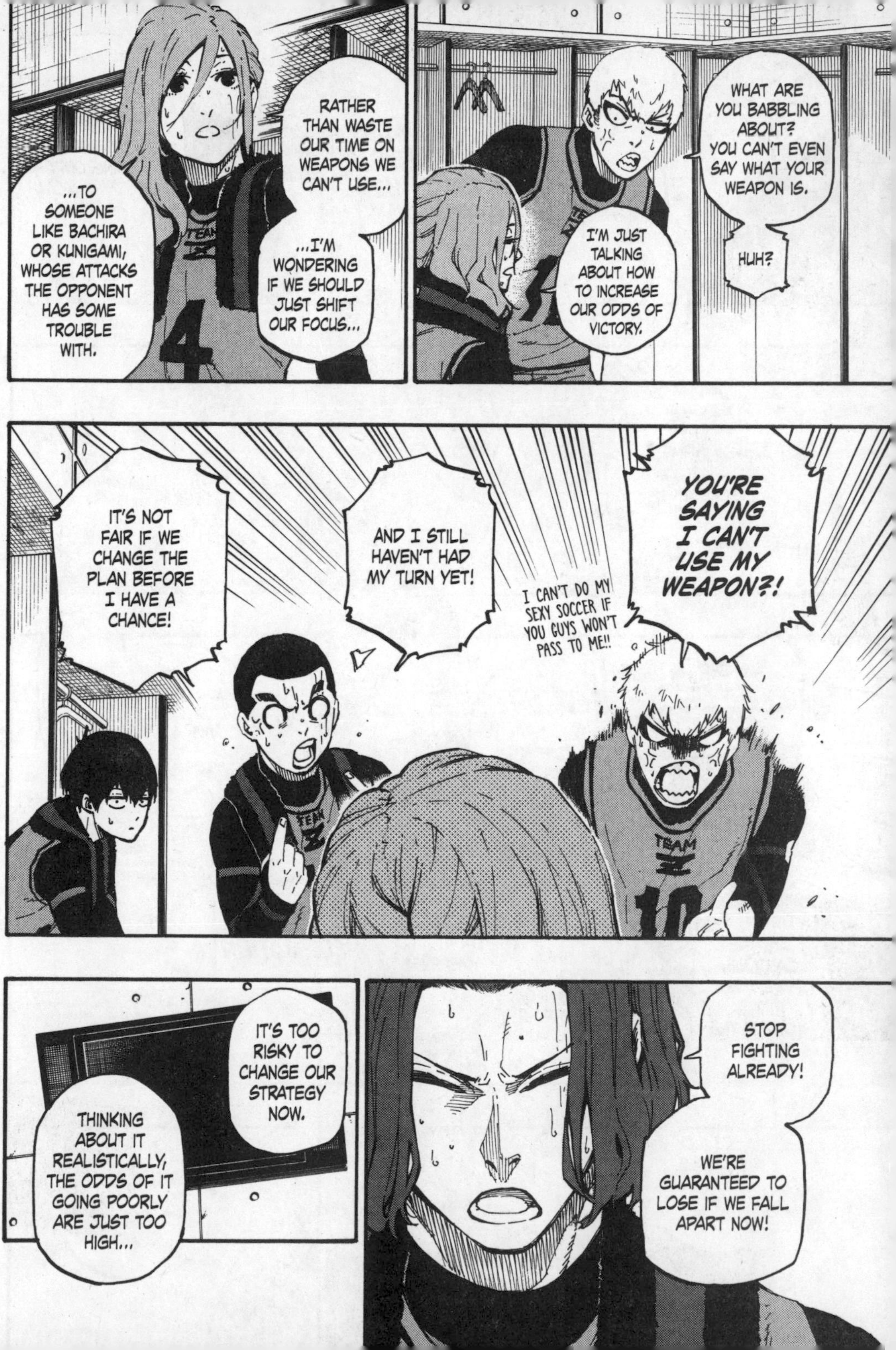
WHAT ARE YOU BABBLING ABOUT? YOU CAN'T EVEN SAY WHAT YOUR WEAPON IS.
HUH?
I'M JUST TALKING ABOUT HOW TO INCREASE OUR ODDS OF VICTORY.
RATHER THAN WASTE OUR TIME ON WEAPONS WE CAN'T USE...
...I'M WONDERING IF WE SHOULD JUST SHIFT OUR FOCUS...
...TO SOMEONE LIKE BACHIRA OR KUNIGAMI, WHOSE ATTACKS THE OPPONENT HAS SOME TROUBLE WITH.
YOU'RE SAYING I CAN'T USE MY WEAPON?!
I CAN'T DO MY SEXY SOCCER IF YOU GUYS WON'T PASS TO ME!!
AND I STILL HAVEN'T HAD MY TURN YET!
IT'S NOT FAIR IF WE CHANGE THE PLAN BEFORE I HAVE A CHANCE!
STOP FIGHTING ALREADY!
WE'RE GUARANTEED TO LOSE IF WE FALL APART NOW!
IT'S TOO RISKY TO CHANGE OUR STRATEGY NOW.
THINKING ABOUT IT REALISTICALLY, THE ODDS OF IT GOING POORLY ARE JUST TOO HIGH...

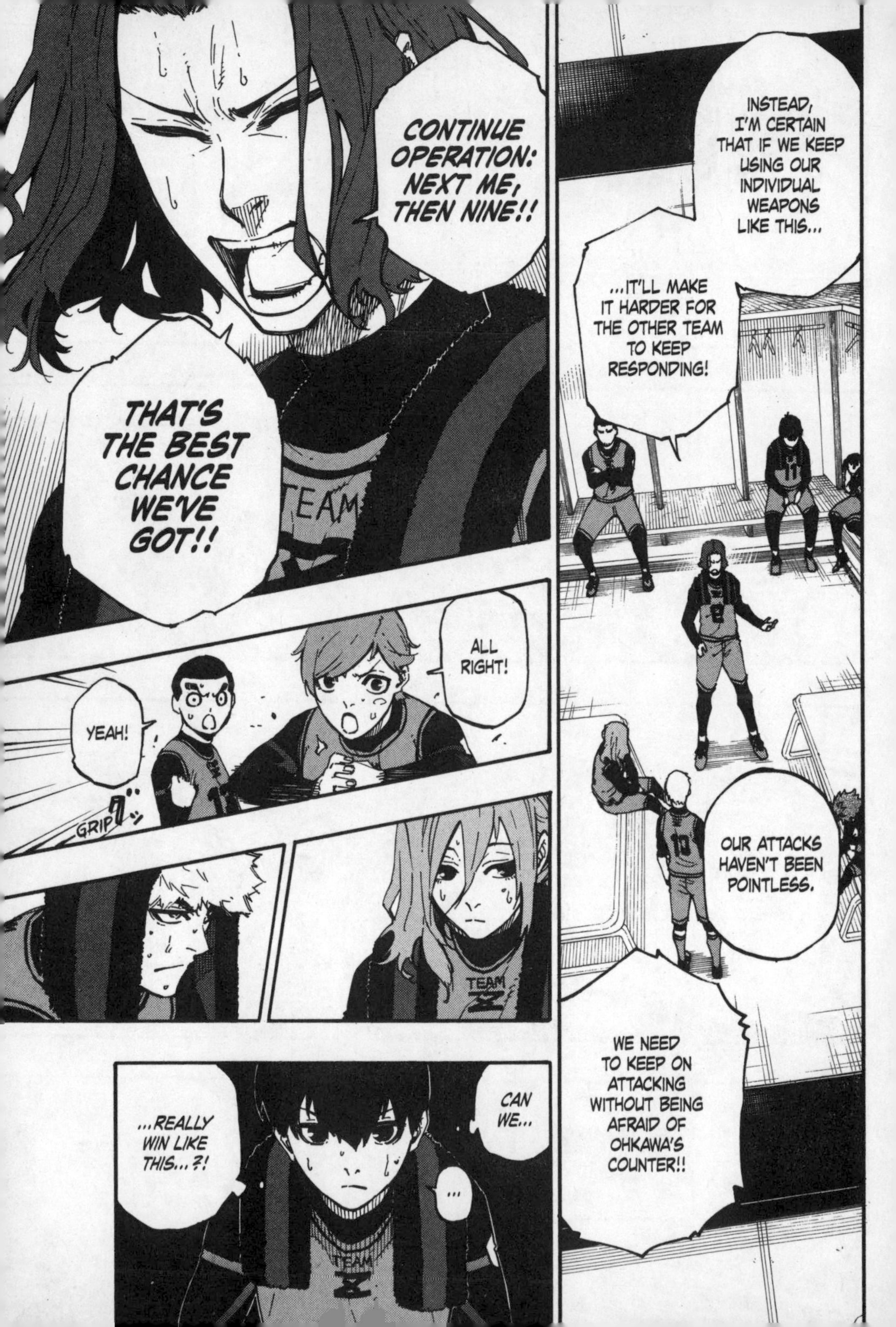
INSTEAD, I'M CERTAIN THAT IF WE KEEP USING OUR INDIVIDUAL WEAPONS LIKE THIS...
...IT'LL MAKE IT HARDER FOR THE OTHER TEAM TO KEEP RESPONDING!
OUR ATTACKS HAVEN'T BEEN POINTLESS.
WE NEED TO KEEP ON ATTACKING WITHOUT BEING AFRAID OF OHKAWA'S COUNTER!!
CONTINUE OPERATION: NEXT ME, THEN NINE!!
THAT'S THE BEST CHANCE WE'VE GOT!!
ALL RIGHT!
YEAH!
GRIP
CAN WE...
...REALLY WIN LIKE THIS...?!
...

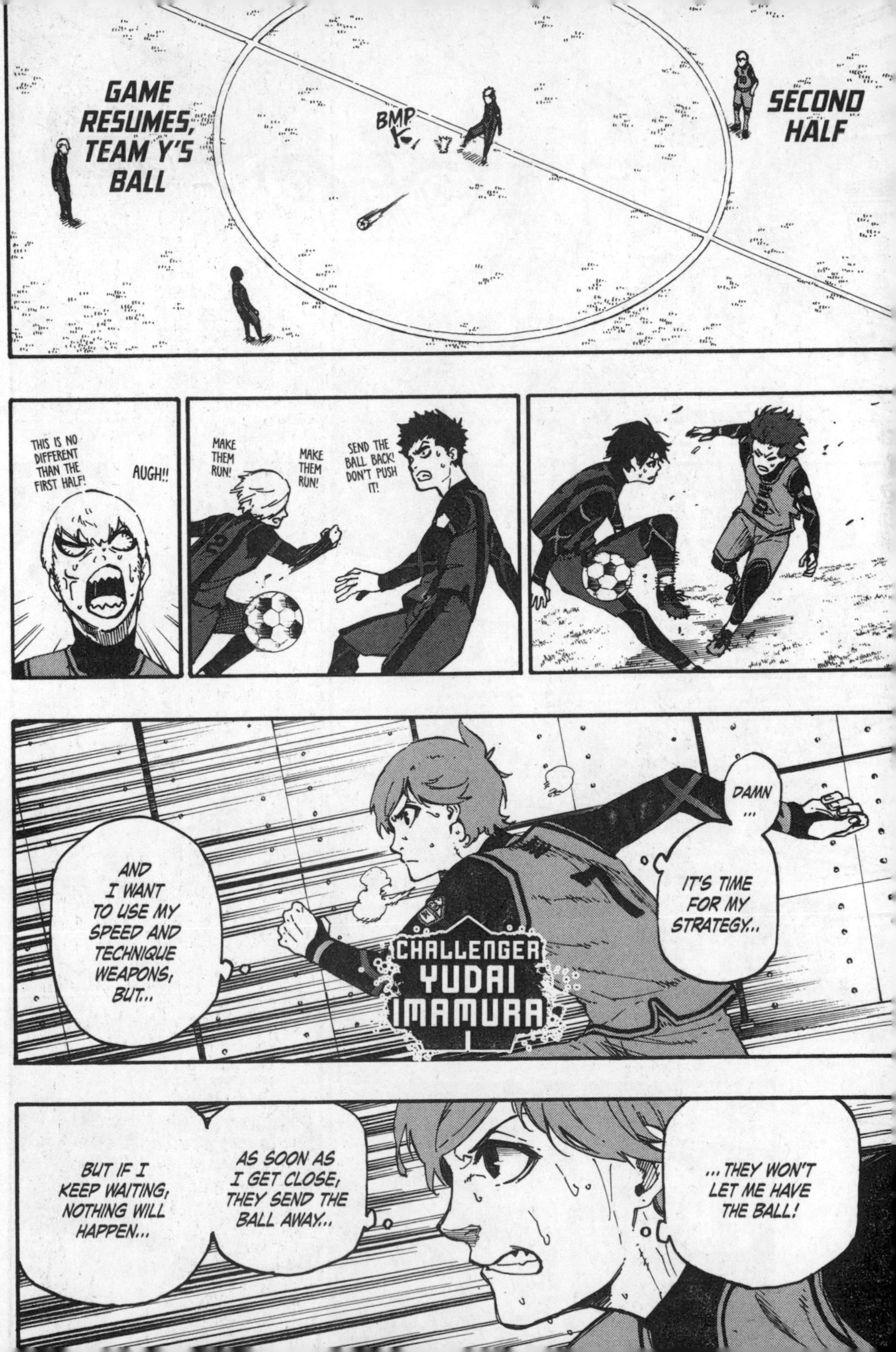
SECOND HALF
GAME RESUMES, TEAM Y'S BALL
BMP
SEND THE BALL BACK! DON'T PUSH IT!
MAKE THEM RUN!
MAKE THEM RUN!
AUGH!!
THIS IS NO DIFFERENT THAN THE FIRST HALF!
DAMN ...
IT'S TIME FOR MY STRATEGY...
AND I WANT TO USE MY SPEED AND TECHNIQUE WEAPONS, BUT...
CHALLENGER YUDAI IMAMURA
...THEY WON'T LET ME HAVE THE BALL!
AS SOON AS I GET CLOSE, THEY SEND THE BALL AWAY...
BUT IF I KEEP WAITING, NOTHING WILL HAPPEN...

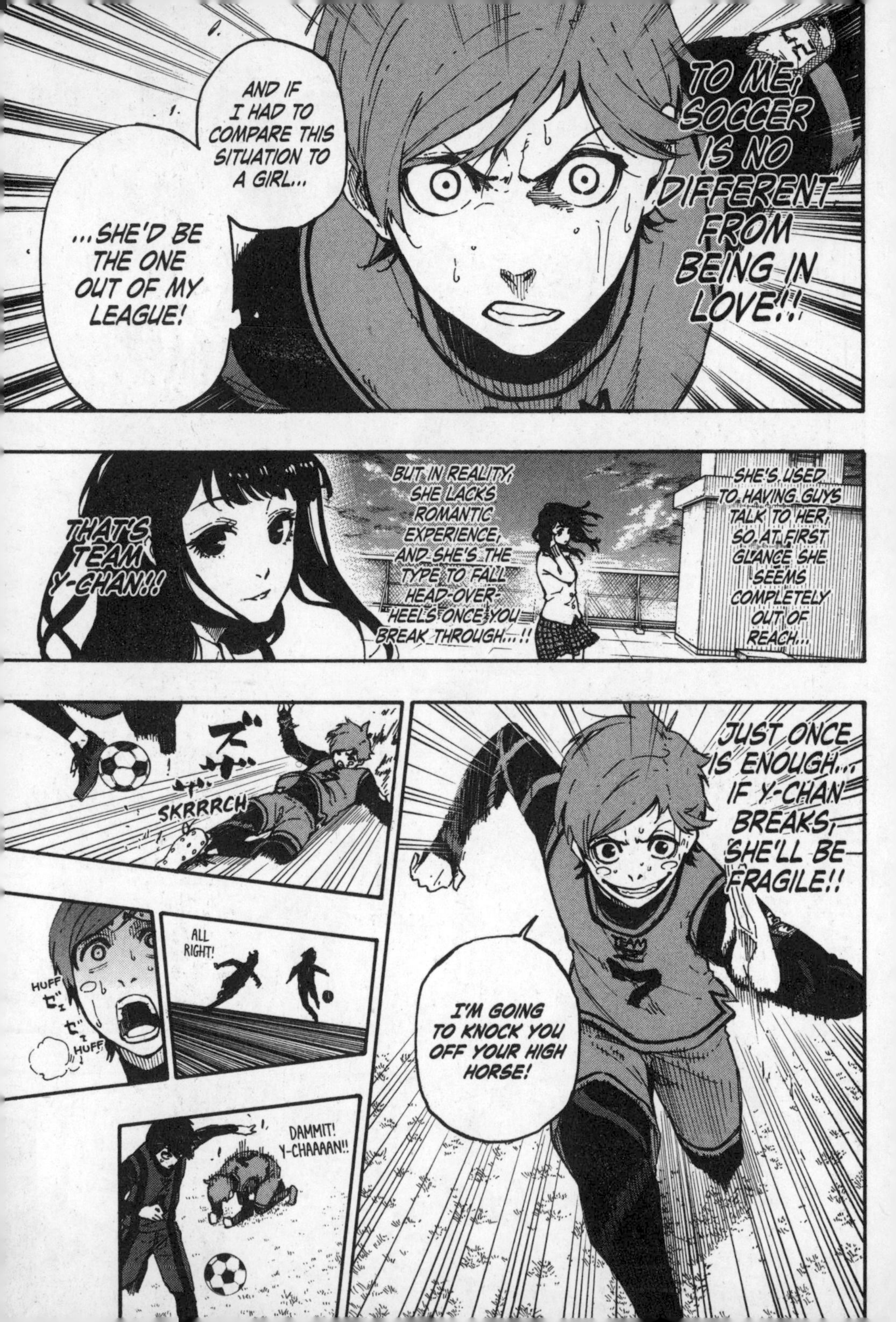
TO ME, SOCCER IS NO DIFFERENT FROM BEING IN LOVE!!
AND IF I HAD TO COMPARE THIS SITUATION TO A GIRL...
...SHE'D BE THE ONE OUT OF MY LEAGUE!
SHE'S USED TO HAVING GUYS TALK TO HER, SO AT FIRST GLANCE SHE SEEMS COMPLETELY OUT OF REACH...
BUT IN REALITY, SHE LACKS ROMANTIC EXPERIENCE, AND SHE'S THE TYPE TO FALL HEAD-OVER-HEELS ONCE YOU BREAK THROUGH...!!
THAT'S TEAM Y-CHAN!!
JUST ONCE IS ENOUGH... IF Y-CHAN BREAKS, SHE'LL BE FRAGILE!!
I'M GOING TO KNOCK YOU OFF YOUR HIGH HORSE!
ズザ
SKRRRCH
ALL RIGHT!
HUFF
ゼェ
ゼェ
HUFF
DAMMIT! Y-CHAAAAN!!

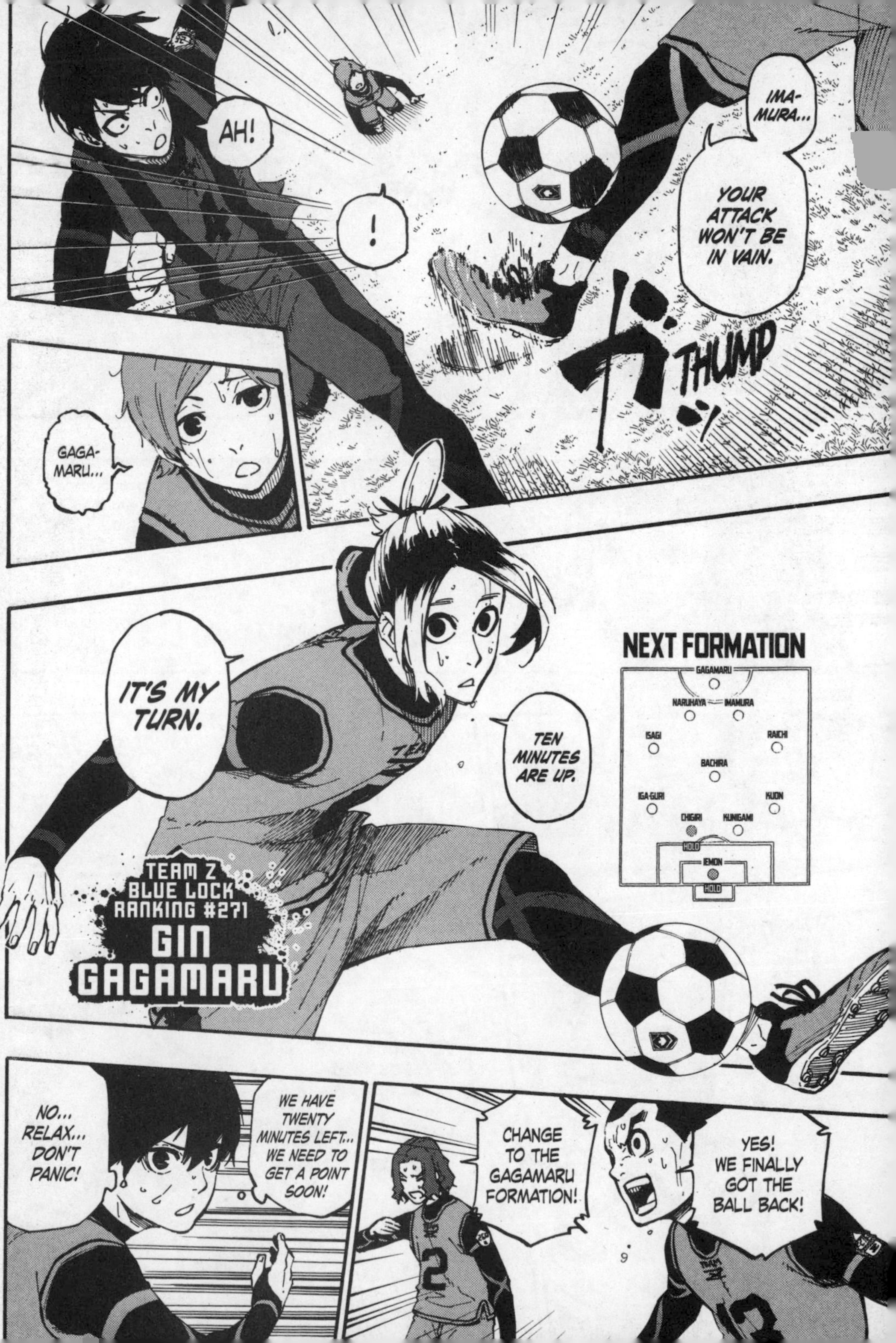
IMA-MURA...
YOUR ATTACK WON'T BE IN VAIN.
THUMP
!
AH!
GAGA-MARU...
NEXT FORMATION
GAGAMARU
NARUHAYA
IMAMURA
ISAGI
RAICHI
BACHIRA
IGA-GURI
KUON
CHIGIRI
KUNIGAMI
HOLD
IEMON
HOLD
TEN MINUTES ARE UP.
IT'S MY TURN.
TEAM Z BLUE LOCK RANKING #271
GIN GAGAMARU
YES! WE FINALLY GOT THE BALL BACK!
CHANGE TO THE GAGAMARU FORMATION!
WE HAVE TWENTY MINUTES LEFT... WE NEED TO GET A POINT SOON!
NO... RELAX... DON'T PANIC!

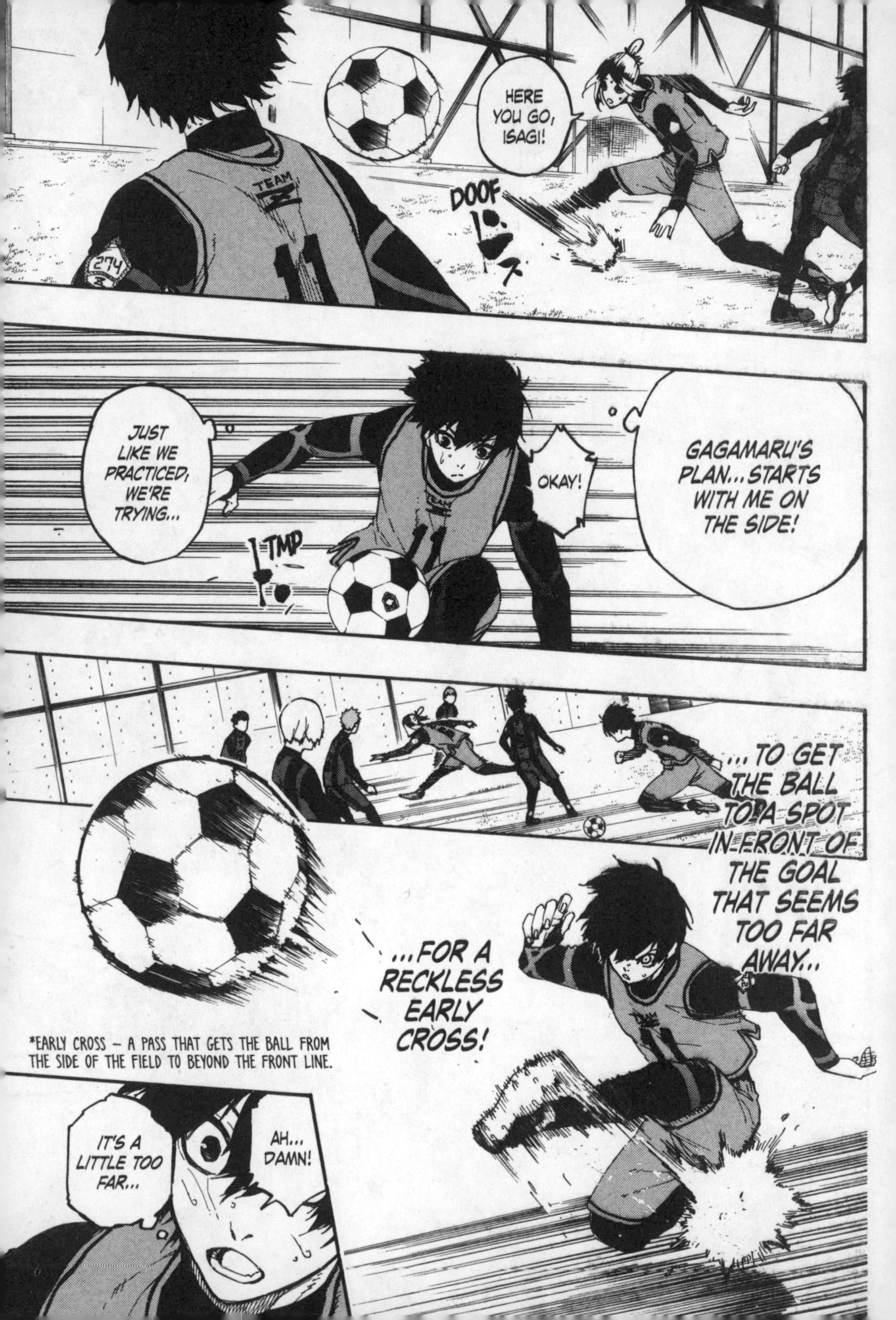
HERE YOU GO, ISAGI!
DOOF
GAGAMARU'S PLAN...STARTS WITH ME ON THE SIDE!
OKAY!
JUST LIKE WE PRACTICED, WE'RE TRYING...
TMP
...TO GET THE BALL TO A SPOT IN FRONT OF THE GOAL THAT SEEMS TOO FAR AWAY...
...FOR A RECKLESS EARLY CROSS!
AH... DAMN!
IT'S A LITTLE TOO FAR...

*EARLY CROSS – A PASS THAT GETS THE BALL FROM THE SIDE OF THE FIELD TO BEYOND THE FRONT LINE.

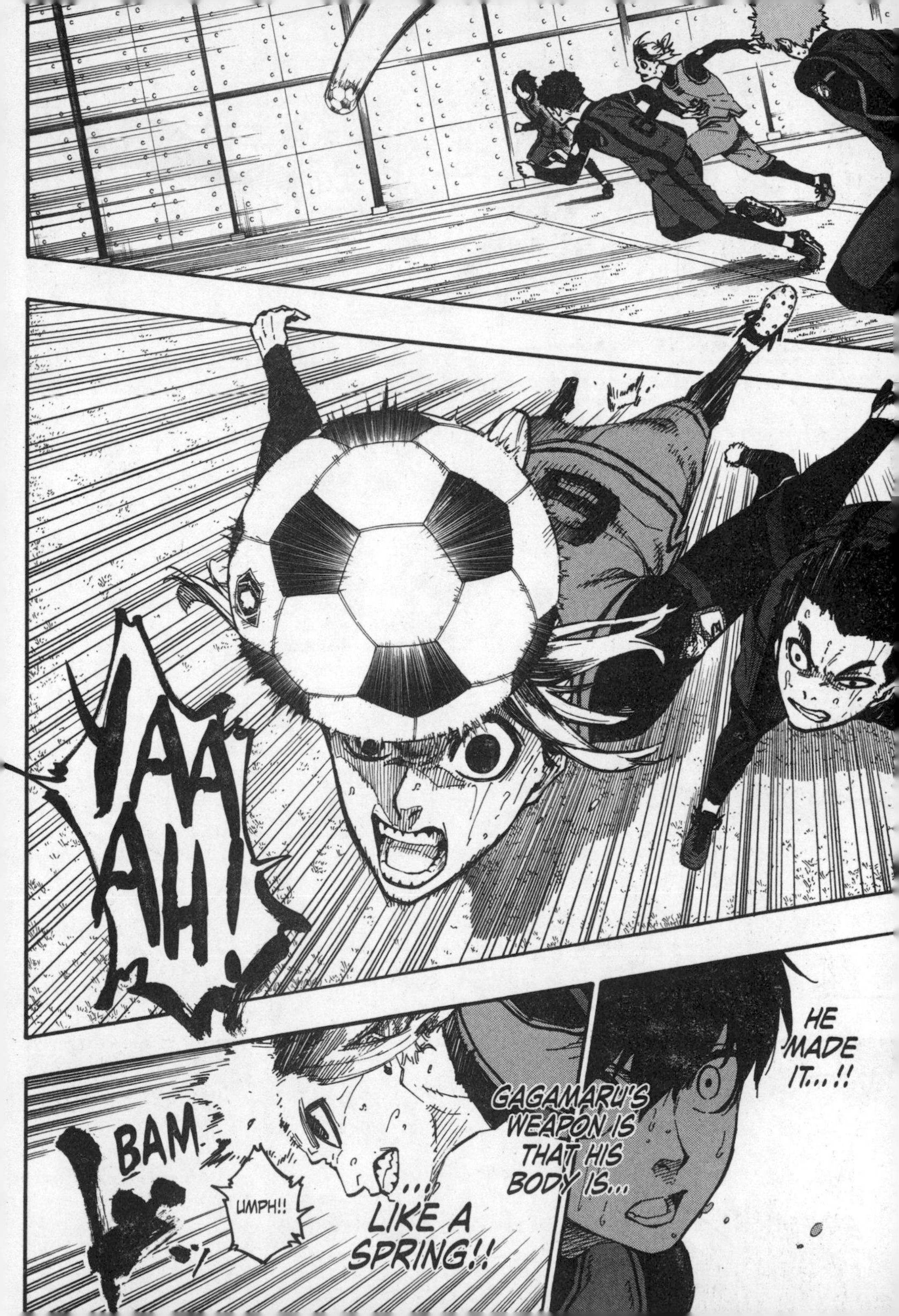
YAAAAH!
HE MADE IT...!!
GAGAMARU'S WEAPON IS THAT HIS BODY IS...
...LIKE A SPRING!!
UMPH!!
BAM

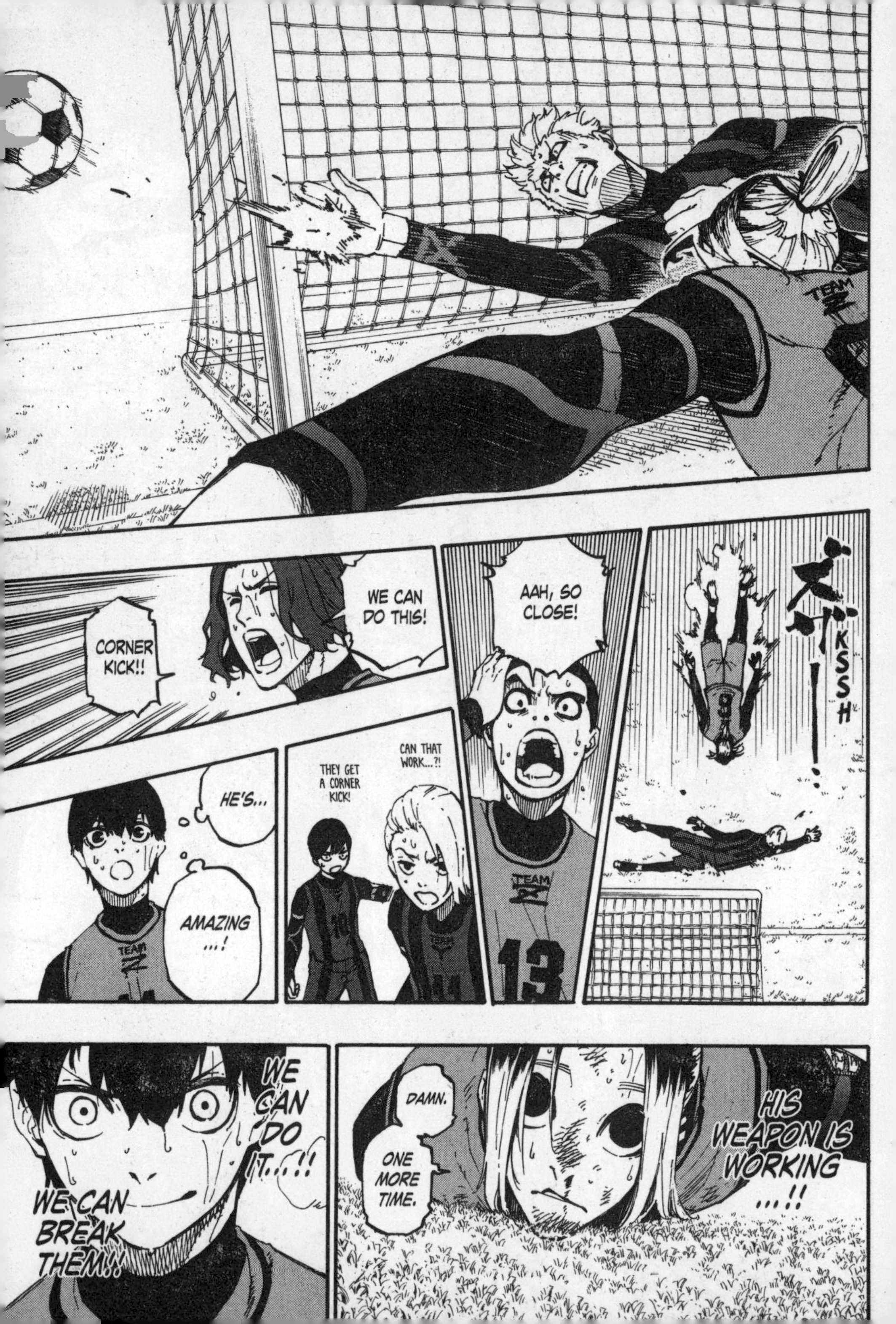
KSSH
AAH, SO CLOSE!
WE CAN DO THIS!
CORNER KICK!!
CAN THAT WORK...?!
THEY GET A CORNER KICK!
HE'S...
AMAZING ...!
HIS WEAPON IS WORKING ...!!
DAMN.
ONE MORE TIME.
WE CAN DO IT...!!
WE CAN BREAK THEM!!

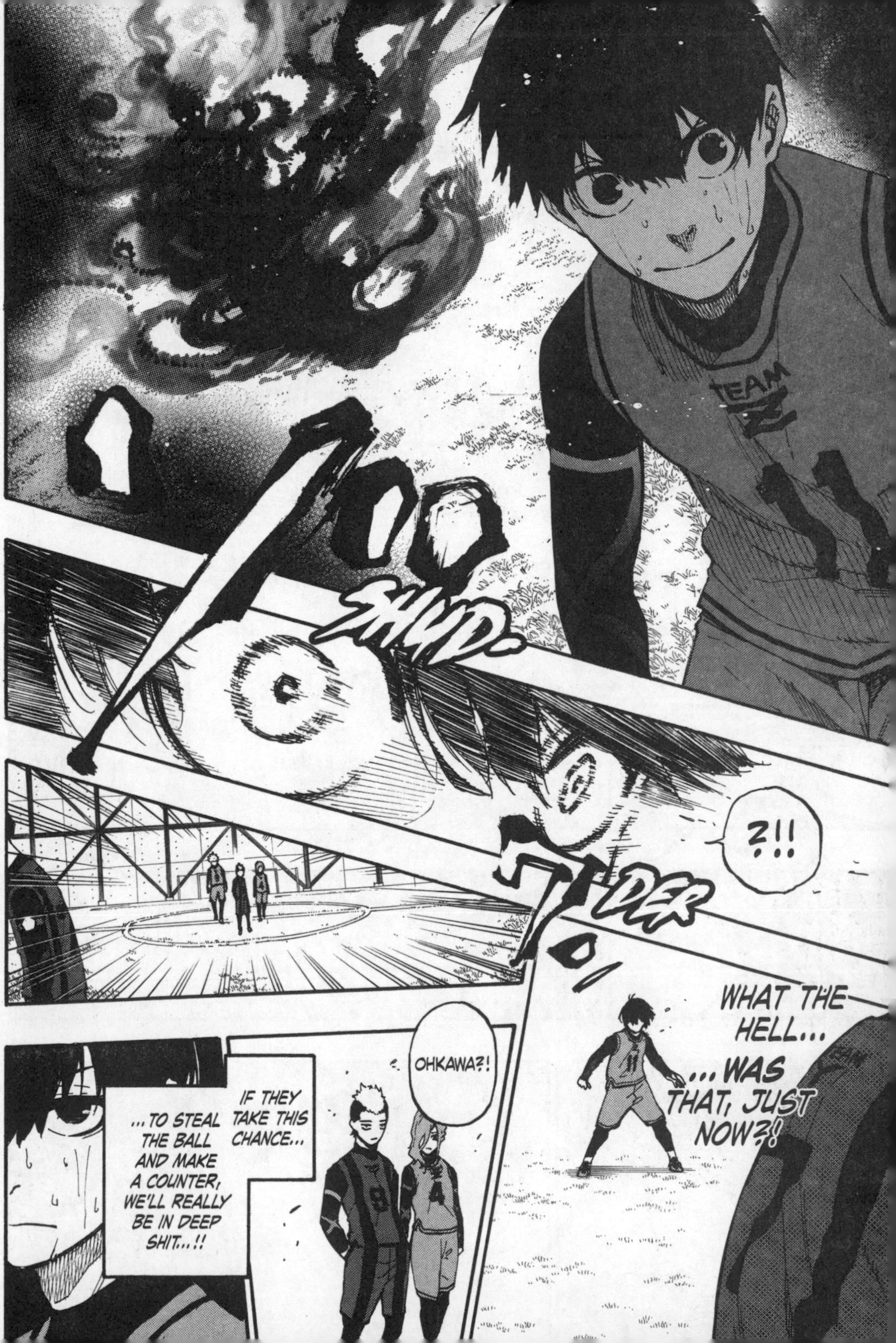
SHUD
?!!
WHAT THE HELL...
...WAS THAT, JUST NOW?!
OHKAWA?!
IF THEY TAKE THIS CHANCE...
...TO STEAL THE BALL AND MAKE A COUNTER, WE'LL REALLY BE IN DEEP SHIT...!!

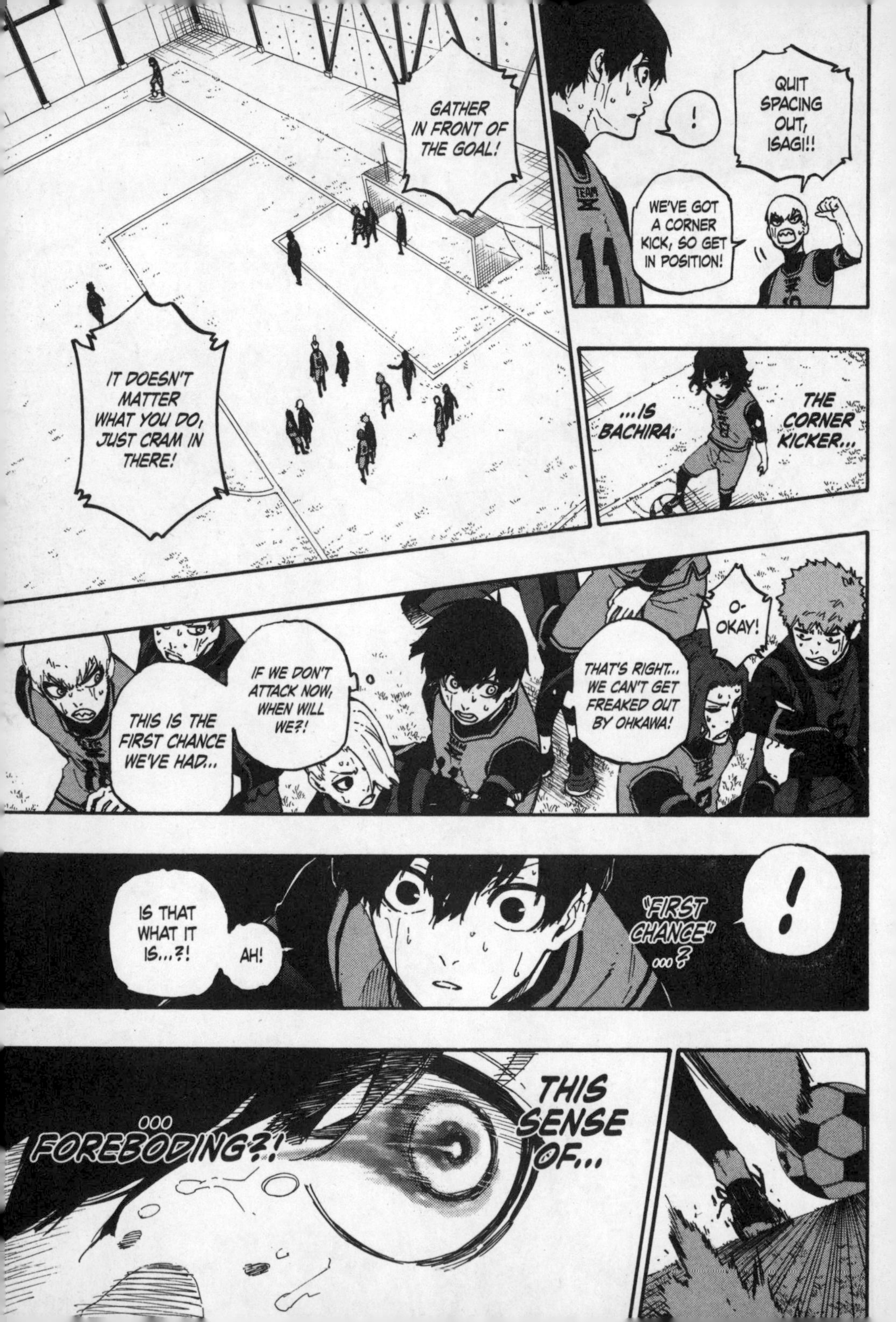
QUIT SPACING OUT, ISAGI!!
!
WE'VE GOT A CORNER KICK, SO GET IN POSITION!
THE CORNER KICKER...
...IS BACHIRA.
GATHER IN FRONT OF THE GOAL!
IT DOESN'T MATTER WHAT YOU DO, JUST CRAM IN THERE!
O-OKAY!
THAT'S RIGHT... WE CAN'T GET FREAKED OUT BY OHKAWA!
IF WE DON'T ATTACK NOW, WHEN WILL WE?!
THIS IS THE FIRST CHANCE WE'VE HAD...
!
"FIRST CHANCE"...?
AH!
IS THAT WHAT IT IS...?!
THIS SENSE OF...
...FOREBODING?!

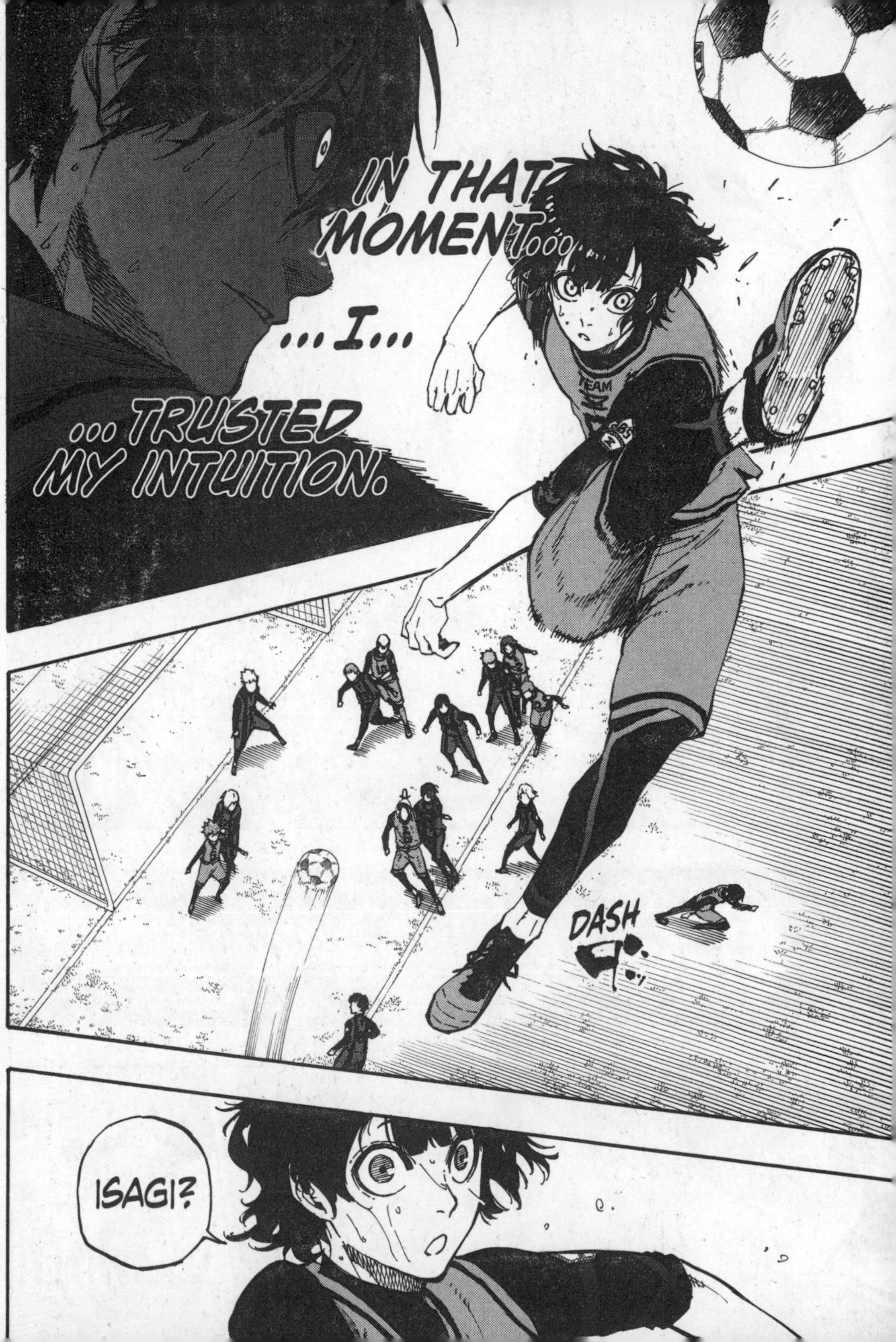
IN THAT MOMENT...
...I...
...TRUSTED MY INTUITION.
DASH
ISAGI?

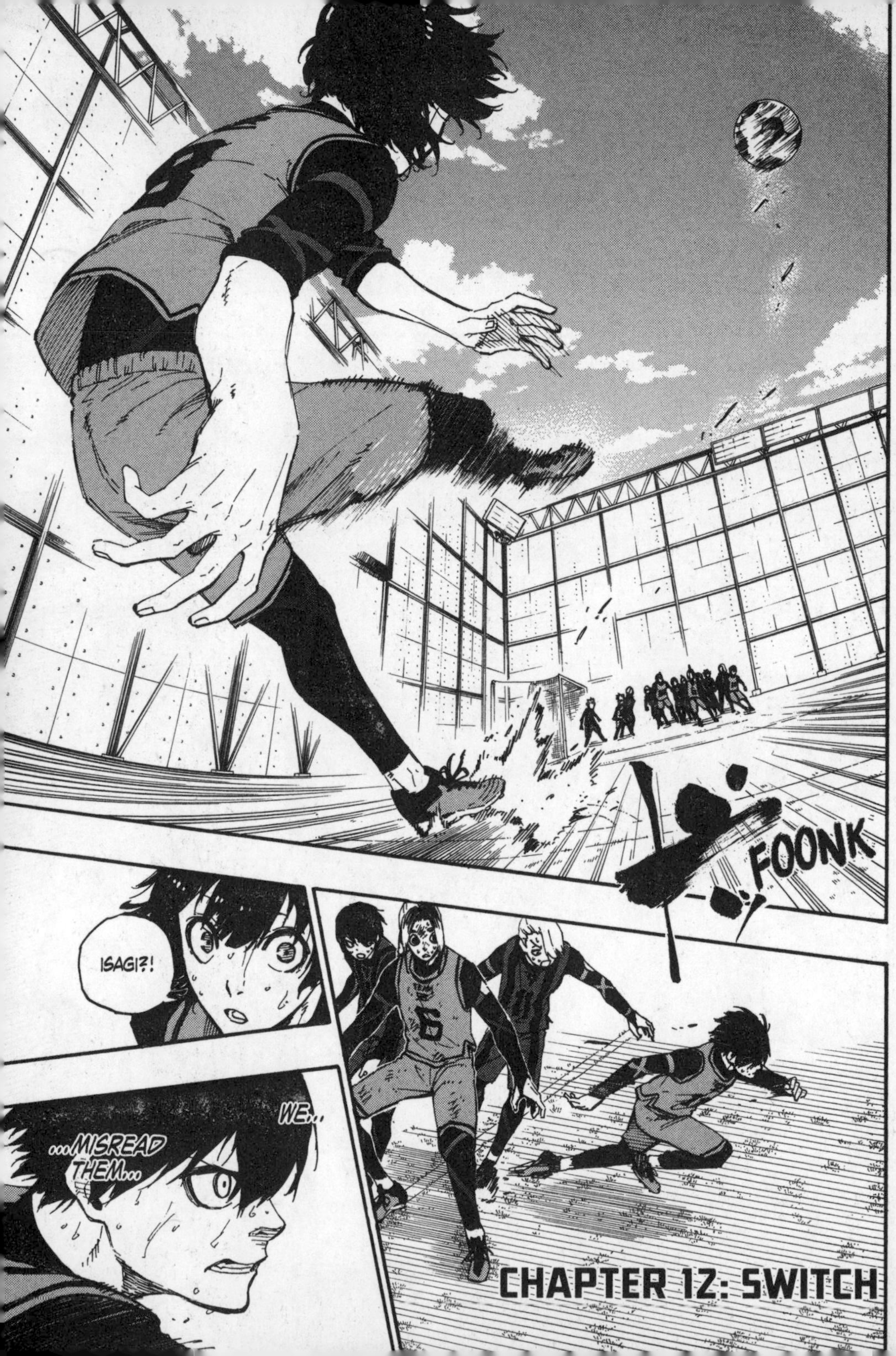
FOONK
ISAGI?!
WE...
...MISREAD THEM...

CHAPTER 12: SWITCH

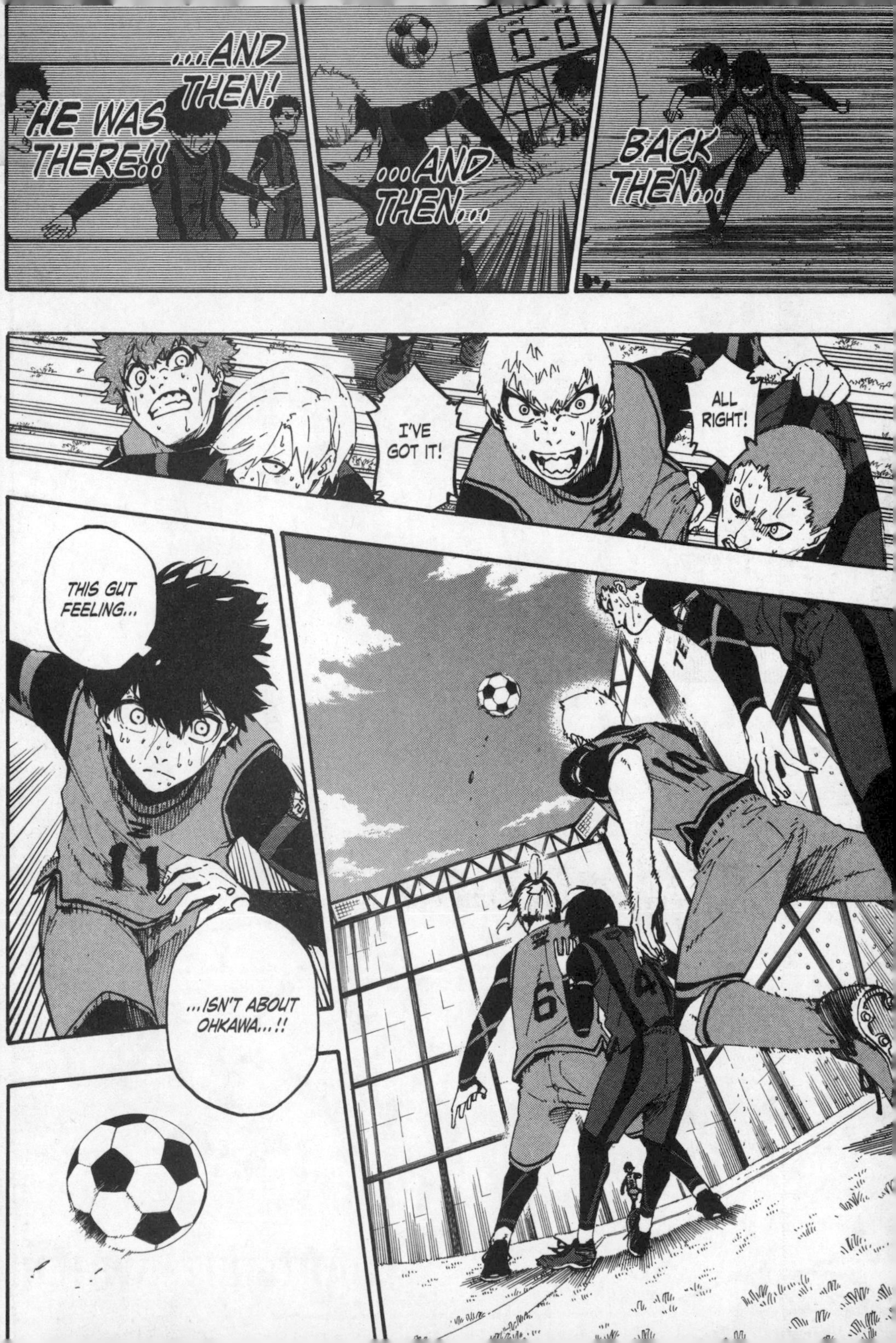
BACK THEN...
...AND THEN...
...AND THEN!
HE WAS THERE!!
ALL RIGHT!
I'VE GOT IT!
THIS GUT FEELING...
...ISN'T ABOUT OHKAWA...!!

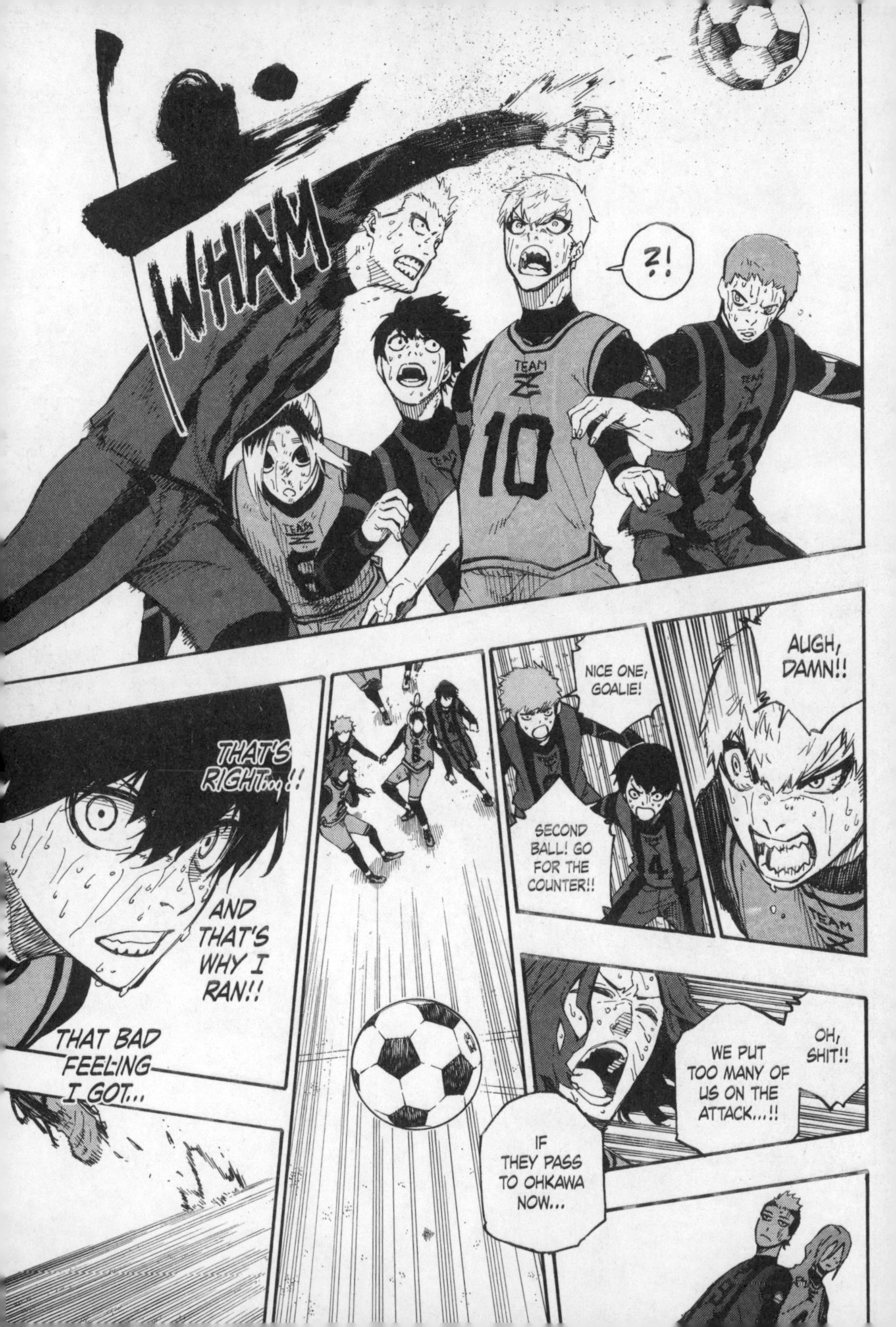
WHAM
?!
AUGH, DAMN!!
NICE ONE, GOALIE!
SECOND BALL! GO FOR THE COUNTER!!
THAT'S RIGHT...!!
AND THAT'S WHY I RAN!!
THAT BAD FEELING I GOT...
OH, SHIT!!
WE PUT TOO MANY OF US ON THE ATTACK...!!
IF THEY PASS TO OHKAWA NOW...

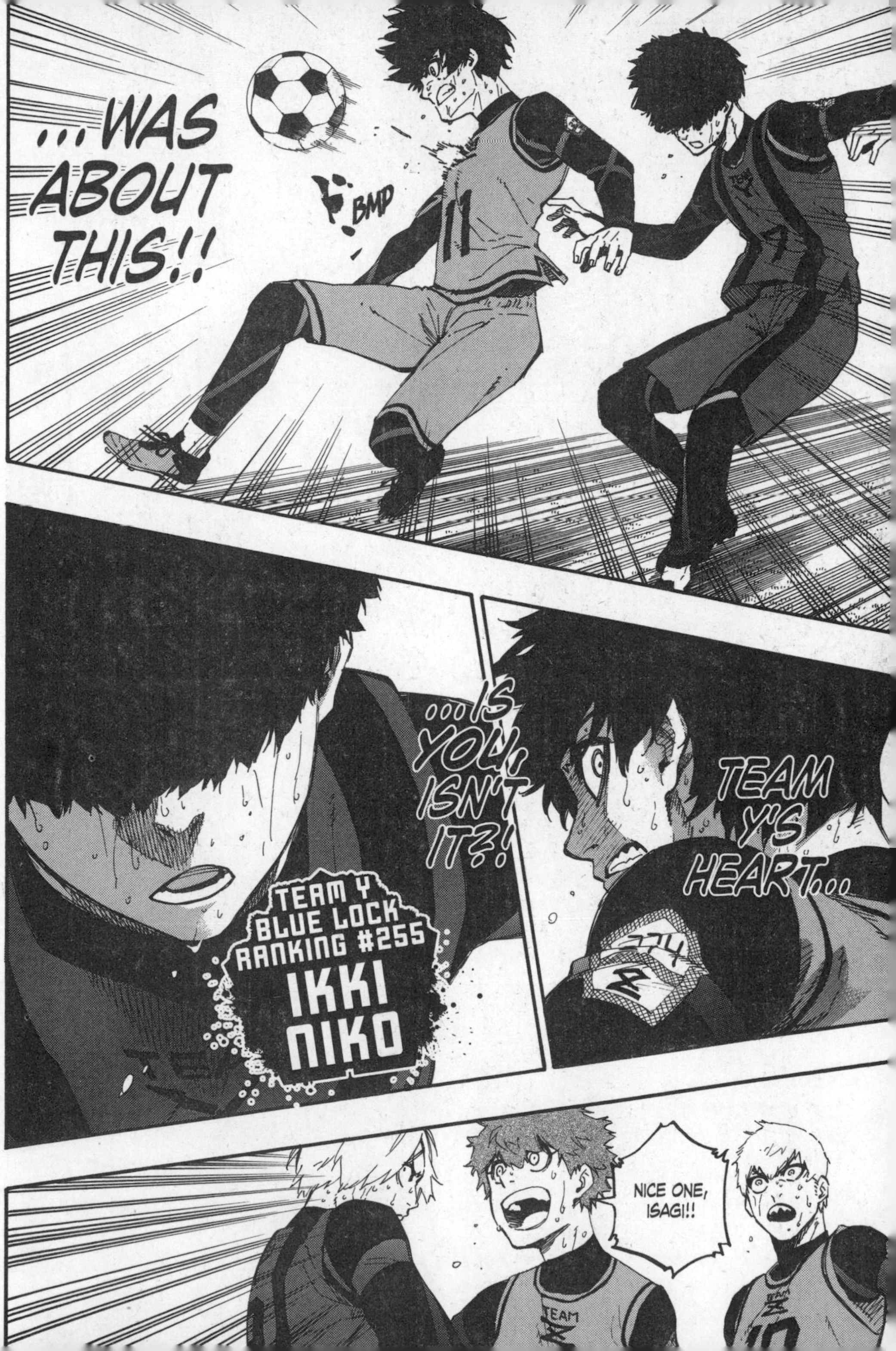
...WAS ABOUT THIS!!
BMP
TEAM Y'S HEART...
...IS YOU, ISN'T IT?!
TEAM Y BLUE LOCK RANKING #255
IKKI NIKO
NICE ONE, ISAGI!!

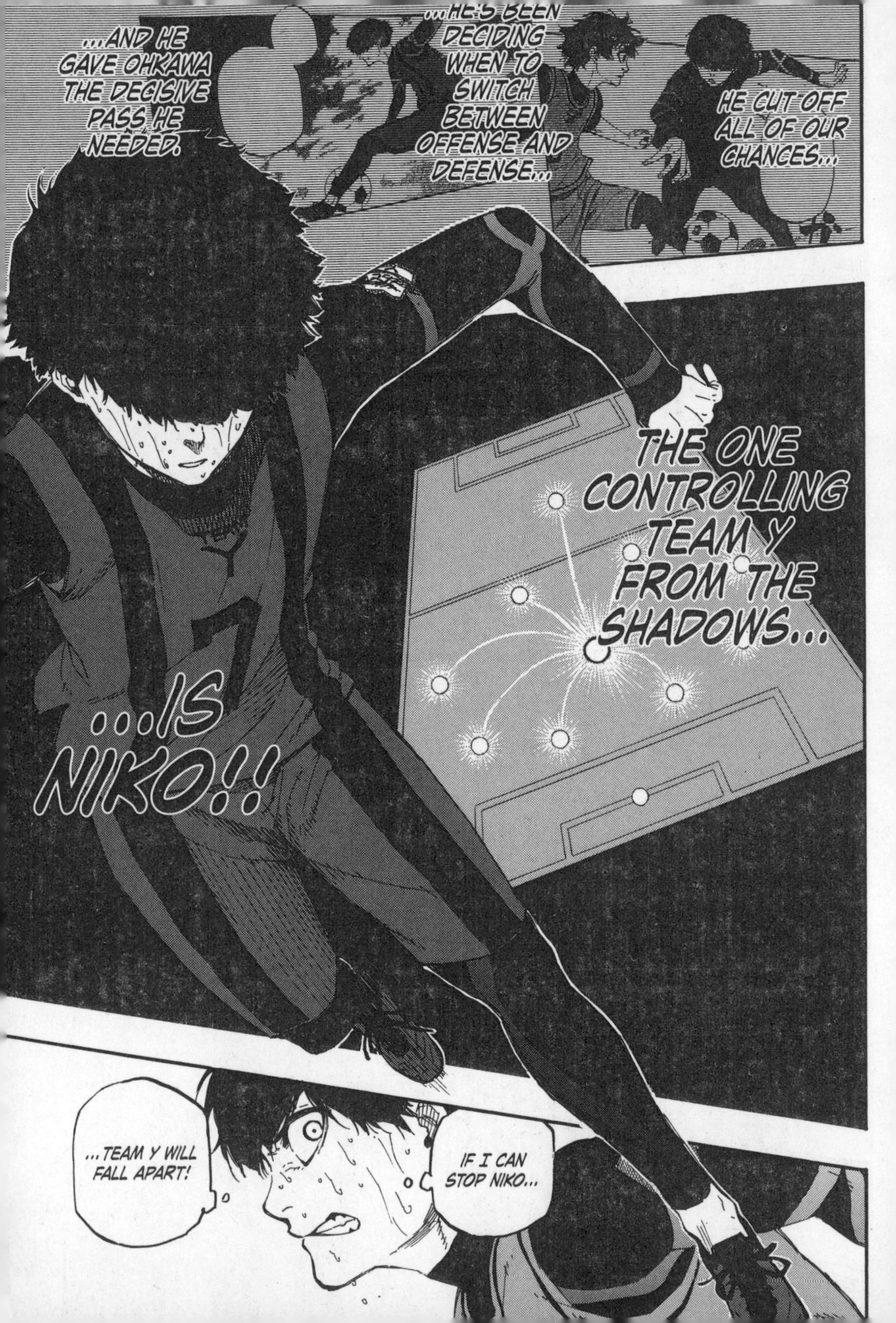
HE CUT OFF ALL OF OUR CHANCES...
...HE'S BEEN DECIDING WHEN TO SWITCH BETWEEN OFFENSE AND DEFENSE...
...AND HE GAVE OHKAWA THE DECISIVE PASS HE NEEDED.
THE ONE CONTROLLING TEAM Y FROM THE SHADOWS...
...IS NIKO!!
IF I CAN STOP NIKO...
...TEAM Y WILL FALL APART!

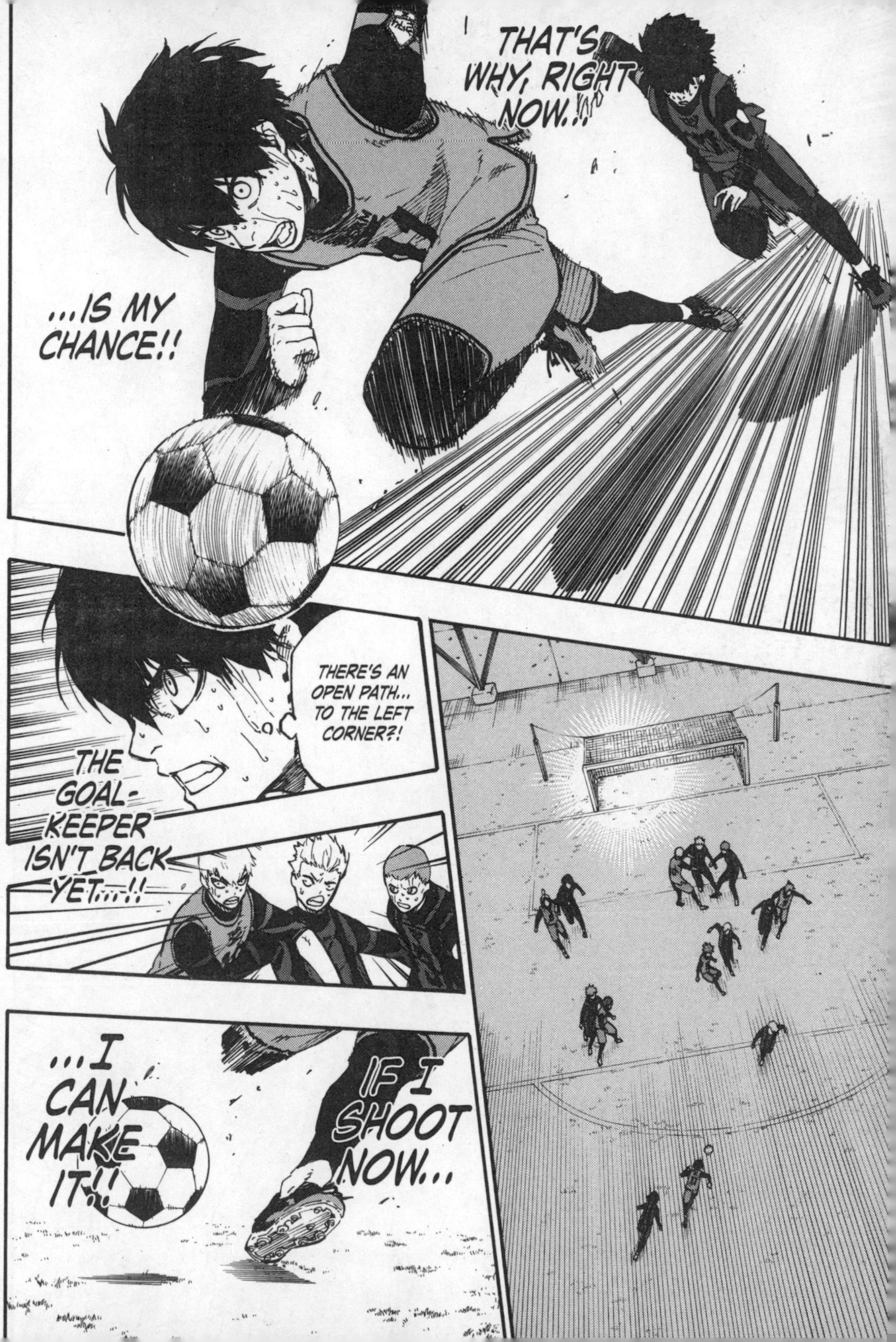
THAT'S WHY, RIGHT NOW..!!
...IS MY CHANCE!!
THERE'S AN OPEN PATH... TO THE LEFT CORNER?!
THE GOAL-KEEPER ISN'T BACK YET...!!
IF I SHOOT NOW...
...I CAN MAKE IT!!

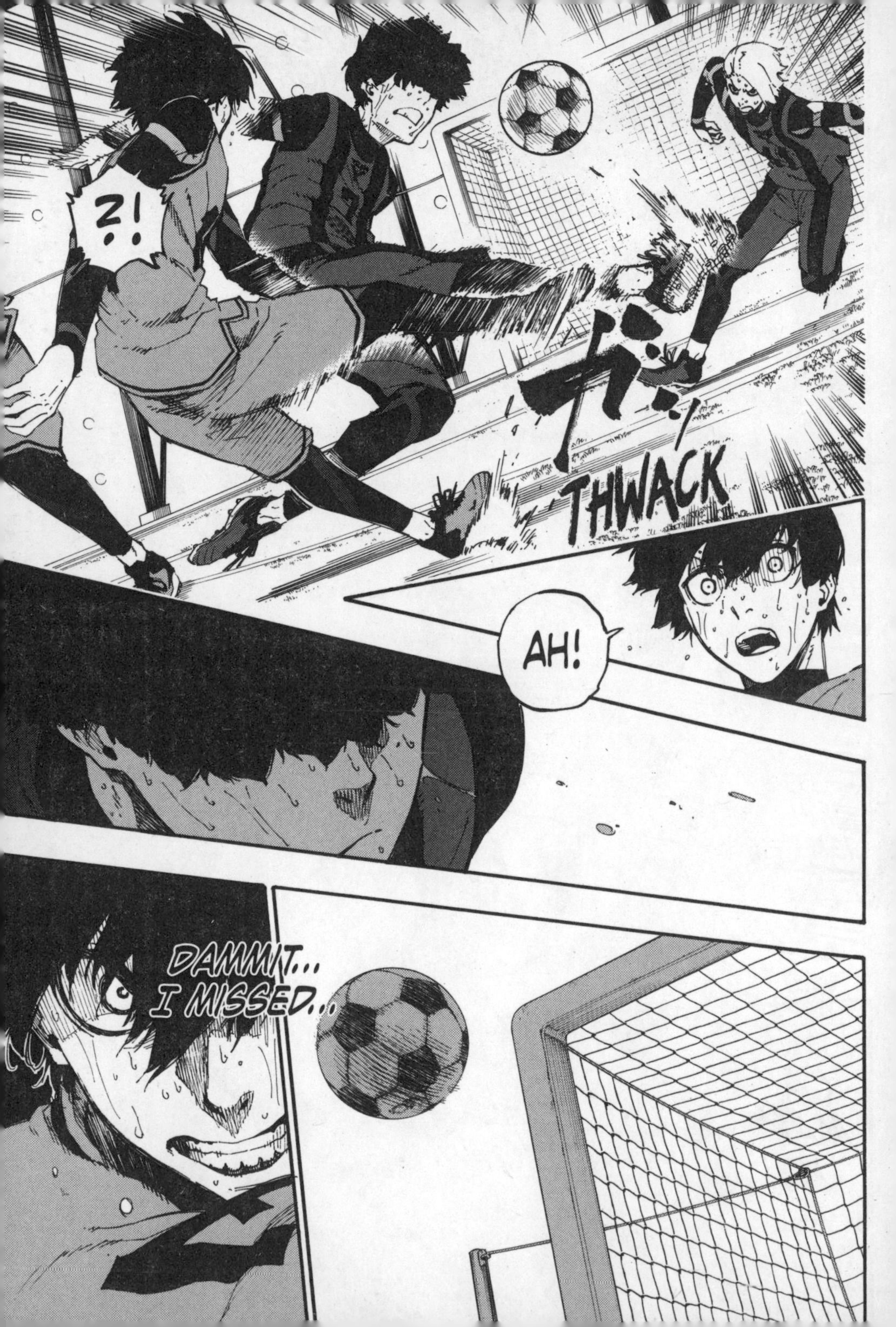
?!
THWACK
AH!
DAMMIT... I MISSED...

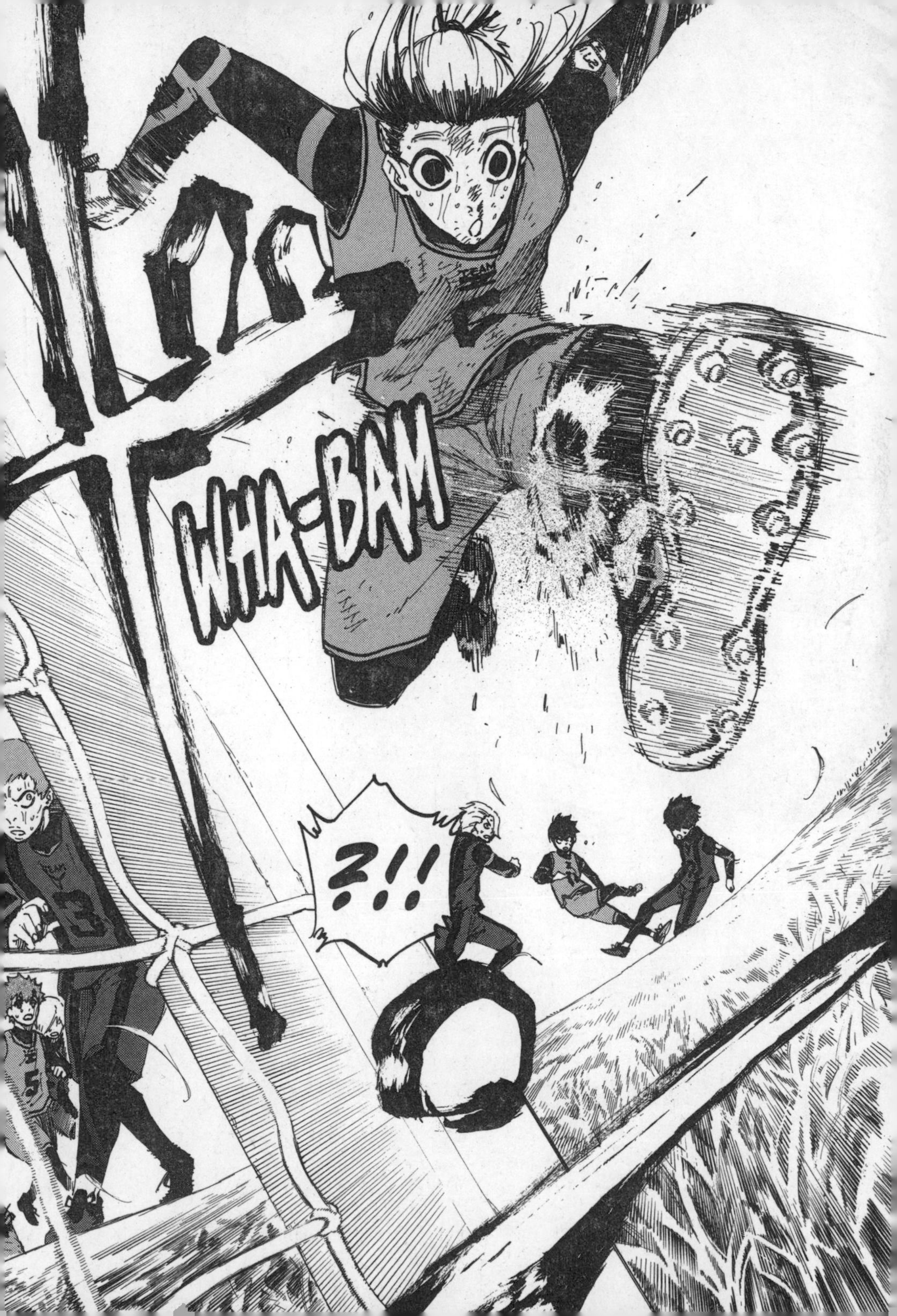
WHA-BAM
?!!

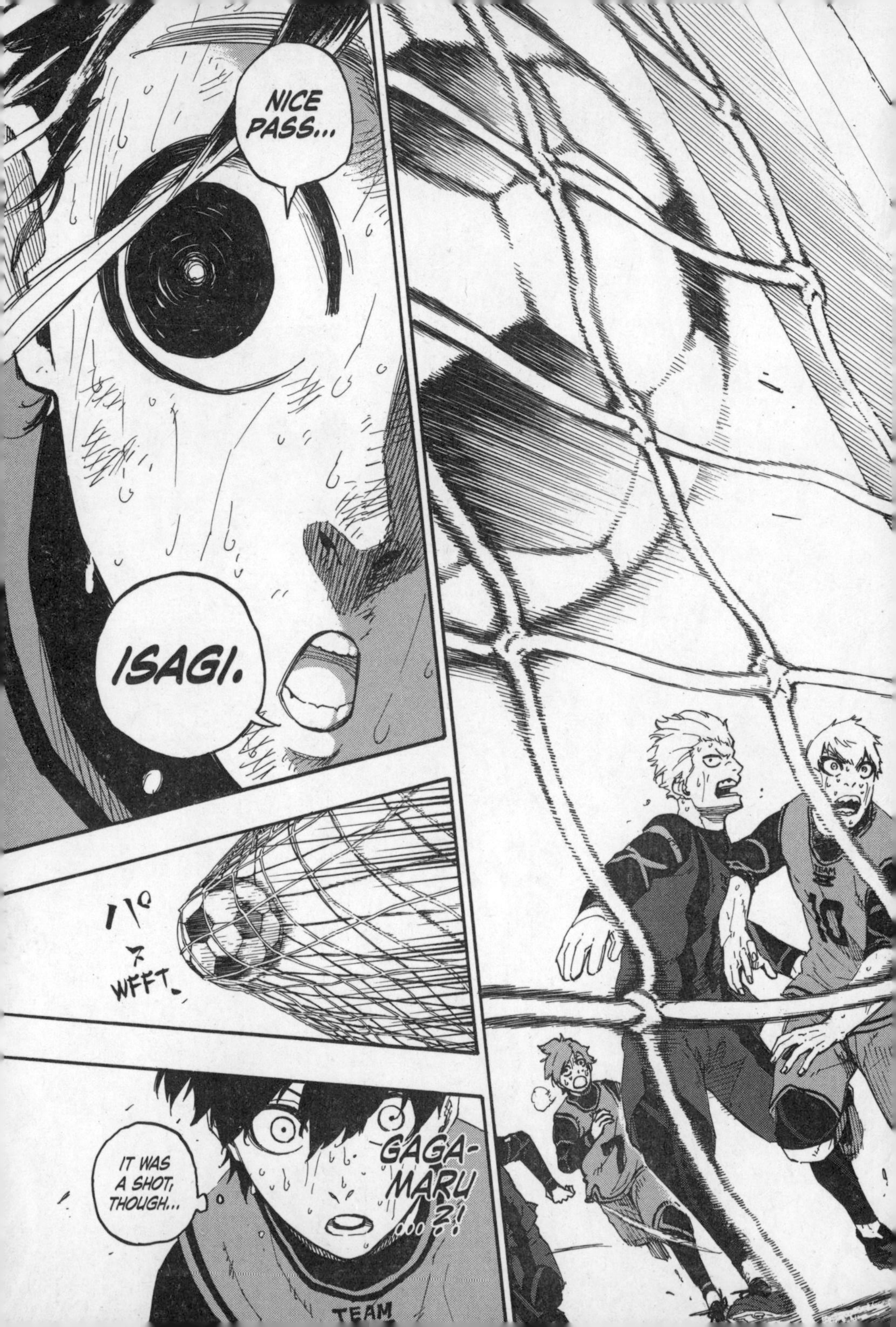
NICE PASS...
ISAGI.
WFFT
IT WAS A SHOT, THOUGH...
GAGAMARU...?!

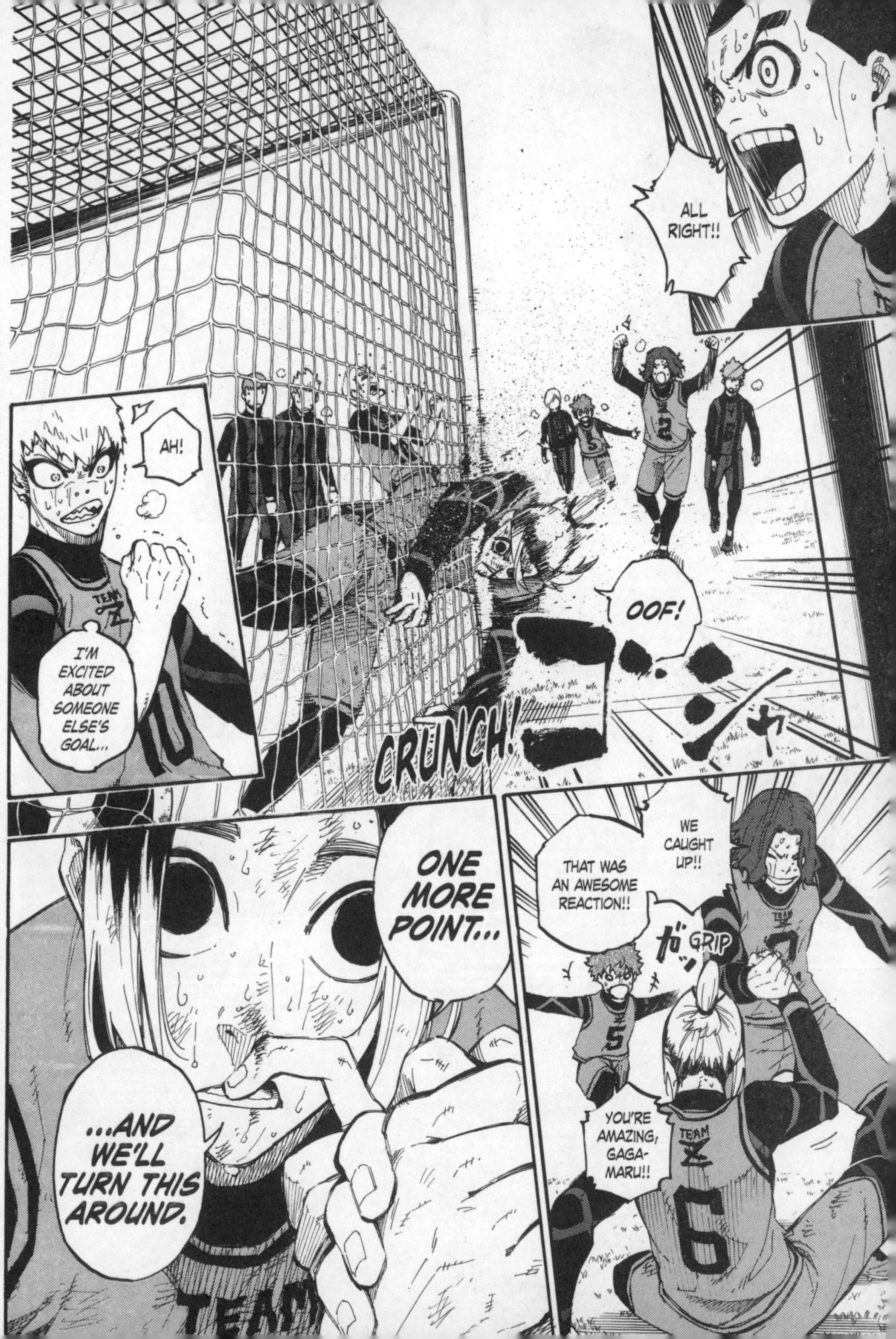
ALL RIGHT!!
OOF!
CRUNCH!
AH!
I'M EXCITED ABOUT SOMEONE ELSE'S GOAL...
WE CAUGHT UP!!
THAT WAS AN AWESOME REACTION!!
GRIP
YOU'RE AMAZING, GAGAMARU!!
ONE MORE POINT...
...AND WE'LL TURN THIS AROUND.

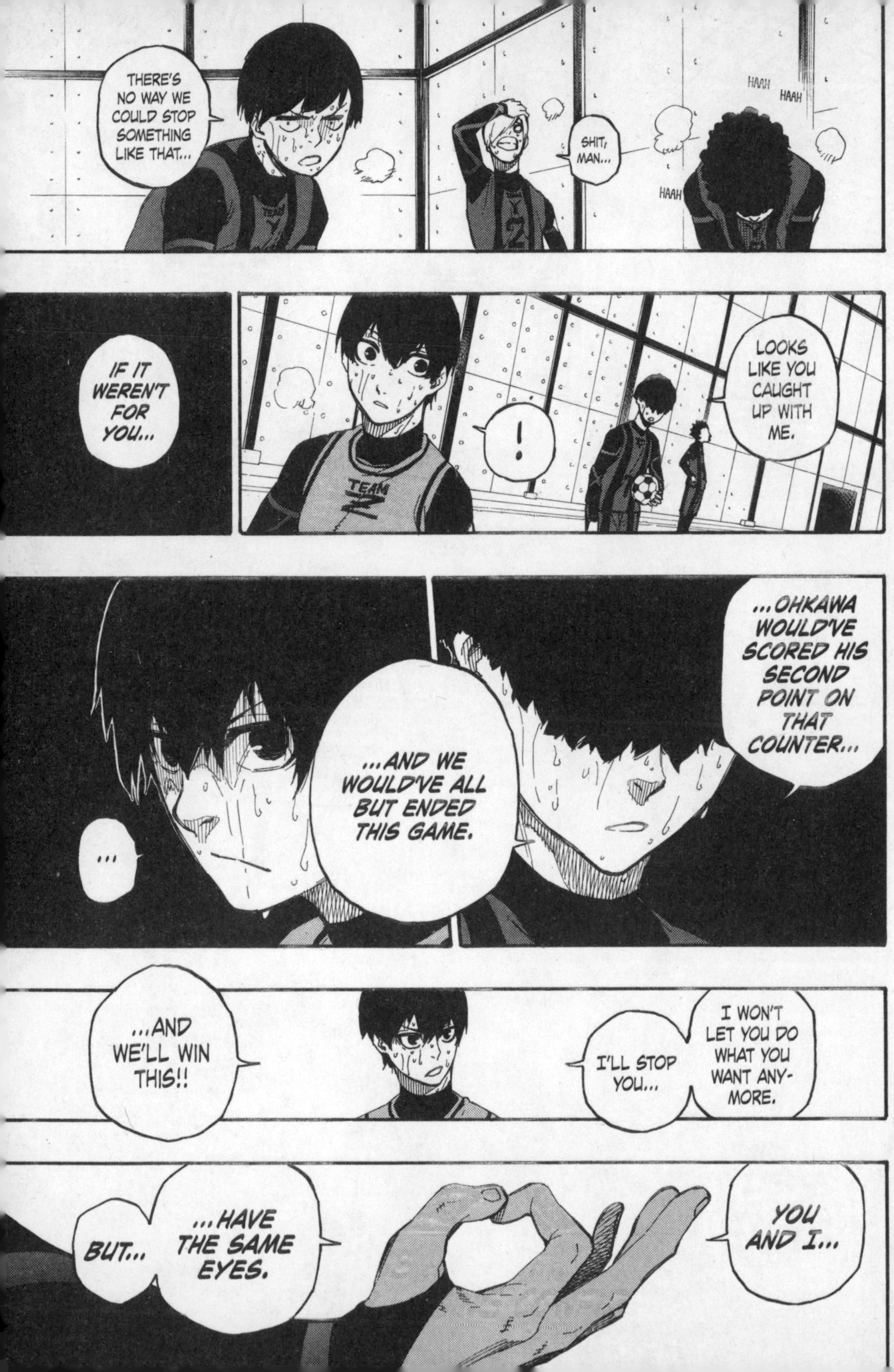
HAAH
HAAH
SHIT, MAN...
HAAH
THERE'S NO WAY WE COULD STOP SOMETHING LIKE THAT...
LOOKS LIKE YOU CAUGHT UP WITH ME.
!
IF IT WEREN'T FOR YOU...
...OHKAWA WOULD'VE SCORED HIS SECOND POINT ON THAT COUNTER...
...AND WE WOULD'VE ALL BUT ENDED THIS GAME.
...
I WON'T LET YOU DO WHAT YOU WANT ANY-MORE.
I'LL STOP YOU...
...AND WE'LL WIN THIS!!
YOU AND I...
...HAVE THE SAME EYES.
BUT...

...YOU CAN'T WIN AGAINST ME.
I'M THE ONE IN CONTROL OF THIS GAME.
JUST YOU WATCH... YOU BANGED BASTARD.
TEAM
1-1
45
SECOND HALF 15 MIN.
NEXT FORMATION
NARUHAYA
ISAGI
GAGAMARU
IGA-GURI
IMAMURA
KUNIGAMI
BACHIRA
RAICHI
CHIGIRI
KUON
HOLD
IEMON
HOLD
ALL RIGHT!!
LET'S GO ALL IN ON THIS ATTACK!
TEAM Z BLUE LOCK RANKING #272
ASAHI NARUHAYA

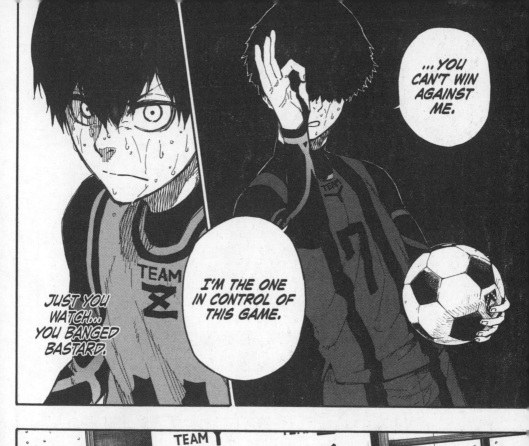

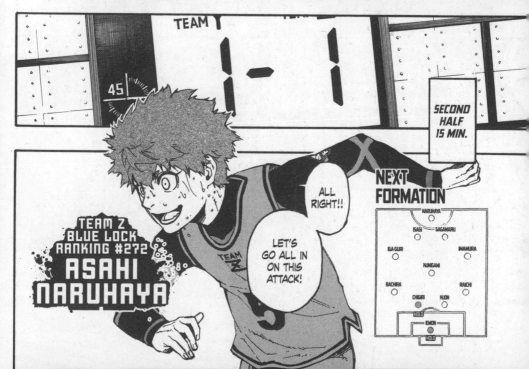

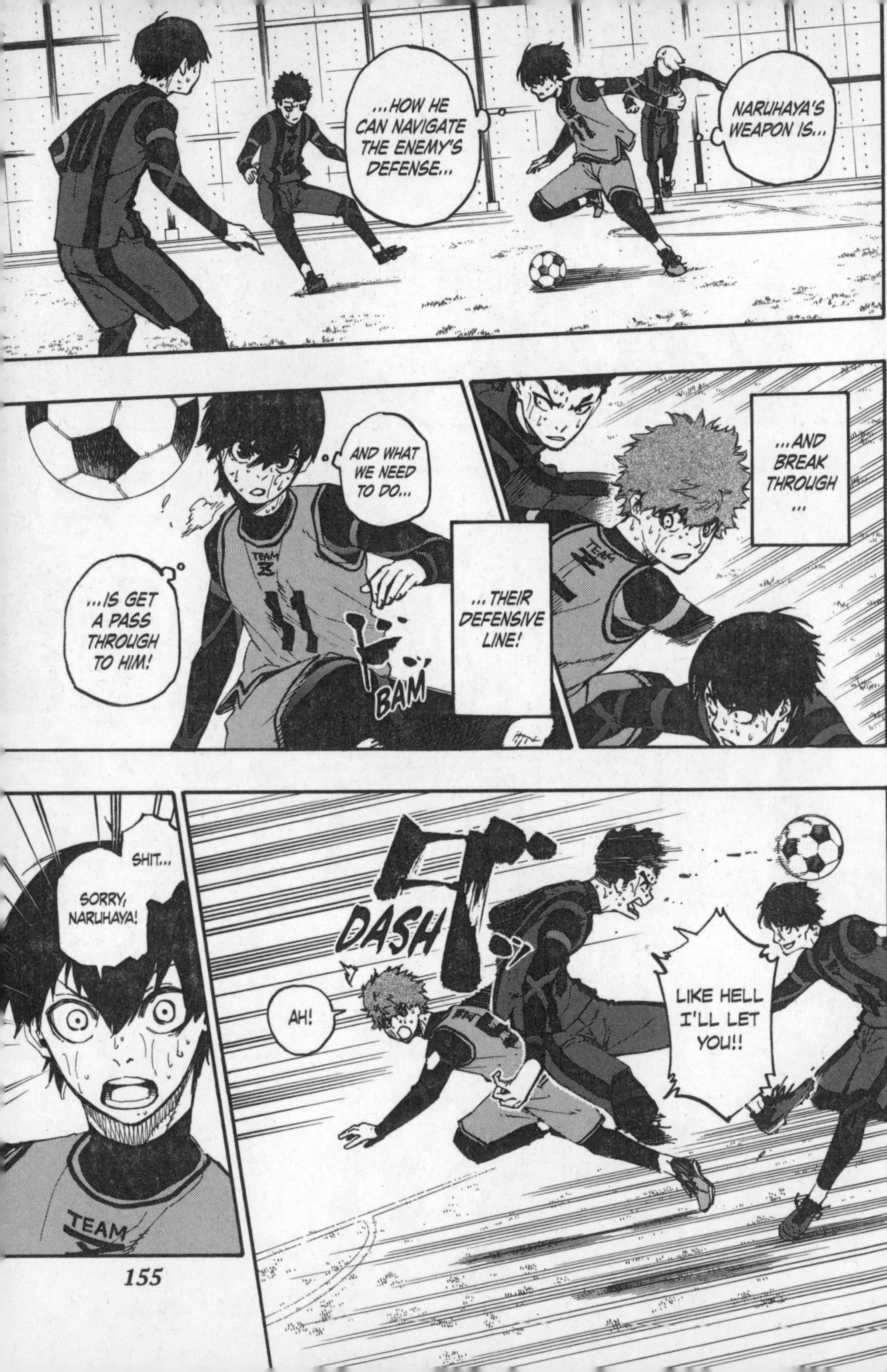

NARUHAYA'S WEAPON IS...
...HOW HE CAN NAVIGATE THE ENEMY'S DEFENSE...
...AND BREAK THROUGH ...
...THEIR DEFENSIVE LINE!
AND WHAT WE NEED TO DO...
...IS GET A PASS THROUGH TO HIM!
BAM
DASH
LIKE HELL I'LL LET YOU!!
AH!
SHIT...
SORRY, NARUHAYA!

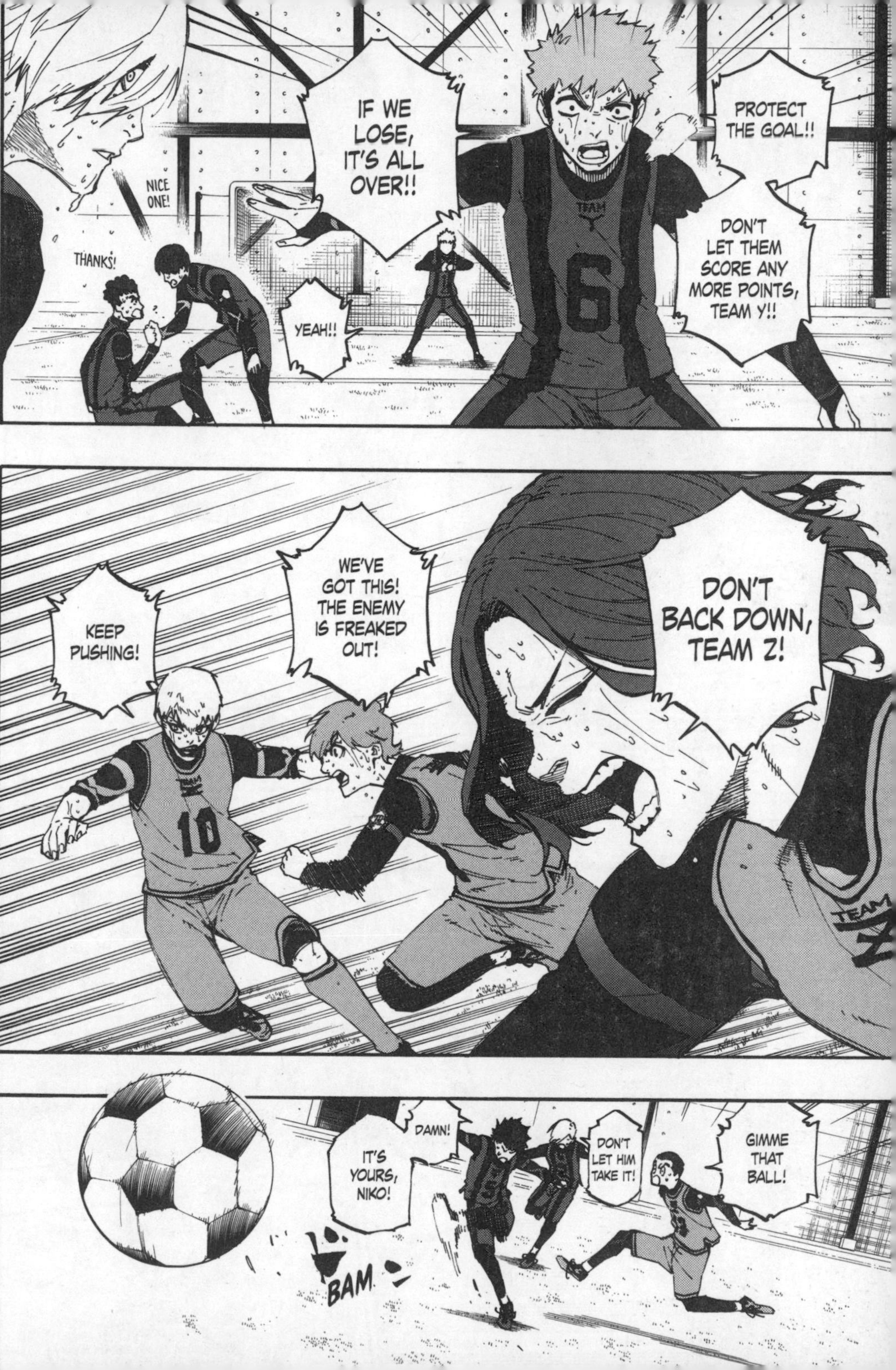
PROTECT THE GOAL!!
DON'T LET THEM SCORE ANY MORE POINTS, TEAM Y!!
IF WE LOSE, IT'S ALL OVER!!
YEAH!!
NICE ONE!
THANKS!
DON'T BACK DOWN, TEAM Z!
WE'VE GOT THIS! THE ENEMY IS FREAKED OUT!
KEEP PUSHING!
GIMME THAT BALL!
DON'T LET HIM TAKE IT!
DAMN!
IT'S YOURS, NIKO!
BAM

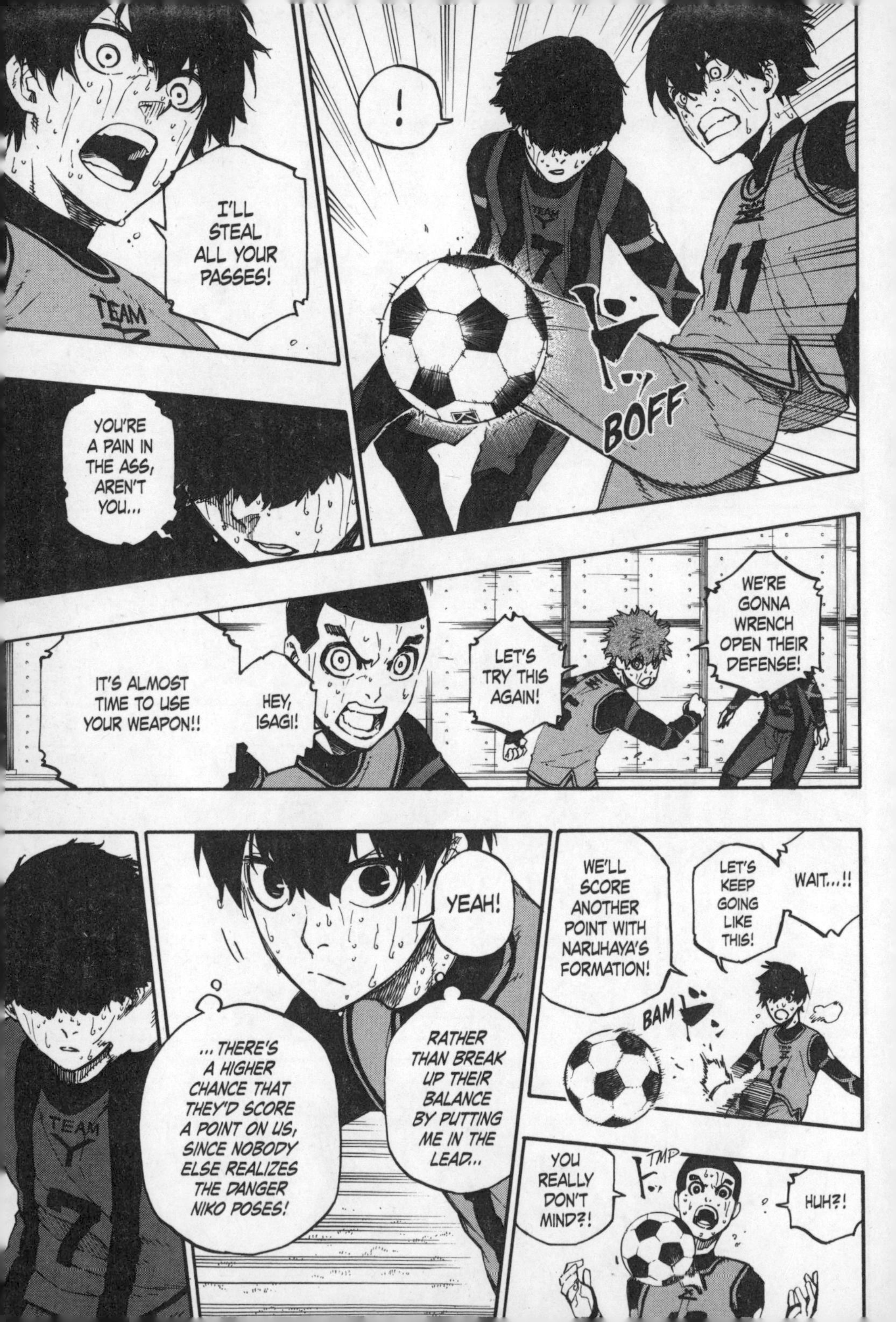
!
BOFF
I'LL STEAL ALL YOUR PASSES!
YOU'RE A PAIN IN THE ASS, AREN'T YOU...
WE'RE GONNA WRENCH OPEN THEIR DEFENSE!
LET'S TRY THIS AGAIN!
HEY, ISAGI!
IT'S ALMOST TIME TO USE YOUR WEAPON!!
WAIT...!!
LET'S KEEP GOING LIKE THIS!
WE'LL SCORE ANOTHER POINT WITH NARUHAYA'S FORMATION!
BAM
HUH?!
TMP
YOU REALLY DON'T MIND?!
YEAH!
RATHER THAN BREAK UP THEIR BALANCE BY PUTTING ME IN THE LEAD...
...THERE'S A HIGHER CHANCE THAT THEY'D SCORE A POINT ON US, SINCE NOBODY ELSE REALIZES THE DANGER NIKO POSES!

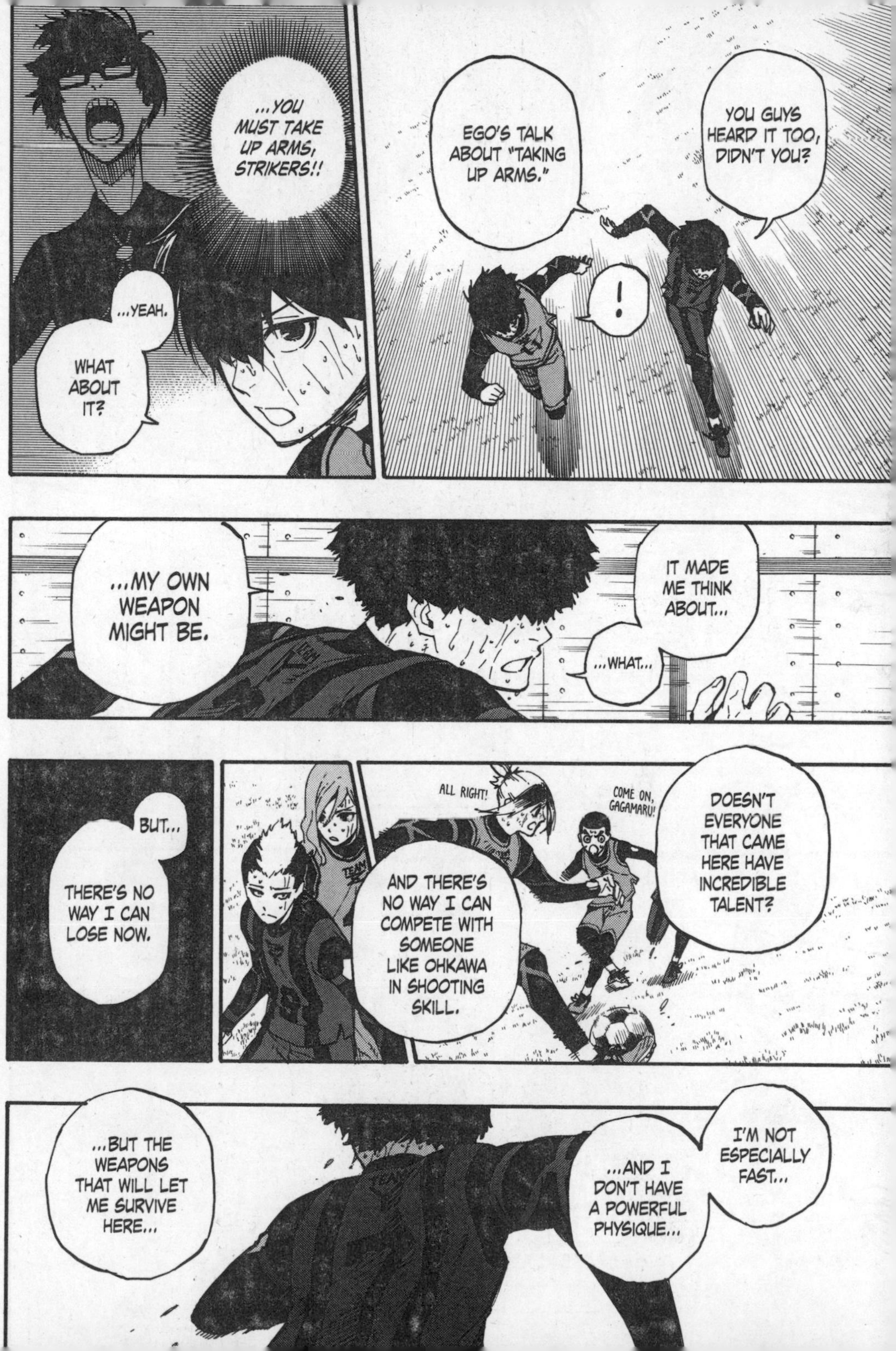
YOU GUYS HEARD IT TOO, DIDN'T YOU?
EGO'S TALK ABOUT "TAKING UP ARMS."
!
...YOU MUST TAKE UP ARMS, STRIKERS!!
...YEAH.
WHAT ABOUT IT?
IT MADE ME THINK ABOUT...
...WHAT...
...MY OWN WEAPON MIGHT BE.
DOESN'T EVERYONE THAT CAME HERE HAVE INCREDIBLE TALENT?
COME ON, GAGAMARU!
ALL RIGHT!
AND THERE'S NO WAY I CAN COMPETE WITH SOMEONE LIKE OHKAWA IN SHOOTING SKILL.
BUT...
THERE'S NO WAY I CAN LOSE NOW.
I'M NOT ESPECIALLY FAST...
...AND I DON'T HAVE A POWERFUL PHYSIQUE...
...BUT THE WEAPONS THAT WILL LET ME SURVIVE HERE...

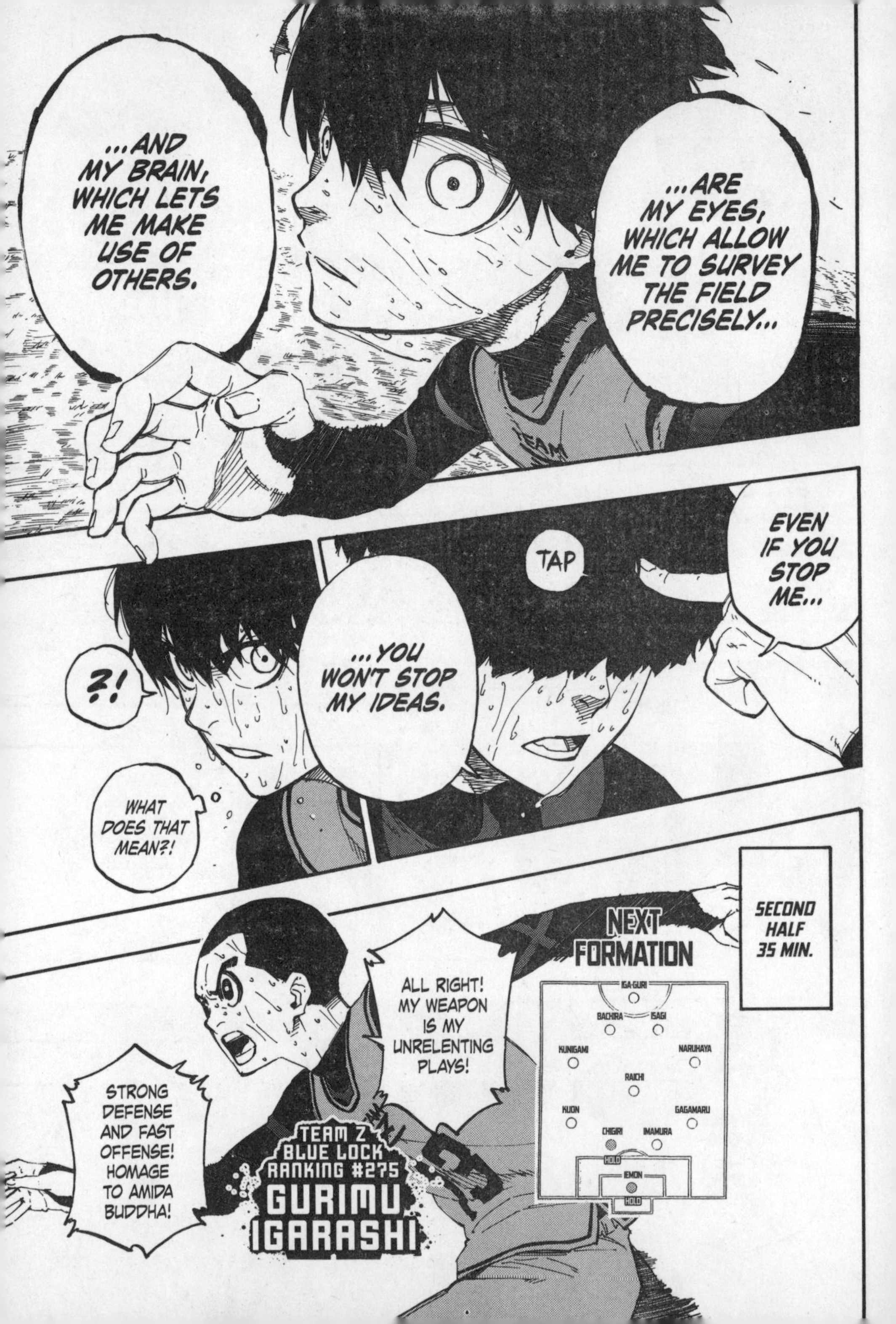
...ARE MY EYES, WHICH ALLOW ME TO SURVEY THE FIELD PRECISELY...
...AND MY BRAIN, WHICH LETS ME MAKE USE OF OTHERS.
EVEN IF YOU STOP ME...
TAP
...YOU WON'T STOP MY IDEAS.
?!
WHAT DOES THAT MEAN?!
SECOND HALF 35 MIN.
NEXT FORMATION
IGA-GURI
BACHIRA
ISAGI
KUNIGAMI
NARUHAYA
RAICHI
KUON
GAGAMARU
CHIGIRI
IMAMURA
HOLD
IEMON
HOLD
ALL RIGHT! MY WEAPON IS MY UNRELENTING PLAYS!
TEAM Z BLUE LOCK RANKING #275
GURIMU IGARASHI
STRONG DEFENSE AND FAST OFFENSE! HOMAGE TO AMIDA BUDDHA!

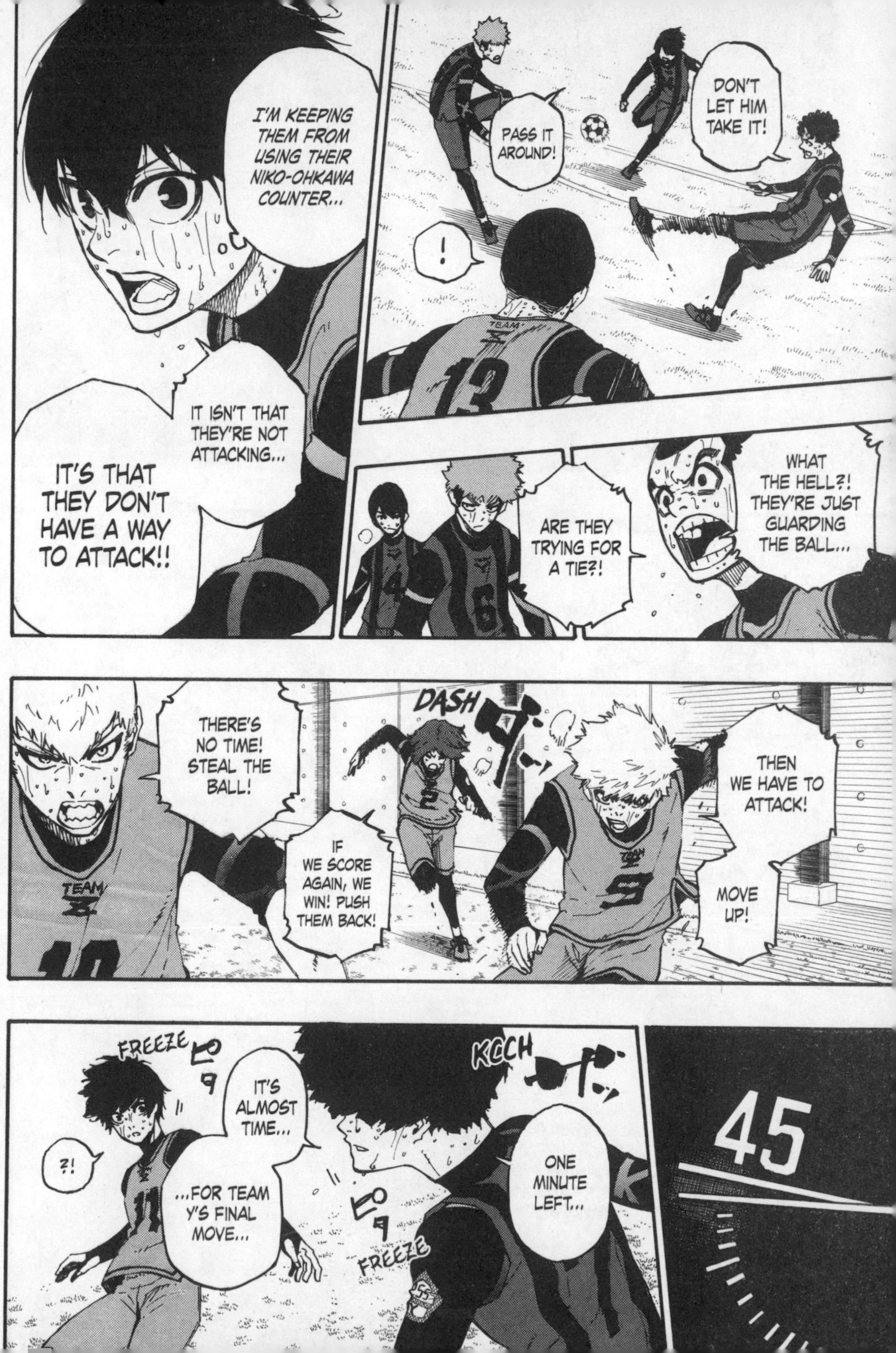
DON'T LET HIM TAKE IT!
PASS IT AROUND!
!
WHAT THE HELL?! THEY'RE JUST GUARDING THE BALL...
ARE THEY TRYING FOR A TIE?!
I'M KEEPING THEM FROM USING THEIR NIKO-OHKAWA COUNTER...
IT ISN'T THAT THEY'RE NOT ATTACKING...
IT'S THAT THEY DON'T HAVE A WAY TO ATTACK!!
THEN WE HAVE TO ATTACK!
MOVE UP!
DASH
THERE'S NO TIME! STEAL THE BALL!
IF WE SCORE AGAIN, WE WIN! PUSH THEM BACK!
45
KCCH
ONE MINUTE LEFT...
IT'S ALMOST TIME...
FREEZE
...FOR TEAM Y'S FINAL MOVE...
FREEZE
?!

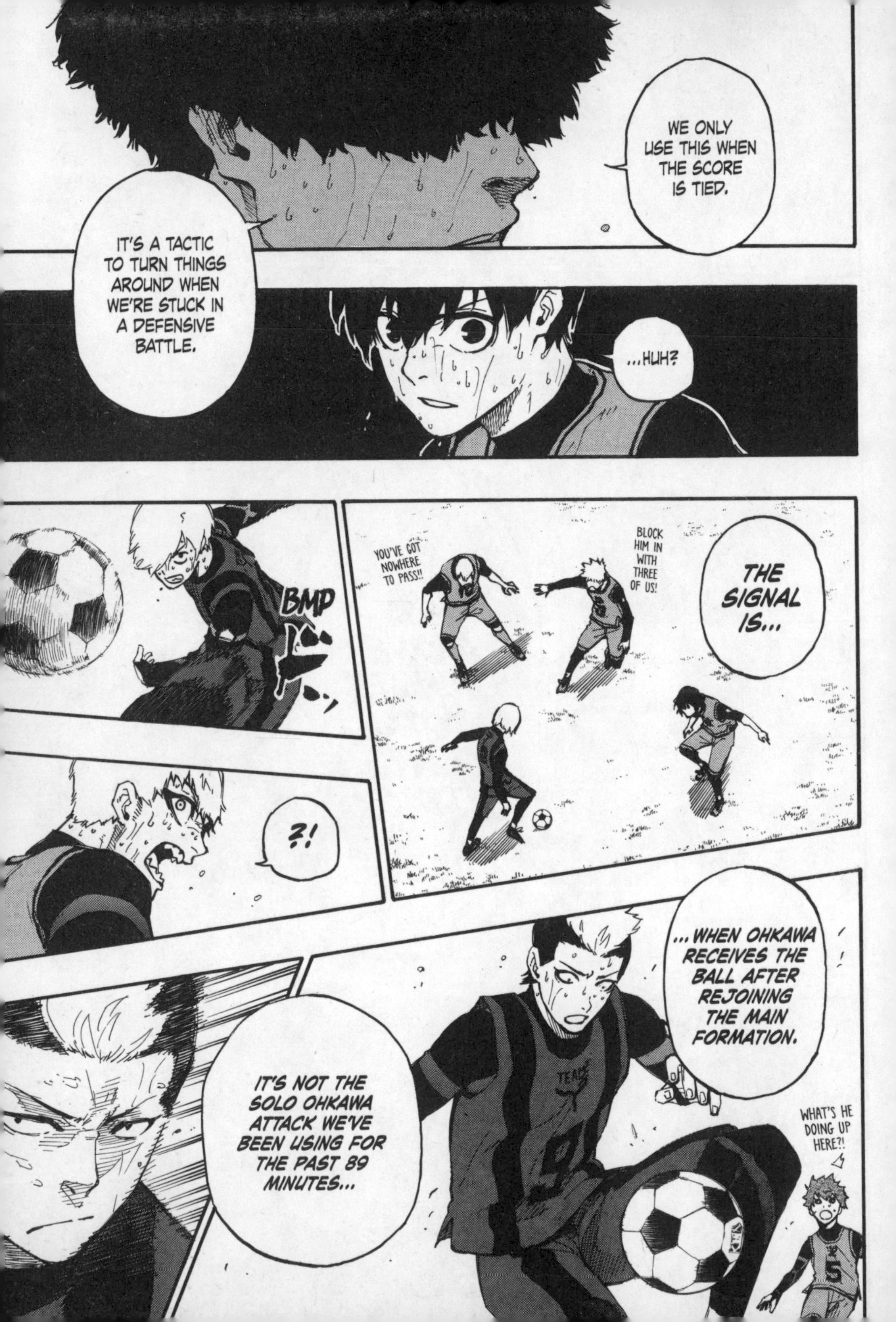
WE ONLY USE THIS WHEN THE SCORE IS TIED.
IT'S A TACTIC TO TURN THINGS AROUND WHEN WE'RE STUCK IN A DEFENSIVE BATTLE.
...HUH?
THE SIGNAL IS...
BLOCK HIM IN WITH THREE OF US!
YOU'VE GOT NOWHERE TO PASS!!
BMP
?!
...WHEN OHKAWA RECEIVES THE BALL AFTER REJOINING THE MAIN FORMATION.
WHAT'S HE DOING UP HERE?!
IT'S NOT THE SOLO OHKAWA ATTACK WE'VE BEEN USING FOR THE PAST 89 MINUTES...

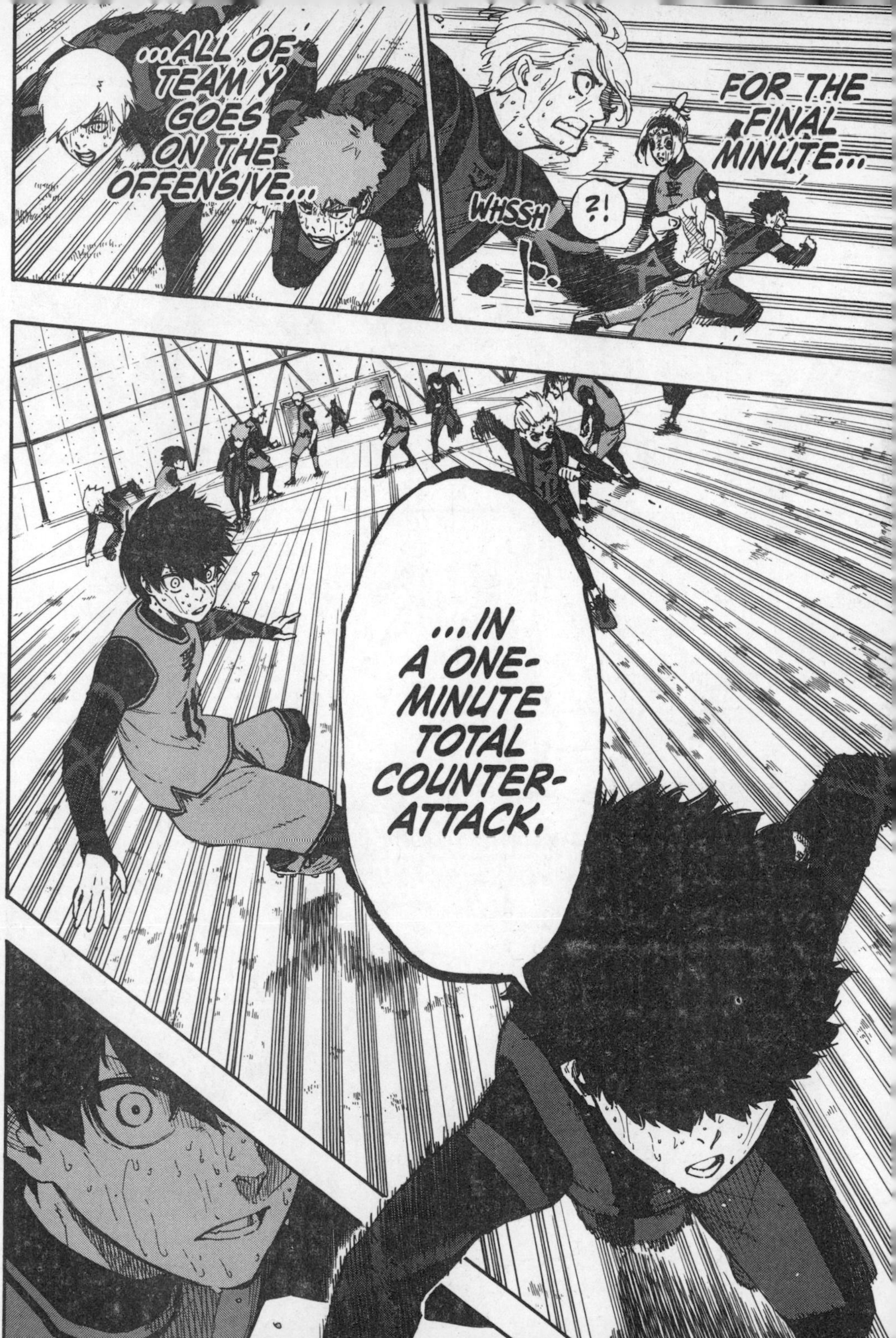
FOR THE FINAL MINUTE...
?!
WHSSH
...ALL OF TEAM Y GOES ON THE OFFENSIVE...
...IN A ONE-MINUTE TOTAL COUNTER-ATTACK.

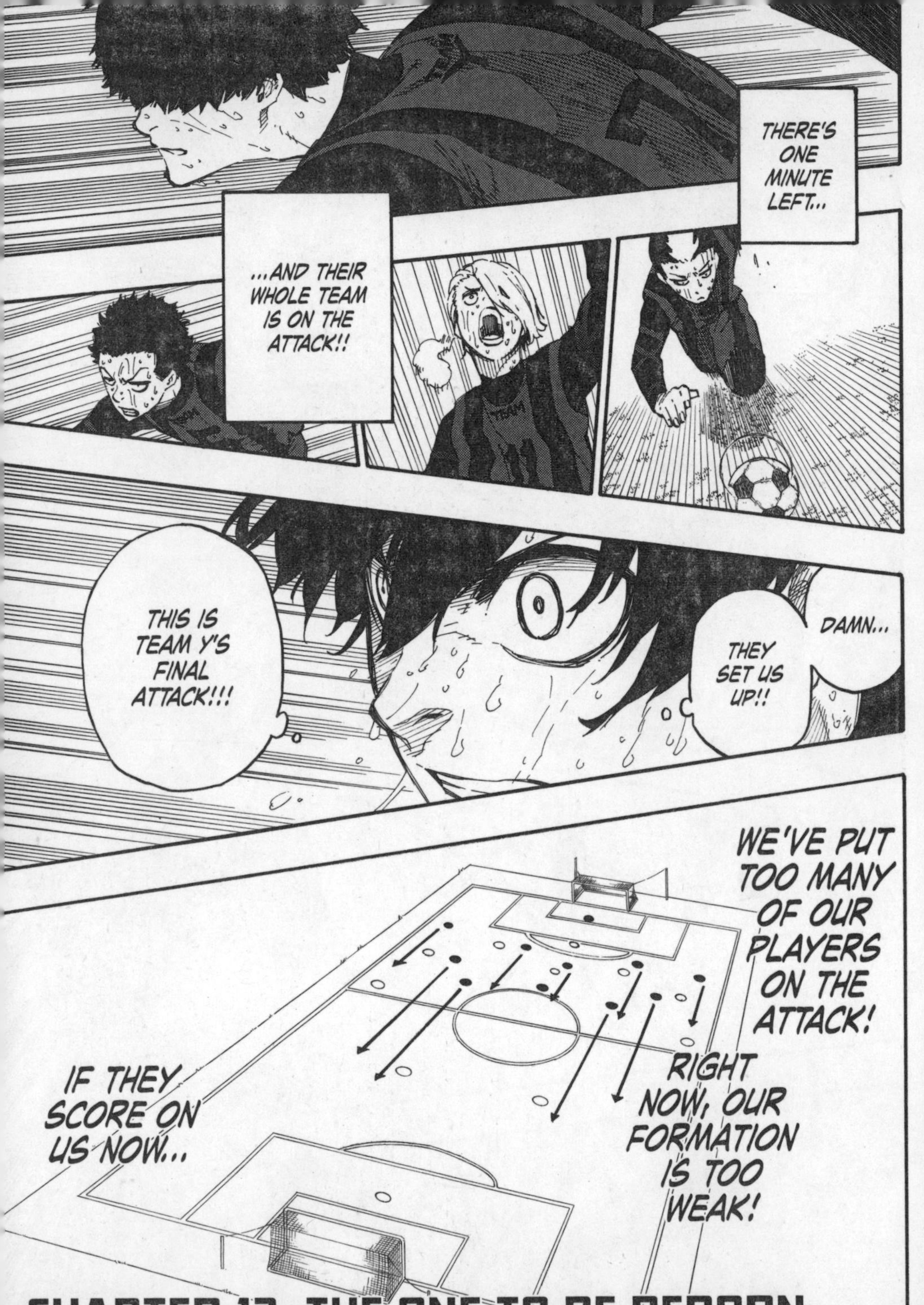
THERE'S ONE MINUTE LEFT...
...AND THEIR WHOLE TEAM IS ON THE ATTACK!!
TEAM
DAMN...
THEY SET US UP!!
THIS IS TEAM Y'S FINAL ATTACK!!!
WE'VE PUT TOO MANY OF OUR PLAYERS ON THE ATTACK!
RIGHT NOW, OUR FORMATION IS TOO WEAK!
IF THEY SCORE ON US NOW...

CHAPTER 13: THE ONE TO BE REBORN

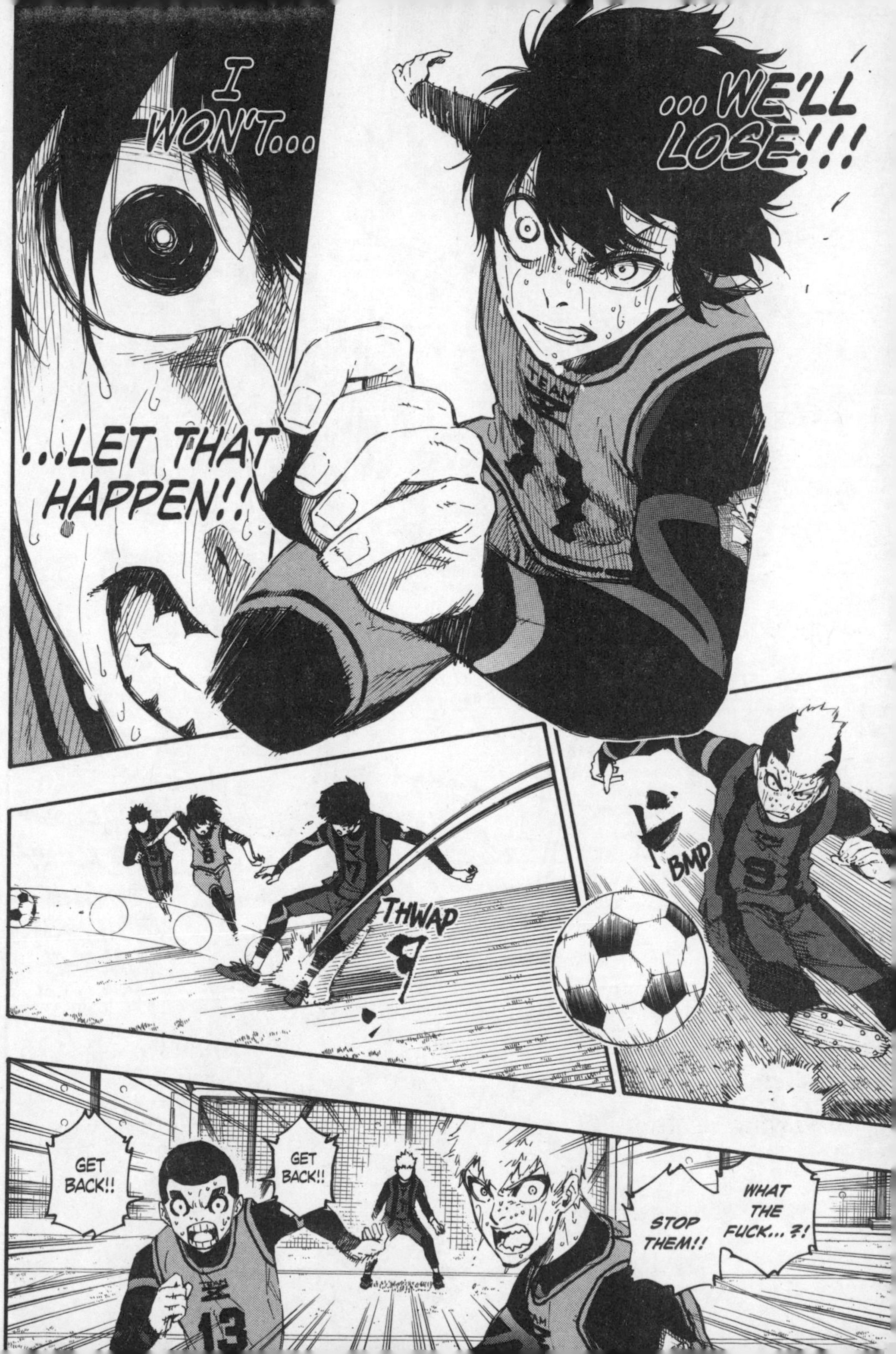
...WE'LL LOSE!!!
I WON'T...
...LET THAT HAPPEN!!
BMP
THWAP
WHAT THE FUCK...?!
STOP THEM!!
GET BACK!!
GET BACK!!

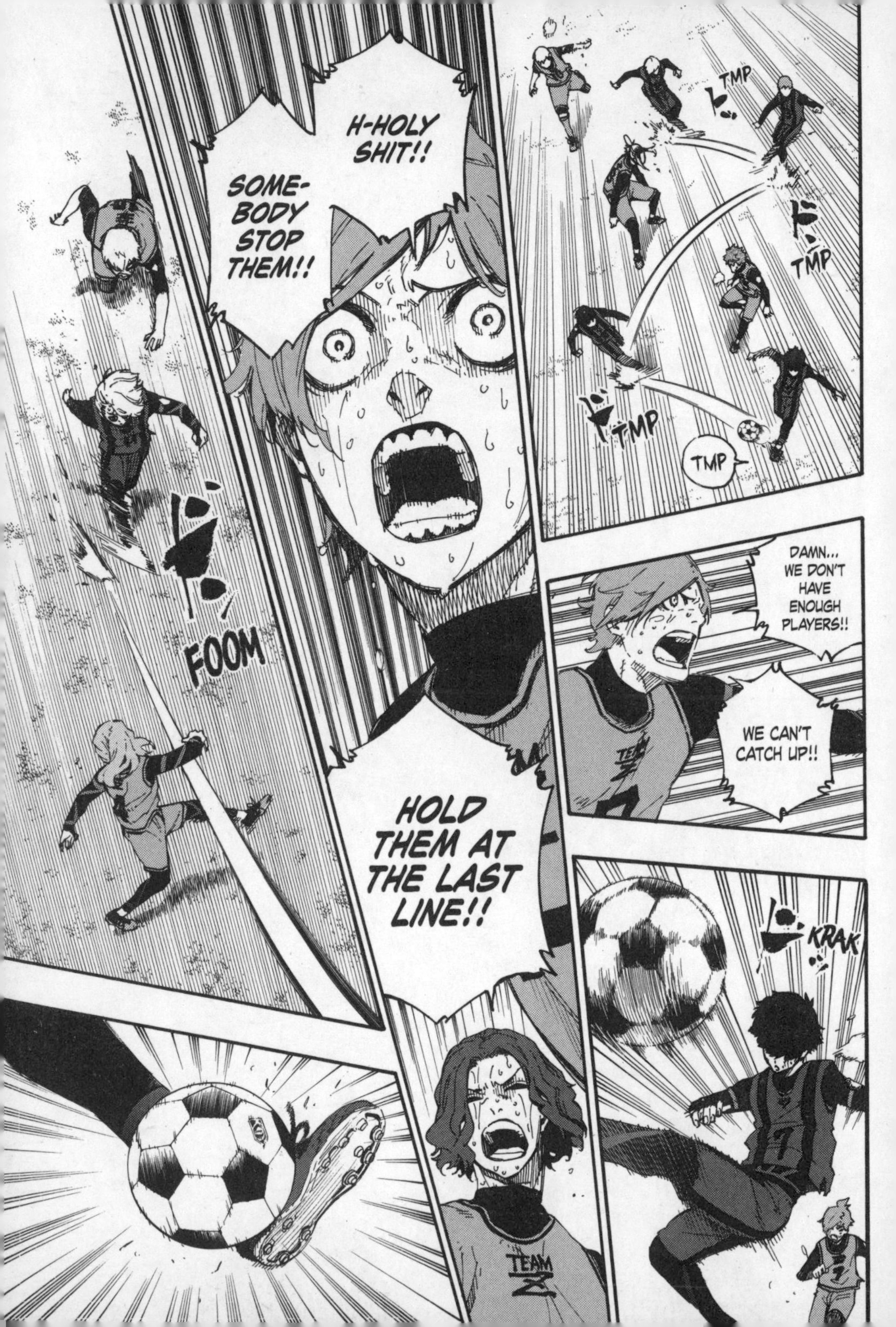
TMP
TMP
TMP
TMP
H-HOLY SHIT!!
SOME-BODY STOP THEM!!
FOOM
DAMN... WE DON'T HAVE ENOUGH PLAYERS!!
WE CAN'T CATCH UP!!
KRAK
HOLD THEM AT THE LAST LINE!!
TEAM Z
TEAM Z

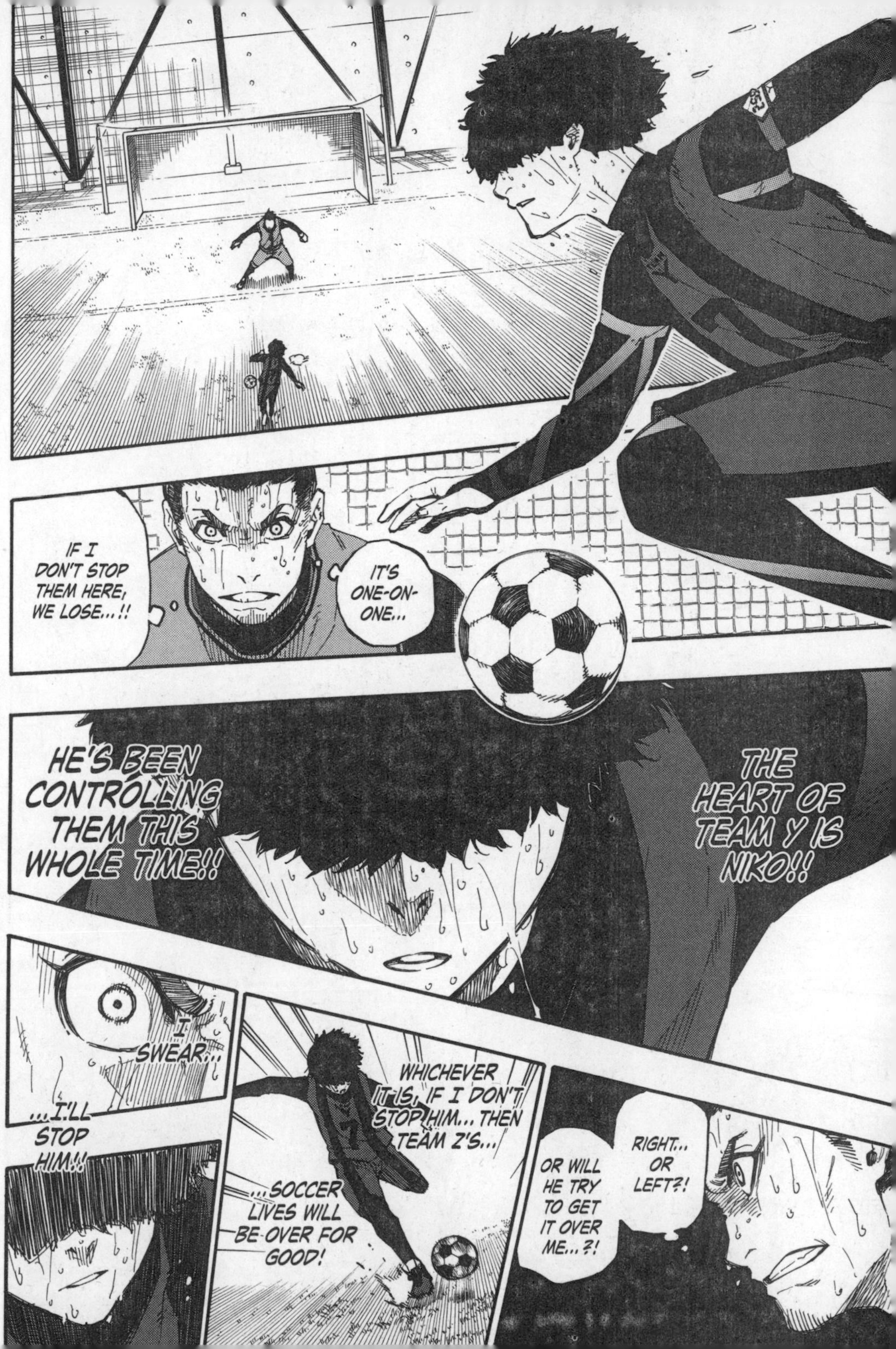
IT'S ONE-ON-ONE...
IF I DON'T STOP THEM HERE, WE LOSE...!!
THE HEART OF TEAM Y IS NIKO!!
HE'S BEEN CONTROLLING THEM THIS WHOLE TIME!!
RIGHT... OR LEFT?!
OR WILL HE TRY TO GET IT OVER ME...?!
WHICHEVER IT IS, IF I DON'T STOP HIM... THEN TEAM Z'S...
...SOCCER LIVES WILL BE OVER FOR GOOD!
I SWEAR...
...I'LL STOP HIM!!

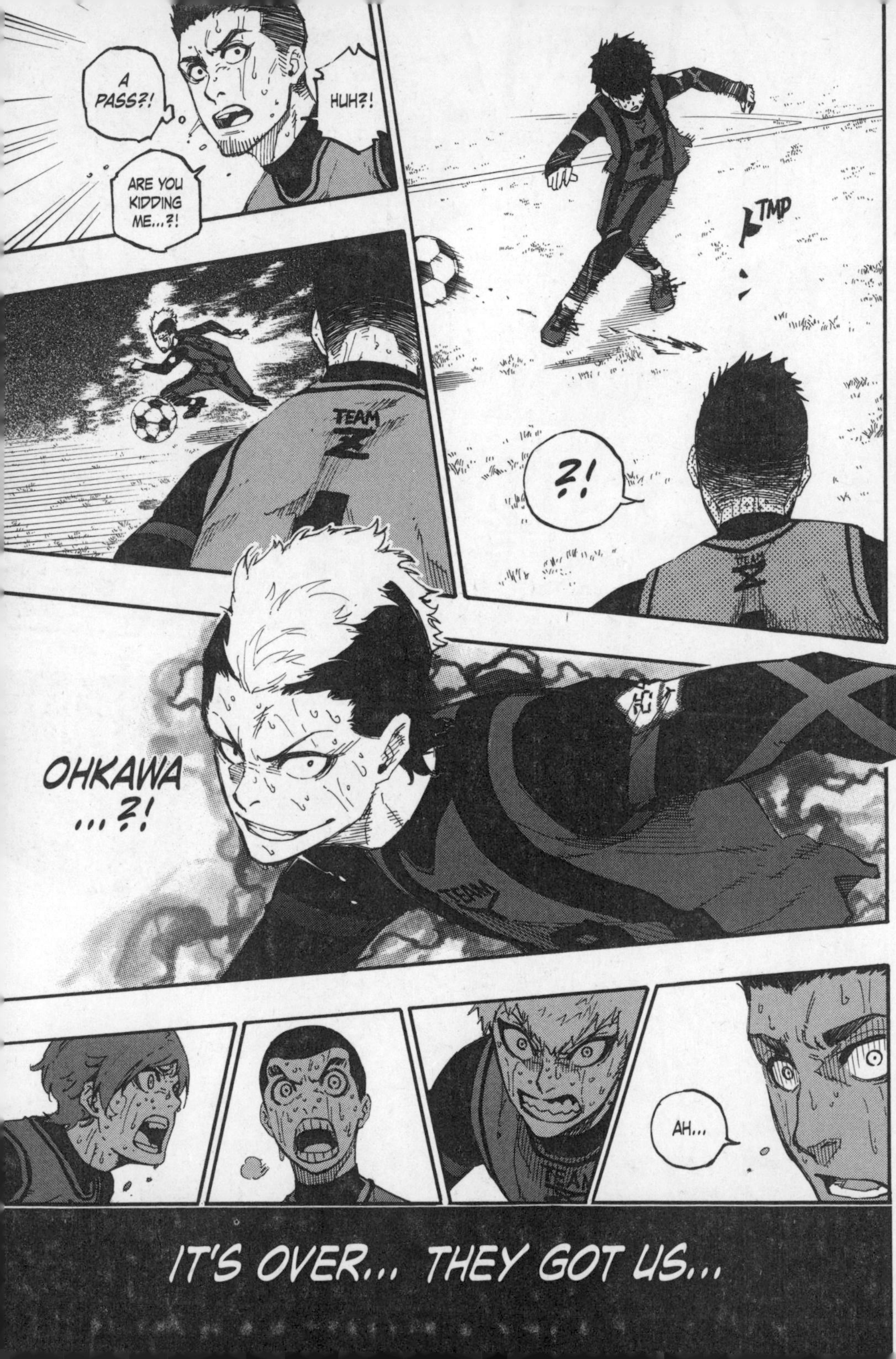
TMP
?!
HUH?!
A PASS?!
ARE YOU KIDDING ME...?!
OHKAWA ...?!
AH...
IT'S OVER... THEY GOT US...

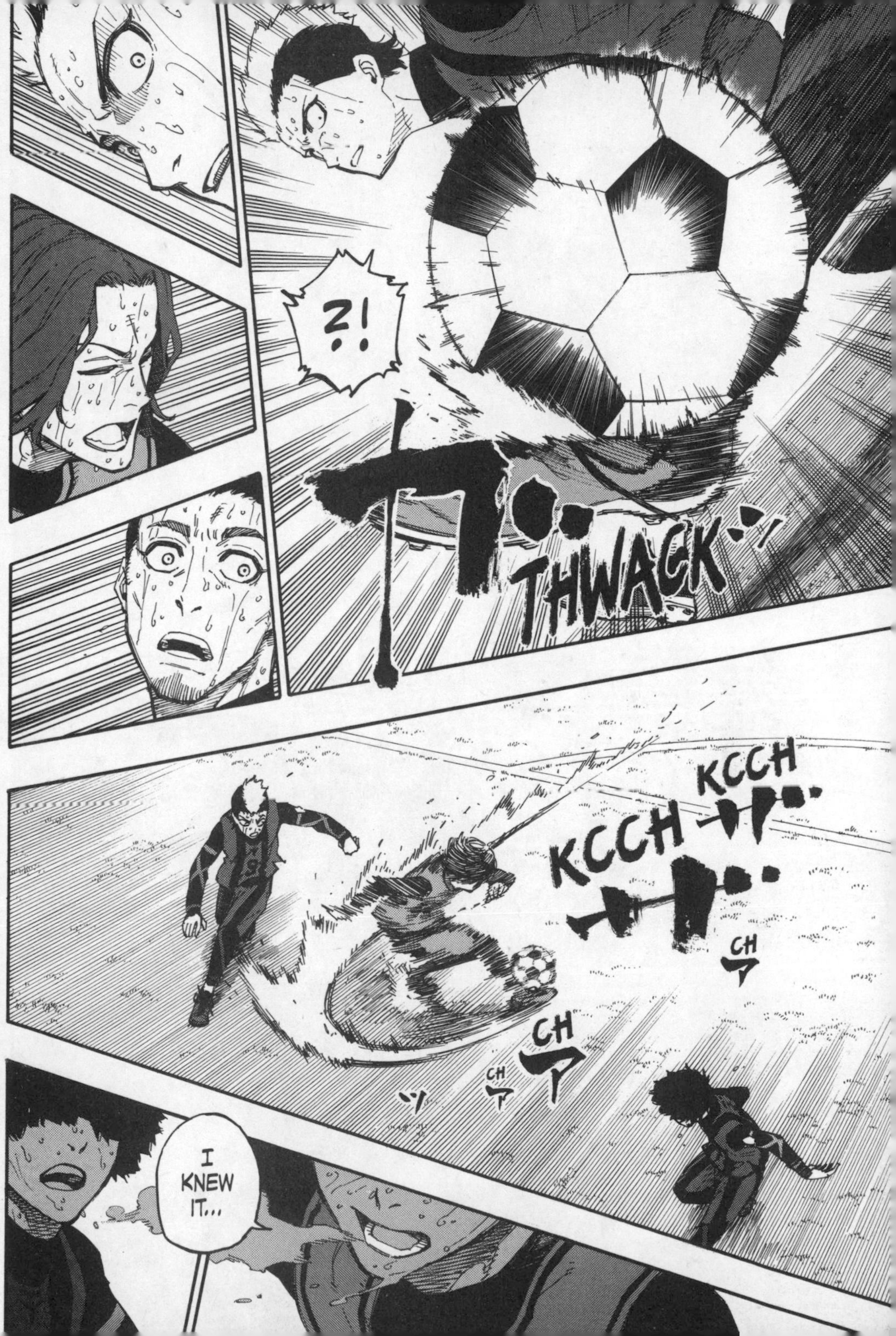
?!
THWACK
KCCH
KCCH
CH
CH
CH
I KNEW IT...

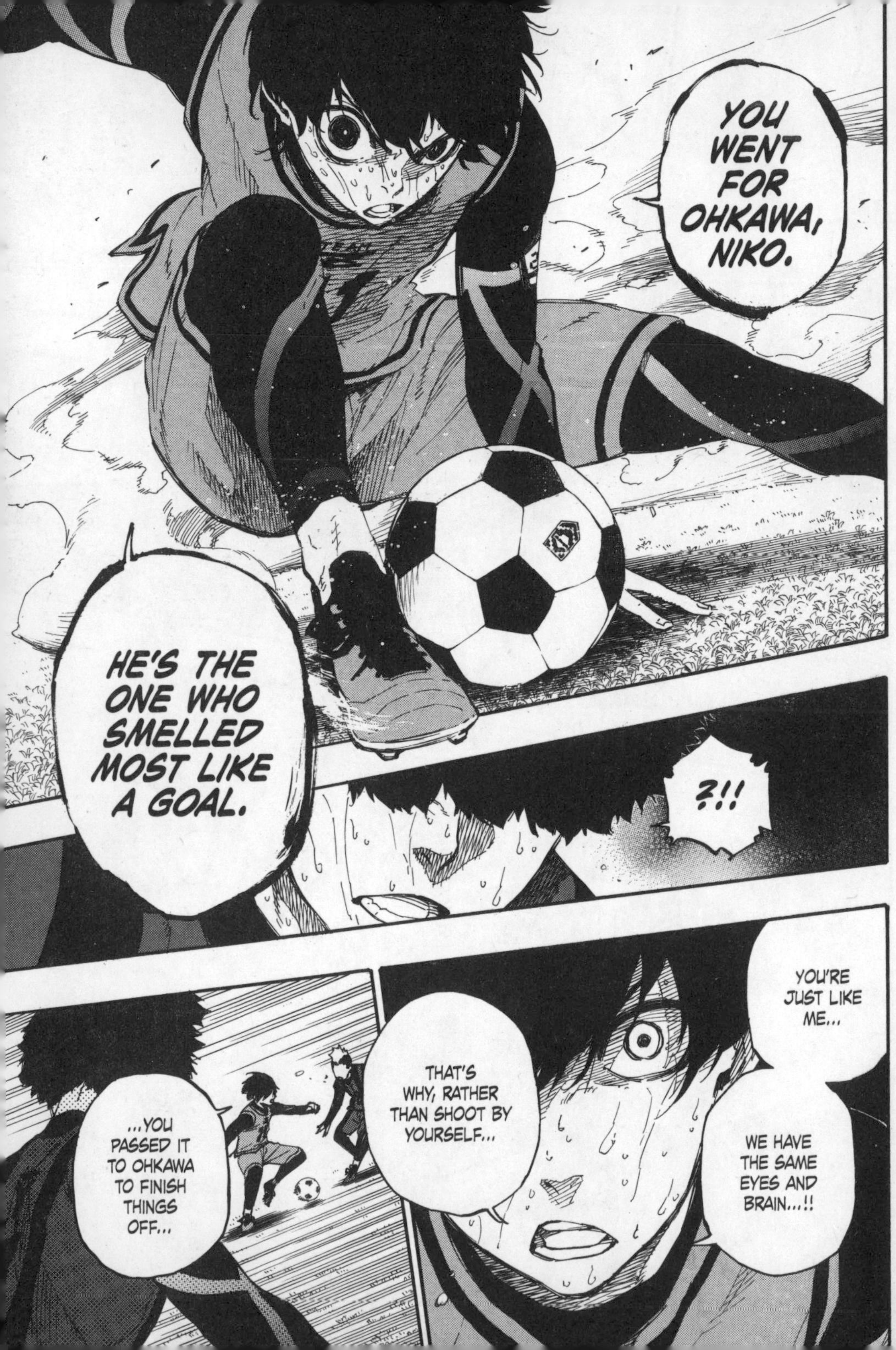
YOU WENT FOR OHKAWA, NIKO.
HE'S THE ONE WHO SMELLED MOST LIKE A GOAL.
?!!
YOU'RE JUST LIKE ME...
WE HAVE THE SAME EYES AND BRAIN...!!
THAT'S WHY, RATHER THAN SHOOT BY YOURSELF...
...YOU PASSED IT TO OHKAWA TO FINISH THINGS OFF...

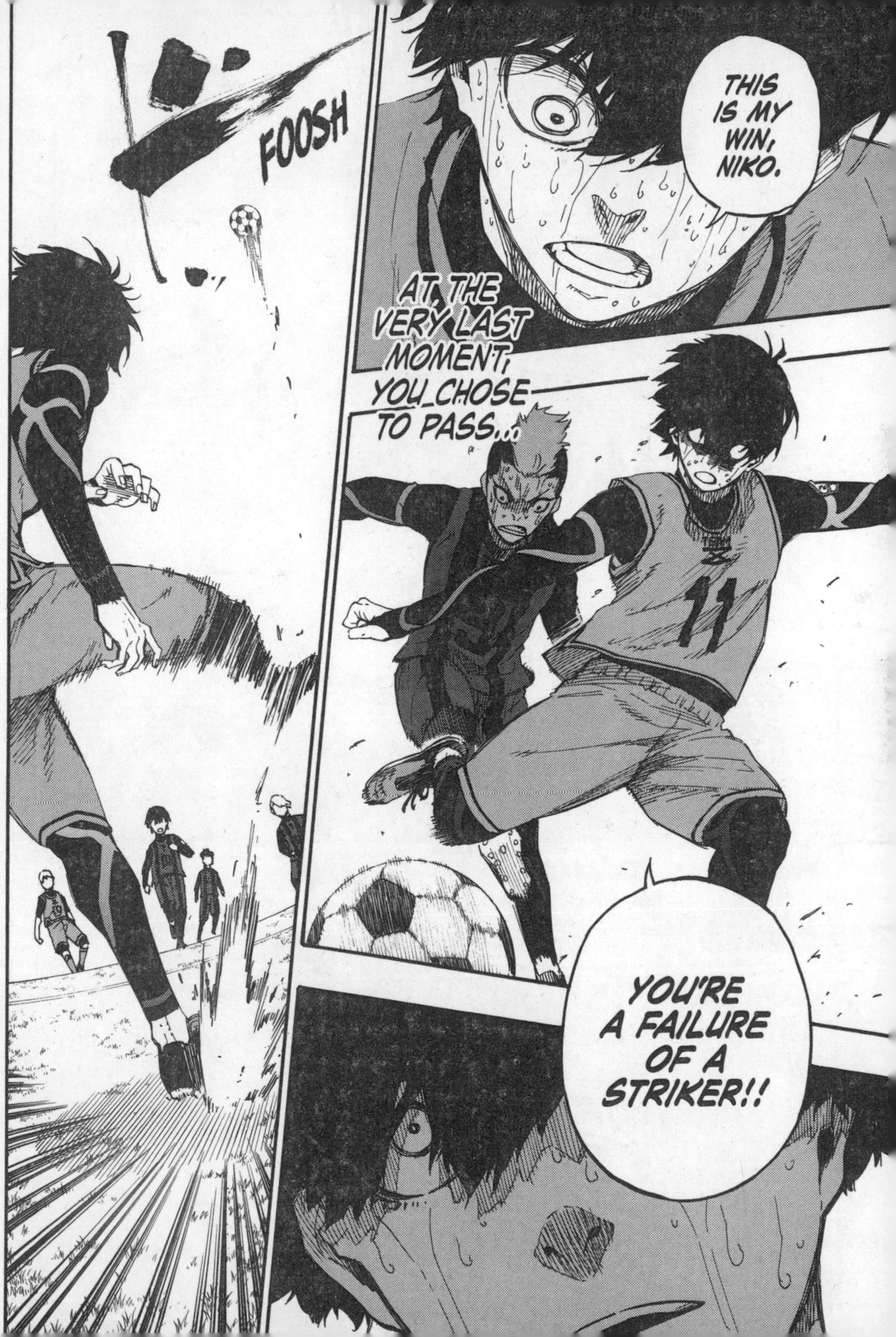
THIS IS MY WIN, NIKO.
AT THE VERY LAST MOMENT, YOU CHOSE TO PASS...
YOU'RE A FAILURE OF A STRIKER!!
FOOSH

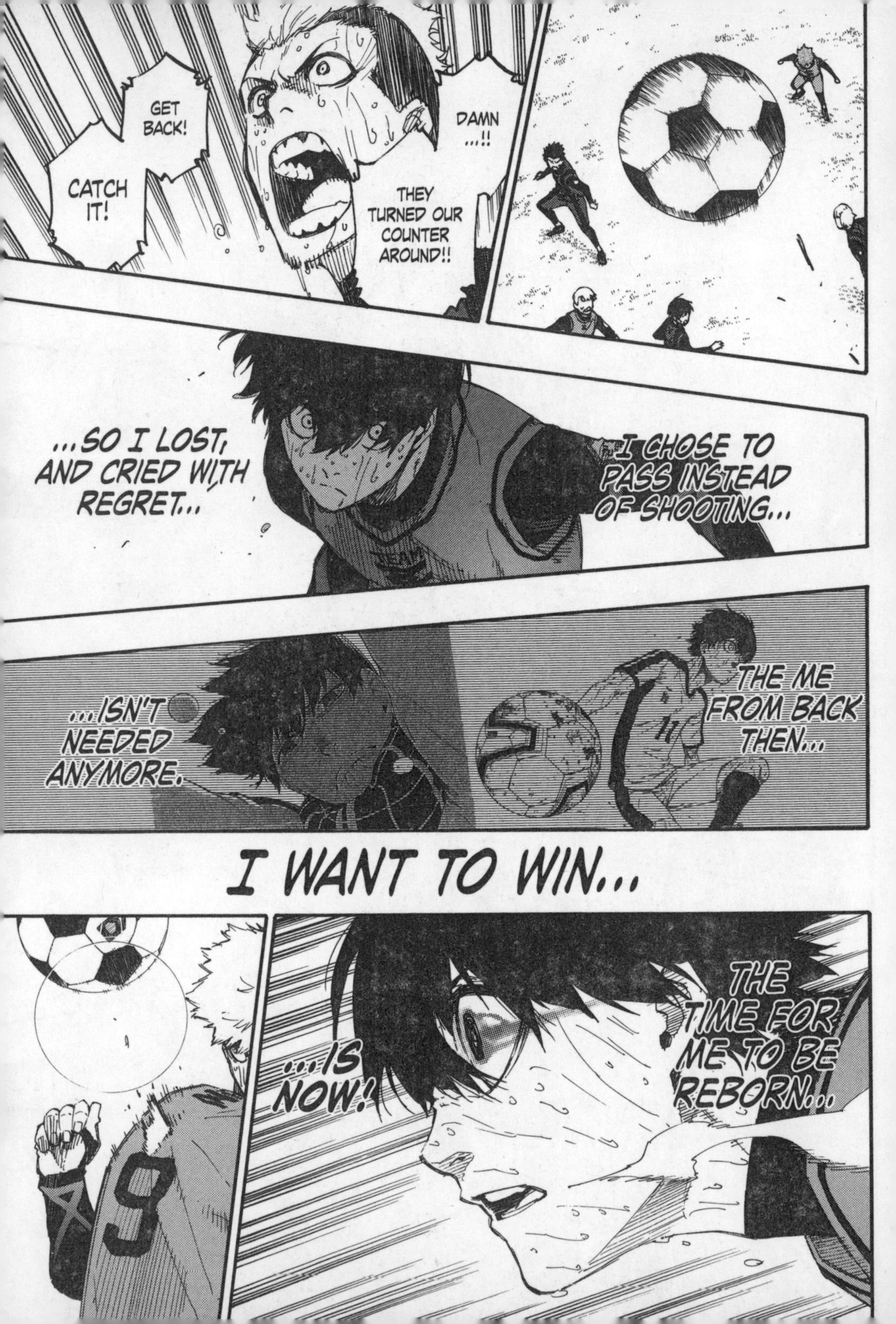
DAMN ...!!
GET BACK!
THEY TURNED OUR COUNTER AROUND!!
CATCH IT!
I CHOSE TO PASS INSTEAD OF SHOOTING...
...SO I LOST, AND CRIED WITH REGRET...
THE ME FROM BACK THEN...
...ISN'T NEEDED ANYMORE.
I WANT TO WIN...
THE TIME FOR ME TO BE REBORN...
...IS NOW!

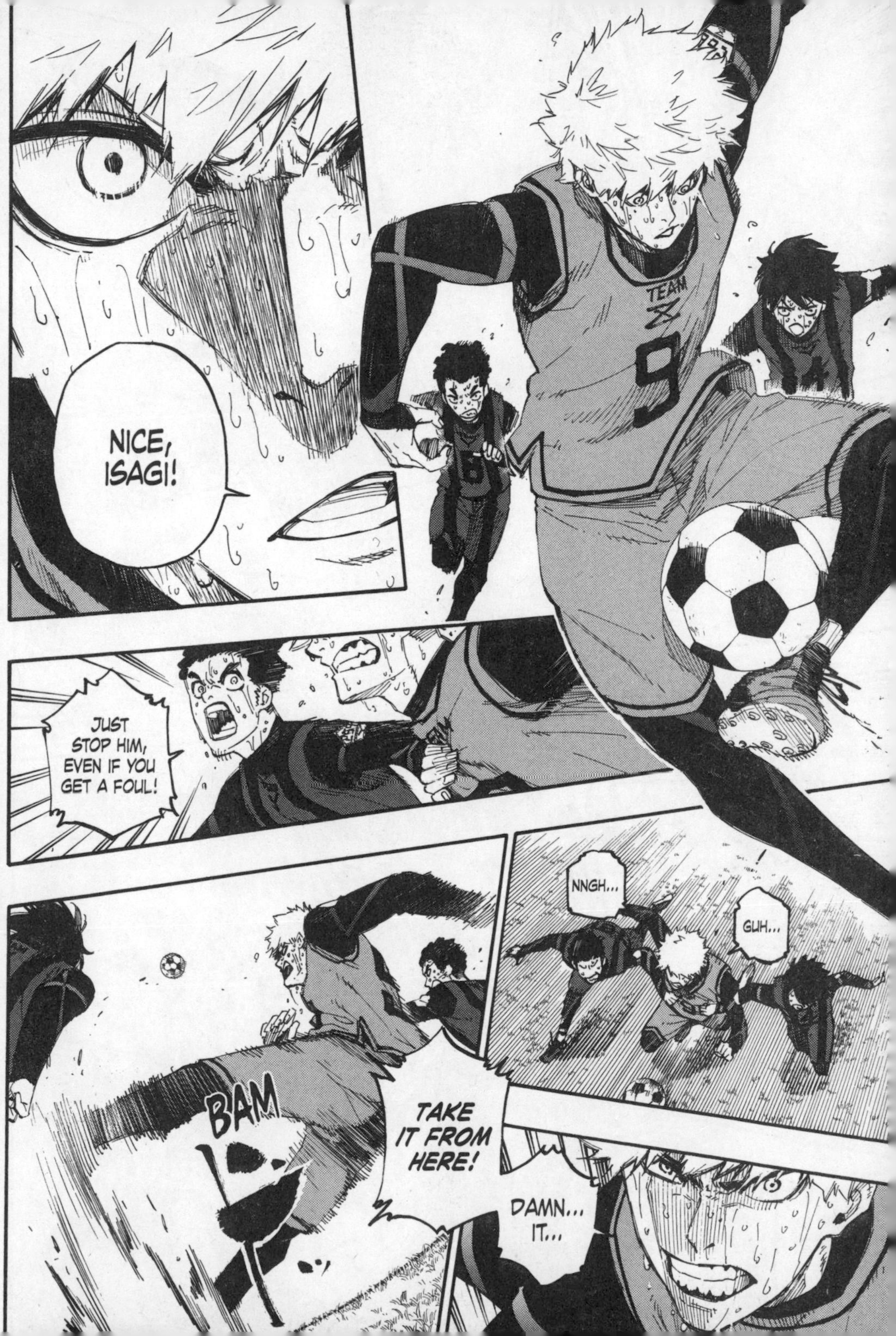
NICE, ISAGI!
JUST STOP HIM, EVEN IF YOU GET A FOUL!
NNGH...
GUH...
DAMN... IT...
BAM
TAKE IT FROM HERE!

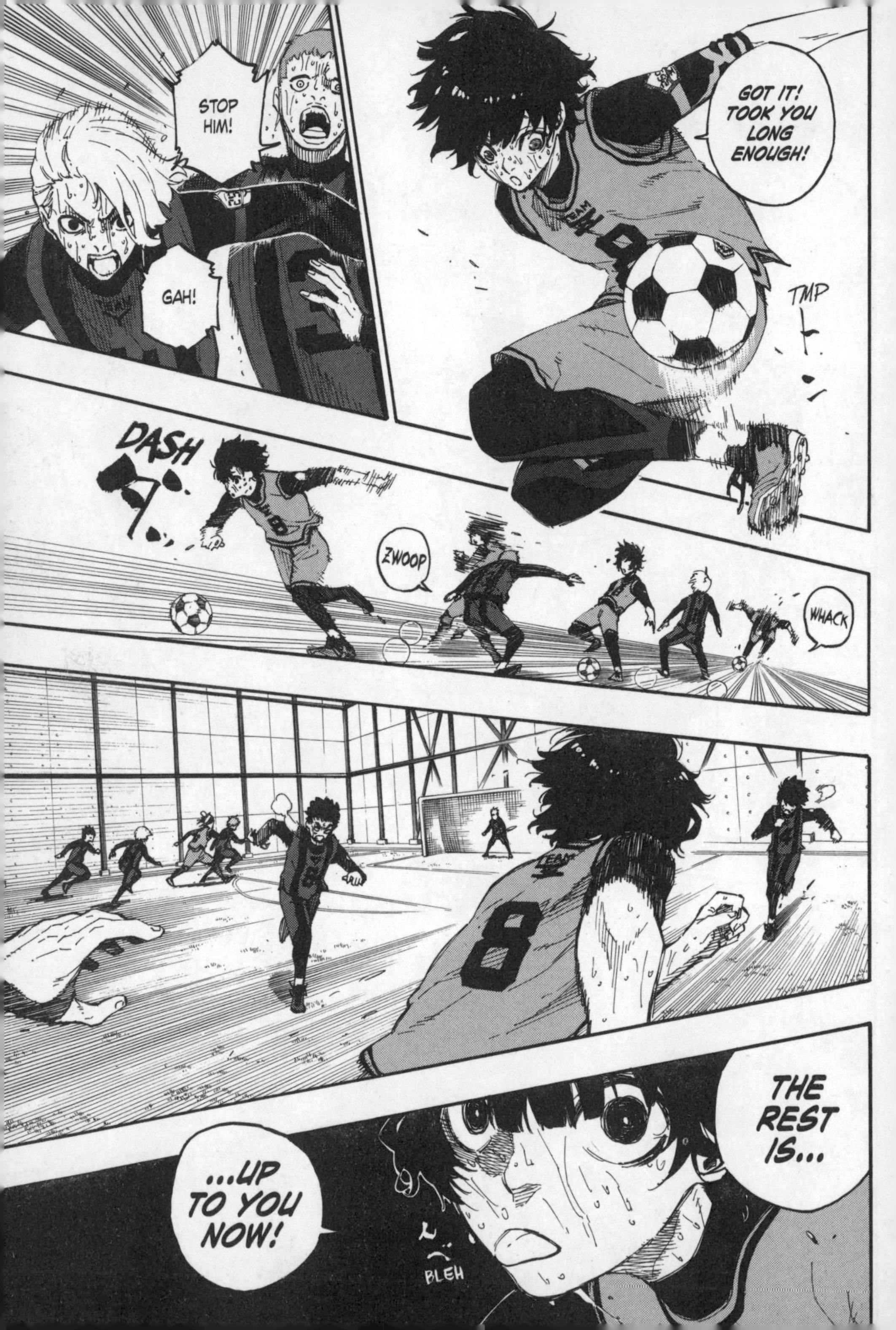
GOT IT! TOOK YOU LONG ENOUGH!
TMP
STOP HIM!
GAH!
WHACK
ZWOOP
DASH
THE REST IS...
...UP TO YOU NOW!
BLEH

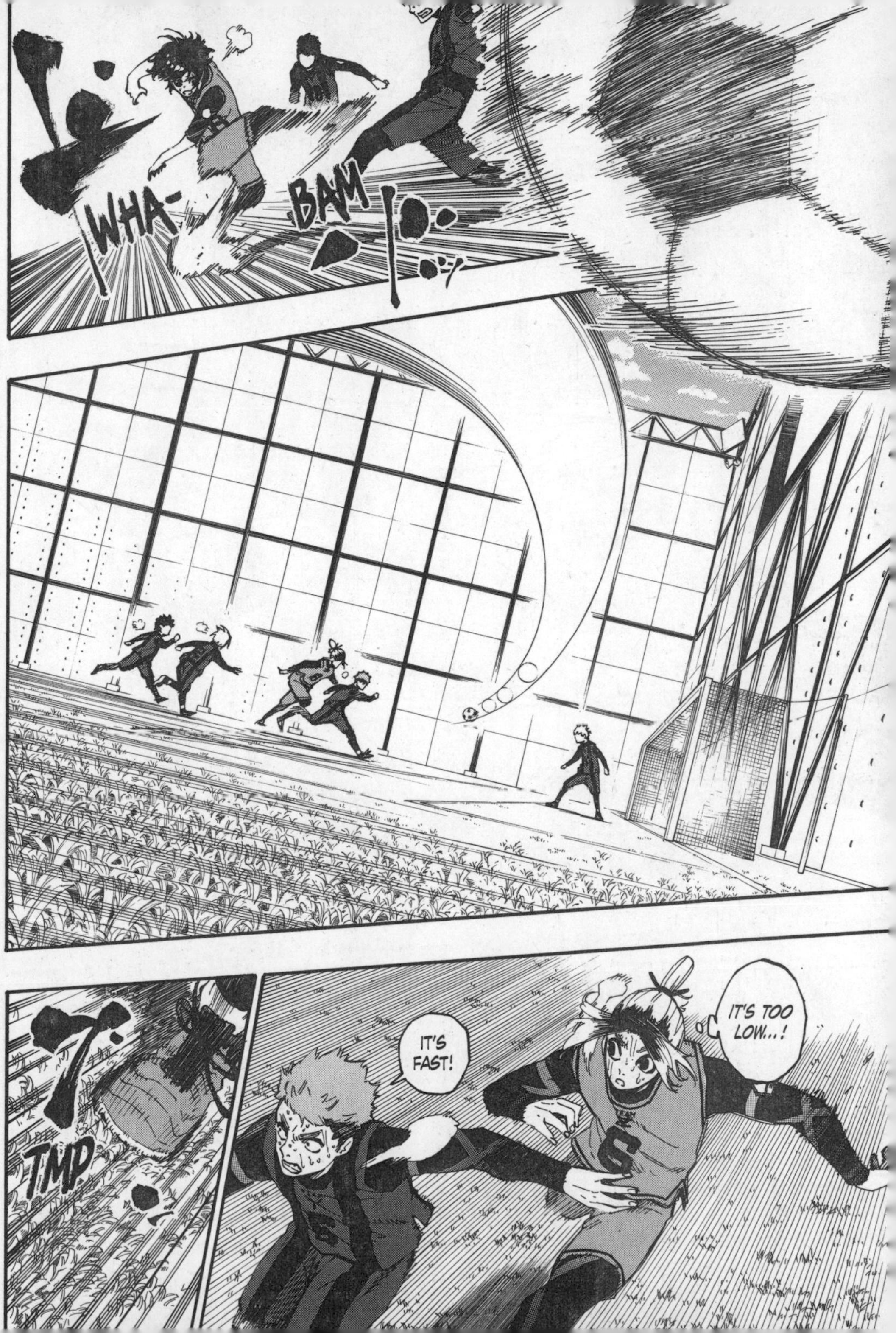
BAM
WHA-
IT'S TOO LOW...!
IT'S FAST!
TMP

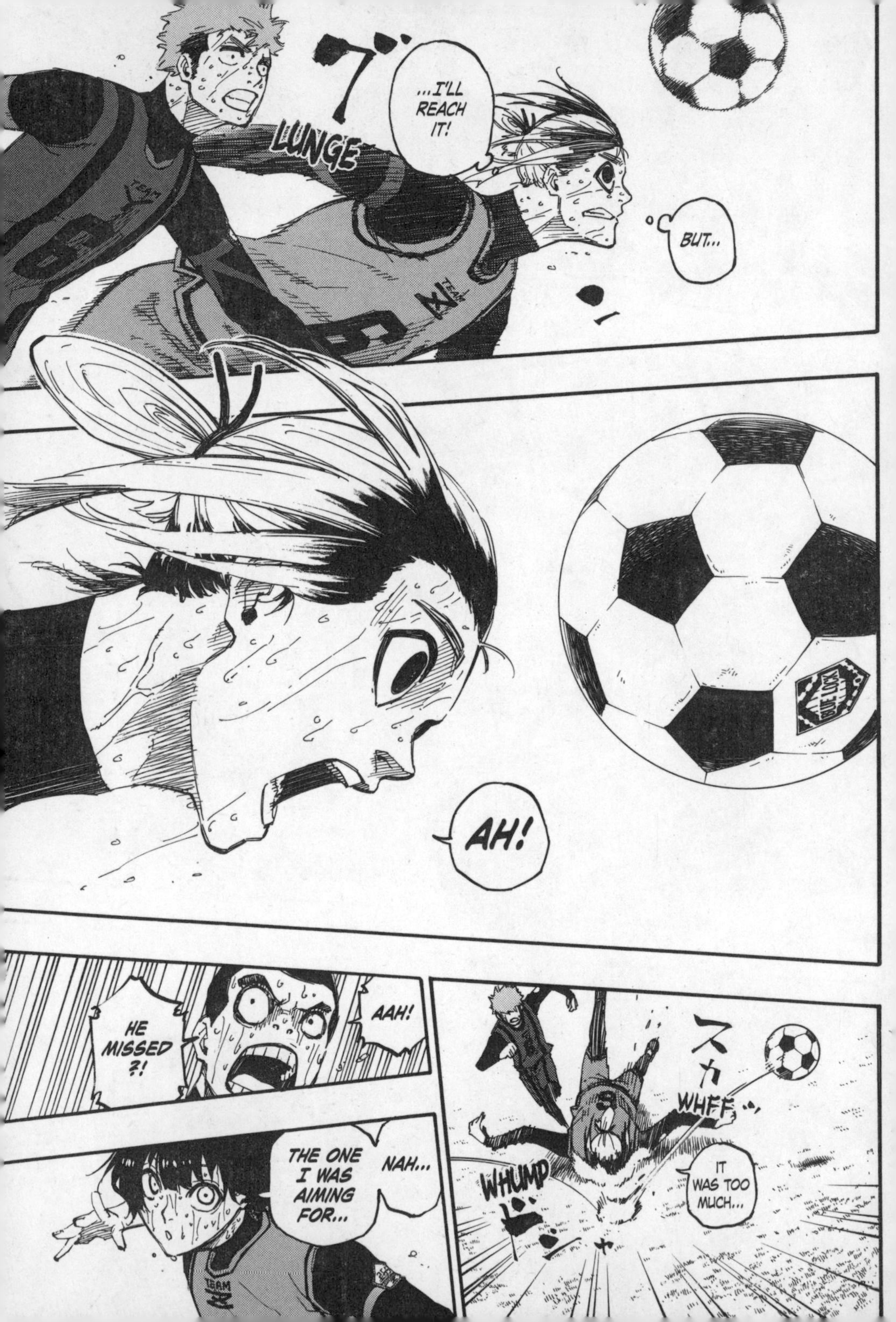
...I'LL REACH IT!
LUNGE
BUT...
AH!
スカ
WHFF
IT WAS TOO MUCH...
WHUMP
ド
AAH!
HE MISSED?!
NAH...
THE ONE I WAS AIMING FOR...

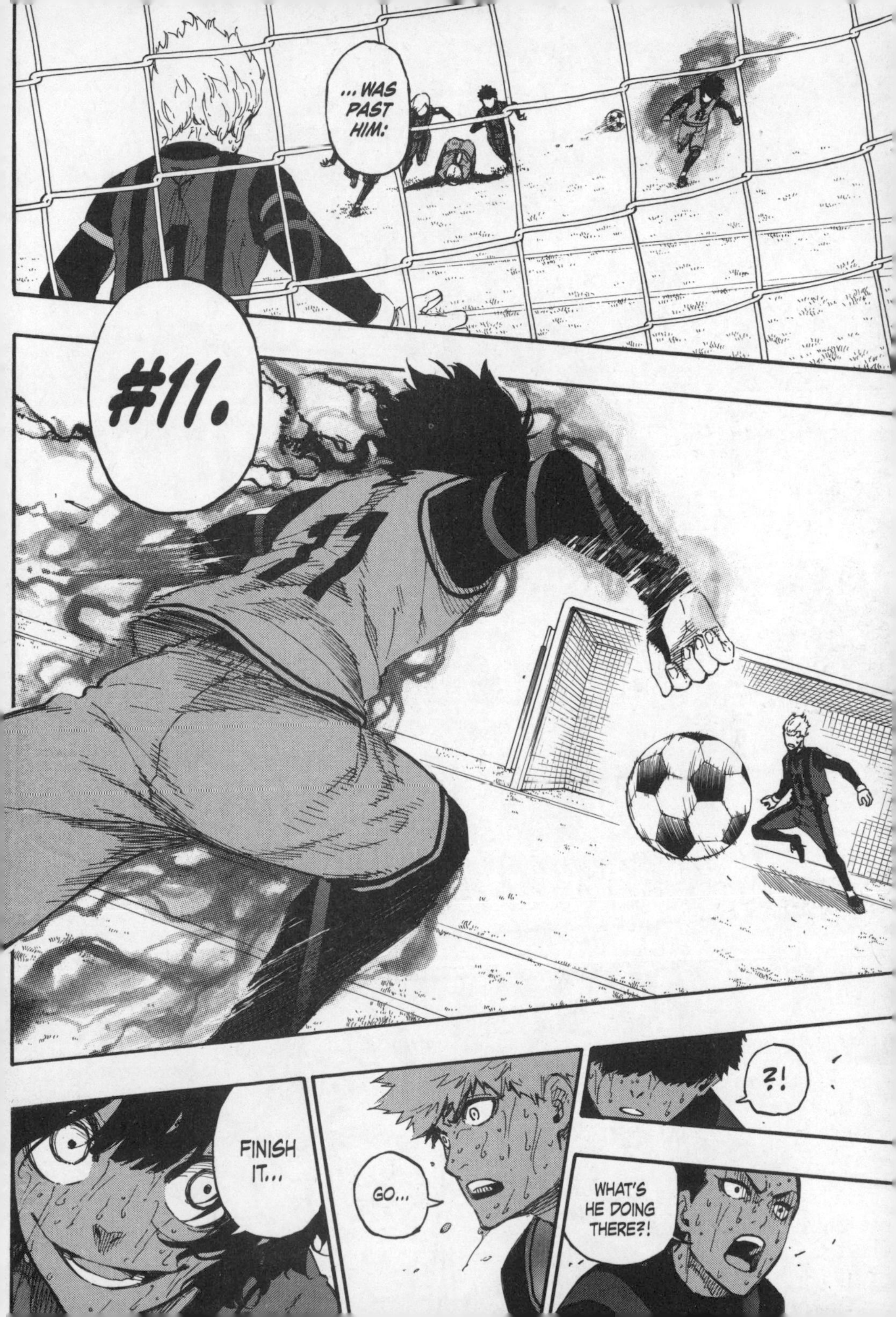
...WAS PAST HIM:
#11.
?!
WHAT'S HE DOING THERE?!
GO...
FINISH IT...

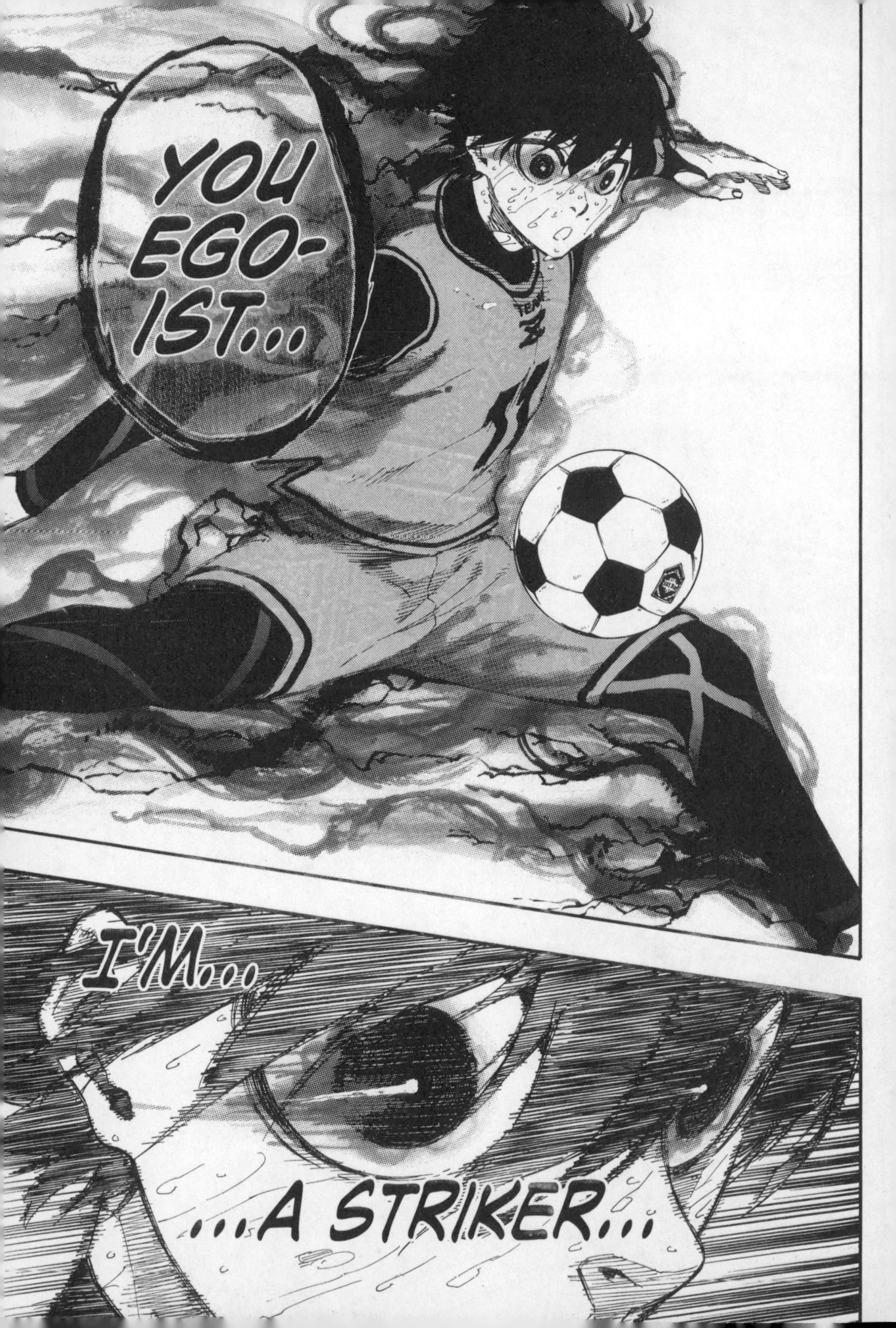
YOU EGO-IST...
I'M...
...A STRIKER...

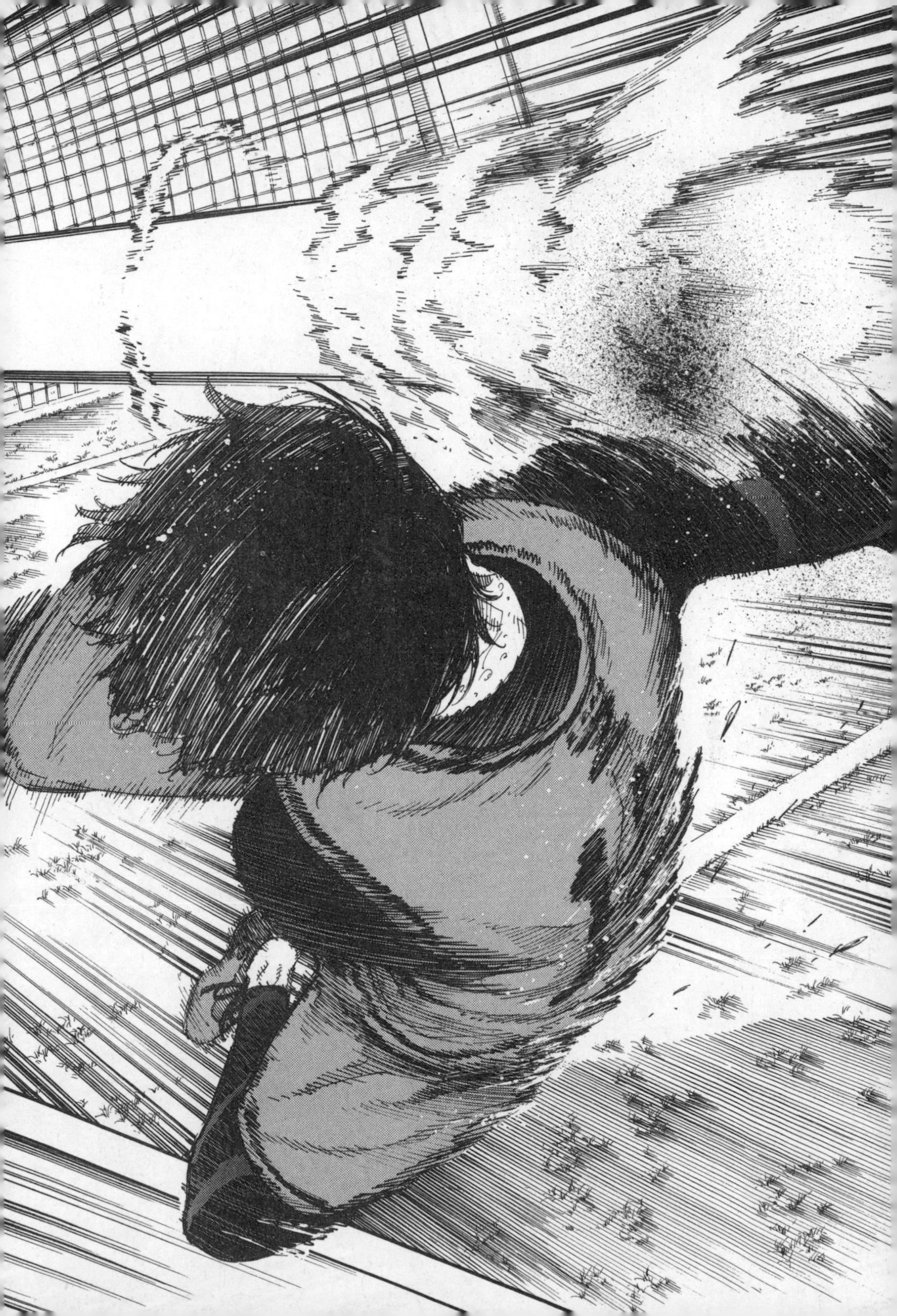

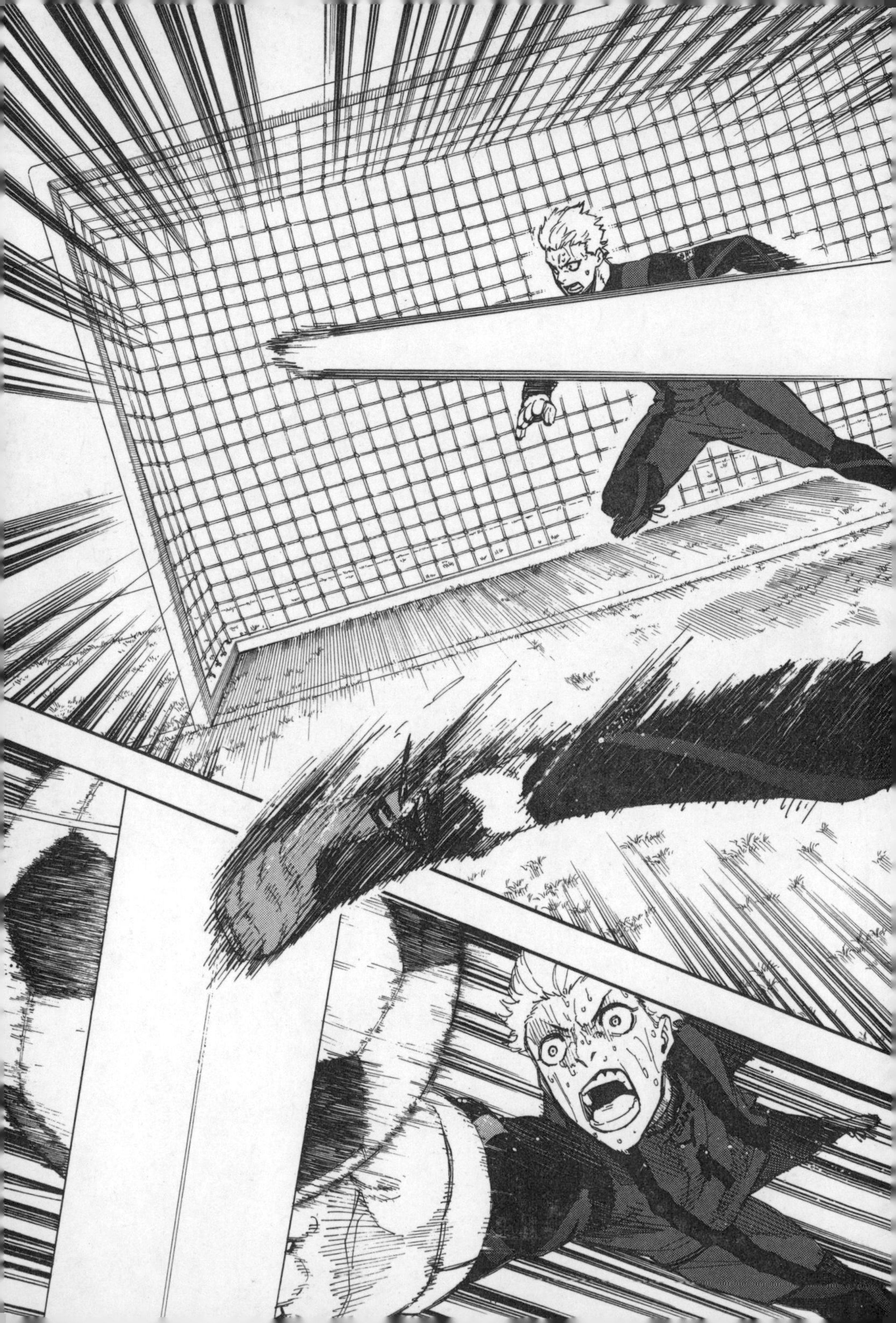

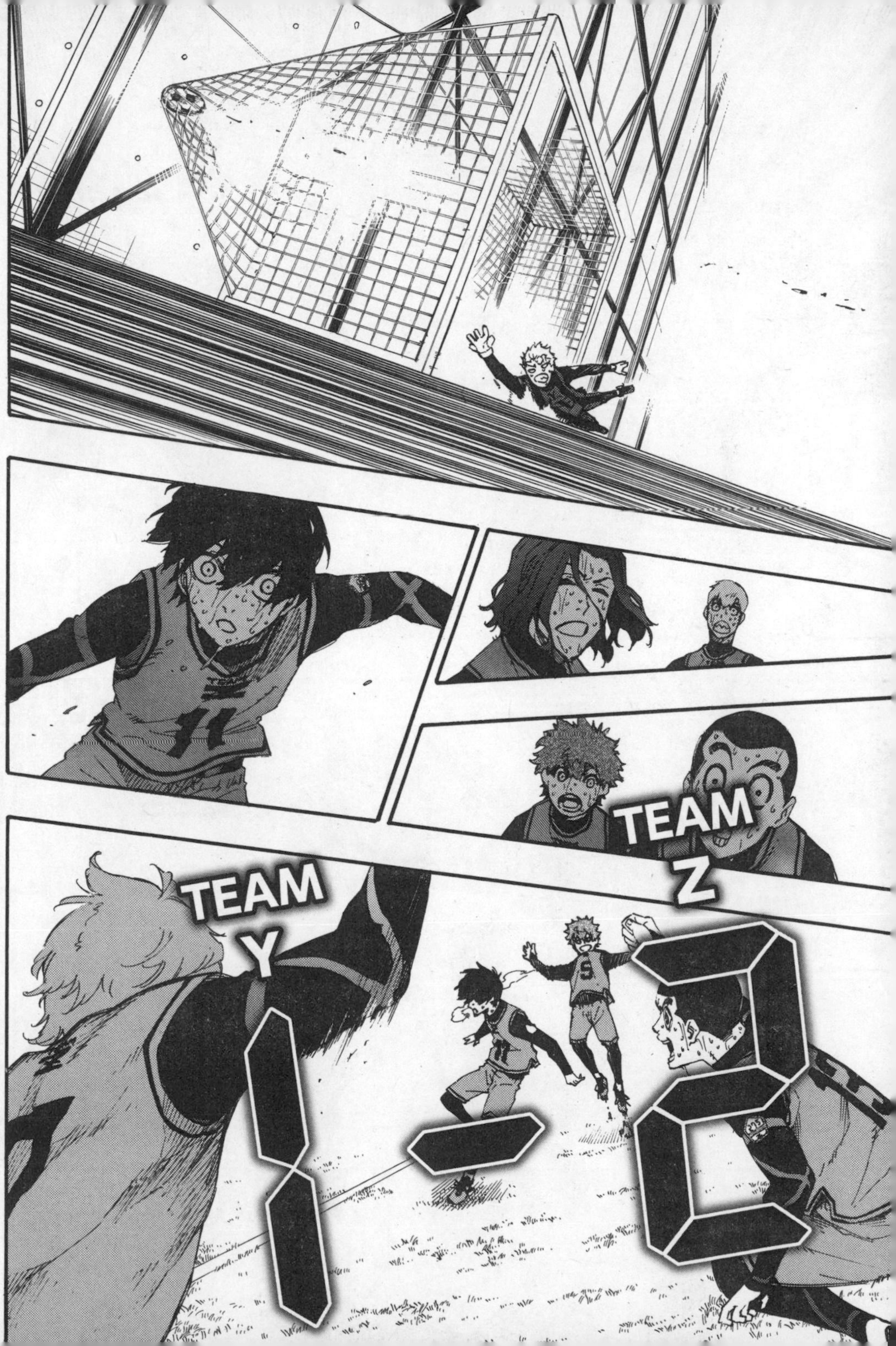
TEAM Z
TEAM Y
1 - 2

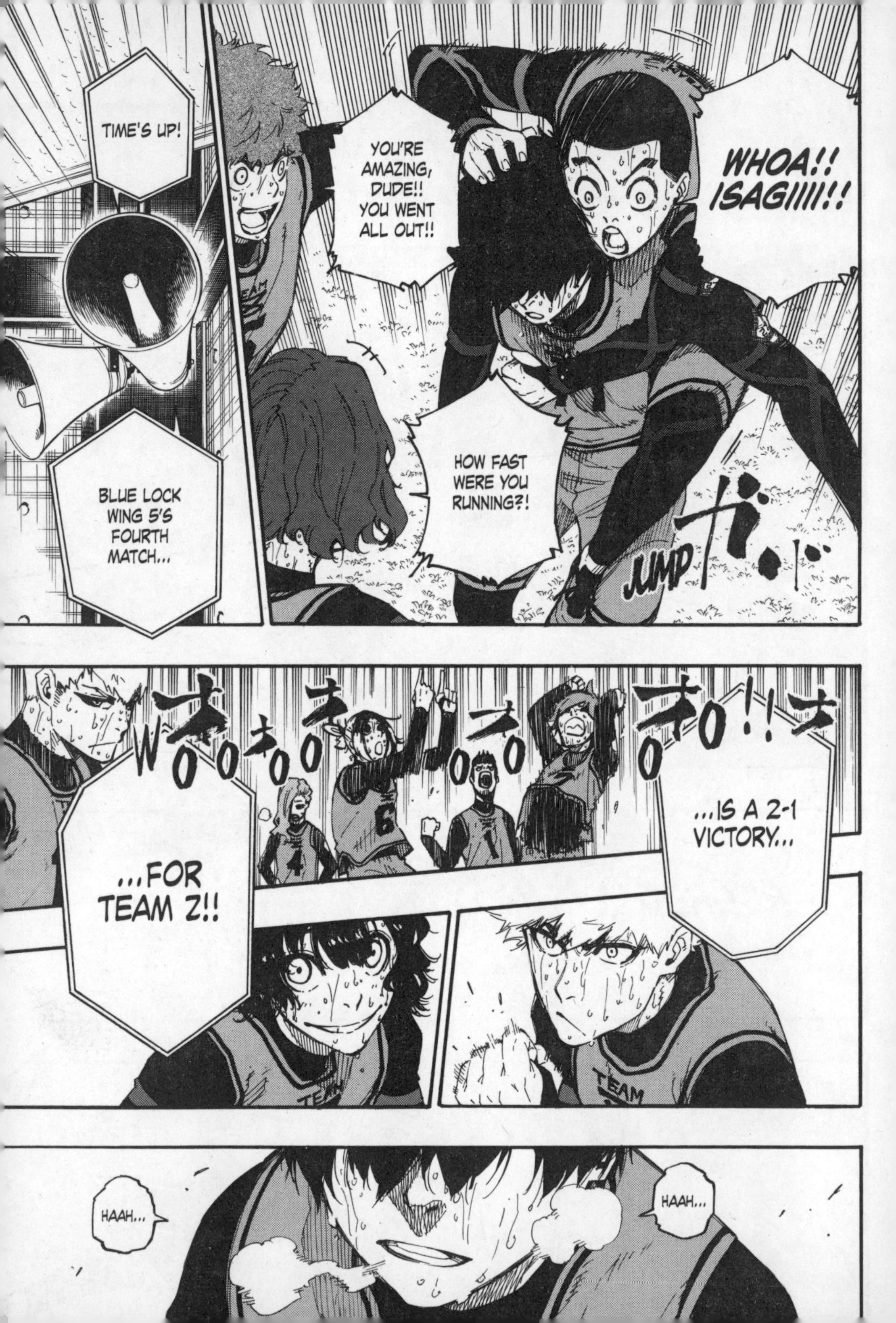
WHOA!! ISAGIIIII!!
YOU'RE AMAZING, DUDE!! YOU WENT ALL OUT!!
HOW FAST WERE YOU RUNNING?!
JUMP
TIME'S UP!
BLUE LOCK WING 5'S FOURTH MATCH...
WOOOOOOOOO!!
...IS A 2-1 VICTORY...
...FOR TEAM Z!!
HAAH...
HAAH...

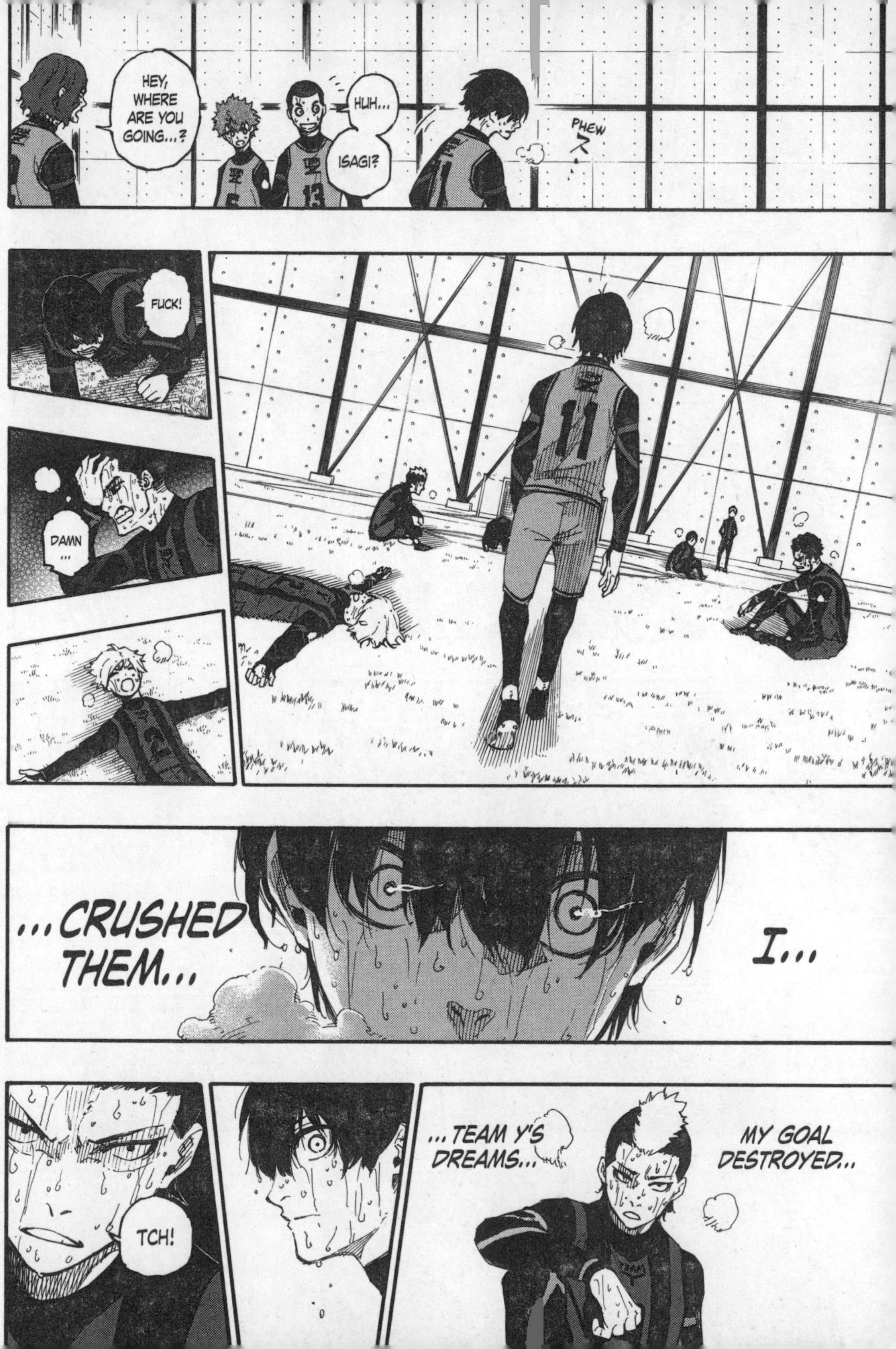
PHEW
HUH...
ISAGI?
HEY, WHERE ARE YOU GOING...?
FUCK!
DAMN ...
I...
...CRUSHED THEM...
MY GOAL DESTROYED...
...TEAM Y'S DREAMS...
TCH!

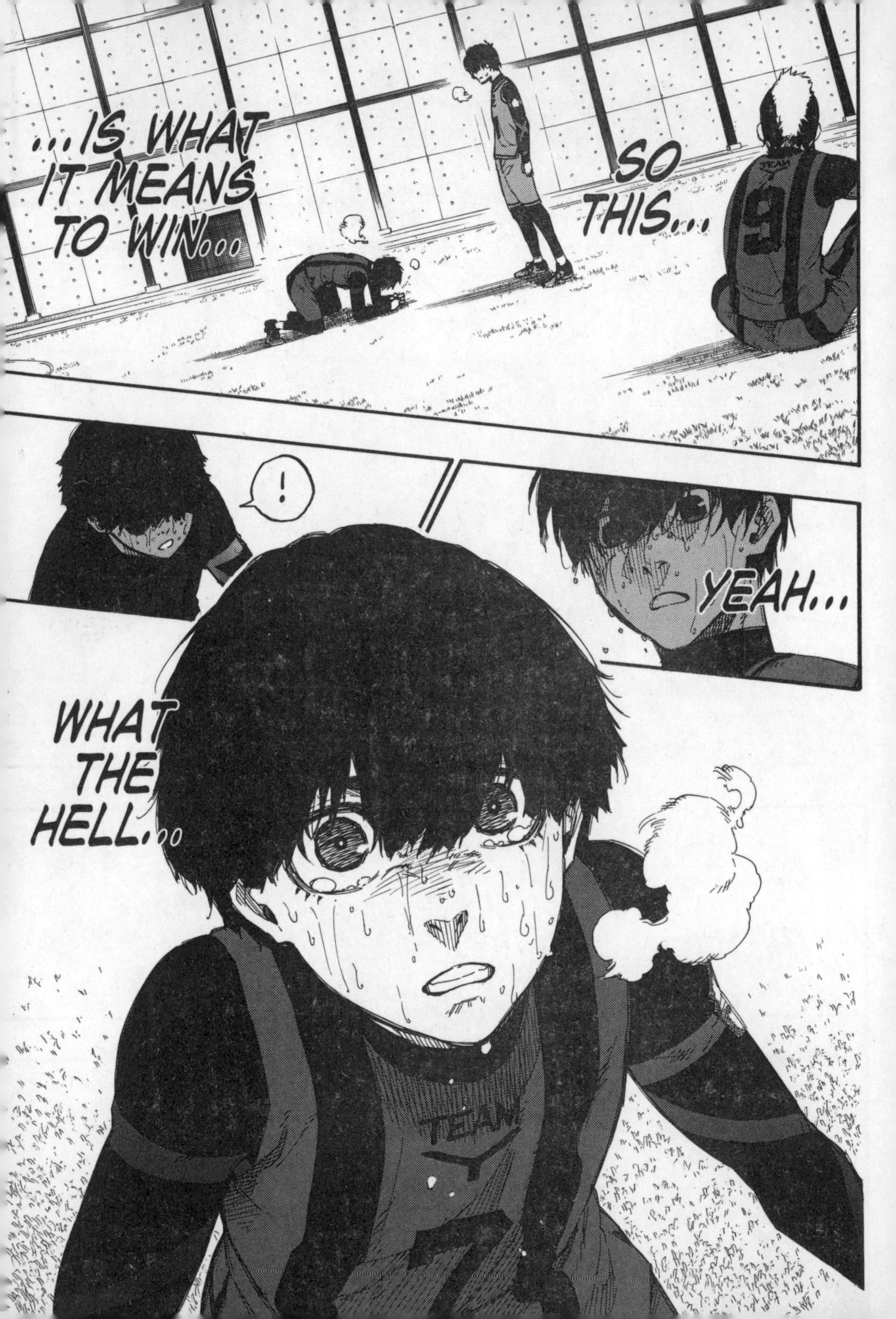
SO THIS...
...IS WHAT IT MEANS TO WIN...
YEAH...
!
WHAT THE HELL...
TEAM

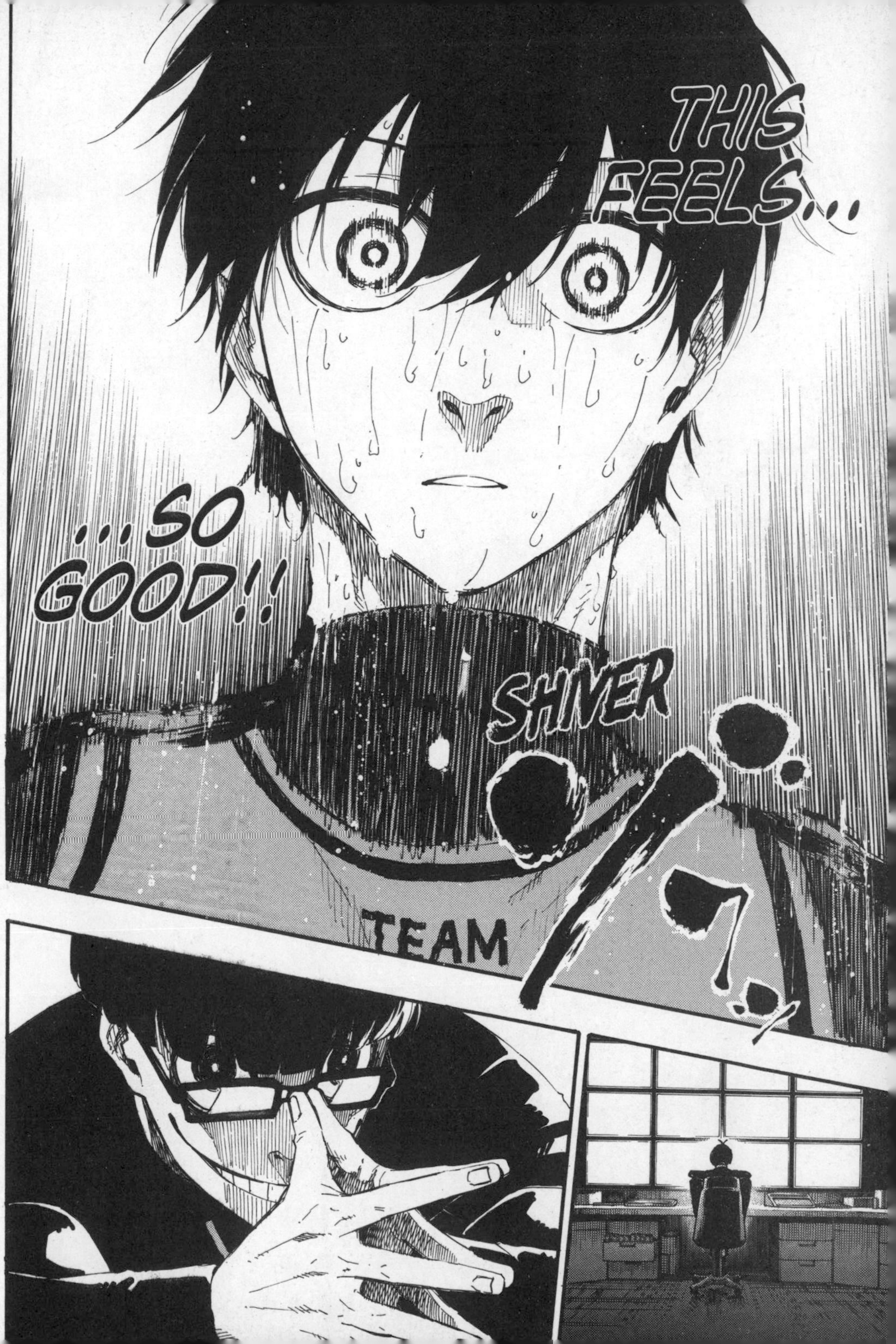
THIS FEELS...
...SO GOOD!!
SHIVER
TEAM

BLUE LOCK

CONTINUED IN VOL. 3

BLUE LOCK FACILITY GUIDE

BONUS SECTION

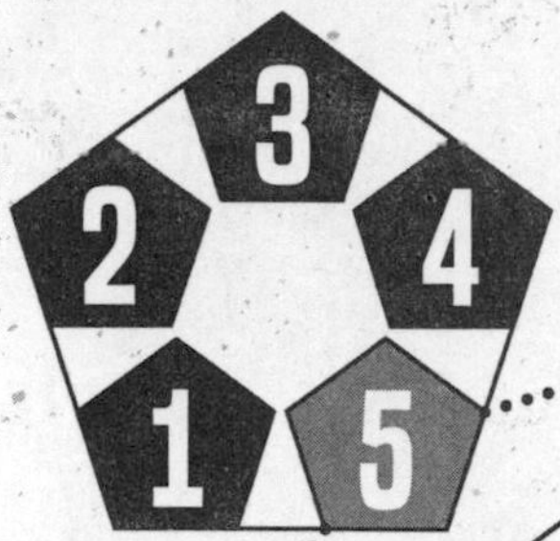
3
2
4
1
5

WING CROSS SECTION

[WING 5]

- BLUE LOCK IS MADE UP OF FIVE OF THESE WINGS GROUPED TOGETHER.

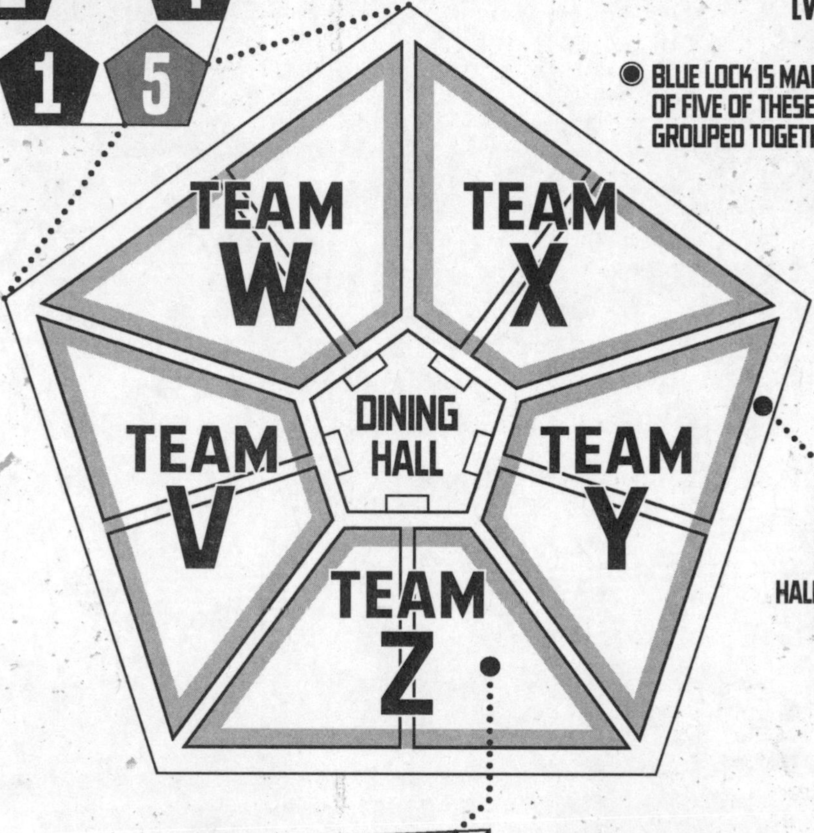
TEAM W
TEAM X
DINING HALL
TEAM V
TEAM Y
TEAM Z
HALLWAY

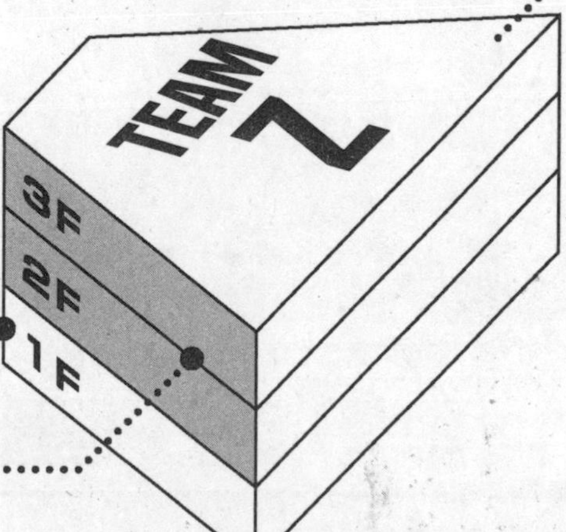
TEAM Z
3F
2F
1F

INDIVIDUAL TEAM SPACES

- THE FIRST FLOOR CONTAINS DORMITORIES AND TRAINING ROOMS.
- THE SECOND AND THIRD FLOORS CONTAIN TRAINING FIELDS.
- ALL FIVE TEAMS IN A WING SHARE THE CENTRAL DINING HALL.

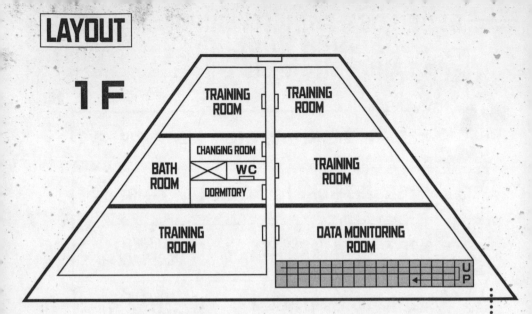

1 F

TRAINING ROOM

TRAINING ROOM

CHANGING ROOM

BATH ROOM

WC

DORMITORY

TRAINING ROOM

TRAINING ROOM

DATA MONITORING ROOM

UP

◉ THE TRAINING ROOMS ARE EQUIPPED WITH STATE-OF-THE-ART FACILITIES.

◉ THE MONITORING ROOMS ARE ABLE TO VIEW GAMES IN THE WING AS WELL AS FOOTAGE FROM PAST GAMES.

2·3F

INDOOR TRAINING FIELDS

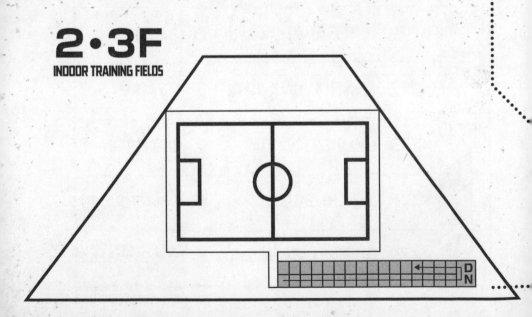

DN

BLUE LOCK RANKING TEAM Z SIDE DISH LIST

BONUS SECTION

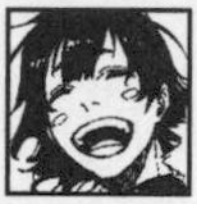	#Z65	MEGURU BACHIRA	[LIVER STIR-FRY]
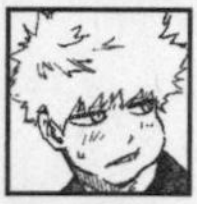	#Z66	RENSUKE KUNIGAMI	[CURRY]
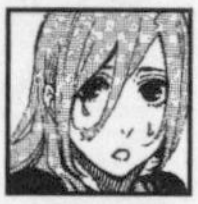	#Z67	HYOMA CHIGIRI	[FRIED VEGETABLES]
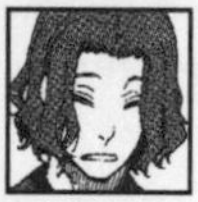	#Z68	WATARU KUON	[GRILLED MACKEREL]
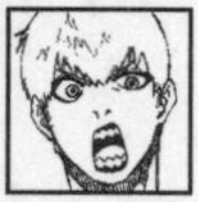	#Z69	JINGO RAICHI	[FRIED CHICKEN]
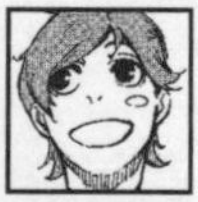	#Z70	YUDAI IMAMURA	[BACON & EGGS]
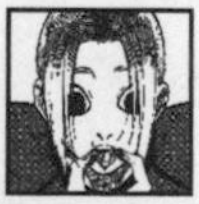	#Z71	GIN GAGAMARU	[GYOZA]
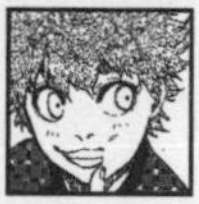	#Z72	ASAHI NARUHAYA	[SALAD]
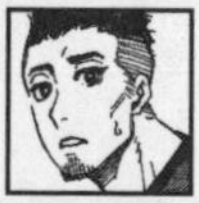	#Z73	OKUHITO IEMON	[OMELETTE]
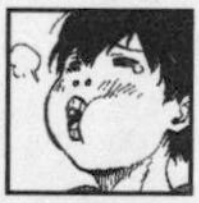	#Z74	YOICHI ISAGI	[NATTO]
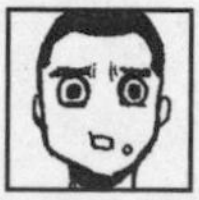	#Z75	GURIMU IGARASHI	[PICKLED RADISH]

STORY — **MUNEYUKI KANESHIRO**

ART — **YUSUKE NOMURA**

ART ASSISTANTS

SUEHIRO-SAN
OTAKE-SAN
FUJIMAKI-SAN
KITANO-SAN
MAEHATA-SAN
FURUMOTO-SAN
ARATAMA-SAN
HARADA-SAN
KIDA-SAN
NAKAMURA-SAN
URATANI-SAN
TAKAHASHI-SAN
TAKANIWA-SAN
KONNO-SAN
SATOU-SAN
(LISTED RANDOMLY)

DESIGN

KUMOCHI-SAN
OBA-SAN
(HIVE)

THANK YOU VERY MUCH...
...FOR READING THIS MANGA.

Yusuke Nomura

"Manga series usually have a shortened acronym. So with Blue Lock, what would it be?
Blue Lock...BL...
B...for Bachira
L...for Lamipus Lamipus Lulululululu!*
BACHIRA TRANSFORM!!"

Yusuke Nomura debuted in 2014 with the grotesquely cute cult hit alien invasion story *Dolly Kill Kill*, which was released digitally in English by Kodansha. Nomura is the illustrator behind *Blue Lock*.

*FROM THE 1960S SERIES, *HIMITSU NO AKKO-CHAN*, AKKO-CHAN IS A MAGICAL GIRL WHO CAN TRANSFORM INTO ANYTHING. WHEN SHE CASTS "LAMIPUS LAMIPUS LULULULULU," SHE REVERSES THE SPELL AND CHANGES BACK TO HER REGULAR SELF.

Muneyuki Kaneshiro

"I recently thought that I was drawing manga because I want people to say 'Wow, so interesting.' This is the second volume. Have a ball!"

Muneyuki Kaneshiro broke out as the creator of 2011's *As the Gods Will*, a death game story that spawned two sequels and a film adaptation directed by the legendary Takashi Miike. Kaneshiro writes the story of *Blue Lock*.

BLUE LOCK

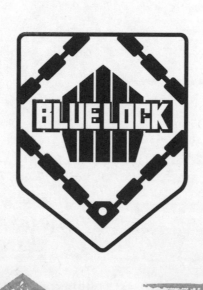

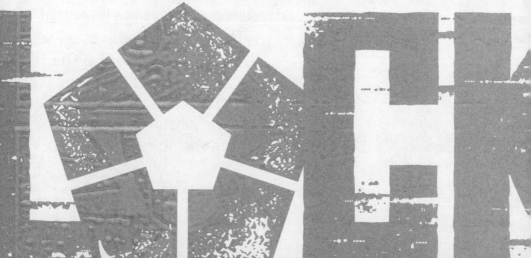

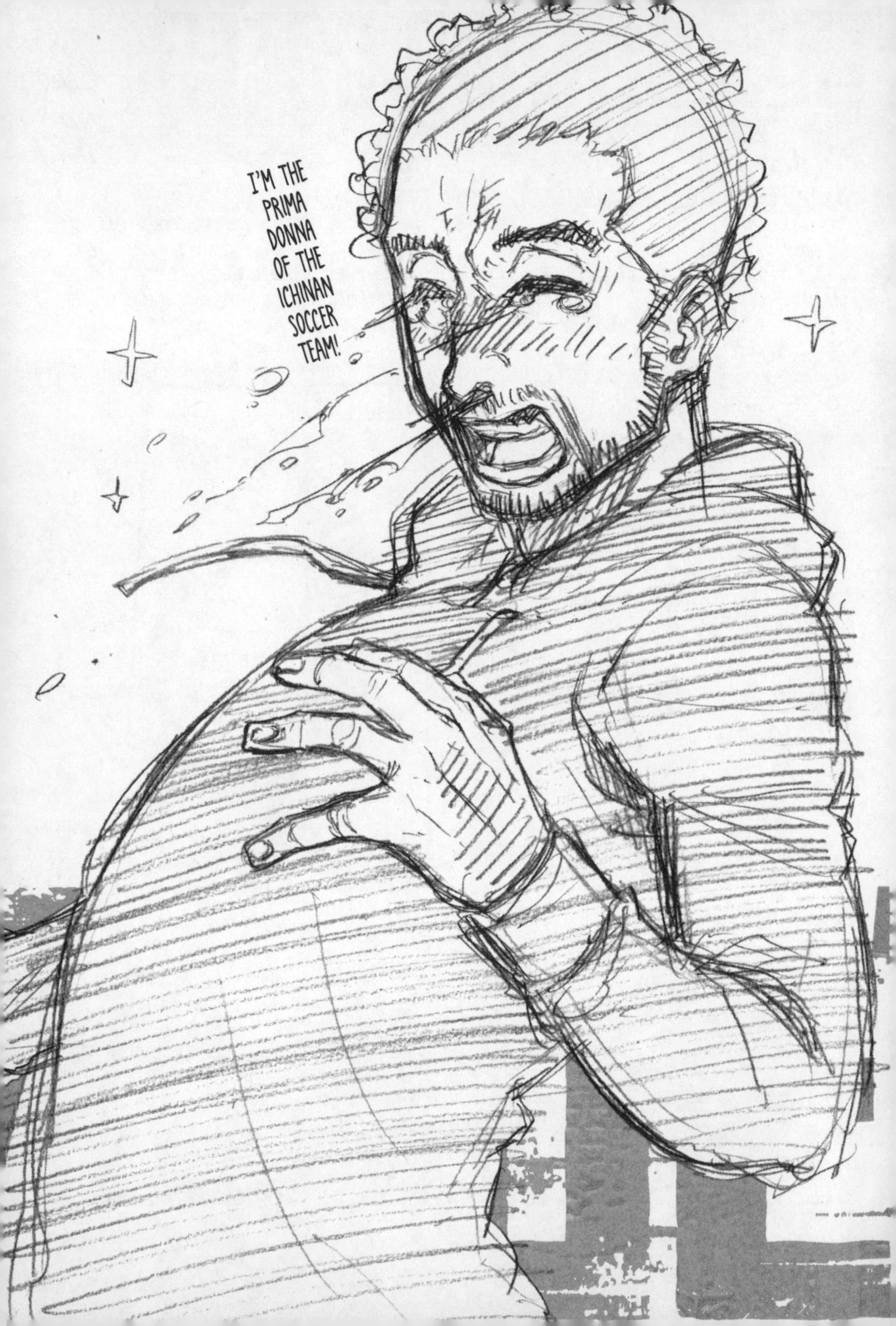
I'M THE PRIMA DONNA OF THE ICHINAN SOCCER TEAM!

TRANSLATION NOTES

BLUELOCK

Y-chan
page 135
The suffix -chan to a name is generally used for young children, close friends, babies, grandparents, and lovers, but it can be attached to objects or ideas to anthropomorphize them. Even though Team Y denotes a group of soccer players, Yudai Imamura alludes the team's characteristics as being that of an unattainable girl [Team Y-chan].

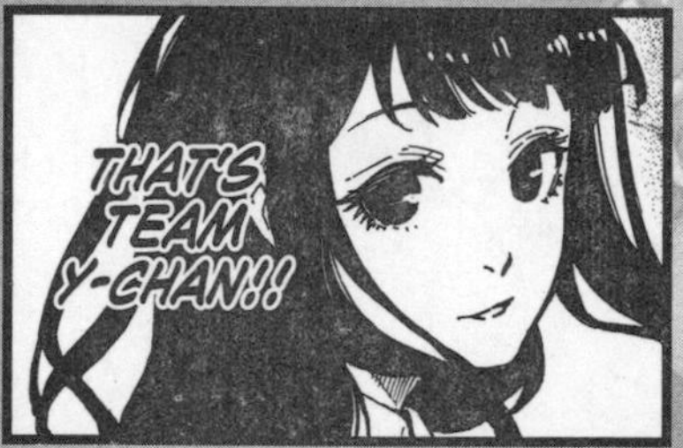
THAT'S TEAM Y-CHAN!!

Homage to Amida Buddha!
page 159
"Namu Amida Butsu," or "Homage to Amida Buddha," is a phrase that is believed to guide the chanter to attain rebirth in the Pure Land of Amida Buddha. This is like Christians doing the sign of the cross or praying, "Lord, have mercy."

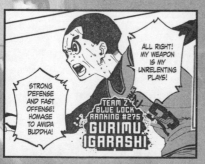

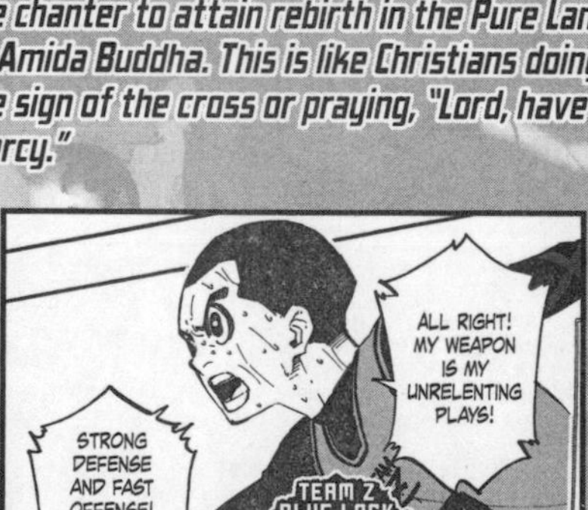
ALL RIGHT! MY WEAPON IS MY UNRELENTING PLAYS!
TEAM Z BLUE LOCK RANKING #275 GURIMU IGARASHI
STRONG DEFENSE AND FAST OFFENSE! HOMAGE TO AMIDA BUDDHA!

-kun
page 7
The suffix -kun to a name is interspersed throughout the story and is generally used among male friends or classmates. It can also refer to someone of junior status or younger age, so it is never used for someone older or in a higher position.

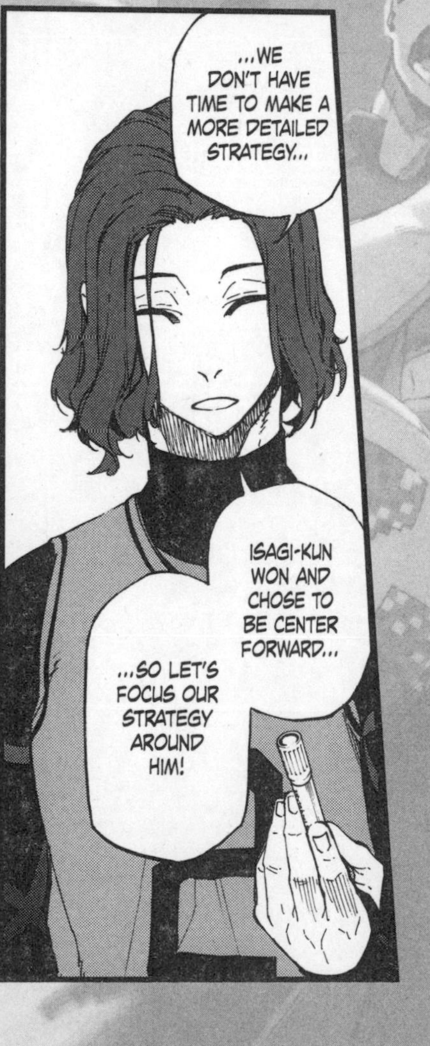
...WE DON'T HAVE TIME TO MAKE A MORE DETAILED STRATEGY...
ISAGI-KUN WON AND CHOSE TO BE CENTER FORWARD...
...SO LET'S FOCUS OUR STRATEGY AROUND HIM!

BLUELOCK

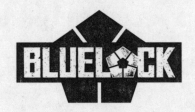

Young characters and steampunk setting, like *Howl's Moving Castle* and *Battle Angel Alita*

Beyond the Clouds © 2018 Nicke / Ki-oon

A boy with a talent for machines and a mysterious girl whose wings he's fixed will take you beyond the clouds! In the tradition of the high-flying, resonant adventure stories of Studio Ghibli comes a gorgeous tale about the longing of young hearts for adventure and friendship!